Liu Xiaobo, Charter 08, and the Challenges of Political Reform in China

Liu Xiaobo, Charter 08, and the Challenges of Political Reform in China

Edited by
Jean-Philippe Béja, Fu Hualing, and Eva Pils

香港大學出版社
HONG KONG UNIVERSITY PRESS

Hong Kong University Press
14/F Hing Wai Centre
7 Tin Wan Praya Road
Aberdeen
Hong Kong
www.hkupress.org

© Hong Kong University Press 2012

ISBN 978-988-8139-06-4 *(Hardback)*
ISBN 978-988-8139-07-1 *(Paperback)*

British Library Cataloguing-in-Publication Data
A catalogue record for this book is available from the British Library.

10   9   8   7   6   5   4   3   2   1

Printed and bound by Goodrich Int'l Printing Co., Ltd. in Hong Kong, China

Contents

Notes on Contributors

Jean-Philippe Béja holds degrees from the Institut d'Études Politiques de Paris (IEP), the University of Paris VII (Chinese), the Centre de Formation des Journalistes (CFJ), and the University of Liaoning (Chinese Literature), and a Ph.D. in Asian Studies from the University of Paris VII. He worked at the Centre d'Études Français sur la Chine contemporaine (in Hong Kong) from 1993 to 1997 and from 2008 to 2010. He is currently a senior researcher at Centre National de la Recherche Scientifique (CNRS), and works at the Centre for International Research (CERI) in Paris. Trained as a sinologist and a political scientist, he works on the relationship between the citizen and the State in the People's Republic of China (PRC). He has also written extensively on the democratization of Hong Kong. Member of the editorial board of *China Perspectives*, which he co-founded, he is also a member of the editorial boards of *Chinese Cross-Currents, East Asia: An International Quarterly, Journal of Contemporary Chinese Studies*, and *Hong Kong Journal of Social Sciences*. He regularly writes for *Esprit*. He supervises Ph.D. dissertations at Sciences-Po (Institute of Political Sciences) Paris, and at École des Hautes Études en Sciences Sociales, Paris.

Fu Hualing is a Professor of Law at the Faculty of Law of the University of Hong Kong. He graduated from the Southwestern University of Politics and Law in Chongqing and received postgraduate degrees in Canada. His research interest includes public law, human rights, and legal institutions in China. He has published widely in media law, the criminal justice system, and dispute resolution with a focus on China.

Eva Pils is an Associate Professor at the Faculty of Law of the Chinese University of Hong Kong (CUHK). She studied in Heidelberg, London, and Beijing, and holds a Ph.D. in Law from the University of London. Her scholarship focuses on human rights and China, with publications addressing Chinese human rights defenders, property law, land and housing rights in China, the status of migrant workers, the petitioning system, and conceptions of rights and justice in China. Eva is co-director of the CUHK Faculty of Law Centre for Rights and Justice and a member of the CUHK Centre for Civil Society Studies, as well as a Nonresident Senior Fellow of the U.S.-Asia Law Institute at New York University's School of Law.

Cui Weiping, a native of Yancheng in Jiangsu province, graduated in 1984 from the Chinese Department of Nanjing University, holds an M.A. in Arts, and is now a professor at the Beijing Film Academy and a scholar of modern Eastern European culture. She is a social as well as a literary critic and well-known public intellectual, and was among the first signatories to Charter 08.

Her major works include *Wounded Dawn* (带伤的黎明), *Invisible Sound* (看不见的声音), *Vita Activa* (积极生活), *Before Justice* (正义之前), and *Thought and Nostalgia* (思想与乡愁). She has translated into Chinese works including Ivan Klíma's 1995 *The Spirit of Prague* (布拉格精神), *Collected Works of Václav Havel* (哈维尔文集), and Adam Michnik's *Toward a Civil Society: Selected Speeches and Writings 1990–1994* (通往公民社会, co-translated).

Michael W. Dowdle is an Assistant Professor at the Law Faculty of the National University of Singapore. Prior to that, he was Chair of Globalization and Governance at Sciences Po in Paris. He was also Himalayas Foundation Visiting Professor in Comparative Constitutional Law at Tsinghua University and a Fellow in Public Law in the Regulatory Institutions Network (RegNet) at Australian National University. His publications include *Building Constitutionalism in China* (with Stéphanie Balme) (Palgrave Macmillan, 2009) and *Public Accountability: Designs, Dilemmas and Experiences* (Cambridge University Press, 2006).

Feng Chongyi is an Associate Professor in China Studies at the University of Technology, Sydney. He is also an Adjunct Professor of History, Nankai University, Tianjin. His current research focuses on intellectual and political development in modern and contemporary China. He has published over sixty articles in academic journals and edited volumes, and numerous articles in newspapers and on the Internet. He is the author of several books such as *Peasant Consciousness and China; Bertrand Russell and China; China's Hainan Province: Economic Development and Investment Environment; From Sinification to Globalisation; The Wisdom of Reconciliation: China's Road to Liberal Democracy; Liberalism within the Chinese Communist Party: From Chen Duxiu to Li Shenzhi*. He is also the editor of many books, including *Constitutional Government and China; Li Shenzhi and the Fate of Liberalism in China; The Political Economy of China's Provinces;* and *China in the Twentieth Century*. He was elected one of the top hundred Chinese public intellectuals in the world in 2005 and 2008.

Michaela Kotyzova started studying Japanese in high school in her native Czech Republic, then added Chinese during her undergraduate studies at the University of Rome, La Sapienza. She has just graduated from an M.A. program in International Relations at the University of Hong Kong. She is interested in music, history, and contemporary affairs.

Willy Wo-Lap Lam is a Professor of China Studies at Akita International University, Japan; and an Adjunct Professor of History and Global Economy at the Chinese University of Hong Kong.

A journalist, author, and researcher with more than thirty years of experience, Dr. Lam has published extensively on areas including the Chinese Communist Party, economic and political reform, the People's Liberation Army, Chinese foreign policy, as well as China-Taiwan and China-Hong Kong relations. He was Senior China Analyst at CNN's Asia-Pacific Office from 2000 to 2004; Associate Editor and China Editor of *South China Morning Post* from 1989 to 2000; and Beijing Correspondent of *Asiaweek* magazine from 1986 to 1989.

Dr. Lam is the author of six books on Chinese affairs, including *Chinese Politics in the Hu Jintao Era* (M. E. Sharpe, 2006); *The Era of Jiang Zemin* (Prentice Hall, 1999); *China after Deng Xiaoping* (John Wiley & Sons, 1995); and *Hu Jintao: The Unvarnished Biography* (in Japanese) (Tokyo: Shogagukan Press, 2002).

Dr. Lam holds degrees in economics and liberal arts from the University of Hong Kong, University of Minnesota, and Wuhan University.

Man Yee Karen Lee (Ph.D., the University of Hong Kong) is an Assistant Professor in the Department of Law and Business, Hong Kong Shue Yan University. Her research covers areas of human rights, law and culture, and law and religion. She is the author of *Equality, Dignity, and Same-Sex Marriage: A Rights Disagreement in Democratic Societies* (Leiden: Martinus Nijhoff Publishers, 2010) and has published articles on human rights issues from cultural and religious perspectives.

Mo Shaoping is the founder and Managing Director of Beijing Mo Shaoping Law Firm. He is also a member of the Human Rights and Constitutional Law Committee of the All China Lawyers Association. Mo specializes in criminal law, and he and his colleagues are well known internationally for defending many politically sensitive cases, including that of Liu Xiaobo. Mo was among the first signatories of Charter 08.

Pitman B. Potter is a Professor of Law at the University of British Columbia (UBC) Law Faculty and HSBC Chair in Asian Research at UBC's Institute of Asian Research. Professor Potter's teaching and research focus on PRC and Taiwan law and policy in the areas of foreign trade and investment, dispute resolution, intellectual property, contracts, business regulation, and human rights. Professor Potter has served on numerous editorial boards for journals such as *The China Quarterly*, *The Hong Kong Law Journal*, *Taiwan National University Law Review*, *China: An International Journal*, and *Pacific Affairs*. He has published several books, including most recently *Law, Policy, and Practice on China's Periphery: Selective Adaptation and Institutional Capacity* (Routledge, 2010), as well as numerous book chapters and articles for such journals as *Law & Social Inquiry*, *The China Quarterly*, and *The International Journal*. In addition to his academic activities, Professor Potter is admitted to the practice of law in British Columbia, Washington, and California, and serves as a consultant to the Canadian national law firm Borden Ladner Gervais LLP. As a Chartered Arbitrator, Professor Potter is engaged in international trade arbitration work involving

China. He has served on the Board of Directors of several public institutions, including Asia Pacific Foundation of Canada, where he is now a Senior Fellow.

Joshua Rosenzweig is a Ph.D. student in Chinese Studies at the Chinese University of Hong Kong. From 2002 to 2011, he was a researcher for The Dui Hua Foundation, where he developed the foundation's comprehensive database of information about Chinese political and religious prisoners, and authored more than a dozen volumes in its series of occasional publications. He is frequently sought out by the international media to comment on China's human rights developments, has given testimony before the US government, and has spoken on a variety of human rights issues before audiences in both the US and China.

Teng Biao is a scholar and lecturer at the Law School of the China University of Political Science and Law, and practices law at Beijing Huayi Law Firm. He holds a Ph.D. from Peking University Law School. In 2003, he was one of the "Three Doctors of Law" who complained to the National People's Congress about unconstitutional detentions of internal migrants in the widely known "Sun Zhigang Case." Since then, Teng Biao has provided counsel in numerous other human rights cases, including those of rural rights advocate Chen Guangcheng, rights defender Hu Jia, the religious freedom case of Wang Bo, and a growing number of death row prisoner cases. He has also co-founded two groups that have combined research with work on human rights cases: "Open Constitution Initiative" (公盟) and "China Against Death Penalty" (北京兴善研究所). He is a signatory to Charter 08.

In February 2011, some months after the submission of this essay, Teng Biao was "disappeared" for seventy days by the authorities, before being returned to his home in Beijing.

Sophia Woodman is a postdoctoral fellow with the Asia-Pacific Dispute Resolution Project at the Institute of Asian Research, the University of British Columbia. Her work focuses on citizenship, human rights and social movements in China. Her most recent publication is: "Law, Translation and Voice: The Transformation of a Struggle for Social Justice in a Chinese Village" (*Critical Asian Studies*, vol. 43, 2011).

Introduction

On the sixtieth anniversary of the Universal Declaration of Human Rights, Charter 08, a manifesto asking for the transformation of the People's Republic into a Federal Republic based on separation of powers, a multi-party system, and the rule of law, was sent to the Chairman of the People's Republic of China (PRC). It was signed by 303 persons from all walks of life: intellectuals and ordinary people, communist party members and dissidents. Two days before it was made public, one of its initiators, Liu Xiaobo, was taken away from his home by the police. After more than twelve months in detention, he was sentenced to eleven years in jail for "incitement to subversion of state power." Two years later, Liu was awarded the Nobel Peace Prize, a decision the Chinese leaders considered a display of hostility by Western powers. But why had they reacted with such severity to a non-violent petition signed by such a small proportion of the population?

This was a puzzle for most observers: the successful organization of the Olympic Games seemed to have reinforced the legitimacy of the Chinese Communist Party (hereafter "CCP" or "Party") both domestically and on the international scene. Those who had forecast the regime's collapse after the 1989 Tiananmen massacre had been proved wrong. Despite the fact that the third wave of democratization[1] had started in China with the spring 1989 demonstrations, the CCP survived the end of communism in Eastern Europe and the collapse of the USSR. In the winter of 2011, it showed its capacity to hold on to power when popular uprisings were sweeping North Africa and the Middle East. The CCP has not only survived; thanks to the double-digit growth of the economy that it has been able to achieve during the last two decades, China's GDP overcame Japan's in February 2011,[2] making the People's Republic the second-largest economy in the world. This has allowed the Party to enhance its legitimacy at home: it can now claim to have achieved the dream which has haunted Chinese elites and masses since the Opium Wars — to make China a prosperous and powerful country (*fuguo qiangbing,* 富国强兵).

In the last few years, the People's Republic has become more assertive on the international scene. Many developing countries' governments see it as a model to emulate, while in the wake of the 2008 financial crisis, most Western countries regard it as the savior of the world economy. During the last two years, thanks to its huge foreign exchange reserves, China has been able to intervene in the European debt crisis and has defended its interests in the South China Sea with unprecedented self-assurance. As a consequence, an increasing number of countries consider China's growing power with increasing nervousness.

These remarkable developments explain why some scholars have described the regime as "resilient authoritarianism"[3] — resilient because of the CCP's willingness and ability to adapt to new circumstances and to change. In fact, at the political level, the Party has modified some of its ideological messages and organizational structures, and not all of these changes have been merely cosmetic.

In order to renew its elites, the CCP has introduced elections at the village level, co-opting many recruits by allowing them to participate in a large number of newly established "consultative" institutions. To overcome bureaucratism, it has introduced mechanisms supposed to promote inner-party democracy. Efforts have been made to enhance the capacity of institutions and improve governance effectiveness and, aware of the dangers of corruption, it has declared its intent to reinforce disciplinary measures. Since the beginning of the reform, it has started to develop a legal system. Changes have also been brought to the media, and control by the propaganda department has become less punctilious. Some scholars view these reform efforts as responses to market developments and new social needs and demands in China's market economy.[4]

Institutional innovation and newly designed mechanisms have allowed the Party to cope with the challenges arising from rapidly expanding information technology, in particular the Internet, and from demands and criticisms articulated by domestic civil society forces and the international community.

The reform measures and institutional adaptation have worked not only in terms of containing social conflict. Some argue that they have also helped to enhance the legitimacy of the Party. For one thing, in today's system, individuals have some measure of economic freedom, even though their economic and social rights are often not well protected. Social media are allowed vibrant growth. The Party has understood that the new information technologies could help develop the economy and make its propaganda more efficient, but it has been keen on preventing them from challenging its authority. It has also allowed the emergence of non-governmental organizations, but has kept them under control — to a point where even the use of the term "civil society" has been prohibited.

Some believe that authoritarian rule has made itself attractive to Chinese citizens who benefit from it and, charmed by its promise of stability and prosperity, widely accept or even welcome it.[5] According to one view of what may be called a "Chinese exceptional mode," social and economic development is therefore possible without political liberalization: there can be rule of law without judicial independence; representation without political participation; freedom without political rights; and accountability without democracy.[6]

In times of relative stability, like many other authoritarian regimes,[7] the Party-state may loosen its control over the economy and society, delegate powers to other institutions, allow a larger social space, and tolerate critical voices. The litmus test is how the Party-state responds to crises — perceived or real. Any existing fault lines between democracies and authoritarian systems become more visible when these systems confront political challenges.

So how can contemporary China pass that litmus test as a post-totalitarian state where judicial independence is absent, where the official media are compliant, where independent media and "citizen journalism" are subdued, and in which civil society organizations remain fragile?

One of the problems which, traditionally, have plagued post-totalitarian regimes has been the question of succession. Despite the fact that since the 1980s, the leaders are not allowed to serve more than two terms in office, the succession process has not yet been institution-alized. Only in 2012, for the first time in the history of the PRC, will a new General Secretary be appointed without the intervention of a charismatic leader.[8] Even though it appears that a consensus has been reached among the top leaders on the name of the future head of the Politburo Standing Committee, tensions seem to have emerged at the highest level — and when there are tensions at the top, the leadership often opts in favor of repression.

The arrest and trial of Liu Xiaobo are a case in point: they have shown that the authorities can react harshly to what appears to most observers as a very mild challenge by a few isolated intellectuals. Seemingly worried that "a single spark can set a prairie fire," the rulers are ready to violate the laws that they have adopted and implemented since the beginning of the reform process. The intimidation of human rights lawyers in the wake of calls for a "Jasmine Revolution" has also revealed that the instruments of control at the disposal of the post-totalitarian regime can be mobilized at any time if the rulers feel under threat. However, these events also seem to show that not everyone in the leadership is convinced that repression is an efficient way to respond to challenges in the long run. The sequence of events in Liu Xiaobo's case points to the fact that there might be divergences in the leadership.

The fact that more than a year had elapsed between Liu's detention and his trial might indicate that some of the top leaders did not agree with such a harsh sentence. Other factors seem to point in that direction: in March 2009, three intellectuals were allowed to go to Prague at the invitation of former Czech president Václav Havel to receive a human rights prize in Liu's name,[9] a decision which was quite surprising as, at the same time, most members of the first batch of Charter 08 signato-ries were summoned for "tea" by the secret police (guobao, 国保), which pressured them to retract their signatures. Besides, despite the strong reaction from the authorities, it took more than three weeks to erase the Charter from the Internet, allowing it to be signed by more than 6,000 people[10] on the Mainland. Although since Liu's trial, immense resources have been invested in the protection of stability (weiwen, 维稳), some leaders have insisted on the necessity to implement political reform,[11] while officials have stressed the need to listen to divergent voices.

Whereas the term "civil society" has been banned from the press, many autonomous organizations have continued to lobby the government, and their leaders have not all been jailed. Finally, after Ai Weiwei's (艾未未) arrest in April 2011, international uproar and critiques by netizens in China have led the authorities to release him.[12] On the other hand, protests by Western leaders against the jailing of Liu Xiaobo have been met with deaf ears.

Undeniably, as we have observed in the post-1989 era, China can react forcefully and repressively without external, institutional constraints in the persecution of Falun Gong (法轮功) and other religious practices, as well as against Chinese Democracy Party (中国民主党) members and other political dissidents, against lawyers and other rights activists, and against Liu Xiaobo and other Chartists. But the problem with views that emphasize the survival skills of the current regime and measure legitimacy by the absence of successful rebellion is that they tend to leave further implications of the system's repressive character in the shadows.

We believe that these should be brought out into the light to allow everyone to assess the system at its full spectrum. It is in this context that this book studies the case of Liu Xiaobo and Charter 08. The Party may have evolved and adapted to new circumstances over the past thirty years, but it remains authoritarian at its core and the authoritarian aspects of the system manifest themselves more clearly when facing a political challenge.

This book is divided into three parts. Part One is about Liu Xiaobo and the criminal process that led to his conviction in December 2009 for "incitement to subversion of state power." Part Two provides discussions and comments on Charter 08 and the political forces it represents. Part Three places Charter 08 in the larger context of contention between protecting rights (*weiquan*, 维权) and maintaining stability (*weiwen*).

The opening chapter by Jean-Philippe Béja introduces Liu Xiaobo as a person, a scholar, an activist. In particular, it highlights the turning points in Liu's life and puts them in political context. As is the case with many activists, Liu's transformation from a bookish scholar into a person at the forefront of the opposition is triggered by political events. In his case, the experience of the bloodshed on June Fourth had a profound impact on his thinking and priorities in life. He moved from literary critique to political critique, engaging in progressively open criticism of the CCP and advocacy for fundamental political reform. Subsequent developments led to his increasingly overt challenges and his participation in the drafting of Charter 08.

Joshua Rosenzweig's chapter turns to Liu as a target of criminal prosecution. It provides a careful and detailed historical review of the offence of inciting subversion, on which Liu was convicted. The chapter traces the legislative change from "counter-revolutionary crimes" to "crimes endangering state security" and the accordingly changing elements and nature of subversion offences. In the second half, Rosenzweig provides an analysis of the defenses that Liu Xiaobo and his lawyers presented in the trial. The chapter concludes that, given the offence of subversion is so vaguely defined, defenses are hard to come up with and of little legal consequence. Rosenzweig's careful analysis thus supports the conclusion that prosecution of "subversion" only serves the purpose of silencing political speech.

In the following chapter, Liu Xiaobo's defense team, led by Mo Shaoping, gives a brief introduction of major subversive cases that the lawyers have defended over the years, including the cases of Yao Fuxin (姚福信), Xu Wei (徐伟), Jiang Lijun (姜立军), Du Daobin (杜导斌), and of course, Liu Xiaobo. By setting out the prosecution evidence and arguments, the authors invite readers to pass judgment on the legality of the prosecution, and the constitutionality and legitimacy of the "subversion" crime at its core. If they do so implicitly rather than explicitly, this by itself is a comment on the difficulties and high risks associated with criminal defense, particularly in "political" cases. Undoubtedly, the answers are straightforward — the argument that crimes subsumed under "subversion" lack any constitutional, legitimate basis has been advanced by others and is put forth in another chapter in this book by Teng Biao. The authors also offer a concise account of the substantive and procedural legal difficulties they have encountered throughout their defense, as well as an analysis of the political causes of these difficulties.

The final chapter in Part One consists of Cui Weiping's account of how she collated the first reactions of famous intellectuals and artists to Liu Xiabo's conviction and eleven-year sentence. Spurred into action by her own outrage and sense of injustice, Cui moved to collect these comments in the form of "Tweets" — short, concise summaries of what people told her over the phone — and later posted them online on her blog. Together, they make for a fascinating testimony to the mood of the intellectual elites in that consequential moment. This chapter shows the strength of China's intellectual community in what may have been one of the country's darkest hours in the past three decades and gives us a sense of the great challenges ahead.

Part Two moves to a substantive analysis of Charter 08 as a text, as well as of the intellectual and political forces it represents. It is composed of five chapters. Potter and Woodman's chapter provides a critical review of Charter 08's compatibility and inconsistency with the existing constitutional and legal order. For Potter and Woodman, Charter 08 is a sophisticated document that both reflects a Western bourgeois agenda in advocating a new liberal order and engages the existing system in calling on the Party-state to live up to its own rhetoric of rights. Because the Charter adopts official rights discourses to challenge the government, the authors argue, it opens a window of opportunity for a possible alliance between the Chartists outside the political system and reformers within the political system. In the end, Potter and Woodman think that the perceived danger of Charter 08 can only be understood within China's "segmented publics," in which "the Chinese government sets formal and informal rules to limit discussions of particular issues to specific institutional spaces." Whether a particular political criticism is regarded as dangerous depends on the identity and circumstances of the critic more than the content of the criticism, and aspects such as foreign contacts or foreign support may play a role. This is an assessment echoed in several other chapters in this book.

For Feng Chongyi, Charter 08 is a significant political manifestation on its own. Similar to the argument put forward by Potter and Woodman, Feng sees Charter 08 as a document that seeks to forge "a grand alliance of Chinese liberal elements 'within the system (*tizhi nei*, 体制内)' and 'outside the system (*tizhi wai*, 体制外)'." Its signatories and supporters include known dissidents as well as officials, retired officials, and others from within the system. More significantly, Charter 08 symbolizes yet another alliance between political dissidence and the *weiquan* movement which is more rooted in Chinese society. The two political forces have been sharply divided since 1989. While the former challenges the CCP directly and calls for a fundamental political change, the latter takes concrete actions in protecting the legal rights of citizens within the framework of the existing political system. Charter 08 provides a common ground for the two forces.

In her chapter, Karen Lee regards Charter 08 as an output of China's long fight for dignity by generations of dissidents. Indeed, despite the different views between Wei Jingsheng (魏京生) and Liu Xiaobo on Charter 08, they are both part of a common intellectual history and political movement. According to Lee, speaking one's mind against the government when called for and fighting for a political system that one believes in is, in essence, what a self-respecting person would do in keeping his or her dignity. After all, as Lee writes, "only human beings are capable of transcending basic animal instincts for the pursuit of higher values." It is that pursuit of higher values that has been motivating dissidents and activists in a hostile environment.

Michaela Kotyzova offers a well-grounded comparison between Charter 08 and Charta 77, the manifesto written by Czechoslovak dissidents, mainly Vàclav Havel and Jan Patocka, to demand the respect of human rights by the Communist Party in Czechoslovakia. The two charters, according to Kotyzova, are similar in their content, both invoking international human rights norms and both attempting to function largely within the existing legal framework. Another related similarity between the two lies in the fact that their objectives are not so much to subvert the regimes as to provide a support structure when the regimes fall. However, despite their similarities, both exist in drastically different political and economic contexts. China in 2008 was different from Czechoslovakia in 1977 in terms of the politics, economy, and soft power that the respective communist parties may have, and those differences affect the impact of the respective charters in society.

The four chapters in Part Three relate Charter 08 to tensions and contradictions between the imperatives of "defending rights" (weiquan) and "preserving stability" (weiwen).

Fu Hualing's chapter, entitled "Challenging Authoritarianism through Law," provides a historical background discussion of the legal rights-based weiquan movement in China, traces what the author characterizes as a tension between the supply and demand of rights, and explains an institutional failure in meeting the increasing demand for rights and the social consequences of that failure. China in the 1990s has been referred to as the "age of rights,"[13] when legislatures at central and local levels passed a large number of laws granting new rights. This is not merely window-dressing in China, as is often argued. Armed with legal rights, citizens of different social and economic backgrounds have started to assert these and engage in a movement of "rightful resistance."[14] Gradually, law has become a rallying point for aggrieved people, and lawyers have become organizers of an emerging social movement. However, as the chapter illustrates, the brutal and drastic social changes and acute conflicts are often beyond the capacity of legal norms and institutions to grasp. As a result, Fu argues, the legal system has failed to serve as a governing tool for the Party-state and to provide remedies for citizens seeking justice — both are giving up on law and resorting to extralegal and illegal measures to settle the score.

Michael Dowdle's chapter places Charter 08 in the comparative and historical context of popular constitutionalism, a concept that Dowdle uses to capture the social meaning of constitutions. For Dowdle, popular constitutionalism does not appeal to the constitutional text or institutional authority, but to the understanding of generations of people who make use of, and give meaning to, the constitutional text. Popular constitutionalism also speaks to the tension and dialogue between the popular and official components in the constitutional development. Putting it in the Chinese context, Dowdle traces the growth of popular constitutionalism from the trial of the Gang of Four, the creeping Parliamentarianism, and public litigation and petition. Significantly, Dowdle explains how popular constitutionalism continues to evolve and develop in the form of online and offline citizen activism even though it is facing the post-2005 crackdown. Charter 08 is part of the evolving popular constitutionalism in China and its significance lies in its attempt and ability to broaden and free the epistemological space.

Eva Pils' analysis of the *weiquan* movement focuses on what the author calls its "dark sides." As Fu also observes, the introduction of rights discourse has given victims of injustice new arguments and mechanisms in their quest for redress. But the Party-state's failure to submit itself to the laws and principles it has recognized has given rise to a worrying trend. Drawing on interviews with lawyers and petitioners, Pils describes the at-times brutal persecution of rights defenders, especially those without fame or professional status, and discusses what she views as increasingly vindictive and violent reactions among some members of the movement. A brief review of attitudes toward violence amongst petitioners, intellectuals, and lawyers shows that beneath an oft-asserted commitment to non-violence in political resistance, there is much doubt and debate within the movement, and that to some, violence seems to be the only last answer. What, they ask, is the argument against violent resistance in circumstances where the state, not its citizens, is the main agent of brutalization? Pils argues that while Charter 08 provides little guidance on how to effect the rational, liberal transformation of Chinese society that is so clearly its vision, its protagonist Liu Xiaobo is perhaps best understood through his noble but hard-to-emulate credo of "having no enemies." In that sense, Charter 08 represents a moral challenge both to the repressive authoritarian state and to the *weiquan* movement.

Willy Lam explores the macro-level political development in China and the possibilities of liberalization in the context of *weiquan* and *weiwen*. For Lam, the government is resorting to both hard and soft measures to maintain stability and legitimacy. On the one hand, a "scorched earth policy" is used against dissidents who may be perceived to challenge the CCP directly, as demonstrated by the prosecution and heavy punishment of Liu Xiaobo and his comrades-in-arm. On the other, Lam argues that the CCP has taken a reconciliatory approach in dealing with the poor, the liberal elements within the CCP, and the Uighurs in Xinjiang. In general, however, Lam is of the view that, when facing color revolutions that have occurred elsewhere, frequent social unrest in different parts of China, and political challenges posed by likes of Liu Xiaobo and Charter 08, the CCP is retreating to a conservative comfort zone ideologically and institutionally. This means that there are only slim chances of further political reform.

Teng Biao's chapter concludes the book. His is a powerful and passionate voice from the heart of someone who has been at the forefront of rights defense and who has experienced first-hand the pains and suffering of *weiquan*. Teng is thus perhaps best situated to explore the psychology of resistance that explains why and how some people — always but a few — refuse to back down, acquiesce, accommodate official lies, and reach arrangements with the system. In a largely "neo-totalitarian" system like that of China today, the problem is no longer naked fear such as might be induced by a tyrannical regime, he argues. Rather, it is the ability to avoid thinking, "that hard-to-attain confusion" that allows people not even to be aware of their deep-down anxieties and constraints. While some observers, as pointed out at the beginning of this introduction, believe that the government has won "legitimacy" in the sense of wide social acceptance of its rule, Teng's analysis leaves no room for such a comforting conclusion. He does not even believe that the Party's partial achievements could win it what he defines as *ex post* "justification," while it continues to be as highly repressive as it is; and citizens acquiescing in the Party's rule appear, on Teng's account, to be at some level complicit in its injustices. Teng's chapter is in some ways one of the most somber accounts of China's liberal movements in this book, but in his analysis of China's rapid social change and his account of the great vibrancy of contemporary activism, he also shows the strength of his own optimism and ideals. There is no doubt in the mind of the author that political change will come eventually — "you can destroy the flowers but you cannot prevent spring," he quotes.

Academic institutions in Hong Kong offer platforms for public debate on sensitive issues in Mainland China, such as the case of Liu Xiaobo and Charter 08. This book is the result of a series of conferences and seminars on Charter 08 organized by the Faculty of Law at the University of Hong Kong in the aftermath of Liu Xiaobo's conviction. The editors would like to thank the University of Hong Kong for its generous funding of the event; the French Centre for Research on Contemporary China (CEFC) for co-organizing one of the conferences; and all the participants who contributed to passionate debates over China's constitutional and political future. Hong Kong is the only place where Liu Xiaobo and Charter 08 can be freely, extensively, and seriously discussed on Chinese soil and we are delighted that the Hong Kong University Press has agreed to publish this book.

Jean-Philippe Béja
Fu Hualing
Eva Pils
25 December 2011
Hong Kong

Part One

Liu Xiaobo and the Crime of Inciting Subversion

Chapter 1

Is Jail the Only Place Where One Can "Live in Truth"?

Liu Xiaobo's Experience

Jean-Philippe Béja

On 8 October 2010, for the first time in history, the Nobel Peace Prize Committee awarded the Prize to a citizen of the People's Republic of China (PRC) — Liu Xiaobo. Instead of celebrating the result of decades of efforts, the government of the PRC denounced "a bunch of clowns": "Obviously, the Nobel Peace Prize this year is meant to irritate China, but it will not succeed. On the contrary, the committee disgraced itself."[1] The Chinese Communist Party (Party) not only prevented the laureate, then serving a sentence of eleven years in the Jinzhou (锦州) (Liaoning, 辽宁) jail, from going to Oslo to receive his award, in an unprecedented move, it also kept more than a hundred persons — whose names appeared on a guest list established by Liu's wife, Liu Xia — and their relatives from leaving China between 8 October and 11 December of that year. The Chinese authorities have even placed Liu Xia under house arrest, and at the time of our writing (August 2011), she is still held incommunicado at her home in Beijing. But who is the man who has provoked such anger from one of the strongest governments on earth?

> I still want to tell the regime that deprives me of my freedom: I stand by the belief I expressed 20 years ago in my June 2nd hunger strike declaration: I have no enemies, I have no hatred.

Twenty years after the declaration that he wrote with three friends[2] just before the June Fourth Massacre, Liu Xiaobo reiterated this profession of faith in what he called the "last statement" that he intended to deliver in front of his judges. We will never know whether he could really do so as, in a blatant violation of the law that he was supposed to enforce, the judge decided that the defendant's plea should not last longer than the prosecutor's, which itself spanned only fourteen minutes.

Two days later, on Christmas day 2009, in what was one of the harshest verdicts delivered in the last decade, Liu Xiaobo was sentenced to eleven years in jail for "incitement to subversion of state power" after a mockery of a "public" trial which even his wife was refused the right to attend. In February 2010, his appeal was rejected and, as one more vexation, on 26 May he was transferred from Beijing to Jinzhou jail in Liaoning — making it more difficult for his wife to visit him — as the authorities do not recognize him as a Beijing resident.

His crime consisted of having written six articles[3] criticizing the Communist Party rule and posting them on the Internet, and in having contributed to the drafting of Charter 08, a manifesto demanding respect for the rule of law and human rights and the enforcement of separation of powers in China.

On the day of the trial, more than a dozen diplomats who wished to attend were left out in the freezing weather, while petitioners who had come to the capital to denounce government abuses spent the morning in front of the Beijing Intermediate Courthouse and, as a token of solidarity with the defendant, tied yellow ribbons to the barriers keeping the public out.

The verdict was condemned by the European Union and the United States, petitions were circulated abroad to protest its severity, and it triggered a bout of indignation on the Chinese Internet. Liu Xiaobo, already one of the most famous Chinese dissidents, had become a symbol of the struggle for free speech in the Middle Empire.

How could this "public intellectual" continue to be without hate despite having been illegally deprived of his right to speak or to publish his writings in his own country, after having endured an exhausting police surveillance for two decades, and having been detained illegally for six months without the right to see his wife or write to her? He himself gave the answer in his "last statement":

> For hatred is corrosive of a person's wisdom and conscience; the mentality of enmity can poison a nation's spirit, instigate brutal life and death struggles, destroy a society's tolerance and humanity,

and block a nation's progress to freedom and democracy. I hope therefore to be able to transcend my personal vicissitudes in understanding the development of the state and changes in society, to counter the hostility of the regime with the best of intentions, and defuse hate with love.[4]

Such moderation seems miles away from Liu's personality of a "black horse" whose denunciation of "scar literature" writers had caused an uproar in the mid-eighties.[5]

Born in Changchun (长春) in the former Manchuria on 28 December 1955, Liu Xiaobo has undergone the woes of his generation. The son of a university professor, he followed his disgraced parents in their exile to the Mongolian countryside from 1969 to 1973. In 1974, like most of his fellow urban residents, he was sent to a people's commune, where he worked for two years before being appointed a worker in a Changchun construction company. When the entrance examinations to the university were re-established, he was admitted to the Chinese department of Jilin University (吉林大学). After graduation in 1982, he went to Peking University where he obtained a Master's degree in 1984. The same year, he became a lecturer at Beijing Normal University (北京师范大学) and obtained his Ph.D. in literature in 1988.

As with most of the intellectuals who have influenced the evolution of modern China, Liu Xiaobo started his career studying literature. One should remember that the principal activists of the May Fourth movement, which introduced Marxism in China, had begun their path by fighting for the establishment of a literature written in the vernacular language as a basis for a "new culture."

This special role of writers has continued through the rest of the twentieth century and, in the wake of Mao Zedong's death, especially after the repression of the Democracy Wall in 1979, the fiercest critiques of the Maoist past have been writers and poets. In works labeled "scar literature," they wrote about the sufferings of the intellectuals sent to May Seventh schools, the torments of the rusticated youths, and the suffering endured by the victims of Mao's political movements. These novels, plays, and poems often attracted the wrath of the Central Propaganda Department, which launched campaigns of criticism[6] to denounce them. Faced with the danger of a new round of persecutions, many writers and artists decided to support the Party reformers in their struggle against the conservatives and neo-Maoists. Former rightist Wang Meng (王蒙) went so far in his support of the reformers that he accepted to become Minister of Culture in 1986.

Therefore, when Liu Xiaobo denounced the shyness of contemporary writers, and their obsession with the fate of members of their caste — although the latter had not always displayed exemplary behavior during those years — and when he stigmatized their Confucian aspirations to become "counselors to the prince," he caused an uproar in progressive writers' circles.[7] While he spared the "misty" (menglong, 朦胧) poets who, breaking with socialist realism, expressed the spleen of the youth instead of the revolutionary enthusiasm which had been de rigueur since 1949,[8] he "reserved his most acerbic comments for the atavistic 'roots' literature[9] that had been in vogue among both up-market authors and readers since 1984. He saw this literary trend as a dangerous and reactionary retreat into traditionalism."[10]

In a vehement article which rocked the literary establishment, he accused them of lacking individual conscience and therefore of betraying their duty as modern intellectuals. He was adamant: for him, literature should preserve its autonomy and writers should not, for strategic reasons, keep silent on certain subjects. If intellectuals were to contribute to the establishment of an autonomous public sphere, they had to cut the umbilical chord that linked them to the State. He was unyielding in his conception of the intellectual, whose essence, he thought, was critical thinking. In order to defend his right to exercise it, he should not be afraid of losing his freedom, or even his life.

Liu's radicalism shocked his readers. It should not have, as his attitude was directly in line with the iconoclastic tradition of May Fourth. This article brought Liu immediate fame and he came to be known as the "black horse" of the literary scene. He was invited to give lectures in many universities in China and abroad. But to establishment intellectuals, including "liberals,"[11] he was a nihilist.[12] Whereas the Chinese reformers were eager to get international awards, he denounced their quest for respectability. When read today, his words seem ironical:

> Contemporary Chinese have been infected with a "Nobel Complex", an "Oscar Complex" to the point of obsessiveness. When Tagore won the Nobel Prize, the Chinese presented him as "the first Asian to win the Nobel Prize for literature" . . . But

> in recent years, Asians have broken the record by not getting any
> prize at all . . . It is obvious, then, that winning a foreign prize is an
> Oriental's passport to the world, bringing lasting fame and consid-
> erable stature in his own country.[13]

Despite his acute criticisms, Liu Xiaobo, who had not taken part in the Democracy Wall movement in 1978–79, was not a political activist. He was above all an independent intellectual who refused to be attached by loyalty to a political patron and who did not shy from criticizing those who were then considered radicals.

But when confronted with a mass movement, to the difference of many an activist, he did not think twice: despite the fact that he was living in New York as a visiting professor at Columbia University when the 1989 pro-democracy movement erupted, he decided to go back to China and immerse himself in the movement although he had analyzed it with a critical eye. He was the only famous intellectual who made this decision and, after his return to Beijing at the end of April 1989, he spent most of his time on Tiananmen Square. He wrote *dazibao* (大字报, big character posters) to express his ideas, which often diverged from the students'. While the latter demanded that the Party reverse the "counter-revolutionary" verdict passed on the student movement by a famous *People's Daily* editorial,[14] he posted a *dazibao* in which he wrote:

> Why do our fellow citizens feel so grateful towards reversal of
> verdicts? To send a righteous person to hell is an exorbitant privi-
> lege, to reverse the verdict is so too . . . We do not starve ourselves
> so that the government may rehabilitate us, but in order to erase
> "reversal of verdicts" from China's political life forever.[15]

Although he kept criticizing the movement, he was one of the few intellectuals who enjoyed a high degree of esteem among the students.[16]

Liu's criticisms were only a minor aspect of his view of the movement. The events made a deep impression on him: the enthusiastic support for the students displayed by Beijing citizens, especially after martial law was declared, convinced him that a new kind of citizen was emerging in China: "June 1989 was the major turning point in my 50 years on life's road";[17] "the martyrs' deaths have opened my eyes and now, each time I open my mouth, I wonder whether I am worthy of them."[18]

His attitude during the pro-democracy movement represented a serious break from the image of the "black horse" who had shocked the progressive intelligentsia. The day before the massacre, he had launched a hunger strike with three friends — Zhou Duo (周舵), Hou Dejian (侯德健), and Gao Xin (高新) — to prevent the repression of the movement. The hunger strike declaration that he mainly authored appealed to the courage of Chinese intellectuals. Their duty was to "take action to oppose military control, to demand the advent of a new political culture, to redeem their fault of having acted cowardly for such a long time. The Chinese nation is backward, and we are all responsible." Even at this crucial time, he continued to use his critical mind:

> The students' main mistake is that they have let antidemocratic practices develop in a movement for democracy . . . Of course, the goal of their movement is democracy but the methods and processes they have used to reach it have been undemocratic . . . However, we think that, as a whole, the most serious mistakes are on the side of the government (which) ignored the basic rights of the people as guaranteed by the Constitution.[19]

He also restated his conviction that violent struggle cannot be a way to achieve democracy.

When the army arrived on Tiananmen Square, Liu and his three comrades tried to negotiate the peaceful evacuation of the square by the students. After the massacre, he could have escaped and even entered the apartment of a diplomat who had taken him to his Embassy, but the Robin Hood (*haohan*, 好汉) in him could not bear to be safe while his hunger-strike partners were out in the streets. Despite the omnipresence of martial law troops, he decided to go out, to try and find out what had happened to them, biking in the streets of Beijing until abducted by the police on June 6th. He was then denounced as one of the "black hands" behind the movement and articles were published in the official press to criticize him.[20] He spent the next twenty months in detention at Qincheng prison (秦城监狱) and was released after having written a self-criticism. It is quite probable that this had haunted him for a long time, and this trauma explains in part his behavior thereafter.

> The souls of June 4th have been watching me from the sky, for fourteen years. To me, a participant in the '89 movement, that

night and that dawn pierced by bullets and crushed by tanks, the memory of lightning-like bayonets have, to this day, been engraved in my memory.[21]

Liu, the lonely radical intellectual, was transfigured by the movement. After his release, he stopped writing about literature and focused on political analysis. Once more, his attitude differed from mainstream pro-democracy intellectuals. For him, the best way to fight what he called the "post-totalitarian regime" consisted of "living in truth." It is not by chance that the act which has led him to be sentenced to eleven years in jail was inspired by the Czechoslovak Charta 77, a manifesto designed by Jan Patocka and Václav Havel, which demanded respect of international treaties on human rights (including, of course, the Universal Declaration of Human Rights). Whereas most radical intellectuals, very much like Liu himself before June Fourth, denounced the intellectuals' attitude that remained prisoners of the literati's traditional posture based on Confucian ethics and encouraged their colleagues to reach high academic standards to guarantee their autonomy, Liu Xiaobo reasserted the importance of ethics:

> To stick to the bottom line which consists of behaving sincerely like a man in daily life doesn't require so much courage, nobility, conscience, or wisdom; such an attitude does not necessarily suppose that one pays the high personal price of jail, of hunger strike … it only requires that one refrain from lying in public speeches; and that when one is confronted with the State's "carrot and stick" tactics, one doesn't lie in order to survive.[22]

If all the Chinese people start to tell the truth, it will be "a deadly threat to a system based on lies." These words definitely have a Havelian touch. The fierce critic of the traditional obsession with ethics diverged with the pro-democracy scholars who explained that democracy was a rational system that allowed various interest groups to express and defend their interests.[23] Whereas the skeptical intellectual he had been in the eighties did not deny the need to be guided by reason in politics, he now acknowledged the importance of ethics in the establishment of a democratic regime: "It is only because of the large mobilization grounded in ethics that the 1989 pro-democracy movement has become the people's movement aimed at transforming China which has bred the biggest hope."[24]

Whereas more and more pro-democracy analysts inside or outside China launched critical reflections over the 1989 movement and came to the conclusion that it had been, to a certain extent, a mistake that triggered a "great leap backwards" and that it was time to say "Farewell to Revolution,"[25] Liu Xiaobo insisted that it was a milestone in the history of contemporary China:

> On the one hand, it has deeply shaken the political legitimacy of the Chinese communist system — Deng Xiaoping's 1992 Southern Tour which launched the second economic reform clearly aimed at repairing the considerable damage caused to the regime's legitimacy and to his personal prestige by the June Fourth massacre; on the other hand, although at an excessively high cost, it has ushered the era when citizens have become aware of their rights; and once this awareness had been awakened, the birth of a civil rights defense movement was inevitable.[26]

The 1989 movement convinced him that the Chinese were no longer the "masses" that Mao Zedong could mobilize at will, but that they had become citizens capable of giving their lives to achieve their ideal of democracy: "The greatness of the 1989 pro-democracy movement is that it has revealed the courage, the sense of justice and the spirit of sacrifice of the silent majority."[27] After June Fourth, Liu Xiaobo, who had always been pessimistic about his fellow humans, became convinced that democratization necessitated not only the sacrifice of conscious intellectuals, but also action by ordinary citizens. He put his faith in unofficial society (*minjian*, 民间) rather than in State power and the elites:

> Most of the reforms are the result of the accumulation of pressure from society, and to defuse the crisis resulting from the moral flaws of the system and from the lame reform, the leaders are forced to make some adjustments to their ideology and to implement partial systemic reforms.[28]

This position put him on a collision course with most intellectuals who kept bragging about the "low quality" (*suzhi tai di*, 素质太低) of the Chinese people and tried by all means to become advisors to the rulers. He did not hesitate to denounce what he termed the "philosophy of the pig," which he said characterized these self-appointed "elites" (*jingying*, 精英). He renewed his fight with the vehemence that had made him famous in the 1980s:

> [T]he mainstream elites have become advocates of the official positions of "priority to stability," "priority to the economy."[29]

He explained further:

> Now it is hard to imagine that this social class which has benefited from State power and depends on it — be they private entrepreneurs or cultural elites — will put its position at risks for moral reasons. Yet, without the spontaneous participation of elites, it is almost impossible to launch a bottom-up popular reform movement.[30]

The elites, including mainstream intellectuals, have a vested interest in keeping things as they are:

> However, the emergence among Chinese elites of hedonism that places the economy above everything else, is not the natural product of their difficulties, but the result of their submission to institutionalized terror, the result of a critical reflection on the 1980s.

Chinese intellectuals in the 1990s insisted on the necessity to become competent specialists rather than to be obsessed by their duty to speak for the people or by their "sense of mission" (*shiming gan*, 使命感). They thought it was the only way to adapt to the challenges of the twenty-first century. Liu Xiaobo begged to differ: "In China, almost everybody has the courage to challenge ethics, whereas one can find almost nobody who has the moral courage to challenge reality."[31] He overtly criticized the "liberal intellectuals" (*ziyou zhishifenzi*, 自由知识分子) who glorified "negative liberty" and denounced the 1989 pro-democracy movement as just another example of the vain struggle for "positive liberties."[32] Liu reminded those thinkers who also defined themselves as "cultural conservatives" that "they ha[d] overlooked the fact that there is a difference in the meaning of conservatism in the West which has a long tradition of liberalism, and in China which has never known it."[33] For him, all these theories were pretexts for those who did not dare rise against tyranny.

Mainstream Chinese intellectuals do not refrain from criticizing the Party; on the contrary, they do, sometimes vehemently, but always in private. They know the limits, and when the Central Propaganda Department threatens them and denounces the "hostile forces," they back off.[34] They know that, as long as they do not create organizations, do not support peasants or workers in their struggles against officials, and refrain from taking part in activities organized by dissidents, they are not seriously at risk: they are aware that the Party will let them enjoy their privileges, travel abroad, and take part in international conferences. Their cautious attitude shocked Liu Xiaobo who reminded them that even in the United Kingdom so dear to these advocates of "negative liberty", men had fought and risked their lives to conquer the freedom their compatriots now enjoyed:[35] "When the famous members of the elite refuse, at the most dangerous moment, to rise in order to defend their ethics and their conscience, when they refuse to pay the individual price, the masses do not have the duty to support them."[36]

This did not mean that Liu had become a populist. He never failed to remind his readers that, to be effective, the pro-democracy movement must involve both the "masses" and the "elites." He vigilantly observed the emergence of resistance among these groups:

> The demand for freedom of expression by intellectuals has been expanding … The intellectuals' resistance to the repression of freedom of expression by the Communist Party, especially the denunciation of the regulation of the Internet, the movement to protect the rights of Liu Di [刘荻], Du Daobin [杜导斌],[37] Jiang Yanyong [蒋彦永],[38] etc., have achieved some measure of success … This would, of course, have been unthinkable without the pressure from the civil rights defense movement.[39]

Whenever members of the elite dared shake the shackles of censorship, he tried to launch movements to support them. He was instrumental in the launching of petitions to support Du Daobin and Liu Di. As soon as the civil rights defense movement appeared in the early twenty-first century, Liu supported it actively: he did everything he could to rally support for the victims of injustice at the grassroots level, as in the case of child slave labor in Shanxi's brick kilns;[40] to denounce the repression of those who dared speak out such as Shi Tao (师涛);[41] and to support workers' struggles, as when he wrote about the organizers of the Liaoyang Ferro-Alloy Factory demonstrations in 2003.

His activism has been impressive and it has earned him the esteem of those who care about the future of China, not only in dissident circles but also in the establishment. Most acknowledge and admire his courage. During his stay at Qincheng prison in Beijing, his first wife asked him to apply for a divorce for the sake of their son's future. He accepted, although this caused him a lot of trouble as his official residence permit (*hukou*, 户口) was therefore transferred to Dalian (大连) where his father resided. This also led him to be imprisoned in Liaoning after his sentencing in 2009.

Liu Xiaobo has always acted in conformity with his ideas, whatever the costs. After his liberation in 1991, he refused to move to the northeast and he settled in the capital without a *hukou* and without a position in a production unit (*danwei*, 单位), a very uncomfortable situation at the time. Because of his situation, he was not allowed to marry Liu Xia with whom he had been living since 1994.[42] Most of the time, he refused to write under a pen-name: having been branded a "black hand" behind the 1989 movement, he was not allowed to publish his works in his motherland, and he survived by writing articles on the political evolution of China for the overseas Chinese-language press.

From January to April 1993, he was a visiting professor in Australia and in the United States. Although his situation in China was precarious, he decided to return home to continue to write and to take part in the fledgling pro-democracy movement, launching petitions to defend human rights and to support the Tiananmen Mothers' demand for the rehabilitation of June Fourth victims. The petitions were made public through the foreign press as the Chinese media were not allowed to reprint them. His marginal situation and his refusal to compromise with the authorities drove him to join the unofficial circles and he became one of the major figures of dissent, a position which came at a cost.

His repeated demands for the government to acknowledge its responsibility in the June Fourth massacre and give compensation to the victims' families, and his actions in defense of human rights exasperated the authorities. From May 1995 to January 1996, he was confined to a residence owned by the Security in Fragrant Hills (香山) in the suburbs of Beijing. However, his conditions of detention were not harsh and after some time, his future wife, Liu Xia, could visit him regularly despite having no legal relation with him. After the end of this peculiar kind of house arrest, he was sent to Dalian, but did not stay there for long and went back to Beijing where he settled with Liu Xia. There, Xiaobo proposed to Liu Xia, but the post-totalitarian regime

once again interfered with their lives. Without a residence permit in
the capital, he could not get married there and the authorities in Dalian
refused to accede to his demand. The two therefore decided to act in
their private life as in their political life: unofficially. They invited their
friends and relatives to celebrate their unregistered wedding — what
the Chinese call "eat candies" (*chi tang*, 吃糖) — in the All Sage bookstore owned by their friend and comrade Liu Suli (刘苏里), an activist
who had been jailed after June Fourth.

Being married did not deter Liu Xiaobo from engaging in activism.
In late 1996, he signed a petition with veteran dissident Wang Xizhe
(王希哲) that asked for co-operation between the *Guomindang* (国民党,
Nationalist Party) and the Communist Party: "I was not convinced by
this demand, but I had a great respect for Wang Xizhe, so I signed."[43]
However, once the petition was made public, Wang fled to the United
States while Liu stayed in Beijing. He was abducted from his home on
8 October 1996 and sentenced to three years of re-education through
labor. This time, the conditions were harsher: as their marriage had not
been acknowledged by the authorities, Liu Xia was not allowed to visit
him and he could not write her letters. Thanks to the intervention of his
lawyer, she was allowed to marry him officially in 1998 and could then
visit him every month.

On 7 October 1999, Liu Xiaobo was released and went straight
back to Beijing where he resumed his action in favor of democracy.
For the following nine years, he was harassed by the authorities, often
followed by the police, or prevented from leaving his home, but this
did not deter him from acting according to his ideas and he became a
central figure in China's political opposition.

Liu was very close to Bao Zunxin (包遵信), the historian who
cofounded the Beijing Autonomous Association of Intellectuals during
the 1989 pro-democracy movement, and they worked hand in hand to
mobilize the intelligentsia in support of human rights. Both thought
that the major task consisted of making the government acknowledge its responsibility in the June Fourth massacre. They actively and
wholeheartedly supported the fight of Ding Zilin (丁子霖), the mother
of a seventeen-year-old student killed by the army, and the founder of
the Tiananmen Mothers.

Liu's behavior, very much in accordance with his ideas, earned him
the esteem of almost all those who had once risen against the regime.

Perhaps because he was once a professor, he is immensely respected by activists of the younger generation. Yu Jie (余杰), a bright literature graduate from Peking University who had worked with him at the Independent Chinese PEN club, considers him his mentor and has written extensively to support him since his arrest. Liu Di, whose satirical posts on the Internet under the pen-name "Stainless Steel Rat" landed her in jail for a year, has had constant contact with him. Liu Xiaobo has also earned the respect of the older generation: of those fifteen years his senior such as Bao Zunxin and Zhang Xianyang (张显扬) — an intellectual close to Hu Yaobang (胡耀邦) and who was expelled from the Party in 1987 — and of ninety-year-old Party elders such as Li Rui (李锐) and Hu Jiwei (胡绩伟), who showed their support for him by writing an open letter to protest his sentencing in January 2010.[44] Petitioners, workers fighting corruption, land activists — he was able to relate to all the militants of the fragmented "people's movement" and to enlist their support in the causes he embraced.

This can be explained by his real charisma. Despite his stutter that gets worse when he gets immersed in a discussion, he is a very convincing and very articulate speaker. Life under the ceaseless surveillance of the *gong'anju* (public security bureau, 公安局) has shaped his behavior. He always meets people openly and tells the truth to all.

He has been one of the first Chinese activists to understand the importance of the Internet, which he called "a gift by God to China," and has used this new technology to circulate petitions in the whole country. Despite the comments by many an observer that dissidents are isolated from society, Liu Xiaobo has been able to maintain contact with professors, journalists, lawyers, and concerned Party members. When he launched a petition to demand the release of Du Daobin, who had been accused of having criticized Jiang Zemin online, he succeeded in obtaining the signatures of prominent establishment intellectuals.

During all those years, Liu Xiaobo has consistently opposed violence, insisting that what he did was legal under the Constitution. He is anything but an extremist, and has acknowledged the progress that has been made since the beginning of the reforms. He has praised the Party when it displayed a minimal amount of sensitivity to the pressures exerted by society, and in one of his books,[45] showed that the situation of human rights had improved and that freedom of expression had made big strides during the last three decades.

Ever since his involvement in politics, he has always refused to take part in underground activities, consistently acting in broad daylight. The case of Charter 08, the drafting of which led him to be jailed on 8 December 2008,[46] is a clear illustration of this attitude. He was convinced that the manifesto, which was written through an elaborate consultation process with hundreds of persons — many of whom were Party members or, at least, members of a *danwei* — was legal under the Constitution. It represented the result of years of discussion by prominent political scientists, activists, and intellectuals who thought it was time to point to a possible way out of the crisis confronting China. When it was made public, the Charter appeared with the signatures of 303 persons among whom were dissidents, establishment intellectuals, and Party members. Liu Xiaobo had not been the main drafter of this Charter, but during his trial, never tried to shed his responsibility and, faithful to his philosophy of *"zuo ren"* (做人, to behave like a man), he defended his right to write it as it was legal and came within the realm of his right to freedom of expression.

The Charter was to be released on the sixtieth anniversary of the Universal Declaration of Human Rights adopted by the United Nations on 10 December 1948. The majority of those who had taken part in its drafting were convinced that, as with most previous petitions, it would have a very limited impact. However, Liu Xiaobo's arrest two days before it was made public gave it a very large echo and, although it was taken off from the Internet after three weeks, it was signed by twelve thousand persons from all walks of life, mostly Chinese, and so became the most widely supported manifesto since 1989. Many among the signatories had been summoned by the agents of public security who put pressure on them to retract their signatures, but almost none of them did.

If by inflicting a heavy sentence on Liu Xiaobo the authorities had intended to deter citizens from joining his struggle, they have miserably failed. The presence of petitioners at his trial has shown that he is more and more considered a defender of ordinary citizens. This image has been reinforced by his being awarded the Nobel Peace Prize. Despite the official silence, the impact of the Oslo Ceremony — when the prize was placed on an empty chair — has been important in China, and many gatherings had symbolic empty chairs in the days that followed.

Times have changed since the 1950s. In 1957, those who were labeled "Rightists" were ostracized, their wives or husbands divorced them, and their children drew a line of demarcation (*huaqing jiexian*, 划清界限) between them. On the contrary, in October 2009, 165 persons signed a public letter expressing their solidarity with Liu: "If Liu Xiaobo is 'guilty of a crime,' it means that everyone of us is a 'criminal.' We must be punished in the same way as Mr Liu Xiaobo."[47]

In the age of the Internet, dissidents are not as isolated as they seem. Liu's struggle is now better known in China, and perhaps his last statement will become true in a not so distant future: "I hope I'll be the last victim of China's unending imprisonment of writers and no one else will be made a criminal for what they say."[48]

Chapter 2
The Sky Is Falling

Inciting Subversion and the Defense of Liu Xiaobo

Joshua Rosenzweig*

When Liu Xiaobo was sentenced to eleven years' imprisonment by the Beijing Number One Intermediate People's Court on Christmas Day 2009, the case focused the world's attention anew on China's laws against "inciting subversion of state power." The lengthy prison term — the longest known since the crime entered the books in 1997 — shocked observers for its harshness and left people scouring the court's verdict for some clue, some justification of the conviction as anything other than a politically motivated punishment passed on a longtime critic of the Chinese Communist Party (hereafter "CCP" or "Party").

The search for a legal explanation turned up little. The Beijing court offered only a cursory explanation of how Liu's alleged offenses — publishing a handful of articles on overseas websites and helping to draft the political manifesto "Charter 08" — could be construed as a "major" threat to national security deserving of such serious punishment. As in other political cases in China, the case against Liu suffered from many flaws: weak evidence and flimsy logic, facts averred rather than proven, and punishments far out of proportion to any reasonable measurement of social harm. The team of two lawyers defending Liu put forth a strong, rights-based argument on behalf of their client, but their efforts appeared to have little effect on the court, whose terse state-

* The author would like to thank The Dui Hua Foundation for providing access to its database of political prisoner information and Tom Kellogg, Otto Malmgren, Glenn Tiffert, and Andrea Worden for valuable comments on an earlier version of this article.

ment that Liu's acts fell "outside the scope of freedom of expression" offered no guidance as to where precisely those boundaries lie.

This chapter seeks to understand the prosecution of Liu Xiaobo by placing it in a broader context. The crime of "inciting subversion" is directly descended from previous prohibitions against "counter-revolution" and, despite changes in nomenclature, has lost little of its original nature as a political instrument. Looking at other cases involving "inciting subversion" in recent years, one finds a number of common threads as well as important differences. The spread of the Internet in China has changed the nature of both the original acts of expression and the assessment of their potential threat to national security. Perhaps more significant has been the emergence of a core group of criminal lawyers who have developed new strategies for defending freedom of expression cases in China. Taking inspiration from both domestic and international law, these lawyers increasingly use their arguments to mount a stirring challenge to the Communist Party's interpretation of the law — a challenge no less significant for the court's limited capacity to engage with it.

Historical-Legal Context of "Inciting Subversion"

Article 105 of the Criminal Law of the People's Republic of China (Criminal Law) covers two separate offenses involving "subversion of state political power and overthrow of the socialist system." The first paragraph focuses on the acts of "organizing, plotting, or carrying out" subversion, whereas the target of the second paragraph is the incitement of others to commit subversion. One of the primary differences between the two offenses is that some act of organization, however loose, is necessary to charge under Article 105(1), whereas charges of incitement under Article 105(2) do not presume any such organizational structure. The former involves demonstrating an act of conspiracy, whereas the latter is focused on demonstrating the socially harmful nature of an act of expression — either verbal or in writing — directed at an unspecified audience without any need to show explicit attempt at conspiracy.

In order to understand the nature of these prohibitions against subversion, one must recognize their roots in earlier laws covering "counter-revolutionary" crime. The idea of "counter-revolution" entered

Chinese political discourse in the 1920s, a period of vigorous debate during which three parties contested the proper course of political change in China. As this contest grew fiercer, one's identification as being on the side of "revolution" grew more important, and increasingly the label of "counter-revolution" began to be applied to one's opponents or even those attempting to remain neutral. It proved to be an extremely flexible label of condemnation, one whose meaning lacked objective definition and depended ultimately upon the position of the person or organization wielding it.[1]

It was in this context that "counter-revolution" was transformed from a category of Chinese political rhetoric into a category of Chinese criminal law. Not long after the unraveling of the revolutionary coalition between the Nationalist Party (*Guomindang*, 国民党) and the CCP during their 1926–27 military campaign to defeat military warlords and unify the nation under a single government, the newly formed Nationalist government under Chiang Kai-shek (蒋介石) established laws to punish counter-revolution as part of the *Guomindang*'s efforts to exclude their former Communist allies and "purify the party."[2] For its part, the CCP retreated to the Jiangxi (江西) countryside, established the "Chinese Soviet Republic," and enacted its own regulations to punish counter-revolution.[3]

After seizing national power in 1949, the CCP used these regulations from the Jiangxi Soviet period as the basis for the 1951 Regulations of the People's Republic of China for the Punishment of Counter-Revolutionaries, provisions targeting those who committed crimes "with the goal of overthrowing the people's democratic dictatorship or undermining the cause of people's democracy." With respect to restrictions on expression, these regulations explicitly prohibited "incitement of the public to oppose or undermine the orders of the People's Government regarding grain levies, taxation, military conscription, or other orders," "sowing dissension between ethnic groups, democratic classes, democratic political parties, or people's organizations, or driving a wedge between the people and the government," or "carrying out counter-revolutionary propaganda and incitement or fabricating and disseminating rumors."[4]

Enactment of the 1979 Criminal Law was meant to elevate the status of law in a China that had been ruled by politics for most of the previous three decades. In fact, however, China's first criminal code remained

infused with political ideology and the language of class struggle. At
the head of the new code's enumeration of specific crimes in the code,
counter-revolution was defined as those "acts intended to overturn the
political power of the dictatorship of the proletariat and the socialist
system and endangering the People's Republic of China."[5] The crime of
"counter-revolutionary propaganda and incitement" (Article 102) prohibited "use of counter-revolutionary slogans, leaflets, or other means
to propagandize and incite overthrow of the political power of the dictatorship of the proletariat and the socialist system."[6]

From Counter-Revolution to Endangering State Security

"Counter-revolutionary propaganda and incitement" became "inciting
subversion of state power" in October 1997, as a major revision of
the Criminal Law was rolled out and counter-revolutionary offenses
replaced with new offenses under the category of "endangering state
security." Though the change of name has made relatively little difference in the practice of Chinese law enforcement, the shift from
"counter-revolution" to "endangering state security" has had a significant impact on the way that such expression offenses are viewed in the
broader context of international human rights law.

The shift has been justified on a number of grounds by Chinese commentators. Over the years since the eleventh CCP Party Congress, the
period of class-based revolutionary struggle officially gave way to a
new stage of "concentrating efforts to promote socialist modernization
construction."[7] From the Party's perspective, the old exploiting class
had been successfully eliminated, meaning that the concept of counter-
revolution was no longer in accord with China's political conditions
and social structure. As a political idea, "counter-revolution" was
prone to change definition based on the evolving environment. To use
such a "malleable" concept to define a category of the criminal law, it
was argued, would be detrimental to the "stability, rigor, and scientific
nature" required in the realm of law.[8]

Experts also cited the practical difficulties involved in establishing
"counter-revolutionary motivation."[9] Under the laws against counter-
revolution, murder, assault, arson, and other crimes could be punished
as counter-revolutionary if it could be determined that the crime was

motivated by the goal of overthrowing the dictatorship of the proletariat and socialist system. Under the new laws against "endangering
state security," the key determination was shifted to whether an act
was a threat to national security or state interests, meaning that acts
like arson or murder not targeting state security directly would hence-
forth be treated strictly as threats to public safety or infringements of
rights of the person — regardless of what the perpetrator's motivations
in carrying out the act might have been.

A more pragmatic reason to do away with "counter-revolution"
was its inadequacy with respect to international law. Since the launch
of the policies of reform and opening in 1978, China had increased its
contacts and co-operation with other countries and was quickly developing awareness of international law and practices. Drafters of the new
legislation observed that many foreign governments viewed counter-
revolution as a "political crime" and, following international practice,
would refuse to extradite suspects facing charges of counter-revolution.
Changing the law to criminalize endangering state security — a concept
with a much more universal basis in international law — would, it was
believed, ease international law-enforcement co-operation and enhance
China's jurisdiction to enforce its criminal law.[10]

Behind all of these reasons for change in legal nomenclature was the
assurance that doing so would have absolutely no detrimental effect
on China's ability to fight crime and ensure stability.[11] All acts previously criminalized by laws against counter-revolution continued to
be prohibited under the revised law, although some crimes — such as
"using a cult or sect to undermine implementation of the law" (Article
300) — were nominally recategorized as "ordinary" crimes, rather than
state security crimes.[12] Moreover, the law made clear that the change in
name would not result in any change for those who had been punished
under the laws of counter-revolution since 1980, including those still
serving sentences when the new law came into effect.[13]

Nowhere is the sense of continuity greater than in the criminal
prohibition against "inciting subversion of state political power," in
which the restrictions on political speech is at least as broad as it had
been under the law prohibiting counter-revolutionary propaganda and
incitement. Article 105, paragraph 2 of China's Criminal Law reads:

> Whoever incites others by spreading rumors or slanders or any
> other means to subvert state political power or overthrow the
> socialist system shall be sentenced to fixed-term imprisonment of
> not more than five years, penal servitude, public surveillance or
> deprivation of political rights; and the ringleaders and others who
> commit major crimes shall be sentenced to fixed-term imprison-
> ment of not less than five years.

Less than half of this provision is concerned with defining the elements
of the offense, and the lack of specificity of these definitions has contributed to controversies that have plagued prosecutions over its entire
history.

For one thing, the key determinative element of motivation or intent,
which should determine whether the acts in question are subject to this
particular criminal sanction, remains elusive. For most crimes, Chinese
law requires there to be intent before an individual can be held criminally responsible for a given action.[14] With respect to inciting subversion, the court must find that a defendant acted despite knowing that
his or her actions could lead others to engage in acts of subverting state
political power or the socialist system. Yet in practice, establishing the
malevolent intent, motivation, or purpose (i.e., *mens rea*) of an act of
expression is not a particularly well-developed area of Chinese judicial
practice. Chinese courts tend to infer malicious intent from the content
of the offending expression; in other words, the nature of the act proves
the subjective motivation of the defendant, making a separate investigation of intent unnecessary.[15]

The law offers similarly little guidance regarding the objective
elements that determine the crime, or what types of acts may or may
not be considered incitement. Specifically mentioned are the use of
"spreading rumor" (defined in one legal treatise as "concocting and
disseminating rumors to deceive and hoodwink the public") and the
use of "slander" (defined by the same source as "fabricating facts and
allowing them to be disseminated in order to defame or viciously
attack").[16] However, the law's inclusion of the phrase "or any other
means" expands the scope of possible acts well beyond these two
explicitly stated.[17] In order to make a judgment about what constitutes
rumor or slander, it is necessary to establish clear distinctions between
facts and opinions, distinctions that have proven in practice to be
highly arbitrary and prejudicial against defendants in incitement cases.

Most cases of inciting subversion of state political power face a maximum sentence of five years in prison, although the maximum possible sentence for "major" offenses is a fixed-term sentence of fifteen years (assuming that the defendant is not simultaneously found guilty of any other charges). Lighter punishments of penal servitude or public surveillance (also known as "control") are also permitted, as are suspended sentences. As with all state security crimes, fixed-term sentences of imprisonment under Article 105(2) carry with them mandatory "supplementary" deprivations of political rights for between one and five years.[18] During this period, an individual is subject to frequent police monitoring and loses the right to vote and stand for election; the rights of freedom of speech, of the press, of assembly, of association, of procession and of demonstration; the right to any job in an organ of the state; and the right to hold a leading position in any state-owned company, enterprise, institution, or people's organization.[19]

Other than the distinction between ordinary and "major" cases, there are no other explicit criteria for determining sentencing in Article 105(2) cases. There are three natural ranges for fixed-term imprisonment: one to five years, five to ten years, and ten to fifteen years. Most sentences fall in the first range, with Liu Xiaobo's being the only known case since the law came into being in 1997 where a sentence of more than ten years' imprisonment was passed. Since most cases of inciting subversion do not result in actual acts of subversion or other tangible harm, courts are left to rely on the facts of the case or an evaluation of the nature of the crime in determining sentencing.[20] Many courts have cited things such as the length of the period during which the alleged incitement took place or some measure of the extent of an offending article's dissemination. However, there do not appear to be any formal standards for application of these metrics, giving the final decision an added sense of subjectivity and arbitrariness.

The Constitutional Context

On paper, at least, China's Constitution provides strong protection for individual expression, but these rights are severely circumscribed by complementary obligations enumerated elsewhere in the document. Under the section of the Constitution entitled "Fundamental Rights and Duties of Citizens," Article 35 states that Chinese citizens "enjoy freedom of speech, of the press, of assembly, of association, of procession and of demonstration." Article 41 also grants citizens the rights to "criticize and make suggestions to any state organ or functionary" and to "make to relevant state organs complaints and charges against, or exposures of, violation of the law or dereliction of duty by any state organ or functionary." The same provision goes on to note, however, that "fabrication or distortion of facts with the intention of libel or frame-up is prohibited." Under the category of "duties," Article 51 places a sweeping restriction on the aforementioned individual rights, stating: "The exercise by citizens of the People's Republic of China of their freedoms and rights may not infringe upon the interests of the state, of society and of the collective, or upon the lawful freedoms and rights of other citizens." Article 54 imposes further limits in the name of national security, stating: "It is the duty of citizens of the People's Republic of China to safeguard the security, honor and interests of the motherland; they must not commit acts detrimental to the security, honor and interests of the motherland." This tension between rights and obligations in the Constitution has not diminished, even after the addition of a 2004 amendment asserting, "the state respects and preserves human rights."[21]

These limitations on individual rights are not the only reason why China's Constitution provides little refuge to those facing criminal sanctions for the exercise of their putative rights. In the Chinese legal system, courts do not apply constitutional principles directly; rather, their role is to apply laws, which in theory are the embodiment of those constitutional principles. Since 1955, China's courts have been bound by a directive of the Supreme People's Court prohibiting direct application of the Constitution to the "determination of guilt and sentencing" in criminal trials. A 2005 "guiding opinion" issued by the Beijing High People's Court prohibits direct citation of the Constitution in verdicts for all criminal, civil, or administrative proceedings. Though some recent evidence points toward attempts by Chinese courts to engage constitutional arguments in the course of adjudication, this appears to have been primarily limited to civil or administrative proceedings, rather than criminal trials.[22]

Likewise, Chinese courts do not have authority to interpret the Constitution or rule on violations of constitutional provisions — such as rights. Instead, responsibility for enforcement and interpretation of the Constitution is granted, respectively, to China's legislature — the National People's Congress (NPC) — and its Standing Committee. As both institutions are dominated by the ruling Communist Party, any hope of appealing to the Constitution in matters where the Party has a strong political interest — as in, for example, cases of individuals charged with challenging the Party's monopoly on power — is faint indeed.

Prosecution of Inciting Subversion

Given the lack of transparency in China's criminal justice system, it is impossible to ascertain what proportion of all cases of inciting subversion are known. Published statistics in China only allow insight into the numbers of individual arrests, prosecutions, and cases (not individuals) adjudicated for the entire category of "endangering state security," but there is no way to break this down further by specific offenses.[23]

As of the end of 2010, seventy-four individuals were known to have been convicted by Chinese courts for inciting subversion since the law came into force in October 1997.[24] Figure 1 shows the distribution of known convictions by year, revealing that more than two-thirds took place in the first half of the period under consideration, and Figure 2 reflects that the median length for a fixed-term sentence is four years. The decrease beginning in 2004 roughly corresponds to the beginning of a three-year period of fewer arrests and indictments for endangering state security overall. That the subsequent upward rebound for state security arrests and prosecutions has not been reflected in more prosecutions for inciting subversion further confirms that, while not exactly rare in the context of state security crimes, prosecutions on charges of inciting subversion do not appear to be as common as cases involving espionage (Article 110) or the "boundary-change threats" of "splittism" (Article 103(1)) and "inciting splittism" (Article 103(2)).[25]

At the time the prohibition against inciting subversion came into being in 1997, Chinese society was still relatively unaffected by the Internet. Acts committed by individuals charged with inciting subversion during the first years after the offense was established actually differed little from what had been punished under the prohibition against "counter-revolutionary propaganda and incitement." For

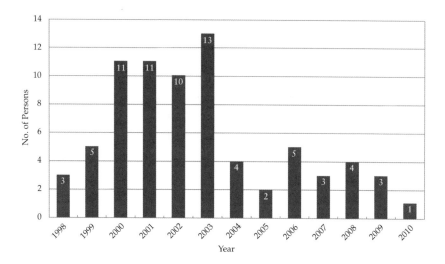

Figure 1

Individuals Convicted of Inciting Subversion (October 1997–December 2010)

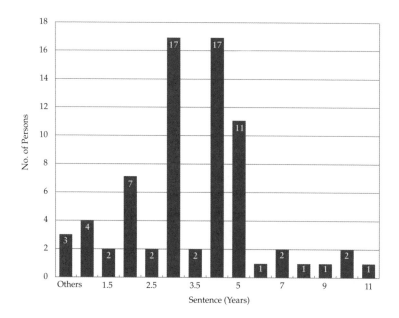

Figure 2

Penalties for Inciting Subversion in China (October 1997–December 2010)

example, in a case in Guangdong (广东), Zhang Chenglin (张成林) was sentenced to five years in prison in 1998 for disseminating a parody of the national anthem, satirical couplets, leaflets, posters, and letters critical of the government.[26] In 1999, Li Zhiyou (李志友) received a three-year sentence in Guangxi (广西) for writing political graffiti in public toilets.[27] That same year, Yuan Yongbo (袁拥波) was sentenced to a year in prison by a Hubei (湖北) court for putting up posters commemorating the tenth anniversary of the 1989 pro-democracy movement.[28] In 2002, Li Huanming (李焕明) was given a stiff sentence of nine years in prison for dropping political leaflets from the top of overpasses in the busy urban centers of Guangzhou and Shenzhen.[29]

Over the last decade, however, the Internet has rapidly developed into a ubiquitous tool of communication and an integral part of daily life for many Chinese. The number of Internet users in China exploded during this period, from 8.9 million in 2000 to 450 million by the end of 2010.[30] As is true elsewhere in the world, email, BBSes, blogs, web games, and social networking platforms have all become the preferred media for many different forms of sociability and self-expression in China. This has had a profound impact on the modes of oppositional political expression and organization in China — and on the state's response. The Internet enables any individual's writings to cross boundaries and reach an audience far wider than any printed leaflet ever could, all with unprecedented immediacy. Activists from different parts of China are more aware of each other than ever before and have more opportunities to share their opinions with others — regardless of physical location — and absorb new ideas and information in "real time."

Simultaneously, however, the Internet has also made the job of authorities in charge of eliminating political dissent considerably easier. Despite the proliferation of voices, with so much of China's political "space" concentrated online, the deployment of police manpower and technology makes it relatively easy for authorities to monitor specific targets. Rarely these days do domestic security police spend their time tracking down political pamphlets; now the collection of evidence in political cases tends to be a matter of downloading some articles from a few well-known websites and checking the hard drives of suspects for incriminating documents and emails.

The new direction began to be seen in 1998, when a 30-year-old software entrepreneur named Lin Hai (林海) was arrested by police on charges of inciting subversion for allegedly collecting the email addresses of nearly thirty thousand computer users throughout China and sending them to the publisher of a US-based daily electronic newsletter, *Chinese VIP Reference News* (*Dacankao*, 大参考), thereby enabling the latter to disseminate a large number of politically inflammatory articles.[31] The case of Sichuan webmaster Huang Qi (黄琦) was among the first major Internet-related cases of political crime to attract widespread international attention and showed that the authorities would not only go after the authors of "subversive" speech but also those who, through their websites, gave a forum to those expressions.[32] Most of those, however, who have been punished under the provisions of Article 105(2) are individuals like Liu Xiaobo, Guo Qinghai (郭庆海), Du Daobin (杜导斌), or Zhang Lin (张林) who have written prolifically for overseas online forums such as Democracy Forum, Democracy and Freedom, or Boxun, or on one of many publications associated with the outlawed Falun Gong organization.

Chinese law enforcement authorities take such links to foreign entities very seriously, even though almost all of these online forums are hosted overseas and blocked by China's "Great Firewall." One new provision added to the 1997 Criminal Law's section on crimes of endangering state security was Article 106, which calls for heavier punishment for those who engage in separatist or subversive activity in collusion with organizations or individuals overseas — something that the new global communications capabilities introduced by the Internet made more possible than was perhaps imagined at the time the law was drafted. In echoes of what used to be called "counter-revolutionary correspondence" (*fan'geming guagou*, 反革命挂勾), Article 106 has been used to impose heavier penalties on a number of individuals — such as Xu Jian (许健), Xu Weikang (徐伟康), and Badun (巴敦) — convicted of making contact with "hostile" broadcasters like Radio Free Asia or Voice of America.[33] In 2003, Beijing resident Wang Xiaoning (王小宁) was given one of the longest sentences ever for inciting subversion — ten years in prison — in part because he made contact with overseas political activists.[34]

The vast majority of individuals prosecuted for inciting subversion have, like Liu Xiaobo, expressed opinions rooted in what could be generally called a liberal democratic critique of the Chinese political system. Chief targets of this critique are the CCP monopoly on political power and limited electoral democracy. Attacks on corruption and other abuses of power have also been a common theme, as have calls for release of political prisoners and reversal of the official assessment of the 1989 pro-democracy demonstrations. But the CCP's liberal critics are not the only ones in danger of prosecution under the provisions of Article 105(2). In 2000, a Hebei man named Wang Shiji (王士吉) was sentenced to three years in prison for launching neo-Maoist attacks on Deng Xiaoping (邓小平) and Jiang Zemin (江泽民).[35] In 2003, Zhang Zhengyao (张正耀) and Zhang Ruquan (张汝泉) were initially arrested on charges of inciting subversion for similarly attacking Jiang Zemin in articles commemorating Mao Zedong, but authorities in Henan (河南) subsequently decided to try them on criminal defamation charges — charges for which they were convicted and sentenced each to three years' imprisonment.[36]

The Defense of Liu Xiaobo

In a short, simple indictment, the prosecution's case against Liu Xiaobo focused on selected statements from six articles published between 2005 and 2008 on websites hosted overseas, as well as passages from Charter 08.[37] Following the constitutive formula for Article 105(2), four passages were identified as involving "fabrication of rumors," defamation, or libel. Each of these statements describes the CCP regime as "autocratic" or "authoritarian" in nature and suggests that the CCP is concerned most with preserving its own rule and has brought great misfortunes to the Chinese nation and its people. For example, the indictment cites this passage from Charter 08:

> We stand today as the only country among the major nations that remains mired in authoritarian politics. Our political system continues to produce human rights disasters and social crises, thereby not only constricting China's own development but also limiting the progress of all of human civilization.[38]

The indictment also identified several "inciting" statements, such as Charter 08's calls for an end to one-party rule and establishment of a federal system of government. Though these passages each touch on changing the political order in China, prosecutors did not put forth any mention of violence or even suggestion that the political change would have to take place immediately. Aside from establishing Liu's authorship or connection to these texts, the rest of the prosecution's case focused on allegations that the widespread dissemination of Liu's writings through the Internet caused "great" harm to national security — harm that ought to be punished more severely in accordance with the levels of penalty set out in the law.

In response to the prosecution's charges, Liu and his attorneys — Shang Baojun (尚宝军) and Ding Xikui (丁锡奎) of the Mo Shaoping Law Firm (莫少平律师事务所) — readily conceded nearly all of the facts set out in the indictment. They did not dispute Liu's authorship of the statements in question but did raise a serious challenge to the prosecution's interpretation of those statements as "inciting subversion" and mount a defense based firmly on the grounds that Liu's speech should be protected as a fundamental right, both under China's Constitution and under international law.[39]

Technical Arguments: Subjective and Objective Elements

The defense statement in Liu Xiaobo's trial of first instance starts as most defense statements have in such cases: by challenging the prosecution's allegation of intent. Indeed, the indictment simply states that Liu's actions were motivated by "unhappiness with the People's Democratic Dictatorship and socialist system," without offering anything (other than the content of the texts themselves, perhaps) as evidence. This ignores, the lawyers argue, the statements Liu made to police indicating that he saw his actions as furthering the development of democracy and rule of law in China, motivations that can only be viewed as beneficial to society, rather than harmful. If one were to look at the totality of Liu's writings, they continue, it would only be reasonable to grant him benefit of the doubt that he did not intend to incite subversion.

Later in the statement, the defense takes issue with the prosecution's characterization of Liu's statements as "rumor," "libel," and "defamation" — thereby challenging three essential constitutive elements established in Article 105(2). Noting that fabrication of facts is an essential characteristic of all three acts, they insist that the offensive statements are "merely [Liu's] personal political opinions and views on newsworthy events, a matter of 'value judgment' rather than 'factual judgment,' with no fabrication of facts." Failure to recognize the distinction between "value judgments" and "factual judgments" is a fatal flaw in the prosecution's argument, they contend.

Arguing for the Importance of Context

Liu's lawyers then assert that prosecutors have taken their client's statements out of context and insist that it is impossible to interpret the meaning of any textual passage without considering its background, context, the issues it concerns, and the conventional views and phrasing of the author. Having written more than eight hundred articles and over five million words over his lifetime, it is unjust to extrapolate the views of a writer as prolific as Liu Xiaobo from the mere 350 or so words cited in the indictment. To make their point, the lawyers show how statements made by Mao Zedong and Deng Xiaoping could, if similarly taken out of context, be used as the basis for criminal prosecution.

Quotation of historical figures — particularly first-generation Party leaders — has been a feature of many defense arguments against charges of inciting subversion. For one thing, it shows how an author's meaning can easily be misconstrued by taking quotes out of context. Though Mao Zedong wrote in 1920 that China should split into twenty-seven separate republics, it is argued that it would be a mistake (or at least a serious political error) to conclude that Mao advocated separatism.

Yet Liu's lawyers take statements out of context as well, as when they marshal statements made by Party leaders like Mao or Liu Shaoqi (刘少奇) during the 1940s as sharing Charter 08's goals for an end to one-party rule and establishment of a federal system.[40] Similarly, in their 2004 defense of Du Daobin, Mo Shaoping (莫少平) and Lü Xi (吕曦) pointed out that Party leaders have also had much to say about the importance of listening to criticism, arguing: "The attitude with which a ruling party treats dissenting opinions (even critical attacks) is a reflection of its breadth of mind and tolerance, and historically the CCP has in fact not lacked in magnanimity in its tolerance of critical views."[41] To illustrate, Mo and Lü cited a famous story Mao Zedong told about the Party's days in Yan'an (延安), when he chose not to retaliate against a peasant woman who said she thought he should be struck by lightning.[42] Mao explained the moral of the story bluntly: "Let people speak — the sky won't fall down!"[43]

Lawyers employ a complex strategy when they try to invoke history and context in defense of their clients. On the surface, one might expect that quoting Party leaders in support of defendants charged with challenging the Party's rule might have some effect on the court, considering how important it is for Party members to study Party history and the collected writings of leaders like Mao and Deng. But one could easily counter that defense lawyers are as guilty of taking statements and anecdotes out of context as prosecutors are. The CCP line on things such as constitutional government or free speech has shifted course several times since its founding in 1921, and historical circumstances have had a major influence over those positions. Even if tolerance for criticism was, as Mo Shaoping has argued, one of the reasons why the CCP successfully won the hearts and minds of many Chinese in the years preceding the revolution, the more tolerant statements and policies made during that period have to be considered in light of the CCP's political contest with the Nationalist government. Since taking power, the CCP has generally kept challenges to one-party rule or criticism of government policy under control.

But when Liu Xiaobo's lawyers make another reference to history, comparing their client's critical statements about the government with "reactionary" statements singled out during the Anti-Rightist Campaign launched in 1957, they are actually making an effort to recontextualize the case against Liu. They ask: "Shouldn't we learn the lessons of history, instead of following the same disastrous historical path of 'criminalizing speech' and 'literary inquisitions'?" For them, the lesson is clear enough, and they claim that "history has proven" that the Anti-Rightist Campaign was "mistaken." Certainly the lawyers are aware, however, that official CCP history has not yet repudiated the campaign, maintaining that it represented a necessary rectification of the Party but that excesses and abuses could be attributed to "leftist deviations." As they do when they highlight the irony of Mao's erstwhile support for policies forbidden in the contemporary context, the lawyers' invocation of the sensitive Anti-Rightist Campaign and questions of "historical verdicts" aims to create discomfort and encourage the court to consider the prosecution of Liu Xiaobo in a broader context. This is one of many rhetorical strategies employed by Chinese defense lawyers that seems to be targeted at an audience beyond the three-judge panel deciding the case.

The Free-Expression Argument

Liu's lawyers anchor their defense statement to the court with a spirited defense of free speech that draws inspiration from Chinese constitutional principles and international human rights law. Liu's statements, they insist, are nothing more than "relatively trenchant, intense criticism," personal views that even if in error should be granted protection under Articles 35 and 41 of China's Constitution and Article 19 of the Universal Declaration of Human Rights. They acknowledge that the International Covenant on Civil and Political Rights (ICCPR), which China signed in 1998 but has not yet ratified, does not establish absolute freedom of expression and that there are legitimate grounds for imposing restrictions on expression, one being national security.[44]

However, any restriction on a fundamental human right like freedom of expression should, argue the lawyers for Liu Xiaobo, be strictly limited. On this point, they seek support from the "internationally recognized" Johannesburg Principles on National Security, Freedom of Expression and Access to Information (Johannesburg Principles), a set of guiding principles drafted in 1995 by a group of thirty-six international experts. This distillation of international and comparative law and human rights protection practices demands that restrictions on expression be in response to legitimate threats to national security, be the least restrictive means possible for protection of the interest, and be compatible with democratic principles.[45] Protection of the government from criticism or embarrassment or the entrenchment of a particular ideology are both explicitly mentioned as illegitimate grounds for restricting expression.[46] Freedom of expression can only be restricted if it can be demonstrated that: (a) the expression is intended to incite imminent violence; (b) the expression is likely to incite such violence; and (c) there is a direct and immediate relationship between the act of expression and the possibility or occurrence of such violence.[47] In their defense statement, Liu's lawyers argue that their client's writings display no intent to incite imminent violence, no likelihood that such violence could occur, and no direct or immediate threat to national security. On the contrary, they argue, Liu repeatedly advocates "peaceful," "rational," "non-violent," and gradual reform.

The centrality of the free-expression argument in defense against charges of inciting subversion is something that has developed over time. The phrase "freedom of expression" does not appear in many of the defense statements that can be found from the years immediately following 1997, even in situations where it seems logical to do so.[48] Early mentions of the right to free expression remained relatively simple, rooted primarily in the protections of China's Constitution. Fu Kexin (付可心), one of the lawyers for political activist He Depu (何德普), articulates this most clearly in 2003, saying:

> As everyone knows, a fundamental principle of the Constitution is its granting to citizens of the People's Republic of China the rights to free speech, publication, gathering, and association. Any time there is an issue over whether a citizen's speech violates the law or constitutes a crime, we must proceed with a sober and serious attitude, take the facts as our basis and the law as our criterion, and clarify the boundaries between rumor and fact, slander and criticism, and the right of a citizen to exercise free speech and the crime of inciting subversion of state political power. Otherwise, it is trampling on the fundamental rights that the Constitution bestows on citizens.[49]

In more recent years, however, defense lawyers have rarely missed an opportunity to mention the Universal Declaration of Human Rights, the ICCPR, and the Johannesburg Principles as support for the free-expression defense. This change coincides with two related developments. One is the inspiration of the 2004 constitutional amendment including explicit language about the state safeguarding human rights — and, thus, implicitly extending the foundation for protection of free expression to include international human rights law as well. Around the same time, one starts to be able to identify a growing rights-consciousness among the Chinese people in general and especially within a core group of lawyers who see their mission as defending rights.[50] As defense of politically sensitive criminal cases has become concentrated in the hands of these "rights defense" (*weiquan*, 维权) lawyers, arguments on behalf of defendants charged with inciting subversion have become more consistent and predictable.

Though defense arguments have become more sophisticated in their use of the discourse of rights, Chinese courts remain relatively constant in refusing to engage the arguments on any but the most basic of levels. In its verdict against Liu Xiaobo, the Beijing Number One Intermediate People's Court merely says that Liu's offending statements fell "outside the scope of free expression."[51] This is in fact a fairly standard response in such cases, but courts have occasionally offered a bit more explanation of what is meant by this. In its 2003 conviction of Huang Qi, the Chengdu (成都) Intermediate People's Court responded to the argument that the content of Huang's website should be protected by the Constitution with the following rebuttal:

> Freedom of expression is a political right of Chinese citizens, but in exercising this right one may not damage national interests or security or employ rumor or slander to incite subversion of state political power. Defense counsel only emphasizes the rights of the defendant and not his obligations; therefore, the court cannot accept [the argument].[52]

Several months later, in response to a free-speech argument made on behalf of Cai Lujun (蔡陆军), the Shijiazhuang (石家庄) Intermediate People's Court again explained that Article 41 of China's Constitution only protects the "use of normal channels to make reasonable suggestions or offer measures for improvement to relevant government organs."[53] Similar refrains about the need for balance between rights and obligations appear over and over in other verdicts and reflect the limits within which Chinese courts are willing (or able) to rebut the free-expression argument. When it comes to engaging arguments based on international human rights law in freedom of expression cases, Chinese courts simply maintain a deafening silence.

Necessity of Legislative Reform

In the summary of their defense of free speech, Liu's lawyers cite the legal principles of "the defendant should have benefit of the doubt" and *nullum crimen, nulla poena sine lege* ("there is no crime and no punishment without a law"). They argue that since Liu is in the best position to interpret the meaning of his own work, even if there are other possible explications of passages in question, he should be given the benefit of the doubt. And since neither China's legislative organs nor the Supreme People's Court or Supreme People's Procuratorate have ever issued any authoritative interpretation to set out a persuasive standard setting the boundary between free expression and criminal behavior, Article 105(2) is prone to subjective, arbitrary, and vague application, and individuals cannot rationally predict whether their behavior might be criminal. In the absence of any such legislative guidance or judicial interpretation, they conclude, the principle of *nullum crimen* should be upheld.

The idea of calling for legislative or judicial interpretation of Article 105(2) took root in mid-2003, a result of multiple coincident events. First, there had been an unusually high number of activists arrested over the previous year as the growing popularity of the Internet combined with efforts to urge newly selected CCP general secretary Hu Jintao (胡锦涛) to take more active steps towards political reform.[54] Among those arrested on charges of inciting subversion was a young Beijing college student named Liu Di (刘荻) — known online as "Stainless Steel Rat" (不锈钢老鼠) — whose case became an immediate cause célèbre and soon found those campaigning on behalf of her and other detained activists facing charges of their own.[55]

A more positive development came in June 2003, when Hu, who became president of the People's Republic of China three months earlier, announced the abolition of the system known as "custody and repatriation" (*shourong qiansong*, 收容遣送). This system of administrative detention, by which individuals without proper proof of local residence could be detained pending forcible repatriation to their place of household registration, had come under attack following the mysterious death in detention of Sun Zhigang (孙志刚) the previous month. Constitutional law scholars issued appeals challenging the legality of the system, appeals that were widely seen as having influenced the decision to eliminate the controversial system. It was a heady moment, one in which it seemed China might be taking a major step in the direction of constitutionalism, a more responsive system of government, and more rule of law.[56]

It was in this context that a Qingdao (青岛) lawyer named Li Jianqiang (李建强) and a Shanghai lawyer named Guo Guoting (郭国汀) teamed up with more than a dozen lawyers, academics, and others to issue an appeal to Hu Jintao and the NPC Standing Committee for the abolition or reform of Article 105(2).[57] Pointing out that young, idealistic, socially conscious Chinese were being unjustly punished, they argued that "aside from abuses of authority by law enforcement [authorities] that have infringed on the constitutional rights of citizens, legislative deficiencies must not be overlooked." "Subversion of state power" or "overthrow of the socialist system" are acts that require the use of violence, they contended, meaning that without calls for violence, those being punished for "instigatory" speech were really doing nothing more than demanding reform. Moreover, they argued, any calls for violence against the state could easily be interpreted as violations of Article 105(1), the crime of subversion. In the interest of the security of the people (not, significantly, "national security") they called on President Hu to act boldly and, in the spirit of the decision to abolish custody and repatriation, abolish or revise Article 105(2). Even though this public appeal for review of the provision outlawing inciting subversion did not achieve its immediate goal, the proposal made an important contribution by strengthening the "arsenal" of arguments available to defense lawyers.

Procedural Justice

Finally, Liu's attorneys raise their objections to serious procedural violations during the handling of his case. In particular, they cite the improper use of "residential surveillance" during the first six months of the investigative phase. Instead of being confined to his residence in Beijing, where he would be under police monitoring and subject to questioning but otherwise able to maintain a relatively normal existence, Liu was held by police in an unspecified location under conditions that were largely indistinguishable from custody in a detention center. The laws and related regulations governing coercive measures call for suspects placed under residential surveillance to be kept in their "place of fixed abode"; if they have none, they may be confined to an alternative location designated by police.[58] Since Liu has a home in Beijing, his lawyers contend, there is no justification for holding him anywhere else in the name of residential surveillance.

The primary purpose of the defense argument about residential surveillance is pragmatic: Liu's lawyers seek to ensure that, if convicted and sentenced to imprisonment, their client gets credit for time already served — as he would if he had been placed in a detention center. The controversy over the "illegal" use of residential surveillance is actually more complicated than it seems to be on the surface. Because the criminal procedure law does not define what is meant by "abode," there are a number of plausible interpretations available. One draws upon the civil procedure code to define it as the place of household registration (*hukou*, 户口), which for Liu Xiaobo is in Liaoning Province.[59] The court ultimately defers to this interpretation, frequently referring to Liu's home in Beijing as his "temporary" residence, regardless of how long he had actually lived there. Although never stated explicitly, it appears that the court also defers to the police interpretation of Liu's conditions of detention as less than "total restriction of personal liberty" and thus not eligible for credit for time served under the relevant regulations.[60]

When Chinese defense lawyers raise procedural violations with trial courts, they do so knowing that it is not the court's role to render opinions about whether defendants' rights have been protected during the course of investigation. Unlike in other jurisdictions, procedural violation is not grounds for dismissal in a Chinese criminal trial. (Serious procedural violations in the course of interrogation, collection of witness statements, or obtaining of other kinds of evidence could, in theory, lead courts to exclude certain evidence.) Knowing that their claims are likely to fall on deaf ears, these defense lawyers realize that each time law enforcement officials neglect to notify a suspect's family of his or her detention, prevent a defense lawyer from meeting with a client on questionable grounds that the case "involves state secrets," refuse to respond to requests for bail or medical parole, or fail to provide defense lawyers access to evidence or even the prosecution's bill of indictment, it belies the Chinese government's claims to operate according to rule of law.[61]

Other Defense Strategies

There are, of course, a number of other strategies that defense lawyers employ in their efforts on behalf of clients charged with inciting subversion. One is making an appeal on the grounds of good faith co-operation by the defendant during the criminal investigation. On a couple of occasions, at least, this argument has succeeded in getting courts to issue suspended prison sentences. In these cases, however, suspended sentences have not turned out to be quite as lenient as one might have originally hoped — in part because of the continued outspokenness of the individuals concerned.

Du Daobin was given a four-year suspension of his three-year prison sentence in 2004 on the grounds that he had been co-operative with police and "expressed guilt and a willingness to submit to the law" at trial.[62] Du did not accept the court's lenience, however, and chafed under the restrictions placed on him during the suspension period. In July 2008, one month before his probation period was set to expire, Du was remanded to custody for violating the terms of the suspension and forced to serve out most of the original three-year sentence.[63] The suspension of Gao Zhisheng's (高智晟) three-year prison sentence in 2006 similarly placed him in a five-year period of limbo, during which he was rarely free from police surveillance and was effectively "disappeared" under extremely suspicious circumstances from February 2009 until also being placed back in custody in December 2011.[64] In these two cases, at least, one could argue that the defendants might have been better off if the court had shown less lenience and simply sentenced them to prison.

Biography as Defense

On a few occasions, defense lawyers in political cases have attempted to justify their clients' more extreme criticisms of the government in part by appealing to details of biography. For instance, Li Jianqiang described the twelve years of frustration Guo Qizhen (郭起真) experienced after being unjustly convicted of assault and losing his job. Guo went from being "an ordinary clerk, the kind of person the Party and government rely on" to "someone unhappy with society, a victim and petitioner ... [who] as time went on developed suspicions, disgust, and even resentment toward China's political system and leaders and expressed his anger through writing."[65] Li continued:

> Actually, this evolution has much to do with the repeated failure of the relevant departments, including judicial departments, to deal with [Guo's] problems properly. In a certain way, one can say that it is because of these repeated failures that he became disconnected from (and doubtful of) the government. If one does not consider this history and places all of the responsibility on his shoulders alone, pushing him into opposition to the government and using criminal sanctions to punish him heavily, this would clearly be unjust and unwise.[66]

Similarly, rights-defense lawyer Li Fangping (李方平) reminded the Beijing court trying Hu Jia (胡佳) that several of his client's more outspoken criticisms of the government were made in a span of over a year in which he had been subject to continual police harassment:

> During this period and the period just before it, he found himself in a situation without rule of law, losing his liberty or freedom of movement for long periods and even disappearing for a short while. His personal experience led him to lose confidence in the rule-of-law situation in this country and develop a negative evaluation of the human rights situation in China, and ultimately this escalated into attacks on the systemic level.[67]

These kinds of biographical justifications do not occupy a major position in the defense strategy, but they can play an important role of contextualizing defendants' more strident criticisms. Chinese law enforcement officials often describe defendants in political cases as having committed acts out of "dissatisfaction with society," and, in a way, the lawyers for Guo and Hu embrace that characterization but turn it back against the government, issuing a warning that conviction will only compound their sense of unjust treatment.

Li Jianqiang, who during his time as a defense lawyer in China was known to take risks and radical positions, took this admonition one step further by warning courts more than once that convicting his clients might result in negative consequences. In his defense of journalist Li Yuanlong (李元龙), he noted that International PEN, Reporters Without Borders, and the Committee to Protect Journalists had all issued appeals on Li Yuanlong's behalf and warned that a conviction could "create serious damage to China's international legal image."[68] Noting that Guo Qizhen's purpose in publishing his critical articles had been to draw attention to his grievances, Li warned that convicting him would create a storm of public opinion and damage the image of China's legal system or even the nation as a whole. Though Guo might be silenced for a time, others would likely step in to criticize the handling of his case. At the very least, Guo would likely pick up right where he left off as soon as he was released.[69]

Measurement of Social Harm

Measurement of social harm is another area of controversy that surrounds the crime of inciting subversion. Under Chinese law, there is no requirement that the act of incitement lead to any subversive acts, so the harm is located merely in the potential for such acts to take place. It does not matter whether the scope of the incitement can be measured or not. Before the Internet became widely used in China, the lawyer for anti-corruption activist An Jun (安均) argued in 2000 that the prosecution could not charge his client with incitement for letters that An had sent to a select group of recipients by fax, because the letters had been sent with requests for comment (i.e., as drafts) and were not intended to be re-circulated (and, in fact, they were not).[70] That same year, Mo Shaoping argued that an article Jiang Qisheng (江棋生) had given to three close friends in his home could not be used as evidence of inciting subversion, since an act needs to be carried out in the open before it goes from being a thought (which cannot be punished) to an act of public expression (which can, under the proper circumstances).[71]

With the advent of the Internet, measurement of social harm takes on a different focus. Liu Xiaobo's attorneys ask a question that comes up repeatedly in trials of so-called "cyber-dissidents": Considering the intensive efforts undertaken by the Chinese government to control access to information via the "Great Firewall," can articles posted on websites that are ordinarily blocked in China possibly incite subversion? The answer, in their view, is obviously no, but this line of argument tends to ignore the ease with which texts published on the Internet get reposted elsewhere or sent by email. It is notable that the

verdict in Liu's case makes an effort to quantify the damage done by
Liu's articles by referencing the number of links made to particular
articles or the number of "hits" posted.[72] This attempt at quantification
seems to be based on the analogy of laws concerning illegal publications, which set different levels of punishment based on the number of
copies printed.[73] But these are not particularly reliable measures of an
online article's reach, and the extent of distribution is but one variable
in the assessment of whether an article carries the potential to incite
subversion.

Distinction between "State Power," "Government," and "Ruling Party"

Perhaps the most controversial challenge defense lawyers have posed
in opposition to prosecutions under Article 105(2) is the lack of clarity
surrounding the meaning of "state political power" (*guojia zhengquan*,
国家政权). Article 2 of the Criminal Law states that one of the aims
of that legislation is to "defend the political power of the people's
democratic dictatorship and the socialist system," a nod to the "Four
Cardinal Principles" formulation set out by Deng Xiaoping in 1979 and
later enshrined in the preamble to China's Constitution. Foremost of
these four fundamental principles over which no debate can be allowed
is the leadership of the CCP and adherence to Marxism-Leninism and
Mao Zedong Thought. Though one might question how descriptive
concepts like "people's democratic dictatorship" and "socialist system"
are in twenty-first century China, in practice the definition of "state
political power" is inextricably linked to a political system led by the
CCP. Merely positing alternative arrangements is precisely wherein
lies the threat to the Chinese political system — and, in the view of the
law, the threat to national security.

Liu Xiaobo's lawyers challenge this head-on in their defense statement before the Court of Second Instance, advancing an argument
that has been raised in one form or another many times before.[74] They
maintain that "state political power," "government," and "ruling party"
should be treated as three separate concepts. "State political power"
is the broadest of the concepts, "the embodiment of the country" or
"the political organization in possession of national sovereignty and its

political powers used to sustain rule and control over society," usually thought of as being comprised of the military, the police, the court system, and organs of the government. The "government" executes the administrative authority of the state, while the "ruling party" is the political party (or parties) coming to possess state political power through elections or other means. Problems are bound to emerge in the course of governance, and it is to address such problems that China's Constitution guarantees citizens the right to criticize or expose short-comings or errors, and citizens also have the right to criticize, even oppose, the government or the ruling party — even if that criticism or opposition is in error.[75]

Conclusion

Broadly speaking, defense strategies in Article 105(2) cases and other cases involving political defendants have been evolving in a direction that goes beyond technical arguments over application of the law to raise wider constitutional challenges and accuse law enforcement agents of violating defendants' procedural rights. The argument put forth by Liu Xiaobo's lawyers bears witness to this trend, as they make use of constitutional arguments, place emphasis on rights, and draw inspiration from international human rights law. In recent years, all of these have become routine elements of an elaborate challenge to the government's reliance on national security as a legal justification for restricting the right to free expression.

That courts seldom engage with the substance of such arguments does not at all lessen their impact. Lawyers acting on behalf of political defendants like Liu Xiaobo have been increasingly searching out ways to articulate their defense arguments publicly, often by posting them directly on the Internet. Knowing full well that their vigorous arguments are likely to fall on deaf ears in the courtroom, they seek alternative venues for obtaining justice — rousing support from academics and activists who are also engaged in pushing boundaries, and going to the foreign media in hopes of mobilizing international pressure, for example. In so doing, they are themselves acting in highly political ways, publicly challenging the Party's authority over the interpretation of the law and constitution.

Ultimately, it is only by viewing China's prohibition against inciting subversion as an instrument of pure political power that its use against someone like Liu Xiaobo makes sense. Despite some minor changes in terminology, the lack of specificity and potential for broad interpretation of Article 105(2) are directly inherited from the laws against counter-revolutionary propaganda and incitement that preceded it. And there is little doubt that, as with those earlier laws, the purpose of the provision against inciting subversion is the silencing of political speech. At the time the new Criminal Law was about to take effect, an authoritative source explained the rationale for prohibiting the incitement of subversion in this manner:

> At present, some unlawful elements, acting under the influence of bourgeois liberal thought, have been actively aiding hostile foreign forces in engaging in political and ideological infiltration and peaceful evolution. Inside and outside the country, they clamor for overthrow of the Communist Party's political power [sic] and establishment of a wholly liberal democratic bourgeois political power, and they recklessly advocate bourgeois liberalization. … Their incitement and propaganda [aimed at] subverting the state political power is rampant and is for them a major method of [promoting] "peaceful evolution."[76]

Fear that the political order faces threats from the combined forces of domestic and foreign enemies has been a feature of revolutionary societies throughout history. Though Chinese society is officially no longer revolutionary, the ruling Communist Party still clings to the idea of lurking political conspiracies threatening to topple "its" political power and that, with the advent of the Internet age, opportunities for such conspiracies to develop and spread have multiplied.

A discourse about free expression as a fundamental human right has come to be an essential element of such arguments, especially since respect for human rights became part of China's Constitution in 2004. These arguments appear to have had limited impact on the individual cases concerned, however, both because adjudication of such cases have been driven primarily by political, rather than legal, rationales and because China's judicial system is not designed to consider questions of fundamental rights. Growing rights-consciousness among the Chinese people and pressure for China to conform to international standards regarding civil and political rights may combine to influence the balance of politics and law in the criminal justice system, but as long as the Communist Party's over-riding principle is "stability above all else," one can expect to see more Chinese critics — and perhaps more rights lawyers, as well — charged with inciting subversion for the indefinite future.

Chapter 3
Criminal Defense in Sensitive Cases

Yao Fuxin, Yang Jianli, Jiang Lijun, Du Daobin,
Liu Xiaobo, and Others

Mo Shaoping, Gao Xia, Lü Xi, and Chen Zerui

As the defense lawyers in several politically sensitive cases, we would like to share our view with people interested in China's criminal justice system on problems that we have encountered in defending political offenders in Chinese courts. In this chapter, we evaluate both the laws and the enforcement of those laws with the aim of providing constructive criticisms for reforming the criminal justice system in China.

Political Cases

This section introduces some of the political cases that we have defended.

The Case of Yao Fuxin (姚福信)

Yao Fuxin was a worker of Liaoyang Metal Alloy Factory, an iron factory in Liaoyang City. Because of the corruption of senior personnel in the factory, it was forced into winding up in October 2002. Yao and others had petitioned many times because of this matter. Along with tens of thousands of workers from this and other factories, he had also demonstrated on the streets on 11 and 12 March 2002. In addition, Yao took the lead in writing four open letters to the leaders at the central, provincial, and city levels, reflecting to them the relevant problems and requesting them to duly implement the principle of "Three Represents" (三个代表)[1] and to punish corruption in order to safeguard the legal rights and interests of thousands of laid-off workers.

On 17 March 2002, Yao was put under criminal detention by the Baita Public Security Sub-Bureau of Liaoyang City for illegal procession and demonstration. Formally arrested on 20 March 2002, he was prosecuted for subversion of state power by the People's Procuratorate of Liaoyang City on 27 December 2002. The case was tried by the Intermediate People's Court of Liaoyang City on 15 January 2003, and Yao was sentenced to fixed-term imprisonment of seven years and deprivation of political rights for three years. His appeal was dismissed and the verdict of the first instance trial was upheld under the judgment of the second instance trial delivered on 25 June that same year.

The Case of Xu Wei (徐伟)

Xu Wei, M.Phil. student of Beijing Normal University, was accused of forming the "New Youth Association" with others, with the intention to explore the path of reforming society. He was also accused of writing articles on the Internet asserting viewpoints such as "the democracy that is being implemented in China is false democracy" and "ending the old-man politics, establishing a young China."

Xu was put under criminal detention together with Yang Zili (杨子立), Zhang Honghai (张宏海), and Jin Haike (靳海科) for subversion of state power on 13 March 2001. On 20 April, they were formally arrested and confined in the Detention Center of the Beijing State Security Bureau. A prosecution was initiated against them on 29 August 2001. Under the judgment of the first instance trial, pronounced on 28 May 2003, Xu and the others were convicted of subversion of state power and sentenced to fixed-term imprisonment of ten years and deprivation of political rights for two years. Dissatisfied with the judgment, they appealed, but this was dismissed by the Higher People's Court of Beijing on 10 November 2003.

The Case of Jiang Lijun (姜立军)

Jiang Lijun was a worker of a heat supply company in Diaobingshan City of Liaoning Province. On 8 November 2002, the Beijing Public Security Bureau placed Jiang under criminal detention, alleging that he had been actively participating in "democratic movements" since 1988;

promoting Western-styled democracy and liberty; and attempting to falsely report to the police that there were bombs in the venue where the Sixteenth National Congress of the Communist Party of China (hereafter "CCP" or "Party") was being held.

Jiang was formally arrested on 14 December of the same year. On 14 July 2003, his case was transferred to the Second Branch Procuratorate of the Beijing People's Procuratorate for prosecution. On 26 September 2003, the Second Branch Procuratorate prosecuted Jiang for subversion of state power. The judgment of the first instance trial was pronounced by the Second Intermediate People's Court of Beijing: Jiang Lijun was found guilty and sentenced to fixed-term imprisonment of four years and deprivation of political rights for one year. Jiang appealed against the decision; on 18 December 2003, the Higher People's Court of Beijing dismissed his appeal.

The Case of Du Daobin (杜导斌)

Du Daobin worked in the Yingcheng City Medical Insurance Management Center. Between July 2002 and October 2003, he posted twenty-six articles on the Internet, including: "Subverting the Government is Legal," "Congratulations to Democracy Forum on Its Fourth Anniversary," and "My Consciousness Does not Allow Me to Remain Silent."

Those articles expressed Du's concerns over the problems in Chinese society (such as the prevalence of corruption, great disparity between the rich and the poor, the hard life of the peasants, and the problem of large-scale unemployment) and his discontent with the failure of the Chinese people to enjoy democracy, liberty, and rights. In his articles, Du asserted that people should have the right to elect a government and a ruling party that could genuinely represent their interests. He hoped that democracy, liberty, and social progress could be enhanced in China, thus improving the lives of the people.

On 28 October 2003, the Xiaogan City Public Security Bureau placed Du under criminal detention for inciting to subvert state power. On 10 November of the same year, he was formally arrested. The Xiaogan City People's Procuratorate prosecuted him on the charge on 20 April 2004 and the case was tried in open court on 18 May 2004. On 11 June of the same year, the Intermediate People's Court of Xiaogan City convicted Du of the charge and sentenced him to fixed-term imprisonment of three years with a four-year suspended sentence and deprivation of political rights for two years. Du appealed, but on 3 August of the same year, the court of second instance dismissed the appeal.

Critiques of the Substantive Law

Paragraph 2 of Article 105 of the Criminal Law of the People's Republic of China (Criminal Law), which creates the offence of incitement to subvert state power, provides that:

> Whoever incites others by spreading rumors or slanders or any other means to subvert the State power or overthrow the socialist system shall be sentenced to fixed-term imprisonment of not more than five years, criminal detention, public surveillance or deprivation of political rights; and the ringleaders and the others who commit major crimes shall be sentenced to fixed-term imprisonment of not less than five years.

This provision violates the Chinese Constitution and international human rights law, because it fails to draw a clear distinction between criminal incitement on the one hand and citizens' right to freedom of expression on the other. Such a vague provision gives neither certainty nor guidance to both law enforcement agencies and ordinary citizens in this potentially dangerous zone. More importantly, it has often been abused by the authorities to persecute political dissidents.

In Du's case, for example, the Intermediate Court of Xiaogan City held that his act had far exceeded the permissible scope of freedom of expression that can be enjoyed by citizens and thus endangered national security. However, the court, in convicting Du, failed to identify this scope, in particular, the perimeter of freedom of speech. Given the lack of a clear delineation, there was no legal basis for the court to find that Du's articles had overstepped the boundary of legally protected expression. The view of the court in Du's and other similar decisions were extremely subjective and arbitrary.

Likewise, in the Bill of Prosecution of the Liaoyang City Procuratorate, Yao Fuxin's listening to the broadcast of Voice of America and his contact with foreign journalists and media such as Agence France-Presse were listed as evidence of his collusion with hostile forces outside the territory of China. But under the existing laws of China, there is no provision prohibiting citizens from doing so.

When the Criminal Law was revised in 1998, hundreds of prominent experts and scholars jointly issued an open letter to the Supreme People's Court (SPC) and the Standing Committee of the National People's Congress (NPC), calling for a judicial interpretation to provide a clear and feasible legal standard for paragraph 2 of Article 105 of the Criminal Law.

We believe that this paragraph contravenes several articles of the Constitution, for example Article 33 ("The state respects and protects human rights"), Article 35 ("Citizens of the People's Republic of China enjoy freedom of speech, of the press, of assembly, of association, of procession and of demonstration"), and Article 41 ("Citizens of the People's Republic of China have the right to criticize and make suggestions regarding any state organ or functionary").

Even if the views expressed in the articles of Du Daobin and others are wrong, they still fall within the scope of a citizen's right to freedom of expression. The authors were simply exercising their right to freedom of expression as guaranteed by the Constitution, and should not be considered as having committed the offence of inciting to subvert state power.

International conventions that China has signed also expressly protect citizens' right to freedom of expression. For example, Article 19 of the Universal Declaration of Human Rights provides that "Everyone has the right to freedom of opinion and expression; this right includes freedom to hold opinions without interference and to seek, receive and impart information and ideas through any media and regardless of frontiers." Article 19 of the International Covenant on Civil and Political Rights (ICCPR) provides that "(1) Everyone shall have the right to hold opinions without interference. (2) Everyone shall have the right to freedom of expression." Clearly, Article 105, paragraph 2 of the Criminal Law contravenes these two international convention provisions.

Procedural Difficulties in Handling Political Cases

In our experience in handling political cases, we have encountered the following procedural difficulties as a matter of routine.

Failure to Notify the Family of the Criminal Suspect

While the duty of informing a suspect's family after detention is relatively straightforward, it has been routinely ignored by the investigative organs. Although Article 64 of the Criminal Procedure Law of the People's Republic of China (Criminal Procedure Law) provides that "[w]ithin 24 hours after a person has been detained, his family or the unit to which he belongs shall be notified of the reasons for detention and the place of custody," the family members of Yao Fuxin did not receive the Notice to the Family or Unit of the Detainee until three days after Yao was put under detention. Similarly, Jiang Lijun's family had never been notified of his detention or arrest.

Failure to Allow the Accused to Meet with His Lawyer Promptly

According to Article 11 of the Provisions on Several Questions in Implementing the Criminal Procedure Law (关于刑事诉讼法实施中若干问题的规定) (Six Departments Provisions),[2] when a lawyer requests to meet with a criminal suspect, a meeting should be arranged within forty-eight hours. According to Article 43 of the Provisions on the Procedure of the Public Security Organs in Handling Criminal Cases (公安机关办理刑事案件程序规定) (Ministry of Public Security Procedural Provisions), "When a public security organ disapproves a lawyer to meet with his client, it should explain the reason of disapproval to the lawyer." However, the rules authorizing lawyers' access to clients in custody are barely observed, if at all.

The police, without providing any justification, routinely deny lawyers' applications to meet their clients in detention. When a reason is given, it would often be either "the officer in charge of the case is not in the office" or "inability to obtain permission because the leader is not in office." Another common excuse is that "state secrets are involved in the case." Indeed, involvement of state secrets has been routinely cited as the excuse to deny lawyers' access to clients in custody in a wide-range of cases. But when the case went to the court, there would always be no claim of state secrets.

During Yao Fuxin's nine-month detention, the Public Security Bureau of Liaoyang City at first refused the lawyers' application for meeting without giving any reply. Later, the denial was justified on the ground that state secrets were involved in the case. However, the trial was actually held in open court without any involvement of state secrets.

Some police officers have gone even further by advising suspects not to retain the services of lawyers. According to Jiang Lijun, the public security officers in charge of his case had expressly told him that "there is no use to hire a lawyer during the investigation stage." Such an act is not only an infringement of the right of the criminal suspect, but also a serious illegal act in violation of Article 96 of the Criminal Procedure Law.[3]

Even if a meeting is successfully secured, lawyers still have difficulty in effectively communicating with the accused because of numerous obstacles imposed by the investigative organs. These include restrictions on frequency of meetings (e.g., only one meeting is permitted during the investigation stage) and the number of lawyers present (e.g., each meeting should be attended by two lawyers). Time limits are also imposed (e.g., each meeting can only last for half an hour), and there have even been cases where investigative organs arrange for appointments at 11:20 a.m — knowing full well that lunch is in ten minute's time — thus rendering the meeting nothing more than a mere formality.

Personnel of the investigative organs are usually sent to monitor the meeting and to restrict the contents of the conversation between the lawyers and the accused. For example, lawyers are not permitted to discuss the case with their clients during the meetings — how could lawyers provide legal services if they are not allowed to do so? Some detention centers even require lawyers to bring with them handcuffs to the meeting in order to prevent the suspects from escaping.

Difficulty in Investigation and Collecting Evidence

Article 37 of the Criminal Procedure Law provides that: "Defence lawyers may, with the consent of the witnesses or other units and individuals concerned, collect information pertaining to the current case from them" and "with permission of the People's Procuratorate or the People's Court and with the consent of the victim, his near relatives or the witnesses provided by the victim, defence lawyers may collect information pertaining to the current case from them."

In other words, if a lawyer cannot obtain the consent of the relevant persons, he cannot collect evidence from them, and this actually means giving them the right to refuse to give evidence to defense lawyers. When a lawyer requests to collect evidence from a victim or the witnesses provided by the victim, he is also required to seek the permission of the procuratorate and the court concerned. All these arrangements make it almost impossible for lawyers to exercise their right to collect evidence.

Restrictions on Lawyers' Access to Case Files

According to Article 36 of the Criminal Procedure Law, lawyers do not have access to the case materials during the investigation stage; during prosecution, they can only have access to the "judicial documents pertaining to the case and the forensic reports" (诉讼文书、技术性鉴定材料); and during the first instance trial, they can only have access to the "major evidence" (主要证据) of the alleged offences that were transferred by the procuratorate to the court. What is "major evidence" is determined by the procuratorate concerned.[4]

In practice, it is common that the procuratorates do not submit to the court evidence that is advantageous to the accused. Due to this reason, the provisions with regard to lawyers' right to have access to the case materials as provided for in the amended Criminal Procedure Law is a retrogression. Under the original law which was promulgated in 1979, the procuratorate was required to submit all the case materials to the court before trial. Now, lawyers can have access to these only at the second instance trial. In some cases, such as in Xu Wei's, lawyers are still prohibited from reading and making copies of some of the case materials even at this stage — the very same ones used by the court as major references and bases to convict and sentence the criminal suspects.

Extended Detention during the Trial Stage

According to the Criminal Procedure Law and the relevant judicial explanations, the standard time limit for detention (i.e., time limit for adjudication) for the first instance trial should be one-and-a-half months; but can be extended to a maximum of six months. For the second instance trial, the time limit is one-and-a-half months with a one month extension in special circumstances.

However, the first instance trial of Xu Wei's case lasted for twenty months, exceeding the time limit for detention. From the time Xu filed his notice of appeal to the time the court of second instance pronounced its judgment, another five-and-a-half months had lapsed, exceeding the time limit for detention.

Lack of Public Supervision over the Impartiality of Adjudication

The trial of Xu Wei was said to be in the form of a public trial. Yet, when the families and friends of the accused went to court to get passes to attend the trial, court officials told them that the court had not notified them that the trial would be open to the public; consequently, no passes would be distributed. When Xu's lawyers entered the courtroom to discuss this matter with the judges, they discovered that only a few seats in the public gallery were occupied. The judges had previously told them that all the passes had been distributed, the public gallery was full, and the families of the accused could not attend the trial. Journalists who arrived at the court very early in the morning were also barred from entering the courtroom.

Failure of Witnesses to Testify in Court

Witnesses, as a matter of routine, do not testify in court. Normally, only the witness statements will be read out by the prosecutor. Such a practice prevents defense lawyers from cross-examining the witnesses in court and is in violation of the principles of criminal law.

Article 47 of the Criminal Procedure Law provides that:

> The testimony of a witness may be used as a basis in deciding a case only after the witness has been questioned and cross-examined in the courtroom by both sides, that is, the public prosecutor and victim as well as the defendant and defenders, and after the testimonies of the witnesses on all sides have been heard and verified.

Article 48 of the Criminal Procedure Law provides that: "All those who have information about a case shall have the duty to testify." Thus, according to these provisions, witnesses should testify in court. The confession statements of the accused and witness statements can be used as a basis in deciding a case only after these individuals have been questioned and cross-examined by the prosecution and the defense. The reason for the law imposing such an arrangement is that witness statements and confession statements alone may not be reliable: the facts which are nearest to the truth of the case can be found out only under rigorous examination and cross-examination. For this reason, the credibility of witness and confession statements before cross-examination should be lower than those after; and when there are inconsistencies between these two kinds of evidence, according to the principle of direct evidence, the court should admit the latter. Furthermore, duly applying the principle of direct evidence is also important in balancing the power between the prosecution and the defense in carrying out investigation and collecting evidence, as well as minimizing the risk of defense lawyers being wrongfully prosecuted for the offense of "obstructing the accused/witnesses in giving evidence." However, when the courts implement Article 47, the term "statements of the witnesses" (证人证言) is understood as written testimonies instead of oral evidence adduced in court.

Lawyers do not have the right to compel a witness to testify in court. When a lawyer considers that there are defects in a witness statement and requests the witness concerned to testify in court, this will never be accommodated if the court refuses to exercise its power to summon the witness. Moreover, there is no mechanism to protect the safety of witnesses who testify in court; some procuratorates have even made use of various excuses to arbitrarily arrest witnesses. Finally, even if witnesses agree to testify in court, the judge may still refuse to summon them for reasons such as fear that the predetermined decision of a case will be affected should a witness withdraw previously given evidence. Judges are not required to explain the reason for their refusal, and lawyers do not have any right to challenge their decision.

The case of Xu Wei and his co-defendants illustrates these problems. Witnesses had submitted to the court amendments and explanations to the statements they had provided — revisions that were favorable to the accused. However, because they were not allowed to testify in court, defense lawyers did not have the opportunity to cross-examine them, thus failing to challenge the authenticity of their statements. During the second instance trial, four key witnesses in this case were waiting outside the court before the trial commenced, requesting to testify in court. When defense lawyers requested the judge to summon those witnesses to give evidence and be cross-examined in court, the judge said that they would be called when the court considered it necessary. However, after the whole day's trial had been completed, the court still failed to give its consent.

Illegality in the Verification and Admission of Evidence

Another problem with the evidence in Xu Wei's case is that the written report prepared by the state security organ which investigated the case was used as major evidence for conviction. In fact, this is not a category of evidence as prescribed by the law,[5] nor is it objective in nature.

Failure to Pronounce the Judgment in Public

At the second instance trial of Yao Fuxin, the Higher People's Court of Liaoning Province only read out its judgment to the criminal suspect at the detention center. Neither his lawyer was informed to appear in court nor were his family members allowed to attend the trial. This was a clear violation of Article 163 of the Criminal Procedure Law which provides that: "In all cases, judgments shall be pronounced publicly."

The Liu Xiaobo Case in Focus

Facts of the Case

Liu Xiaobo was a writer, the former president of the Independent Chinese PEN, and a political dissident. He was a lecturer at the Chinese Department of the Beijing Normal University. In the mid-1980s, Liu shocked the writers' community by criticizing Li Zehou (李泽厚). After that, he had been arrested many times for participating in the June Fourth Movement, calling for its vindication, and demanding the

Chinese government to carry out democratic constitutional reform. After release, he published volumes of articles, denouncing contemporary politics and expressing his concerns about the lack of protection of human rights in China. All these acts made him one of the major targets of surveillance of the Chinese government. Each year, during sensitive occasions (such as the anniversary of the June Fourth Movement, as well as meetings of the Chinese People's Political Consultative Conference, the NPC, and the Congress of the CCP), the Chinese authorities would put Liu under house arrest, requesting him not to step out of his domicile and not to visit friends. They even cut off his telephone and Internet connections from time to time.

On 8 December 2008, Liu Xiaobo was put under criminal detention for inciting to subvert state power and was put under residential surveillance the following day. On 23 June 2009, the procuratorate approved Liu's arrest, and on 25 December, the Beijing No. 1 Intermediate People's Court convicted him of the offence, sentencing him to fixed-term imprisonment of eleven years and deprivation of political rights for two years.

In its judgment, the court alleged that Liu had posted seditious articles on overseas websites that were said to "spread rumors and defame" (造谣、诽谤) the Chinese government. These included: "The Autocratic Patriotism of the Chinese Communist Party" (中共的独裁爱国主义), "Are the Chinese People Only Entitled to Accept 'Party-Dominated Democracy'?" (难道中国人只配接受「党主民主」), "Changing the Regime through Changing the Society" (通过改变社会来改变政权), "Multi-Faceted Autocracy of the Chinese Communist Party" (多面的中共独裁), "The Negative Impact of the Emergence of Autocracy on Universal Democraticization" (独裁崛起对世界民主化的负面效应), and "Keep Asking about the Case of Child Labor in the Black Brick Kiln" (对黑窑童奴案的继续追问).

The court also stated that Liu had attempted to incite the subversion of the Chinese government by calling for the "abolition of the privilege of dominance of the ruling power by one party" (取消一党垄断执政特权) and "the establishment of a Federal Republic of China under a democratic constitutional framework" (在民主宪政的架构下建立中华联邦共和国) in Charter 08.

Liu's appeal against the conviction was dismissed by the Higher People's Court of Beijing on 11 February 2010.

Procedural Illegality

Violation of Law through Application of Compulsory Measures

Liu Xiaobo had been put under residential surveillance by the Beijing Public Security Bureau from 9 December 2008 until it arrested him on 23 June 2009. Although he was said to be under residential surveillance, he was treated as if he were under detention — an act which seriously violated the Criminal Procedure Law and the Ministry of Public Security Procedural Provisions. According to these two pieces of legislation, when an investigative organ imposes residential surveillance on a criminal suspect, it has to observe the following rules:

(a) Residential surveillance should be administered in the domicile of the criminal suspect concerned. Only when a criminal suspect has no fixed domicile can the investigative organ administer the residential surveillance in a designated residence;

(b) The person being put under residential surveillance has the right to continue to live with family members he used to live with; and

(c) No approval is required for a person subjected to residential surveillance to meet with his lawyer.

However, the Beijing Public Security Bureau, which was the investigative organ in this case, failed to observe these laws. Despite having legal domicile in Beijing, Liu was not put under residential surveillance at his home. His wife was not informed of his whereabouts, and he was only allowed to meet with her twice. Although Liu's lawyer had expressed many requests to the bureau to meet with Liu, he had not received any reply.

Refusal of Prosecutorial Organ to Listen to Opinions of the Defense Lawyer

Article 139 of the Criminal Procedure Law provides that:

When examining a case, the People's Procuratorate shall interrogate the criminal suspect and heed the opinions of the victim and of the persons entrusted by the criminal suspect and the victim.

Article 12 of the Provisions on Guaranteeing Lawyers' Practice According to Law in Criminal Actions by the People's Procuratorates (关于人民检察院保障律师在刑事诉讼中依法执业的规定) provides that:

> When a People's Procuratorate examines a case transferred to it for prosecution, it shall hear the opinions of the lawyer of the criminal suspect and the lawyer of the victim, and shall note them down carefully and add them to the case files. Where it is difficult to hear the opinions of the lawyer of the criminal suspect and the lawyer of the victim, it may send a written notice to them, asking them to give written opinions.

In Liu's case, the prosecutorial organ gave his defense lawyers the impossible task of reading all the case materials and submitting their opinions within one day, from 8 to 9 of December. By not listening to the views of the defense lawyers, the prosecutorial organ had violated the law and the relevant judicial interpretation.

Failure of Court to Deliver Notice of Trial to Defense Lawyer According to Legally Prescribed Time Limit

At about 2:30 p.m. on 20 December 2009 (Sunday), Liu's defense lawyer received a call from the judge presiding over this case, notifying him that the trial would commence in Court No. 23 at 9 a.m. on 23 December 2009 (Wednesday). According to Article 151, paragraph 1, item 4 of the Criminal Procedure Law, after a People's Court has decided to open a court session, it shall deliver the Notice of the Trial to the defense lawyer no later than three days before the opening of the court session. The "three days" mentioned in that provision should exclude the day of the trial and the day the notice is sent. It is obvious that in this case, the three-day criterion had not been met.

No Legal Basis for Presiding Judge to Refuse Admission of Evidence Submitted by the Defense Lawyer in Court

During the trial, in order to prove that the allegations against Liu as stated in the Bill of Prosecution could not be substantiated, the defense lawyer submitted to the court literature proving that the CCP and its leaders had been objecting to the dominance of power by one party and had proposed to establish a federal republic. However, the court refused to allow the evidence on the ground that the prosecution did not have the time to prepare for the cross-examination. We believe that:

(a)   If the prosecution needed time to prepare for the cross-examination of the evidence presented by the defense in court (the defense lawyer had had a brief communication with the prosecutor with regard to the evidence prior to the trial), the court should have followed Article 155 of the Interpretation of the Supreme People's Court on Several Questions in the Implementation of the Criminal Procedure Law of the People's Republic of China (最高人民法院关于执行《中华人民共和国刑事诉讼法》若干问题的解释): adjourn the trial and, based on the actual situation, determine the time needed for the prosecution to do the preparation. There is no legal basis for the presiding judge to refuse the evidence.

(b)   According to legal principles, the rule of admissibility of evidence in criminal litigation is "beyond reasonable doubt"; as long as the evidence submitted by the defense poses some "reasonable doubt" as to the defendant's guilt, regardless of when that evidence is presented to the court, the court should permit cross-examination.

No Legal Basis for Presiding Judge to Restrict Time for Accused and Defense Lawyers to Make their Submissions

Before all parties presented their submissions, the presiding judge requested the accused and the defense lawyer not to take more time than the prosecutor in making their submissions. He was even counting down the time on his watch while the parties were making their submissions. Since the law requires the prosecution to present its submission first, this ruling gave the prosecutor control over the time allotted to the opposing side for their submissions. We believe that:

(a)   There was no legal basis for the presiding judge to set a time limit for the accused and the defense lawyer to present their submission.

(b)   According to legal principles, what the presiding judge had done constituted an infringement of the right to defense of the accused and his lawyers.

(c) Compared with the defense, the prosecution was in a more advantageous position, legally and politically. So, while it appeared to be fair to give both parties the same amount of time to make their submissions, it was actually biased towards the stronger party.

No Legal Basis for Presiding Judge to Interrupt Accused Thrice during His Final Statement

According to Article 160 of the Criminal Procedure Law, after the presiding judge has declared conclusion of the debate, the defendant shall have the right to present a final statement. When it was time for Liu Xiaobo to present his, the presiding judge interrupted him several times. For example, when Liu mentioned that the June Fourth incident in 1989 was the turning point of his thinking, the presiding judge asked him not to touch upon the June Fourth incident. In fact, Liu had only stated a timeframe — and nothing related to June Fourth. Even if he had, there was still no valid reason and legal basis for the judge to interrupt him.

Lack of Judicial Independence

Given the system design, China is not a country which practices judicial independence. There is no law prohibiting political parties from interfering with the work of the judiciary. Article 5 of the Constitution lists the various categories of sectors that must abide by the Constitution and the law: state organs, the armed forces, political parties, public organizations, enterprises and institutions, and individuals. Article 126 of the Constitution provides that:

> The people's courts exercise judicial power independently, in accordance with the provisions of the law, and are not subject to interference by any administrative organ, public organization or individual.

It is commonly understood that Article 126 does not exclude the CCP from exercising leadership over the judiciary, nor does it provide that judges, as individuals, enjoy independence in adjudicating cases and are free from any interference.

Although there is no mention of such an institution in the Criminal Procedure Law, political-legal committees at the central and various local levels have tremendous political power, and can directly undermine judicial independence and interfere with the court's adjudication. They are subordinated to the Party committees at various levels and exist in each of the administrative regions in China. The secretary of the political-legal committee normally serves concurrently as the vice-secretary of the Party committee in the respective administrative region.

In political cases where decisions are made at a higher or even the highest level, there tends to be a vicious cycle. The biased report of a case by the investigative and procuratorial organs affects the determination of senior state officials, whose decision has great impact on that of the court and the judicial committee. This, in turn, plays a critical role in the judges' final verdict.

Because of the lack of judicial independence, Chinese lawyers can only play a limited role in the criminal process. It is officially acknowledged and widely reported that these lawyers experience multiple difficulties in their criminal defense work.

Aggressive lawyers can also easily get themselves into trouble with the prosecution. Article 306 of the Criminal Law provides that:

> If, in criminal proceedings, a defender or agent *ad litem* destroys or forges evidence, helps any of the parties destroy or forge evidence, or coerces the witness or entices him into changing his testimony in defiance of the facts or give false testimony, he shall be sentenced to fixed-term imprisonment of not more than three years or criminal detention; if the circumstances are serious, he shall be sentenced to fixed-term imprisonment of not less than three years but not more than seven years.

But what constitutes "coercion" (威胁) and "enticement" (引诱) remains largely undefined. The law does not provide a clear and specific objective standard. As long as a witness, a criminal suspect, or an accused changes his testimony or withdraws his previous confession after meeting with a lawyer, the relevant authority will suspect that he has done so under the latter's influence. Regardless of the actual reason, the lawyer may immediately be put under detention. If there is insufficient evidence to support a charge of falsification of evidence, other offenses will be brought against the lawyer in order to ensure that punishment is inevitable. This provision provides a legal justification for the authorities to take revenge on lawyers for discharging their duties as lawyers, and one of the fundamental reasons for the decrease in the percentage of legal representation in criminal cases in China.

Conclusion

As a member state of the United Nations, China should fulfill its international obligations in ensuring that its domestic laws and procedures comply with international human rights standards. Only when the law of China becomes rights-based and law enforcement becomes more impartial, more transparent, and more accountable can the various aforementioned problems in the criminal process be rooted out and the aforementioned abnormalities facing Chinese defense lawyers be changed fundamentally.

To duly implement the principles of fair trial in China, judges must be able to adjudicate independently. For them to do so, the powers and functions of the political-legal committees have to be clearly defined and distinguished from the functions of the courts, the procuratorates, and the police. Such committees cannot over-ride the courts and judges; it also cannot interfere with judges' adjudication. Eventually, a court-centric system should replace the existing police-centric system, and the courts should have the ownership to rule on the legality of police and prosecution decisions, in particular, those in relation to the imposition of detention and other compulsory measures. Only when the court is independent would the legal environment for lawyers improve and the difficulties that lawyers encounter in criminal defense work, as identified in this chapter, be alleviated.

Chapter 4
Breaking through the Obstacles of Political Isolation and Discrimination*

Cui Weiping

The trial of Liu Xiaobo was held on 23 December 2009, a good year after he had been detained.[1] While the authorities claimed that it was an "open trial," not even Liu Xiaobo's wife Liu Xia was allowed to attend. Neither were many others allowed in, whether they had come with the intention of witnessing how the courts of this country tried a "political offender," or as friends of Liu Xiaobo, or just as ordinary people: all were excluded from this trial.[2] News reporting about Liu's trial was also strictly controlled by the government: except for an extremely brief notice about the trial originating from Xinhua News Agency,[3] which other newspapers were supposed to reproduce in inconspicuous places, the media were not allowed to engage in any free reporting on the trial. All these measures of the government were intended to keep the trial low profile and to "disappear" Liu Xiaobo from public view, in order to reduce the "political threat" he was thought to have posed to the government.

The trial thus perfectly illustrated what might be called a policy of political isolation. As one of the punishments the authorities reserve for those considered to have violated their "taboos," neither their writings nor any news about them — nor indeed, even their names — are allowed to appear in media reports. Some but not all of these "banned people" have previously been imprisoned. Upon release, they have

---

* This article was originally written in Chinese and translated into English by Eva Pils.

still not been given the same space for free expression that others enjoy — but then again, such space is, in any case, restricted in this society.

A writer by profession, Liu Xiaobo has been unable to publish any of his works openly with domestic publishers for over twenty years since his release from prison, to which he had been sent after June Fourth, 1989. His name, too, cannot be publicly mentioned. It is just as Liu Xia wrote in her letter to Havel:[4] "When you take a look at any newspaper, any book in China, you will find that citizen Liu Xiaobo does not exist; he has been shut out for twenty years." The text of Charter 08, too — which the government regards as a very serious threat — cannot be published with any domestic publishing house and cannot be made available to society for public debate. On the Internet, anyone who wanted to keep on discussing it was soon forced to use homonyms to replace the term "Charter 08" in order to bypass government censorship. Instead of writing "Charter 08" (*Lingba Xianzhang*, 零八宪章), they had to write "County Head" (*xianzhang*, 县长), because these words sound similar in Chinese.

This kind of isolation is an outward expression of a deeper-rooted form of political discrimination. Those who have independent views and are willing to publicize them, even though they act on their conscience, will be regarded as challenging and provoking the government. They will consequently be treated as political pariahs and not be allowed to enjoy equal treatment with other citizens. Just as certain words and phrases are regarded as "sensitive text" on the Internet and eliminated, so, too, are some people regarded as "sensitive figures." In the past, for instance, we had the so-called "Four Elements" (*silei fenzi*, 四类分子) and the "Five Categories of Black Elements" (*hei wulei*, 黑五类).[5] The use of the word *"lei"* (category), to designate human beings, slighted those so designated: elements belonging in these categories were less than fully human and must not be allowed to lead the lives of normal human beings. During the Cultural Revolution, there was a yet more extreme term to describe certain people: *niugui sheshen* (牛鬼蛇神) or "cow monsters and snake demons,"[6] a phrase that seemed to turn those human beings into mere freakish objects. Today, political discrimination not only takes the form of depriving targeted individuals of their right to freedom of expression and to a public life, but also of not letting them leave the country, not considering them for certain positions or for promotion, not allowing them to change their jobs, as well as banishment from the classroom or suspension from their duties.

And yet, people today are constantly trying to find ways and means to break through this discrimination and isolation. On the eve of Liu Xiaobo's trial, for instance, a lot of young Twitterers added a yellow ribbon to their Twitter profiles, publicly expressing their support; some went so far as to swap their own headshot for one of Liu's. Even more impressively, many young people gathered outside the Beijing No. 1 Intermediate People's Court on the day of Liu's trial, braving the bitter cold of that day, valiantly expressing their standpoint, and not worrying that they might be obstructed openly there and then — or worse, secretly taken to account later. In contrast to previous similar occasions, the majority of Liu's young supporters this time had not had any significant prior "political experience." There were few amongst them who exhibited a spirit of total self-sacrifice for the great aim of achieving democracy in China, and yet, they came forth courageously to express what they felt: "Liu Xiaobo, you are not alone." The scene, the atmosphere on that day was deeply moving.

I too had a duty to express my support for Liu Xiaobo. I differ from those young people in that Liu Xiaobo and I are of the same generation. From the 1980s, we have shared many experiences, we have walked the same paths, and due to our related professional areas we also have met a great many mutual friends and acquaintances. A few years back, he and I and a couple of other friends had gone hiking in Huairou in the countryside around Beijing. During that outing, we had reminisced about old times and about old friends in the literary circles of the 1980s, whom nowadays we did not get to see often. We had sighed and joked over our memories.

On the evening of 24 December 2009,[7] I thought I should call up some of those old acquaintances. At the time, I had this strong feeling that we could not just let one of our friends disappear from within our midst. If we were unable to prevent him from being taken away to a prison cell, the least we could do was not to allow his name never to be mentioned again amongst his friends and acquaintances. We could not just do as directed by the government and from now on treat Liu Xiaobo as taboo, making him another forgotten subject. A year before we had still been reading his essays online; we had met him and chatted together over meals and wine, had listened to him expound his views on all manner of subjects with lively enthusiasm. And now, he was supposed to have vanished all of a sudden; we were no longer to see him for all these many days and years. It was too hard to accept this new form of isolation. Surely he had not posed any threat to this society or any particular person? Of course he had not. Surely he had not gobbled up many state assets, meriting punishment? Not that, either. He was merely a bookish man who had written some things. This had been his only crime.

So I called Qian Liqun (钱理群), who had been a widely known scholar in the 1980s;[8] Tong Qingbing (童庆炳) of Beijing Normal University (北京师范大学), one of Liu Xiaobo's doctoral supervisors and an authority in the field of literature and arts; the poet Mang Ke (芒克);[9] and the literary critic Tang Xiaodu (唐晓渡).[10] I called these particular friends because I knew that they had frequently gathered for drinks and chats in the eighties. I also called Liu Xiaobo's former classmate Dr. Sun Jin (孙津). Dr. Sun was having a meal in a restaurant when I called, and there was a terrible noise in the background. He asked me to call back again that evening — it did not matter how late it was. In our further conversation, I told him that he did not necessarily have to talk about Liu Xiaobo's criminal conviction or appraise what Liu had done, or his work; it would be fine for him just to say whatever came to his mind — his scholarship, his character, any sort of story would do and he could talk about whatever he wanted as long as it was about Liu.[11]

That same evening I posted the comments collected in these conversations on Twitter.[12] Doing so meant that no matter how long the conversation had been, I could post no more than 140 Chinese characters.[13] Tong Qingbing, for instance, talked a lot about the relationship he had had with Liu Xiaobo as his Ph.D. student. He told me that Liu had originally been assigned the prominent Beijing Normal University arts scholar Huang Yaomian (黄药眠) as his principal doctoral supervisor, with Tong as a co-supervisor. However, before the completion of Liu's thesis, Huang passed away, and therefore Liu's *viva voce* defense of his thesis was presided over by Tong. I patiently listened to Tong's recollections. Before hanging up, Tong said, "After all, I was his teacher for a time. He was my student. I hope he will take care of himself." I used just this one short sentence for my post on Twitter.

Later, it turned out that the majority of the people I had called did not know what Twitter was and how it worked. This meant that I had to spend a lot of time explaining it to each one of these people. When they understood, a few among them expressed dissatisfaction with the 140-character limit.

It was only on the following day, 25 December 2009, after the verdict was announced, that the idea of turning myself into a "media outlet" came into my head. An eleven-year sentence for Liu Xiaobo, whatever else it meant, was a big matter, a matter of great concern for the political life of this country in which we all lived. Yet, the domestic media were, of course, not going to be able to interview anyone about it as usual. They could not report even the reactions and comments of the intellectuals — regardless of what those views were, they could not be published. That seemed so unreasonable. Explaining my action on my blog, I cited the words of the philosopher Confucius, saying that poems could "be a source of inspiration and a basis for observation; they can help you to come together with others, and to express a sense of outrage."[14] The point about "observation," I wrote, was that poems allowed people to understand social life; through them, one could gain an understanding of the achievements and failures of a particular era's customs and politics. And that, surely, was why the venerable sage had collected three hundred odes. If I could now manage to collect the views of contemporary intellectuals on this issue by interviewing them and compiling what they said, I, too, would have contributed something for people to "observe."[15]

I decided to focus on interviewing people who had been active since the 1980s and were now roughly in their fifties, for the following reasons.

Firstly, these people had experienced the "thought emancipation" and "political reform" that were called for in the 1980s and then suspended after June Fourth, 1989. In a certain sense, Liu Xiaobo had been holding on to the idealism of that era, and therefore, had things in common with all these people I interviewed; they had a basis for mutual understanding.

Secondly, the people I chose had in the meantime become noted authorities within their respective fields. They had performed outstandingly in their area of professional expertise, and that had also given them a certain social status and reputation. Even though according to an old saying in China, "everyone bears responsibility for the fate of the country," I still think that those who have power, status, and who are in a position to speak should assume an even greater responsibility.

In fact, many of my interviewees had been acting in accordance with their social responsibility all along and had often spoken up publicly, only this time, they lacked a media platform from which to air their views. I could give them one using my Twitter account. Some of the interviewees thanked me on the phone for doing this because they would otherwise not have had a chance to make their views known.

Thirdly, my interviewees could count as being relatively safer than others, in terms of any kind of trouble they might incur because of having given an interview. Comparatively speaking, younger people had not yet completely established themselves or built protections within their lives. I absolutely did not want to see anyone get hurt or punished because they had answered my questions — I absolutely did not want to see anyone be expelled or dismissed or demoted.

Later, I saw some criticisms to the effect that what I was doing was rather similar to the political movements of previous eras, during which everyone was forced to "declare their position" in order to "pass." But I do not think that it was similar at all. I am merely an ordinary scholar and I do not stand on the side of the government; I have no power whatsoever to coerce anyone to do or say anything.

If my interviews could be considered to put anyone under pressure, then that pressure came not from me but from the system — for it is a system that demands complete loyalty, that cannot allow people to speak their views truthfully, even in cases where privately all share similar views. Apart from that, people may have experienced a sort of pressure that originated in their own conscience. They may have felt under pressure to show that their conscience had not yet been suffocated and that all they needed was more courage to show that they were independent, not merely products of the system. In other words, any "pressure" that may have been felt resulted from the tension between the system and the conscience of my interviewees. People are perpetually exposed to that tension, caught up in that uncomfortable space, struggling to cope; my phone calls merely served to expose the awkwardness of that situation.

Some friends later told me that our mutual friends had started to scare each other mockingly, "Cui Weiping will be giving you a phone call tonight." I can understand if people started jokingly referring to my calls as "ominous midnight calls." Why could I not call them during the daytime? It was because almost every day, I would get as far as picking up the handset — and then hang up again without having dialed anyone's number. It was because I had to overcome a psychological obstacle of my own before making any of these calls. Deep down, I knew this was an "unusual" action — dragging people out of the ordinary course of their lives and getting them to leave their accustomed framework to face such a difficult issue. But it was as I said then: "Sometimes, the chain of one's life is torn apart. This has happened with the heavy verdict for Xiaobo, such a serious thing occurring in our midst. We cannot escape from this rupture in our lives, or from our own 'original sin'."

Filled with thoughts like these, I would procrastinate from morning to afternoon and from afternoon to evening, and then after dinner I would think, maybe some people have got a habit of watching the 7 o'clock CCTV evening news; after the news, I would watch the "hot issue interview" news feature, and then wonder if there might not be people watching the TV drama following that. In sum, I would work out a whole number of reasons for not doing it — for putting it off further and further until the day was almost over. When I called rock musician Cui Jian (崔健), it was almost midnight. He told me he was currently preparing for a performance, and that I should call again the following day. Sure enough, I saw a recording of that performance on television the next day. I consoled myself by thinking that my phone call had inspired him to perform extra well.

Given this background, I greatly valued all the comments I got, whatever their content was. I also knew I was but a temporary reporter and that I was not specially looking for people to express their support or like-mindedness; I ought to be happy to record whatever the person I spoke to said. Later, as I got more experienced, I adopted a method of holding the phone with one hand while taking notes with the other, and then immediately negotiating with my interviewee how to publish their comments — whether to sum up their words this way or that way. If the interviewee turned out to suffer from "text addiction" (as I am a sufferer myself), it could take pretty long to arrive at an agreed wording. I am grateful to all my interviewees to this day — even to those who seemed unable to focus and wasted a lot of time talking about all sorts of other things.

It ought to have been comparatively easier to have conducted my interviews through e-mail, so as to avoid any awkwardness that could be felt in an immediate conversation. But when I tried this out, I found that it did not work well. I would send out twenty messages one evening, and if by the third or fourth day I had got two answers, that was already not bad — a success rate of about ten percent. I sent individualized e-mail messages rather than mass e-mails, which meant that I had to spend a long time writing the messages. So, I am particularly grateful to anyone who e-mailed me their views directly and unprompted. Among those are some who are not particularly close friends, and quite possibly some who were not at all familiar with Twitter, but they all placed that much trust in me and put themselves at a certain risk. Later, I may get the opportunity to mention their names and give due praise to them in public. At this point, one young friend I would like to mention in particular is Wang Wo (王我), a documentary filmmaker whose two films — *Renao* (热闹, *Noise*) and *Zheteng* (折腾, *Torment*)[16] — I like very much. He sent me a text message that read: "Professor Cui, I know you may not get round to 'interrogating' me, but I would like to say, eleven years are not a certain person's prison term. Eleven years is the longest a certain doomed group of people have left." There were a couple of other young people who got in touch with me of their own accord in this manner, sending me e-mails or text messages.

Nursing my mixed feelings of guilt and gratitude, I was still surprised, taken aback, and upset about some of the criticisms and condemnations of my interviewees' comments on Twitter, especially at the beginning. I was aware, of course, that I had importuned them and so I felt like a friend toward each person willing to accept the call and share their thoughts. While I had published their views, I had certainly not meant to make them targets of public attacks or exposure. At that time

I felt that I should defend them just as one would defend one's friends. On Twitter and on my blog, I appealed more than once to people to stop these attacks, so that I could overcome my feelings of guilt about my "original sin [i.e. the "sin" of encouraging the targets of such attacks to make their views known]." Actually, the vast majority of interviews had been conducted in a friendly and amiable atmosphere. Only gradually could I come to accept that it was normal for netizens to have all sorts of different views about the celebrities they cared about.

Among the comments from the 148 interviewees I posted on Twitter, there was not a single one that said, "I firmly support the government's action and the verdict of the No. 1 Intermediate People's Court of Beijing Municipality." But had anyone thought of providing a public forum for individuals holding such views? Two groups of friends told me that they were going to try to find people willing openly to express their support for the government's action, but for reasons I am not privy to, they did not follow through with their plan.

I would like to take this opportunity to thank those who provided me with the contact numbers and e-mail addresses of interviewees and helped me to get their friends to speak to me. I would like to thank those friends who advised me, making excellent suggestions when I encountered difficulties and did not know how to handle them. I am much indebted to everyone for their support, without which I would not have been able to see the project through. I would say that the "ominous midnight calls" have been a piece of joint performance art, to which everyone who gave interviews contributed.

Of course, there are some more anecdotes that could be related, but now is not yet the right time. Perhaps I should tell one story that only concerned myself. One day at home after lunch, while I was posting messages on Twitter, my doorbell rang. I saw from my surveillance camera that a person in uniform was standing outside. My first thought at the time was, "Guys, I'm busy now, please come again a little later." Actually, I was working on Cui Jian's comment, which was composed of three lyric segments and had to be broken down into three parts before it could be posted on Twitter. As a former poetry critic, I knew I had to organize it further, for instance by using special symbols to indicate the start of each new line in the poem. It was quite complicated and time-consuming.

The View of Cui Jian (Rock Musician)

"Thoughts"

The situation is more complicated than you or I imagined
The reality is more brutal than you or I imagined.
One could choose to be more emotional
Or choose to be more rational.
I chose the latter.

The latter comes at the expense of
Having to store up the emotions that could have been released
When one's taken a stance one can observe one's living environment more closely.
No country like ours, no history like this
We do not have any place assigned to us, no proper place to go to.

Creation is finding a way where there was no way.
It is always independent.
Perhaps 2020 is a good year.
Before then, each of us can still do something.[17]

As I was typing to the rattling sound of my keyboard, I was suddenly reminded of a film I had watched as a child, entitled "*Yongbu Xiaoshi de Dianbo*" (永不消逝的电波, *An Electric Wave that Will Never Fade Away*).[18] Towards the end of this film, braving great difficulties, the grand old actor Sun Daolin (孙道临), acting as a Communist soldier collecting intelligence in a city occupied by the enemy, calmly sends off his last telegram, refusing to succumb to fear of his imminent arrest. Well, I thought that at that moment I rather resembled Sun Daolin; handling my Twitter message was rather like him handling a telegram, only that Sun's character in the movie is in a genuinely tight situation. As I was sitting there with my headphones on, I could not help chuckling inwardly, because I had never imagined that I could ever come to resemble Sun Daolin.

But then I realized that the person outside my door was just my residential compound's security guard. He had come to my flat because he had a question about my upstairs neighbor. I wondered why I had never paid attention to what uniform those guards wore.

19 August 2010

Appendix: Editors' Selection from Cui Weiping's Collected Tweets:[19]

Qin Hui (秦晖):[20] It is a travesty that people are still being punished for their words. I did not sign the Charter, but I accept the notion that while I might not agree with your point of view, I must defend your right to express it; and I firmly oppose the sentencing of Liu Xiaobo to prison for his writings.

Xu Youyu (徐友渔):[21] The crime Liu Xiaobo was sentenced for was based on Charter 08. The Charter was a reaffirmation of the United Nations [Universal] Declaration on Human Rights, therefore Liu's conviction defies civilized norms widely recognized by humankind. It also defies the current Chinese Constitution, because the Constitution clearly states that Chinese citizens enjoy freedom of speech. It flies in the face of the Chinese people and human conscience.

Zhang Yihe (章诒和):[22] In 1968, I was sentenced to twenty years in prison for the crime of counter-revolutionary actions; in 2009, for the crime of inciting subversion of state power, Liu Xiaobo has been given a sentence of eleven years. We both were made criminals for our words, one forty-one years before the other. This can only make one wonder: this system of ours, has it really improved much? Has our society made any progress at all?

Yuan Weishi (袁伟时):[23] This is the twenty-first century, and people are still being criminally punished for their words. This is a civil rights violation and a desecration of civilization. It is another blemish upon China's name! The authorities' insistence on making Liu Xiaobo a criminal has made him a hero in the hearts and minds of many. With the difference of perception so vast, how will the rulers manage?

Yu Yingshi (余英时):[24] In total, Liu Xiaobo has been sent to prison three times, with each time bringing him more honor than the last, and this present time topping it all. A glorious precedent exists in Chinese history, namely that of Fan Zhongyan (范仲淹),[25] who said he would rather die than live in silence, and who was put away three times in his lifetime. The first time, his friends said, "A star has fallen." The second time, people said, "Now the moon." The final time, "And the sun." He laughed in response: "The three phases of Fan Zhongyan." This is what Liu Xiaobo is today.

He Weifang (贺卫方):[26] Not too long ago, a foreign media outlet phoned for an interview, asking what I thought of Mr. Liu Xiaobo's eleven-year sentence. I replied angrily that I would rather not comment. The person asked: "So you don't think that eleven years is too heavy?" I retorted: "Oh, do you think just three years would have been okay? For someone who hasn't committed any crime, a single day is too much — even one day of imprisonment would be an injustice. But anyway, do you think he will have to serve the full term?"

Guo Yuhua (郭于华):[27] Charter 08 stated demands for basic and legitimate rights and called for social change in a moderate and common-sense way; so where is the crime? Even if its content was completely wrong, this was not the kind of speech that can be criminalized. It is not what he did but convicting Liu Xiaobo for it that was an "incitement to subvert state power" — an act that flew in the face of social conscience and humanity.

Wang Xiaoyu (王晓渔):[28] I cannot circumvent Internet filtering, and I did not see any reports about this in the Mainland media. I firmly believe that this report of an unarmed, defenseless scholar having been sentenced to eleven years in prison is a slanderous fabrication originating from a small number of enemy forces. How could a grand, dignified, and upright nation possibly allow something as unconstitutional as this to happen? I hope that the good masses who do not at this point understand the truth will open their eyes and see the truth for themselves, and not allow themselves to be confused by rumors.

Zhang Yiwu (张颐武):[29] [When I phoned him he said he had not heard about Liu Xiaobo's criminal conviction, and that he was currently focusing on other issues, such as, for instance, Xiao Shenyang. I explained that I only wanted to have people's thoughts on this issue. He said he had] "no thoughts whatsoever."

Zhang Lifan (章立凡):[30] 1. Constitutionalism and democracy are not only solemn historical commitments, they would also allow one to maintain legitimacy through providing mechanisms for social reconciliation and avenues of redress. This Christmas, the government's arrogance and prejudice have once again blocked these avenues. 2. Given this history of repeated dishonesty and the current regress in the economy, in politics and rule of law reform efforts, it has become very difficult to resolve social conflicts. 3. As they have lost their sense of historical reality and are now trying to reverse the trend of history, they are committing suicide. Although I do not love the Revolution, it has now been confirmed to be retarded and beyond hope.

Ai Xiaoming (艾晓明):[31] Facing freedom from behind a barbed wire, Liu Xiaobo rushed toward it without regard to the barbs driving into his flesh until it bled. An eleven-year sentence will bury alive his ability to think freely. Silence is acquiescence, complicity, it harms the conscience, it cuts off all hope, it condemns ten thousand posterior generations to living in lies. Sorry, perhaps there aren't even ten thousand posterior generations left. Perhaps we will finish ourselves off much sooner than that. Chinese people, if you do not speak the truth, if you stay silent until you are all dumb, how can the Chinese coexist with civilizations that gave birth to works such as *Katyń*[32] and *The Lives of Others*?[33]

Bei Dao (北岛):[34] The criminalization of speech makes people once more feel the dark shadows of our ancient imperial regime. I am reminded of a criminal sentence passed thirty years ago that was similar. Will we ever be able to come out of these dark shadows? I am also moved by the love between Liu Xiaobo and Liu Xia. Their love far surpasses the hatred of those who believe that they control others' fates.

Xu Xiao (徐晓):[35] Before Xiaobo's trial I said to the National Security Protection Squad (*guobao*, 国保) police officers: If Liu Xiaobo is convicted because of Charter 08, then as one of its co-signatories, I ask you to send me to prison, too.

Hu Yong (胡泳):[36] Firstly, we are still close to the Cultural Revolution, the Anti-Rightist Movement, and the Anti-Hu Feng Campaign; secondly, we are still far from the civilized world, we are still living in a barbaric country. I am calling for the abolition of Article 105 subsection 2 of the Criminal Law, that infamous legal provision, which means a continuation both of the crime of counter-revolution of the 1979 Criminal Law and of the imperial Chinese practice of imprisoning people for their thought.

Wang Lixiong (王力雄):[37] I hope there will be another sort of change in the coming eleven years. The most effective support for Liu Xiaobo and all the other political prisoners would be quickly to change this society and to set the people free.

Zhang Sizhi (张思之):[38] After reading the Liu Xiaobo case I want to ask Heaven: The great, glorious and correct Party promised to the nation that no one's speech would be treated as crime, that there would be constitutional government, that its words could be relied on and its actions expected to have results. How can this turn out to be mere rhetoric and empty talk? And having once proclaimed People's Democracy and the Four Freedoms, how can it keep violating these principles? For those who amidst helplessness dare to fight for democracy for the whole people and who are willing to sacrifice their own freedom for this goal, I express my heartfelt praise and respect!

Václav Havel:[39] There is nothing subversive of state security or damaging to future prosperity when citizens act guided by their own will and according to their best knowledge and conscience, when they associate among themselves to discuss and express peacefully their concerns and visions about the future development of their society. On the contrary, a country's material and spiritual future is undermined when its citizens are not allowed to act, associate a scholar of modern Eastern European political culture, think and speak freely.[40]

Hu Xingdou (胡星斗):[41] Regarding the Liu case, I have already said in many interviews: by criminalizing speech, China has fallen short of the standards for a civilized or even just a respectable country. No matter how much our economy is flourishing, China remains a barbaric country, and the flourishing economy is no more than a bubble, brought about by a corrupt regime exercising its special powers. At one time, Hitler's economy flourished, too; and so did Stalin's. And yet they foundered eventually. The soul of the people dies under repression of speech.

Liu Zaifu (刘再复):[42] In his book *Meiren Zeng Wo Menghanyao* (美人赠我蒙汗药, *A Beauty Drugged Me*),[43] Liu Xiaobo abused me as a "theory czar" (and before that he several times criticized me harshly as being a nationalist, etc.), but today I, this "czar," want to say: I oppose all criminalization of speech, including that affecting Liu Xiaobo.

Mao Yushi (茅于轼):[44] I heard a few old Party comrades say that at the Second and Seventh Party Congresses federalism was already proposed. If federalism was already proposed at the Second and Seventh Party Congresses, why then can't Liu Xiaobo propose it? If we want to progress as a society, we must allow new thoughts.

Zhang Boshu (张博树):[45] Considering it as a legal decision, the heavy sentence for Liu Xiaobo is ludicrous, it is a typical example of criminalization of speech. The fact that this is happening in twenty-first century China is shameful for our entire people. Considering it in the context of transition, the decision will only make Charter 08 more well-known around the world, and it has created a hero of the opposition. Whether or not any of Charter 08's content is debatable, whether or not Liu Xiaobo as a person has weaknesses or insufficiencies, all that is no longer important. What is important is that because of this verdict the transition is now occurring in a new setting; it has acquired greater force of legitimacy. Sentence is passed right now on those who passed sentence on him. I suppose that those who decided the heavy sentence for Liu Xiaobo could not anticipate that.

Wang Yi (王毅):[46] I used to hope I could persuade myself that China was suffering under too heavy a burden of authoritarian history; that nowadays, "ant people" and "fart people" were a product of this burden as well as various current conditions; and that we should have sympathy with the rulers and their one-step-forward-three-steps-back system of achieving progress, and show full understanding for the fact that China could not possibly complete its journey toward rule of law and constitutional government in one day. But now, it seems that there has to be a limit to such forbearance — namely, that we must expect from the ruler that you will at least show a little honesty. You cannot on the one hand make a commitment to the "International Covenant on Civil and Political Rights (ICCPR)" before the whole world, and tearfully preach about how human rights and democracy represent a manifestation of human civilization and so on and so forth; and then on the other hand continue to treat people the way you treated Yu Luoke (遇罗克), Zhang Zhixin (张志新) and Lin Zhao (林昭).

Part Two

Charter 08 in Context

Chapter 5
Boundaries of Tolerance

Charter 08 and Debates over Political Reform

Pitman B. Potter and Sophia Woodman

Introduction

Dissident intellectual Liu Xiaobo is now serving an eleven-year prison term for his role in the drafting and distribution of Charter 08, and the awarding of the 2010 Nobel Peace Prize to him has been denounced by the Chinese authorities as a "political farce."[1] Yet many of the points made in the Charter have clear echoes in recent remarks on political and legal reform by academics and government officials, including Premier Wen Jiabao (温家宝) himself. This raises important questions about the boundaries of tolerance for proposals on political reform and discussion of politically sensitive issues more generally. An analysis of the scope and locations of recent debates over political reform indicates that the legitimacy of proposals for reform is determined not so much by their content as by the identity and status of the speaker, and the location and time of the speech.

In this chapter, we first consider the compatibility of the content of Charter 08 with established laws, policies, and objectives, including recent pronouncements on political reform. We also point to ways in which the Charter challenges underlying norms and rules. Then we proceed to suggest some of the factors that determine the reception, legitimacy, and persuasiveness of particular proposals for reform, proposing the concepts of "segmented publics" and "differential rights" as ways of analyzing these.

This examination of the debate over political reform provides some insight into broader conditions for freedom of expression, thus addressing the question posed by the drafters of Charter 08: "Where is China headed in the twenty-first century? Will it continue with 'modernization' under authoritarian rule, or will it embrace universal human values, join the mainstream of civilized nations, and build a democratic system?"[2]

The Phenomenon of Charter 08

"Charter 08," a manifesto for political and legal reform in China, was inspired by "Charta 77," in which Václav Havel and others called for political reform and respect for human rights in Czechoslovakia in 1977.[3] Charter 08 was signed by 303 prominent scholars, professionals, lawyers, writers, artists, activists, civil servants, and citizens from across the People's Republic of China (PRC) and released on the sixtieth anniversary of the Universal Declaration of Human Rights, 10 December 2008.

The document begins with a critical review of the past century of political and legal developments in China, focusing on the struggle for democratic accountability and rights and freedoms. It levels particular criticism against political abuses under the PRC, including the Cultural Revolution and the 1989 Tiananmen Massacre. The document recognizes improvements in living conditions in China under the policy of reform and opening up since 1978, and acknowledges the importance of the government's signing the International Covenant on Economic, Social and Cultural Rights (ICESCR) and the International Covenant on Civil and Political Rights (ICCPR), and its promise to draw up a human rights action plan.[4] However these efforts are dismissed as formalistic actions by a regime that is committed first and foremost to maintaining its own power. Continued abuses of human rights result from ineffective and corrupt institutions and insufficient commitment to the rule of law, the Charter asserts, and have led to an epidemic of social conflict. Overall, it concludes that the system of governance is in such decline that "change is no longer optional."[5]

Charter 08 can be seen as an expression of the long-term project of a group of liberal officials, thinkers, and activists in China.[6] This group has members both inside and outside the Chinese Communist Party (hereafter "CCP" or "Party"), spanning the divide between officials and dissidents.[7] At the center of the Charter are liberal principles of constitutional governance, including democracy and the rule of law, and suggestions on how these might be adapted to China's conditions.

Of course, the dominant consensus in the ruling Party is that liberal tenets do not apply to China.[8] The Charter would pose little threat if its principles and proposals could be dismissed as simply reflections of Western bourgeois thinking. More challenging for the Party, however, is the way Charter 08 proposes meaningful enforcement of the rights articulated within the current constitutional framework, thus calling on the government to live up to its own commitments. In essence, the Charter questions the Party's narrow interpretation of human rights and the rule of law, arguing that the fundamental dogmas of Chinese socialism that mandate continued Party supremacy are neither legitimate nor effective, and serve to incapacitate China's socialist law and human rights systems.

Charter 08 puts forward six fundamental principles — freedom, human rights, equality, republicanism, democracy, and constitutional rule — all of which are reflected in existing PRC constitutional doctrine. However, the Charter articulates them in a manner consonant with classic principles of liberal governance.[9]

The principle of *freedom* is described in Charter 08 as a "universal human value," and includes freedom of speech, freedom of press, freedom of assembly, freedom of association, freedom of residence and movement, and the freedoms to strike, to demonstrate, and to protest. The first four of these freedoms are recognized in Article 4 of the PRC Constitution. The rights to strike, demonstrate, and protest are broadly commensurate with the "four big freedoms" enshrined in Article 13 (to speak out freely, air views fully, hold great debates, and write "big-character posters") and Article 28 (the right to strike) of the 1975 PRC Constitution, although these were later removed and did not appear in the 1982 Constitution.[10]

The principle of *human rights* was incorporated into the PRC Constitution in an amendment in 2004 that added the phrase, "the state respects and preserves human rights," to Article 33.

Charter 08's principle of *equality* is also articulated in the PRC Constitution, through such provisions as "equality before the law" (Article 33, paragraph 1), "equality of nationalities" (Article 4, paragraph 1), and equality between men and women (Article 48).

The Charter's principle of *democracy* echoes PRC constitutional references to "socialist democracy" and "democratic centralism,"[11] as well as commitments to local elections.[12] Components of this principle in the Charter include popular sovereignty; people's exercise of political power; and dignity, freedom, and human rights for minorities, which find limited parallels in official rhetoric on these themes articulated in Articles 2, 4, and 33 of the PRC Constitution, as well as in other laws and policies.[13]

Constitutional rule implies the centrality of the legal system and legal regulation, and thus seems consistent with the formal rhetoric of the rule of law as expressed in Article 5 of the PRC Constitution.[14]

Despite this apparent convergence, significant divergences on both normative and substantive levels mean that the extent of enforcement has been questionable.[15] Protection of freedom and human rights, for example, remains subject to the precondition that citizens "perform the duties prescribed by the Constitution and the law" (Article 33, paragraph 3 of the PRC Constitution). These limits are entrenched further by constitutional doctrine that subordinates all rights to the needs of socialism and to the interests of state and society.[16] Protection of equality rights tends to be formalistic, so constitutional and legal expressions of equality have little impact on entrenched socioeconomic inequalities and gender discrimination, for example.[17] The emphasis in PRC constitutional doctrine on "socialist democracy" and "democratic centralism" effectively limits the reach of democratic processes.[18]

In contrast to the preceding five, Charter 08's principle of *republicanism* challenges the presumptions underlying current orthodoxy more directly, as it draws explicitly on liberal discourses and prescribes a political system of institutions and processes ordered by law rather than Party policy, and characterized by an environment of freely competing interest groups, civil society organizations, and individuals. This vision is underpinned by a conception of civic engagement that echoes the roots of republicanism while constraining its majoritarian impulses through procedural rules and minority rights, thus contrasting with provisions of the PRC Constitution that mandate the Party's monopoly on political power. Although recent years have seen the emergence of a variety of interest group politics on a limited scale within the National People's Congress (NPC) and some government rule-making processes,[19] these are not procedurally protected and thus are conducted at the Party's discretion. Charter 08 articulates principles of legal institutionalism that would entrench political arrangements of republicanism.

In sum, the principles set out in Charter 08 put forth ideals of the rule of law and liberal governance, while questioning the limits imposed by Party orthodoxy. Charter 08 challenges the government to make good on its claims to recognize a variety of constitutional and human rights, adopting existing formal language but offering interpretations that are not limited by the Party's political imperatives.

While the Charter's principles draw on current orthodoxy, its specific policy proposals bring into focus the barriers to thoroughgoing political reform within the existing framework. Yet by framing the possibilities for reform in terms of existing political-legal arrangements, Charter 08 leaves open the possibility of reconciliation.

Charter 08's proposals on a *new constitution* and the *separation of powers* run counter to the unitary state design.[20] However, in practice, the unitary state model is already giving way to other arrangements: the literature on fragmented authoritarianism, for example, suggests the limits to its power,[21] while functional federalism approaches recognize the reality of continued balancing of central and regional power.[22] In the ongoing process of administrative and bureaucratic reform, separation of powers has already become an operational norm in certain areas. Thus, jurisdictional contests exist between the power of courts to interpret the meaning of the law and constitutional provisions granting the NPC Standing Committee sole power over legal interpretation.[23] Tensions also arise between administrative bodies under the State Council and organs of the NPC on issues of policy implementation and supervision.[24]

Proposals on *legislative democracy* reflect language that is already contained in the constitutional and legal framework for the PRC state.[25] The same can be said for the proposal on *public control over civil servants and the bureaucracy*, where institutional arrangements on supervision of state organs are already expressed in Article 2 of the PRC Constitution, as well as through legal avenues for enforcement in the Administrative Litigation Law and the State Compensation Law. Related proposals on *elections of public officials* could be carried forward through expanding the current policy of promoting local elections, while the principle of *independence of the judiciary* is already expressed in the PRC Constitution.[26] Related proposals on ensuring *justice and fairness* refer to the establishment of meaningful legal institutions and processes to safeguard these values and ensure fairness, justice, and equality of opportunity. Calls for such institutional reform challenge China's administrative law systems (including provisions for judicial review and the "letters and visits" (*xinfang*, 信访) system), but nonetheless fall generally within the purview of acceptable reform proposals.[27]

The Charter's call for *guarantees of human rights* requires new institutional arrangements for human rights protection. While some courts in China have reportedly established tribunals (*shenpanting*, 审判庭) to hear complaints on matters including human rights, doubts about the capacity of courts is evident in the Charter's proposal for the establishment of a human rights committee. This proposal also reflects long-standing pressure from the human rights system of the United Nations (UN) for states to establish national human rights institutions. The proposed *abolition of "re-education through labor"* has already found growing acceptance among many in society and some in the government and Party leadership.[28] Proposed reforms to ensure *residential equality* among rural and urban residents seem largely unproblematic for the central government, although local governments may be resistant to reforms of the *hukou* (户口, household registration) system that eliminate their role in restricting permanent settlement, particularly of rural-to-urban migrants.[29] While proposals related to *freedoms to form associations, assembly, expression, and religion* challenge official limits on these rights, as discussed above there is considerable room for accommodation within the existing constitutional framework.[30] Policy reforms in areas of *private property*,[31] *financial and tax reform*,[32] *social security*,[33] and *environmental protection*[34] are all nominally compatible with existing state law and policy. The proposal to form a *federated republic* seems broadly commensurate with existing PRC policy. This would extend equality and fairness to Hong Kong and Macau while protecting their existing freedoms; find a peaceful unification solution for Taiwan; and provide a workable framework for China's minority nationality areas in which all ethnic and religious groups can flourish. However, Beijing has retained for itself options to assert the primacy of its political authority in each of the regions discussed.[35]

While the Charter 08 proposals are thus broadly consonant with the aims of the current system, its call for a *"truth and reconciliation"* process presents a more direct challenge. Such a proposal has been under discussion in domestic and transnational dissident circles for some years,[36] and would involve rehabilitating those vilified in the political campaigns of the past, releasing serving political prisoners and prisoners of conscience and paying reparations, as well as establishing an investigative commission to look into the facts of past injustices and atrocities. As with other elements of Charter 08, influences from liberal models are evident — in this case the truth and reconciliation processes associated with political change in Northern Ireland and South Africa.[37] While this is the most dramatic proposal in Charter 08, it could provide an opportunity for building political unity in China. Facing a significant legitimacy deficit, the CCP has consistently refused to open up historical records or engage in serious reflection on events including the Anti-Rightist Campaign, the Great Famine, the Cultural Revolution and, perhaps most crucially for the current leadership, the Tiananmen Massacre of 1989. However, some of those in leadership positions seem keen to strengthen the state's capacity to govern effectively, and Charter 08's proposal on truth and reconciliation offers an opportunity to transcend the limitations of past ideological rigidity and political orthodoxy to confront the errors of the past and build a new consensus on the future.

Thus, while the principles and proposals of Charter 08 certainly challenge Party orthodoxy, they also present multiple possibilities for accommodation. And as might be expected in a relationship that is as much about negotiation on practical implementation as about the articulation of ideals, the most contentious issues, such as the principle of "republicanism" and the call for "truth and reconciliation," could serve as trade-off items to be shelved — at least temporarily — in order to reach agreement on other issues.

Other Voices: Orthodox Calls for Reform

Despite the convergences outlined above, the proposals of Charter 08 are unlikely to be officially accepted, especially given the conviction of Liu Xiaobo. However, components of Charter 08 may well affect debates in expert and official circles on legal and political reform.[38] In fact, calls for political reform from establishment figures reveal that the issues raised in Charter 08 are not withering on the vine.

Most prominently, Premier Wen Jiabao has made a number of recent statements supporting political and legal reform. In September 2010, when Wen spoke at the thirtieth anniversary of the founding of the Shenzhen Special Economic Zone, he said: "Without the safeguard of political reform, the fruits of economic reform would be lost and the goals of modernization would not materialize."[39] In addition, he claimed that allowing more scope for criticism of the government and its officials was important in addressing "the problem of over-concentration of power with ineffective supervision."[40]

These comments echo Charter 08's claim that without political reform, the gains of economic development will be lost:

> The Chinese people, who have endured human rights disasters and uncountable struggles across these same years, now include many who see clearly that freedom, equality, and human rights are universal values of humankind and that democracy and constitutional government are the fundamental framework for protecting these values. By departing from these values, the Chinese government's approach to "modernization" has proven disastrous....
>
> The stultifying results are endemic official corruption, an undermining of the rule of law, weak human rights, decay in public ethics, crony capitalism, growing inequality between the wealthy and the poor, pillage of the natural environment as well as of the human and historical environments, and the exacerbation of a long list of social conflicts, especially, in recent times, a sharpening animosity between officials and ordinary people.... The decline of the current system has reached the point where change is no longer optional.[41]

In an interview with CNN's Fareed Zakaria on 23 September 2010, Premier Wen again stated that political reforms should go ahead in tandem with economic reforms. In particular, he advocated changes towards greater democracy, oversight of government, and judicial independence:

> We need to improve our legal system, run the country according to law, and establish the country under the rule of law and we need to have an independent and just (独立和公正的) judicial system ...[42]

Government should be subject to oversight (监督) by the people and that will require us, call on us to increase transparency in administrative affairs. It is also extremely necessary for government to accept oversight from the news media and other political parties....

There is also another important aspect that when it comes to development of democracy in China, we need to take into account China's national conditions (国情), and we need to introduce a system that suits China's special features, and we need to introduce a gradual approach....

Socialism, as I understand it, is a system of democracy. Without democracy, there is no socialism. And such a democracy first and foremost should serve to ensure people's right to democratic elections, oversight and decision making. Such a democracy should also help people to fully develop themselves in an all-round way in an environment featuring freedom and equality. And such a democracy should be based on a full-fledged legal system. Otherwise there would be chaos. That's why we need to run the country according to law and ensure everyone is equal under the law.[43]

In the portion of the interview aired on Fareed Zakaria's GPS program on CNN, Wen expressed support for freedom of speech and argued that the ruling party should be accountable to the law:

I believe freedom of expression is indispensable (我认为言论自由……都是必不可少的), for any country, a country in the course of development and a country that has become strong. The Constitution of China guarantees (保障) freedom of speech.

I believe I and all the Chinese people have such a conviction that China will make continuous progress, and the people's wishes for and needs for democracy and freedom are irresistible (人民民主和自由要求是无法阻挡的).

I have done some deeper thinking about this topic, since we last met. My view is that a political party after it becomes a ruling party should be somewhat different from the one when it was struggling for power. The biggest difference should be that this political party should act in accordance with the constitution and the law (政党活动应该要符合宪法和法律的规定).[44]

These remarks echoed comments made in Wen's earlier speech to the UN General Assembly and in a roundtable meeting with Chinese and American media in New York, although these were removed from official Chinese media reports.[45] The Premier's comments are broadly in line with statements in Charter 08 around democracy and freedom:

> Without freedom, China will always remain far from civilized ideals.
>
> The most fundamental principles of democracy are that the people are sovereign and the people select their government.
>
> Members of legislative bodies at all levels should be chosen by direct election, and legislative democracy should observe just and impartial principles.
>
> There should be a comprehensive system of democratic elections based on "one person, one vote." The direct election of administrative heads at the levels of county, city, province, and nation should be systematically implemented. The rights to hold periodic free elections and to participate in them as a citizen are inalienable.[46]

Wen Jiabao is not the only prominent person to have spoken out in support of freedom of speech in recent months. In October 2010, twenty-three retired officials led by Li Rui (李锐) (Mao Zedong's former secretary), Hu Jiwei (胡绩伟) (former *People's Daily* editor) and Jiang Ping (江平) (former president of the China University of Political Science and Law) — the group Feng Chongyi (冯崇义) calls the democrats within the Party[47] — submitted an open letter to the NPC Standing Committee calling for removal of restrictions on freedom of speech: "Our core demand is that the system of prior approval be changed to a system of *post-facto* legal responsibility."[48] Once again, the comparisons with Charter 08 are striking: "We should make freedom of speech, freedom of the press, and academic freedom universal, thereby guaranteeing that citizens can be informed and can exercise their right of political supervision."[49]

Yet it is not only those obviously identified with the liberal camp who have expressed such opinions. In November, Zhou Yongkang (周永康), a member of the Politburo Standing Committee and director of the political-legal system (政法系统), called for China to "comply with the universal principles of law."[50]

Clearly the boundaries of tolerance for discussion of universalism are broader when the speaker is the Premier or the chief legal official in the government than when the comments come from a dissident intellectual. When compared with the official response to Charter 08, reactions to political reform proposals from within the establishment have been remarkably muted. Reflecting the extent to which the political elite is divided on these issues, however, there have been a variety of responses to Wen's speeches, ranging from orders to the media not to reprint his remarks to editorials challenging his views. The Party Propaganda Department reportedly issued directives to Chinese media not to report on Wen's CNN interview.[51] *People's Daily* published a series of three editorials on 21, 25, and 27 October 2010, implicitly challenging Wen's call for political reform. These editorials called instead for incremental reform that would not challenge the authority of the Party leadership.[52] This approach echoed the terms of the Communiqué of the Fifth Plenum of the Seventeenth Central Committee on 18 October 2010, which focused on continued economic development and failed to address the key point of Wen's speeches (and of Charter 08) that continued economic and social development would require more thoroughgoing political reform.[53]

Response to a Moderate Challenge

Despite Charter 08's convergences with current law, policy, and objectives, the government's response to it was aggressively repressive. In the first week after its release, forty signatories were questioned, and during the course of the following year, more than a hundred were harassed or detained.[54] Peking University Law School required its students to boycott Charter 08,[55] while Peking University law professor He Weifang (贺卫方) was exiled to remote Shihezi (石河子) in Xinjiang after signing the Charter. The initiators and principal drafters of Charter 08 — Liu Xiaobo, Zhang Zuhua (张祖桦), and Jiang Qisheng (江棋生)[56] — were all detained around the time of the document's public release, but only Liu remains in custody.[57]

One reason for the severe sentence imposed on Liu Xiaobo is evidence of growing support for Charter 08 in a climate of growing public dissatisfaction over corruption and local authoritarianism, as well as increasingly draconian repression of dissent. Beginning with 303 signatures in December 2008, a year later 10,390 people had signed the document, according to the Charter website.[58] This figure was cited in the court's verdict in Liu's trial as "evidence" of his crimes.[59] Chinese people from a wide spectrum of occupations and places are apparently more often framing claims in terms of human rights.[60] In March 2010, a human rights activist in Guangzhou encountered a middle-aged man on a bus giving out copies of the Charter, who said he had already distributed more than ten thousand copies.[61]

The challenge posed by Charter 08 is made even more intense by Liu Xiaobo's conduct throughout his trial and imprisonment, where he adopted the bearing of a patriotic critic of an unjust regime:

> Hatred can rot away at a person's intelligence and conscience. Enemy mentality will poison the spirit of a nation, incite cruel mortal struggles, destroy a society's tolerance and humanity, and hinder a nation's progress toward freedom and democracy. That is why I hope to be able to transcend my personal experiences as I look upon our nation's development and social change, to counter the regime's hostility with utmost goodwill, and to dispel hatred with love....
>
> In order to exercise the right to freedom of speech conferred by the Constitution, one should fulfill the social responsibility of a Chinese citizen. There is nothing criminal in anything I have done. [But] if charges are brought against me because of this, I have no complaints.[62]

The award of the Nobel Peace Prize to Liu in October 2010 did little to dampen the government's hostility to him and the Charter.[63] It had threatened the Nobel Committee with severe consequences if Liu was awarded the prize, and after the announcement, Beijing termed it a desecration and issued a barrage of hostile commentary.[64] Associates of Liu Xiaobo were rounded up and his family put under effective house arrest, while colleagues in China were barred from traveling abroad in case they might attend the award ceremony.[65] At the event, Liu's absence was marked by an empty chair with his photograph on it, and for the first time since 1936, no representative of the Peace Prize recipient was available to accept the award.[66]

Differential Rights, Segmented Publics

While harsh punishment has been meted out to Liu, overall the government's response to the signatories of Charter 08 has been far from uniform, and the comparison of the Charter with comments by Wen and others above also reflect differentials in levels of tolerance accorded to advocates of political reform. Restrictions on expression do not follow a unified logic. While overall freedom of expression has expanded significantly in the reform era, standards for acceptable speech vary enormously depending on the institutional location of the utterance; the identity, status, and history of the speaker; and the time of the event. The combination of all these factors means that determining what may be restricted or allowed is contingent, but certain underlying principles can be discerned. While restrictions on content have frequently been studied, insufficient attention has been paid to other elements through which expression is constrained — and even sometimes enabled. Below we will provide some pointers to analyze the operation of these elements.

Firstly, we propose the concept of "segmented publics" as a way of understanding the element of institutional location. A public is "a space of discourse" defined by those it addresses,[67] while this community simultaneously comprises those who address it.[68] Drawing on Jürgen Habermas' idea of "the public sphere,"[69] these are spaces for deliberation of public affairs and what constitutes the common good, as well as for making claims that are based on these understandings. Yet in contrast to how Habermas envisaged the public sphere, the idea of "segmented" publics indicates that these are divided into separate spaces, and points to how the Chinese government sets formal and informal rules to limit discussions of particular issues to specific institutional spaces.

Here, then, lines of inclusion and exclusion are explicitly drawn. Critiques of Habermas' original "public sphere" conception pointed to *implicit* exclusions and inequality in its operations.[70] In China today, the explicit *intention* is to constrain debate within a particular group of people, usually based on their status. Yet debate may be relatively free within the circumscribed space of a particular segmented public.

There are a number of different types of segmented publics. Within bodies such as universities and think tanks, debates are legitimated due to the expert knowledge of their members. In these spaces — which are themselves divided up according to categories of knowledge and expertise — educated elites are authorized to participate "in the ordering of society as specialists who advise government and business."[71] Here, then, issues such as politics and the rule of law become technical matters on which people with relevant training may advance opinions based on their study of the subject. A related example is how diplomats and government officials deal with UN processes related to China's implementation of its international human rights obligations as a matter of "international co-operation" that is separated from domestic discussion.[72]

In the field of associations that exists on the margins of and even inside state agencies, discussions are authorized among members of organizations that assist the government in carrying out policies and mobilizing the public for shared goals. Here, both expertise and encouraging a certain degree of citizen participation are justifications for allowing freer discussion of the specific issues designated as the concerns of the group in question. The scope such associations are creating for advocacy and debate has been expressed in the idea of "embedded activism." This concept shows how the embeddedness of social organizations — manifested in blurred distinctions between civil society and state, in the formation of groups within the state structure, and the interpersonal connections that make these possible — serve both to constrain and to enable action on a set of shared goals.[73] As Ho and Edmonds write, "[E]mbedded environmentalism is a resourceful and negotiated strategy employed by activists to gain maximum political and social influence ... by professing to uphold the principles of the [CCP] and the state."[74]

A third example is the lowest levels of formal government and the residents' and villagers' committees that are obligated by law to deal with all complaints that come to them, thus being the site for the unrestricted right to express grievances, articulated in Article 41 of the Constitution. Given this role, these institutions are authorized as a venue for a certain degree of public debate. The exercise of the constitutional "right to complain" is conditional on the appropriateness of the venue in which the complaint is made. The *same words* spoken in the wrong venue can bring sanctions on the speaker.

Apart from the latter case, the rules of these segmented publics are largely unwritten and complicate the picture. These should be seen as dynamic spaces where boundaries are permeable, often contested, and constantly in formation. When disputes arise, boundaries of appropriate expression may become politicized, and the right of a person or group to raise a complaint or speak on a certain issue may be challenged.[75] People making contentious claims often need to try to forestall such politicization by articulating the specific laws and policies that make their grievance a legitimate matter for that particular public arena.[76] Even within expert publics, controversial claims often need to be framed in a way that demonstrates how they are supported by existing orthodoxy.

When publics operate through media such as the Internet, academic publications, or limited circulation newsletters, another layer of complication arises. Each medium operates under different levels of constraint.[77] Adding a further level of complexity, individuals may move between segmented publics and simultaneously operate within different ones.

The unwritten rules of segmented publics are supported by cultural norms such as the prohibition on "airing the family's dirt outside" (家丑往外扬) and the idea of "giving face." Both of these norms make public criticism difficult, thus reinforcing segmentation. Elitist conceptions of tutelage over "the masses" also legitimize debate within privileged segmented publics. For example, some Chinese scholars have argued that deliberative democracy can develop among intellectuals first in a closed "public sphere," and then gradually be expanded. Their interpretation of the Habermasian concept emphasizes the *rationality* of deliberation within it, a formulation that privileges the contributions of experts.[78]

The system of constraints (and censorship more generally) is highly personalized, and relies not only on leaders exercising control over the people within their jurisdiction or in their unit, but also in the development of institutional cultures within certain spaces that are favorable to more open debate. Some leaders may allow a lot of debate, and indeed may use their institution to pursue aims at variance with those set by the Party leadership. This flexibility has been increased by decentralization and administrative reforms.[79] As Ho has argued in relation to environmental organizations,[80] the embeddedness of segmented publics within formal institutional spaces and networks can be enabling as well as constraining.

By contrast, the "responsibility systems" that enable debate in this way can also lead to suppression of complaints and discussion in other kinds of environments,[81] with the imprisonment of petitioners in psychiatric hospitals being an extreme example.[82] By punishing officials "responsible" for contentious speech and claims that exceed the bounds of the designated segmented public(s) within their jurisdiction, central government rules for evaluating cadres serve to encourage such repression of complainants.[83]

This focus on the role of individuals points to a second level of analysis, encapsulated in the concept of "differential rights." To a certain extent, this is already apparent in the concept of segmented publics, as these accord members and non-members differing rights to speak. Relative expertise is a key dimension along which entitlement is determined, but age is another important factor, giving retired democrats within the CCP relative latitude to make comments critical of government policy and actions, for example. These officials have continued to publish articles that go against the current consensus in advocating democratic reform, "whereas less privileged authors have been banned from publishing on much less sensitive topics."[84] Thus, differential rights operate along a spectrum of entitlements. While the CCP democrats represent one extreme, the other is illuminated by the outside boundaries of differential rights, in which people can be deprived of their right to speak altogether. The case of Liu Xiaobo is illustrative in this regard.

Despite the disappearance of overt class struggle rhetoric — even an unspoken ban on the idea that Chinese society is divided into classes — as well as the Constitution's guarantee of equality before the law, the idea that variably situated people have differential rights of expression remains a key principle in the Chinese legal order. This is an example of how exceptions are a consistent norm in Chinese law. As Sapio puts it, "[L]egal reform has increased the law's potential to suspend rights."[85] This logic is expressed most clearly in the "deprivation of political rights,"[86] which is a *required* addition to any conviction under provisions of the Criminal Law on endangering national security,[87] and may be applied to people convicted of other specified serious offenses.[88] In addition, those sentenced to death are deprived of these rights in perpetuity.[89]

Such restrictions rest on what might be termed "applied class struggle,"[90] a new variant of the old logic expressed in Mao Zedong's famous classification of disputes as being either among "the people" or between "the people" and "enemies."[91] While this formulation is now more commonly evoked as a rationale for ensuring that "internal contradictions" are promptly addressed so as to forestall unrest,[92] it still implies that there are those outside the pale who cannot be dealt with except through suppression.

In terms of the national legal order, with the shift to "national security" rather than "counter-revolution" as a rubric for prosecution of critics of communist rule, formalized with the amendments to the Criminal Law in 1997, the parameters for determining a person's status as an "enemy" in legal terms have gradually shifted. Now those in the category of enemies must be identified with "hostile foreign forces," as such a connection is inherent in the Chinese legal concept of crimes against national security.[93] Articulating the role of such forces in preventing China from resuming its rightful place in the international arena has been a key theme in the Party's project of patriotic education, which is the mechanism for forming the "spiritual civilization" it aims to build.[94]

The deprivation of political rights — and thus of any right to speak or be heard — is most identified with those found to be "enemies" of national security. Aware of the way such dichotomies are used to challenge the right of critics situated outside China to speak, the drafters of Charter 08 consciously restricted signatories to people inside China to avoid the charge that they had "colluded with hostile foreign forces."[95]

But this did not prevent such charges being leveled against Liu Xiaobo, or his conviction for the crime of "inciting subversion of state power" on 26 December 2009. The main items of "evidence" in the case were six articles he wrote and published online and the Charter. For each of the pieces of writing listed in the court's verdict, the fact that it was published on a website outside the PRC was noted, demonstrating a linkage to "hostile foreign forces" that was central to proving the prosecution's case.[96]

Differential rights do not only apply to the right to speak. The exceptions also extend to procedural protections that should apply to the persons, but do not because of their being identified as belonging to a special category. This was apparent in Liu's case: he was held incommunicado for a long period without having been charged with any crime, and for many months, despite repeated inquiries, his family was not formally notified of his detention as required by Chinese law.[97] He was sentenced to eleven years' imprisonment after a closed trial from which even his wife was excluded, on the grounds that she was a witness in the case.[98] Such exceptions are seen in many cases of detainees facing charges of crimes against the state.

Yet the boundaries between "people" and "enemies," between members and non-members of segmented publics are likewise dynamic, contextual, and contested. They are also historical and cumulative. Liu Xiaobo's record as a former political prisoner is an aspect of understanding why he received such a severe sentence, as is his identification with the events of 1989.

These distinctions apply well beyond high-profile cases like Liu's. The designation of "enemies" can occur at any level of the system. In practice the distinction between the current legally restrictive definition of "enemies" with external links, and old habits of class struggle in which this category was applied more broadly to critics of authority, both central and local, are often blurred. Applying political labels to people is a practice that continues as a key tactic in daily contentious politics, with the aim of discrediting their claims.[99] Those whose complaints threaten the power of local officials can thus find themselves deprived of all rights to raise their concerns, regardless of how mundane. This is evident in the treatment of individuals who persist in petitioning for redress of grievances outside their place of *hukou* registration, where such complaints would be permissible.[100] Both constitutionally and in terms of administrative practice, residents' committees and villagers' committees are required to address all matters brought to them by their constituents, making them a legitimate arena for voicing criticisms and complaints.[101]

Adding another layer of complexity, the scope of expression allowed in various segmented publics and the relative degree of differential rights are also temporally and spatially dynamic. These vary according to the time period and the type of event, whether cyclical or one of a kind; national or local in scope. The run-up to the Beijing Olympics provided a key example of the latter type, while the routine clampdowns around the anniversary of the June Fourth Tiananmen Massacre and the strict control of petitioning in the run-up to the annual "two meetings" of the Chinese People's Political Consultative Conference and the NPC exemplify the former. Béja suggests one factor in the severity of Liu's punishment was the Chinese leadership's fear that the release of Charter 08 on the eve of the significant year of 2009 (marking the twentieth anniversary of June Fourth and the sixtieth of the founding of the PRC) could have a similarly catalyzing effect on the public to open letters calling for democratization issued in late 1988 and 1989.[102]

The dynamic and contested nature of these divisions is obscured by formulations that distinguish between strategies of working "inside" and "outside" the state system, sometimes contrasted as "engagement" versus "confrontation."[103] In fact, the boundaries are blurred and constantly shifting, and the distinctions above are better thought of as situated along a series of spectrums, with multiple versions of the binary of "inside" and "outside." Furthermore, the state and the Party cannot be seen as monolithic, and those who advance contentious claims often seek to take advantage of divisions of opinion and interest within them to press their cause. The actions of those on the edges, those who make "boundary-spanning claims," as O'Brien and Li describe them, can result in sanctions or may serve to enlarge the scope of debate.[104]

Conclusion

Although the proposals raised by Wen Jiabao and other establishment supporters of reform parallel quite closely the ideals and proposals of Charter 08, they also represent a quite different dynamic: that of insiders challenging orthodoxy. It remains to be seen whether this congruence presages real change, or instead results in a retreat to narrower definitions of the permissible parameters of political reform debate, as some have claimed.[105] But it seems unlikely China's leaders have the stomach for the kinds of radical reversals of the past. More probably, the boundaries of legitimacy will be redrawn so as to permit proposals such as those of Wen Jiabao and the intellectuals to be tolerated, if not acted upon. And even if public calls for changes along the lines of the Charter 08 proposals disappear, this does not necessarily mean that they are not under discussion, but indicates that the boundaries of the relevant segmented publics have temporarily become less permeable, making this debate less visible.

Visibility, and rejection of such boundaries, is a principled position taken by Liu Xiaobo and others. In part, this represents a lack of choice: Liu has written of how he was deprived of the right to be heard in his own country, whether as a teacher or a writer, following his involvement in the events of 1989.[106] His active participation in the student demonstrations of 1989 — he dedicated the Peace Prize to those who died in the Tiananmen massacre — ensured his exclusion from the circle of trust. Either he could accept his deprivation of rights (and perhaps eventually win back some limited rights through keeping quiet) or he could make his voice heard in media outside China, thus constantly risking being accused of collaborating with hostile foreign forces.

The punishment of Liu Xiaobo is reminiscent in some ways of the crackdown on "rightists" in 1958 that began when Mao's apparent invitation to criticism of Party and government leadership styles led to condemnations from non-Party members of Party rule more broadly.[107] In both cases suppression was as much about the identity and status of the critics and the location of the speech as it was about the content of the feedback. The Party's constant efforts to enforce boundaries of segmented publics have created multiple arenas and communities for debate, not all of which are seen as legitimate venues for criticisms of the dominant orthodoxy.

The current political and legal arrangements for CCP rule are based on an apparent consensus among top Party leaders that constitutional provisions on rights should be interpreted in a restrictive fashion. It is the effectiveness of this consensus and the institutional mechanisms for enforcing it that led Peng Zhen (彭真), the prime mover of the contemporary PRC legal order, to declare in 1979 that the Party should not intervene in individual court cases — the broader process of indoctrination and consensus within the political and legal systems would ensure conformity to these norms without the inconvenience and risk of direct intervention.[108] But the consensus rests on the willingness of this community to maintain it; some assert that it is eroding from within, as many of the tenets of a more liberal approach are already widely accepted among members of the elite.[109] Perhaps, then, the thrust of Charter 08 in challenging the formalism of the government's current consensus, and demanding that existing rights and freedoms be realized in practice, represents more of an insider position than is apparent from the prosecution and vilification of Liu. The heavy-handed response to the awarding of the Peace Prize could be seen as a last-ditch attempt to forestall the emergence of a new consensus around Charter 08's starting point: "change is no longer optional."[110]

Chapter 6
The Threat of Charter 08

Feng Chongyi

In terms of the text itself, Charter 08 is a moderate proposal using ideas and concepts borrowed either from legal and political documents of the Chinese Communist Party (hereafter "CCP" or "Party") or from well-known international human rights documents universally accepted in the contemporary world, such as Universal Declaration of Human Rights (United Nations), Declaration of Human Rights (France) and Declaration of Independence (USA).[1] Even the most controversial concept of "federal republic of China," which has been singled out by the CCP government as a proof of the "crime of subversion," was also part of the early CCP political program. Why, then, have Charter 08 and its primary organizer Liu Xiaobo been met with such a harsh suppression by the CCP government?

This chapter highlights the contrast between rhetoric and reality in communist China and argues that Charter 08 is a serious threat to the Chinese communist regime in at least three ways: it heralds a grand coalition of liberal forces in China; it presents a viable alternative to the Chinese communist dictatorship in China; and it provides a rallying point and political goal for the amorphous but increasingly vigorous rights defense movement in China.

Charter 08 and the Grand Coalition of Chinese Liberal Forces

To a great extent, signatories of Charter 08 can be seen as the apotheosis of the Chinese liberal camp. In terms of professional and social diversity, the 303 original signatories of Charter identified themselves as: lawyers, writers, journalists, editors, teachers, artists, officials, public servants, engineers, businessmen, workers, peasants, democracy activists, rights activists, and scholars of all disciplines. From the political or ideological perspective, they are liberal leaders in all strata and circles of society.[2]

There are two sources for the development of liberal forces in China today. The first is the revival and renewal of Chinese liberalism dating back to the late nineteenth century, when some Western missionaries and late Qing reformers such as Yan Fu (严复), Kang Youwei (康有为), and Liang Qichao (梁启超) started to introduce the Chinese people to Western liberalism and democratic institutions.[3] This kind of intellectual orientation was also carried on by the revolutionaries led by Sun Yat-sen (孙逸仙/孙中山), although they abandoned the reformers' political vision of a constitutional monarchy for that of a republic, and thereafter succeeded in establishing the Chinese Republic in 1912. Chinese liberalism culminated in the first phase of the New Culture Movement from 1915 to 1919, in which intellectuals of the Chinese enlightenment advocated the idea of supplanting "Eastern ethics" — based on the principles of subordinating individuals to the family, to the clan, and to the state — with "Western ethics" based on individual dignity, individual rights, individual freedom, the development of individuality, and scientific reasoning.[4]

However, this trend did not last for long and was instead sidelined by the rise of nationalism and socialism. By the time of China's war of resistance against Japan, triggered by the latter's full-fledged invasion in 1937, the intellectual trend in China had seen a U-turn from modernization and cosmopolitanism back to conservatism and Sinification. A whole range of traditional Chinese values centered around loyalty and subordination of individuals to hierarchical authority, which had been under severe attack during the May Fourth period, resurfaced with, ironically, the protection of "revolutionary" ideologies such as Marxism and the Three People's Principles (*sanmin zhuyi*, 三民主义). The cause of liberalism was still fought by its believers who eventually constituted "the third force" between the Chinese Nationalist Party (KMT) and the CCP, although most Chinese liberals finally shifted ground from the priority of defending individual freedom toward that of advancing collective and national interests, to the extent where individual freedom became a means to achieve a higher end, such as national unity, defined by stronger political forces, such as the KMT and the CCP, which chose to settle differences through a life-and-death struggle in the battlefield. Liberalism encountered a dead end in the process of civil war between the KMT and the CCP in the late 1940s and as a consequence of the purge by the communist regime in the 1950s.[5]

The second source is the liberal response to the peculiar reality produced by reform and development in China since the 1980s. With the aid of capital, technology, and consumer markets, and facilitated by globalization, China has rapidly evolved into a new order of market Leninism, a useful term coined by *New York Times* correspondent Nicholas Kristof in which the Leninist Party-state is sustained by the combination of relatively free-market economics and autocratic one-party rule.[6] In other words, it is an astonishing paradox, putting together previously incompatible elements of both capitalism and communism, the latter of which by definition aims at eliminating capitalism. To the surprise of many throughout the world, this strange hybrid has produced an economic dynamism parasitic on the exceptionally low cost of productive factors, the growing global market, and the expansion of imported and indigenous technologies and expertise. The enormous wealth generated by this new prosperity has provided greater incentive for Chinese communist power holders to hang on to power and more resources to co-opt other social groups and repress the opposition. The result is a transition to and consolidation of "power elite capitalism (*quangui zibenzhuyi*, 权贵资本主义)," in which capitalism is dominated by the communist bureaucracy, leading to rapid, sustained economic growth on the one hand and endemic corruption, striking social inequalities, ecological degeneration, extensive abuse of human rights, and political repression on the other.

Under these circumstances, the most promising new political force engendered by market Leninism in China is the formation of a liberal camp in the late 1990s, consisting of at least six distinctive but partially overlapping categories: liberal intellectuals, democracy movement activists, liberals within the CCP, Christian liberals, human rights lawyers, and grassroots rights activists.[7] Each of these groups propounded liberalism from its own perspectives through publications and speeches, took part in a variety of social and political activities for the cause of democracy, sometimes expressed mutual support for one another when persecuted by the Party-state, and occasionally joined in issuing joint petitions or open letters on the Internet to express their shared concerns or demands for democratic changes. Their publication and activities have widely spread liberal ideas among the population and profoundly changed the intellectual, ideological, and political landscape of contemporary China.

The publication of Charter 08 marked the unprecedented maturity of Chinese liberalism, which went astray every now and again, and experienced repeated setbacks during modern times. The sophistication as expressed in Charter 08 is shown in at least four senses: a good grasp of the core of liberalism as universal values such as freedom, equality, and human rights plus political institutions based on democracy, power sharing (*gonghe*, 共和), and constitutional government; a whole-hearted embracement of individualism, universalism, and cosmopolitanism as opposed to statism and the nationalist project of "national wealth and power" at the expense of individual freedom; a categorical rejection of planned economy and the dominance of state ownership, in favor of market economy and private ownership; and a sound understanding of the rule of law, making a clear distinction between rule by law (法制, law as a tool for the rulers) and the rule of law (法治, rulers subject to and limited by the law). This is a remarkable development, given that in the past, even Chinese liberals were miserably seduced by nationalism, state socialism, and other ideas running counter to individual rights and liberal democracy.

The signatories and subsequent promotion of Charter 08 have also clearly demonstrated the solidarity of the Chinese liberal force. It must be admitted that not everyone in the diverse Chinese liberal camp endorsed Charter 08. Some leading liberals expressed reservations and did not sign the document. Leading liberals within the CCP, such as Li Rui (李锐) and Zhu Houze (朱厚泽), who prefer to play a critical role as mediators between the CCP leadership and civil society, regarded Charter 08 as a direct confrontation with the Party leadership and politely declined the invitation to join.[8] Their concern is shared by some leading liberal intellectuals such as Zhu Xueqin (朱学勤) and Xiao Han (萧瀚), who maintain that the document should have allowed greater space to accommodate the ruling communist party.[9]

Some leading social democrats within the liberal camp, such as Qin Hui (秦晖), did not sign the document either, on the ground that it did not go far enough in spelling out demands for social welfare and the economic rights of the poor.[10]

However, the Charter 08 Movement represents a grand alliance of Chinese liberal elements "within the system" (*tizhi nei*, 体制内) and "outside the system" (*tizhi wai*, 体制外), as well as an alliance between the citizen movement and dissident movement. Together, they have virtually formed a mature, peaceful, and rational opposition to the ruling CCP. The principal force of the Charter 08 Movement are those "outside the system," but the signatories and supporters of Charter 08 also include officials, retired officials, scholars, and professionals "within the system," such as Li Pu (李普), Du Guang (杜光), Zhang Sizhi (张思之), Mao Yushi (茅于轼), Sha Yexin (沙叶新), Zhang Xianyang (张显扬), Xu Youyu (徐友渔), He Weifang (贺卫方), Cui Weiping (崔卫平), Li Datong (李大同), and Li Gongming (李公明). Furthermore, Charter 08 has put an end to the division between the Chinese dissident movement and the Chinese citizen movement, changing the post-June Fourth situation where the Chinese citizen movement had consciously kept a distance from the Chinese dissident movement, which had been demonized and effectively marginalized by the CCP government.

Charter 08 is a very rare document supported not only by citizens of all walks of life in China, but also by almost all leaders and organizations of Chinese democracy movement in exile — including the China Alliance for Democracy, Initiatives for China, Human Rights in China, and different factions of the Chinese Democracy Party and Federation for a Democratic China — and Chinese dissident journals such as *Beijing Spring*, *China in Perspectives*, *Democratic China*, and *China E-Weekly*, as shown by their signing of Charter 08, their statements in support of Liu Xiaobo, and their participation in the celebration of the awarding of the Nobel Peace Prize to him. The only notable exception is Chinese democracy movement veteran Wei Jingsheng (魏京生) and a dozen of Chinese exiles in the West, who maintain a radical approach of revolution, regard themselves as the only strong and faithful heroes qualified for the leadership of the Chinese dissident movement against the Chinese communist regime, and regard any compromise as an act of collusion and betrayal.[11]

Constitutional Democracy as a Feasible Alternative to the Chinese Communist Dictatorship

A widely accepted proposition put forward by the Chinese communist regime to justify its monopoly on political power is that, without communist control, China would degenerate into chaos and fall apart. In other words, the Chinese communist regime tries in every possible way to eliminate any political alternative to its one-party autocracy, and at the same time uses the lack of a viable alternative as an excuse to maintain its dictatorship. To break this vicious cycle and circular argument, Charter 08 has shown that the choice for China is not between dictatorship and chaos, but between dictatorship and liberal democratic order.

Charter 08 sets constitutional (liberal) democracy as the aim of Chinese political development, and peaceful reform and rational interaction as the means to achieve that goal. It is actually an invitation by the Chinese liberal camp to all Chinese citizens from both the state and the society to join their efforts in democratizing China. In particular, it does not exclude Chinese communist rulers from the process. As concluded in Charter 08,

> We hope that our fellow citizens who feel a similar sense of crisis, responsibility, and mission, whether they are inside the government or not, and regardless of their social status, will set aside small differences to embrace the broad goals of this citizens' movement. Together we can work for major changes in Chinese society and for the rapid establishment of a free, democratic, and constitutional country. We can bring to reality the goals and ideals that our people have incessantly been seeking for more than a hundred years, and can bring a brilliant new chapter to Chinese civilization.

The concept of "constitutional democracy" is a careful choice. In China, as elsewhere, the term "democracy" has been extensively abused to mean many different things, even including outright dictatorship. "Democracy" meant precisely one-party dictatorship when Mao Zedong and other Chinese communist leaders declared they had delivered a "higher form of democracy" in China, as did Lenin and his communist followers in the former Soviet Union. By choosing the concept "constitutional democracy," Charter 08 categorically rejects any dictatorship disguised as "democracy" — variously known as "new democracy," "people's democracy," "socialist democracy," or "proletarian democracy." For drafters, signatories, and other supporters of Charter 08, constitutional democracy is the genuine democracy that is built on basic liberal values of freedom, equality and human rights, practiced through regular elections and free competition for public office, and provided with effective legal protection of constitutional rights and clear limits on the power of the government, which exercises power under the rule of law and the constitution.

Equally important is the peaceful means chosen in Charter 08 to achieve constitutional democracy in China. In stark contrast to Leninists, Stalinists, and Maoists, Chinese liberals resolutely reject the idea that an end itself can justify the means. Based on the assessment that violence employed in successive revolutions led only to worse dictatorship instead of promised freedom and democracy, and convinced of the intrinsic value of peace, the drafters of Charter 08 call for a peaceful political reform rather than a violent revolution to overthrow the current communist regime; they call for dialogue, reconciliation, and co-operation to prevent possible bloodshed and political turmoil in the process of democratization. Mindful about the concerns and fears of revenge among communist government officials and encouraged by the examples set in the peaceful democratic transition in South Africa and elsewhere, Charter 08 proposes to establish, in the process of democratic transition, a Truth Investigation Commission charged with finding the facts about past injustices and atrocities, determining responsibility for them, upholding justice, and, on these bases, seeking comprehensive social reconciliation. In his statement prepared for his trial in Beijing in December 2009, Liu Xiaobo, the primary drafter of Charter 08, emphasized that he did not treat communist officials as his enemies and did not hate them at all:

> [f]or hatred is corrosive of a person's wisdom and conscience; the mentality of enmity can poison a nation's spirit, instigate brutal life and death struggles, destroy a society's tolerance and humanity, and block a nation's progress to freedom and democracy. I hope therefore to be able to transcend my personal vicissitudes in understanding the development of the state and changes in society, to counter the hostility of the regime with the best of intentions, and defuse hate with love.[12]

All the concrete recommendations put forward in Charter 08 convey the liberal voice of Chinese society but do not seek overthrow of the communist government. As a matter of fact, most of these proposals or specific standpoints of Charter 08 are either compatible with CCP agendas or part of CCP policies. The recommendation calling for separation and balance of legislative, executive, and judicial powers reflects a consensus in Chinese society, and experiments in separating and balancing powers have been arranged by the CCP government at different levels and in different localities since the 1980s. The recommendations calling for election of deputies to legislative bodies and public offices of all levels is nothing but an encouragement for the CCP government to upgrade its current practice to a higher level. The recommendation calling for judicial independence is in line with the official promotion of the rule of law and legal professionalism. The recommendations calling for improvement of urban-rural equality, establishment of universal social security, and protection of the environment are in line with the social policies pursued by the Hu Jintao-Wen Jiabao (胡锦涛-温家宝) leadership. The recommendations calling for protection of property and fiscal reform echo the Law of Property Rights passed by the National People's Congress of China (NPC) in 2007 and several rounds of fiscal reforms carried out by the CCP government in recent years.

There is no doubt that some recommendations in Charter 08 are challenging for the CCP regime. The proposal to amend the Constitution of the People's Republic of China may not sound very heretical, as the Constitution has been routinely changed in its existence of less than six decades. However, the call to take away from the Constitution all articles running counter to the fundamental democratic principle of popular sovereignty — those contradictory expressions in the preamble, in particular — amounts to the demand for the CCP to voluntarily relinquish its monopoly on political power. Similarly, the urge for nonpartisan control of public institutions may be resonant of the official drive to modernize the system of civil servants, but the CCP is far from ready to withdraw from the armed forces and the police.

On the surface, the recommendations calling for protection of human rights and implementation of freedom of association, freedom of assembly, freedom of expression, and freedom of religion are lifted from the Constitution, and some of these — such as freedom of assembly, demonstration ("collective walks"), and religion — are already passively accepted by the Party-state. Nevertheless, legal protection of freedom of expression (*kaifang baojin*, 开放报禁) and freedom of association (*kaifang dangjin*, 开放党禁) constitutes nothing less than the transformation of the CCP dictatorship into a multiparty democracy.

The feasibility of China's smooth and peaceful transition to constitutional democracy lies as much in the aspirations, demands, and support of the population as in the enlightenment of the CCP leadership to embrace universal values of humankind and join the mainstream of civilized nations in the contemporary world, as urged in Charter 08. What is required from the CCP government, as summarized in the Charter, is to honor rights enshrined in the Constitution, in line with the International Covenant on Civil and Political Rights (ICCPR) signed by the CCP government and the International Covenant on Economic and Social Rights (ICESCR) ratified by the NPC. Some of the current CCP leaders — Premier Wen Jiabao, in particular — openly embrace the universal values of freedom, equality, and human rights and call for meaningful democratic reform.[13]

It is unfortunate that the CCP leadership, dominated by the hardliners, has not responded positively to Charter 08 but instead launched a new round of open attacks on institutions of constitutional democracy and declared an unprecedented war on universal values. They played the age-old trick of despotic regimes in China and other parts of the developing world to dismiss the universal values, practices, and institutions of liberal democracy as unsuitable or even poisonous "Western" values. Chen Kuiyuan (陈奎元), president of the Chinese Academy of Social Sciences, asserted that in the "competition between China and the West for the commanding ground (*zhigaodian*, 制高点)" in humanities and social sciences, "we must establish our confidence and eliminate blind worship [of the West]. We cannot respect Western values as so-called universal values and cannot play down the values of our Party and state as disputable values (*linglei jiazhi*, 另类价值)."[14] Jia Qinglin (贾庆林), Chairman of the People's Political Consultative Conference of China, urged all political parties and groups in China and Chinese people of all nationalities and all social strata to closely follow the leadership of the CCP and "strengthen the line of defense against the harassment by the two-party system, multiparty system, parliament system, tripartite separation of power, and other wrong ideas of the West."[15] Wu Bangguo (吴邦国), Chairman of the NPC, reaffirmed in his report to the Second Plenary of the Eleventh NPC on 9 March 2009 that China should never copy the West and never practice multiparty competition for power, tripartite separation of power, and a bicameral parliamentary system.[16]

These words are matched by action in reality. While the thought police led by Li Changchun (李长春), a member of the Standing Committee of the Politburo in charge of propaganda affairs, has tightened the control on liberal voices in the media, the security apparatus headed by Zhou Yongkang (周永康), a Politburo Standing Committee in charge of legal affairs, has stepped up persecution of democracy movement leaders, liberal intellectuals, human rights lawyers, and other human rights activists. The systematic crackdown on the Charter 08 movement, the ridiculous sentence of Liu Xiaobo to prison for eleven years on the criminal charge of "inciting subversion of state power," and the arrogant boycott of the 2010 Nobel Peace Prize indicate that the CCP government once again chooses to stand on the wrong side of history and miss yet another golden opportunity to make a fresh start and return to the fold of mainstream civilization in the contemporary world.

Political Vision for the Rights Defense Movement

The construction of a system of universal human rights under the United Nations is arguably the greatest moral and political achievement of the twentieth century. Based on the idea of human equality, the "human rights revolution" — beginning with the Universal Declaration of Human Rights in 1948 — has liberated billions of people from political and social oppression: ranging from decolonization throughout the world to racial desegregation in the USA; from the call for the elimination of all forms of racial discrimination to the advance of multicultural democracy promoting the rights of national, ethnic, religious, and linguistic minorities; and from democratization in the communist world to democratization in the Arabic world. The "human rights revolution" relying on people's power and mainly peaceful means has swept away tyrannical regimes of all colors in all continents, one after another.

Viewed from this perspective, the budding "rights defense movement" (*weiquan yundong*, 维权运动) in China in the 2000s represents a continuous unfolding of the world "human rights revolution." Its emergence foreshadows a new, more optimistic political scenario in which smooth transition to a stable constitutional democracy through constructive interactions between state and society may occur.[17] The current rights defense movement is a comprehensive movement involving all social strata throughout the country and covering every aspect of human rights. Due to a strict ban on organized opposition, rather than taking the form of a co-ordinated nationwide movement, the rights defense movement has instead developed as a diverse and increasingly forceful wave of isolated cases of rights defense reported daily in the media: public interest litigations, in particular, as well as public protests (or "mass incidents," a term coined by the Party-state to describe unapproved strikes, assemblies, demonstrations, petitions, blockages, collective sit-ins, or physical conflicts involving ten or more people). Those "mass incidents" numbered sixty thousand in 2003, seventy-four thousand in 2004, and eighty-seven thousand in 2005, an average of more than two hundred protests a day, according to official figures.[18] Some of them may involve thousands of people and result in police and paramilitary intervention, leading to loss of lives. The movement is not merely "rightful resistance" of the rural poor,[19] but has also become an urban phenomenon facilitated by the growing strength of the middle class and the latest technologies such as the Internet and mobile phone.

It is generally agreed among Chinese political activists and scholars that the rights defense movement proper in China was kick-started in 2003 by two major events: the Sun Zhigang (孙志刚) case resulting in the abolition of State regulations on the detention of migrants and the entire custody and repatriation system targeting migrant workers, and the SARS epidemic leading to a new wave of openness in the media.[20] The year 2003 has also been named "the first year of rights (*quanli yuannian*, 权利元年)" in China.[21]

Most cases of this rights defense movement aim to protect economic and social rights, including protests by peasants against excessive taxes, levies, and forced seizures of farmland; strikes by workers against low pay, arrears of pay, and poor working conditions; protests by laid-off urban workers against unfair dismissal by their employers; protests by homeowners against forced eviction by government and developers; protests by residents against forced relocations; campaigns by citizens against unpaid social entitlements; campaigns for the rights of women and children; and protests by affected residents against environmental pollution.

However, cases of defending civil and political rights are also on the rise. These include campaigns by lawyers, journalists, and writers for freedom of speech and press; campaigns by Christian house churches and Falun Gong practitioners for freedom of religion, belief, assembly, and association; campaigns against arbitrary detention, re-education through labor, torture, and excessive use of the death penalty; campaigns against injustice and abuses of public power by victims of Party-state agents, particularly by the thousands of petitioners who flew to the national capital or provincial capitals from all over the country to seek redress from perceived injustice; protests by migrant workers against the household registration system and other discrimination; and protests by peasants against irregularities and manipulation in village elections.

This claim of 2003 as the first year of the rights defense movement sounds odd, as assertion of a variety of rights has been a theme for the democracy movement and other civil movements in China since the late 1970s. For example, the Educated Youth Returning to Cities Movement (1976–79) was a large-scale movement for the rights of residence and employment by millions of former urban students who were sent to the countryside by the Party-state during the Cultural Revolution. The Democracy Wall Movement (1978–79), which coincided with the Unofficial Magazines Movement that lasted until 1981, was a pro-democracy and human rights movement spearheaded by Chinese democracy activists who demanded and practiced the political rights of free speech, free press, and free association. The 1989 Pro-Democracy Movement, led by students and joined by millions of other citizens, aimed not only to clean the government from corruption but also to establish a variety of political rights, especially the right of association.

The relationship between the current rights defense movement and the Chinese democracy movement deserves further investigation. After the Tiananmen Massacre in 1989, the latter was at its low ebb. "Farewell to revolution" became mainstream thinking among students and intellectuals, who shifted their focus from politics due to fear or despair. In contrast to immediate political change attempted by the democracy movement, the rights defense movement seeks compromise with the government and protection of legal rights within the existing legal-political framework, confining its main scope to social and economic demands either in the form of individual litigations or collective demonstrations. This does not mean that human rights lawyers, liberal intellectuals, and other rights activists taking part in the movement do not cherish political aspirations for democracy. Rather, given that in the early stages of the movement, fundamental political change was far from the horizon and it was impossible to accomplish the quest for democracy at one stroke, even for those who clearly aimed at constitutional democracy, they chose to defer their ultimate goal and tried to make a breakthrough point by point and step by step.

Compared with the Chinese democracy movement, the current rights defense movement is new in two senses. First, rights are grounded in legal framework and legal process. The Sun Zhigang incident was not only a human rights case fought by ordinary citizens against abuses by the state, but also one that led to the positive response of institutional reform by the state to redress human rights abuses. Second, leadership is provided by the legal profession — rights defense lawyers, in particular — and other citizen activists, rather than known Chinese democracy movement leaders.

The identity of Liu Xiaobo is interesting. From his involvement in the 1989 democracy movement and his serving as president of the semi-legal Independent Chinese PEN, he can be broadly seen as an activist in the Chinese democracy movement. However, as he has not played any role in the formal organizations of the movement, he is not considered a leader in the strict sense, either by other leaders of this movement or by the Chinese communist government.

Most leaders of the rights defense movement have not regarded themselves or been regarded by the Party-state as dissidents. It is a classic, well-known story that the petition sent to the NPC by three young graduates holding Ph.D. degrees in law from Peking University and who later became rights lawyers — Yu Jiang (俞江), Teng Biao (滕彪), and Xu Zhiyong (许志永) — played a key role in bringing about a rare review on constitutional violation and subsequent abolition of the notorious Regulations on Detention and Repatriation of Beggars and Floating Population. With their professional knowledge and extraordinary courage, human rights lawyers have fought in the frontline and provided leadership to the emerging rights defense movement.[22] These lawyers have been hailed as "heroes of our times" or "men of the hour," and have enjoyed an increasingly high profile in the Chinese and international media.[23]

There are hot debates and different approaches among rights lawyers regarding the strategy of the rights defense movement.[24] The mainstream have taken a soft line, with a belief or hope that communist bureaucracy is not monolithic and the current top communist leaders, committed to attracting foreign investment and making the country a respected world power, are running the country "according to law." They are of the opinion that the basic duty of rights lawyers is to help citizens exercise the rights granted to them within the current legal framework; through individual litigations against rights violation, these lawyers are effecting positive policy and institutional changes, and raising the awareness of the concept of human rights.

Some notable victories have been won by this approach. The "nail household" (dingzihu, 钉子户), a family who refused to vacate their home to make way for real estate development in Chongqing (重庆), attracted international attention in March 2007, and led to a negotiated settlement with the developers the following month. This was seen as a test case on the government's enforcement of the new Law of Property Rights. Likewise, protests by residents of the coastal city of Xiamen (厦门) in the second half of 2007 forced a US$1.41 billion giant petrochemical plant with strong political connections and government support to be relocated, probably the Chinese government's first direct concession to public demands through demonstrations. Again in January 2008, similar protests by Shanghai residents forced the Shanghai government to reconsider its Maglev Train project to connect Hongqiao International Airport to Pudong International Airport. In November 2008, starting from Chongqing — one of China's four provincial-level municipalities — and extending later to Jingzhou (荆州), Lanzhou (兰州), Sanya (三亚), Dalian (大连), Shantou (汕头), and other cities, thousands of taxi drivers went on strike over high operating costs and traffic fines, shortages of natural gas, and the government's lack of efforts in reining in unlicensed taxi operators who were stealing fares away. Local governments in these cities negotiated with strikers and took emergency measures to address their demands. More recently in December 2011, after three months of protests by villagers against land grabs at Wukan Village (乌坎村), the Guangdong provincial government yielded to villagers' basic demands for the return of the land and a free election of the village leadership.

These examples are significant because the Chinese government, with its tradition of top-down decision-making, secretive deliberations, and little tolerance for dissent, previously had almost no practice of engaging in popular consultation. The encouraging responses from the government were precisely what had been expected by the activists and other participants of the rights defense movement. Apart from striking a balance between violent revolution and obedience to autocracy, the success of this soft approach — also named the "middle-way model of rights defense"[25] — is also predicated on the positive interaction between the government and the society.

On the other hand, for those who take a harder line, it is futile and harmful to seek compromise with the ruling communist party, as even the "enlightened leader" Hu Jintao, in spite of his talk of expanding constitutional rights and strengthening the legal system, tightened the Party's control over the courts and continued to persecute rights lawyers. With the main purpose of lawsuits being to expose the evils of the Chinese legal system and the crimes of the communist government, it is impossible to win political cases for defendants, as courts are strictly controlled by the Party. Faced with such a situation, these activists resort to supporting Internet campaigns and mass demonstrations, including demonstrations involving violence — paying a high price for their beliefs and actions. Gao Zhisheng (高智晟), Guo Feixiong (郭飞雄), and Guo Guoting (郭国汀), three major advocates of this line, have been ruthlessly punished by the Party-state. Gao has been deprived of his license to practice law, convicted of "inciting subversion," repeatedly tortured in prison, and repeatedly "disappeared." Guo Guoting, similarly deprived and convicted, has been forced into exile. Guo Feixiong has been repeatedly beaten by police and sentenced to five years in prison on the charge of "illegal business activities."

There is a tendency for mass demonstrations to become violent when the legal system proves unable to redress widespread social injustice. In 2008, many cases of mass demonstrations involved violence, including the riot of Tibetans in Lhasa on 14–15 March 2008, which later spread to Qinghai (青海), Gansu (甘肃), and Sichuan (四川). According to an official Chinese source, this led to the destruction of many vehicles and buildings, the death of 18 civilians and one police officer, as well as the injuring of 141 civilians and 241 police officers. According to the Tibetan Government in Exile, more than 140 people were killed in the crackdown by the Chinese government. In June, based on the rumor that a schoolgirl had been raped and killed by the son of a local official, thousands of people in Weng'an County (瓮安), Guizhou Province (贵州省) joined together to burn down 160 offices and 42 vehicles belonging to the local government and police. In July, due to disputes over ownership of rubber trees, hundreds of peasants in Menglian Village (孟连), Yunnan Province (云南省) clashed with police, resulting in the death of two villagers, and the injuring of 19 villagers and 41 policemen. Again in November 2008, due to resentment against forced eviction, about thirty evicted households and thousands of other people surrounded the city government of Longnan (陇南), Gansu Province, burning 110 offices and 22 vehicles.

This situation posed a dilemma for the rights defense movement. On the one hand, court litigations within the existing Chinese legal framework can only produce very limited results, as the Chinese authorities choose to ignore their own laws in violating the rights of citizens and refusing to redress the grievances of citizens; on the other, direct calls for the overthrow of the communist regime or protests by force in streets will be met with brutal suppression. It was against this backdrop that Liu Xiaobo and his colleagues drafted and published Charter 08, which to a certain extent can be claimed as the programmatic document of the rights defense movement.

Charter 08 is a result of the rights defense movement, as well as a guide for the future development of the movement, combining appeals for concrete rights and benefits with a political blueprint. It pools together the major demands raised in the movement, ranging from the demand by peasants for land ownership to the demand by migrant peasant-workers for equal national treatment as urban residents; from the demand by the rich for the freedom of establishing enterprises to the demand by the poor for basic social security; and from the specific demand for the abolishment of the re-education through labor system to the general demand for the protection of human rights and the environment. It also provides the movement with a political goal and direction through generalizing the ideas advocated by Chinese liberal intellectuals in recent years. The relative isolation of students and intellectuals is identified as a major setback of the 1989 Chinese Pro-Democracy Movement.[26] In contrast, the main force of the rights defense movement is the mainstream of society, such as workers, peasants, businesspeople, and professionals of all trades, rather than students. By providing political and intellectual guidance; articulating social, economic, and political demands across all social strata; and carrying the spirit of justice, peace, rationality, and the rule of law, Charter 08 heralds a coalition between intellectuals and the "broad masses of the people," and the convergence of social movement and political democratization.

This kind of coalition and convergence is exactly what is needed for China's further development and what is expected by Chinese reformers, when the reform is losing its momentum. Echoing Charter 08 and using milder language more acceptable to Party leaders, sixteen senior Party members presented a petition to the CCP Standing Committee of Politburo on 20 January 2009. They included Du Daozheng (杜导正) (director of *Yanhuang Historical Review* (炎黄春秋), former director of the State Press Bureau, and former chief editor of *Guangming Daily* (光明日报)), Du Guang (former director of the Research Office and librarian at the Central School of the CCP), Gao Shangquan (高尚全) (president of China Economic System Reform Association and former deputy chair of the State Economic System Reform Committee), Li Rui (former deputy chief of the Organization Department of the CCP Central Committee), Li Pu (former deputy director of Xinhua News Agency), Zhong Peizhang (锺沛璋) (former director of the News Bureau, the Propaganda Department of the CCP Central Committee), and Zhu Houze (former Party Secretary of Guizhou Province and chief of the Propaganda Department of the CCP Central Committee). Instead of directly laying down those liberal principles, the petition urges the Party leadership to "guarantee and put into effect the citizen rights stipulated in the Constitution" and "make a breakthrough in reform and opening by overcoming the obstruction of vested interests." The petition also makes several policy recommendations, such as establishing democratic procedure to guarantee the proper use of the four trillion economic rescue package, resuming the program of political reform formulated by the Thirteenth Party Congress, strengthening the independence of supervisory bodies, liberalizing the media, and widening the space for the development of non-governmental organizations (NGOs).[27] Again, echoing the announcement of the award of the Nobel Peace Prize to Liu Xiaobo, and in the run-up to the Fifth Plenum of the Seventeenth Party Congress, twenty-three former ranking CCP members — including Li Rui, Li Pu, Hu Jiwei (胡绩伟) (former director and chief editor of *People's Daily*), and Jiang Ping (江平) (former president of Chinese University of Political Science and Law) — sent an open letter to the Standing Committee of the NPC on 11 October 2010, calling for an end to censorship in China. The letter cites Article 35 of the Chinese Constitution and demands the state to honor its commitment to the freedom of speech and press. It laments that censorship in China has reached such an absurd level as to suppress and muzzle the speech of the head of the Chinese government, Premier Wen Jiabao.[28]

The mainstream of the Party leadership has not been moved by Charter 08, the calls of those liberal retired officials, or the calls of Premier Wen Jiabao. They are still locked in the mentality and desire to maintain the communist autocracy forever, in the disguise of maintaining social stability. They do not see the rights defense movement — the growth of rights consciousness and civil society, in particular — as political progress in the right direction, but continue to view it as a serious challenge to their authority and a serious threat to their survival. As a consequence, the Party-state and Chinese society are moving in opposite directions. Instead of engaging in positive interactions with the liberal forces and Chinese society to move forward, the Party-state has moved backward and upgraded its systematic suppression of social and political activism to a higher level since 2009, coupling minimal concessions with cruel crackdowns by the massive and exceptionally rich repression apparatus.

The concessions included an increase of personnel and budget for mediation in disputes and payments to ordinary victims, but priority was given to comprehensive crackdowns, attacking NGOs, controlling the media, and jailing or monitoring a large number of targets in the state's blacklists, such as separatists, Falun Gong adherents, democracy movement leaders, "house church" priests, human rights lawyers, disobeying journalists, public intellectuals, and petitioners.[29] Rights lawyers and NGOs were particularly hard hit in this new round of state repression. The choice of the Open Constitution Initiative (公盟), a legal NGO run by rights lawyers and legal scholars, as a target of co-ordinated attacks in July 2009 revealed the attempt by the Party-state to roll back the activities of NGOs and rights lawyers. These individuals were typical moderates within the rights defense movement, fighting for social justice, but also rejecting radicalism. They actively cooperated with the pursuit for "good governance" by the Hu-Wen leadership and showed their best intentions and constructive attitude to the government by refraining from taking on cases involving separatists, Falun Gong, and the Chinese democracy movement. However, they eventually became a target of government attack, as they were increasingly influential nationally and internationally in providing essential legal aid to high-profile public interests cases such as environmental protection, food security, freedom of press, forced home eviction, forced land requisition, and "black jails."[30] The comprehensive attacks on rights lawyers also represented a retrogression of Chinese official legal reform and China's march to the rule of law.[31]

This has serious consequences for the state as well as the society. Why does the Party-state see legal assertion of citizen rights in the rights defense movement as a threat rather than a remedy? One possible explanation is that the Party-state's flirtation with the rule of law is nothing but professing love for what it actually fears. It was "not fully aware of the power of the new ideas of rights and law it was promoting. When this power was finally recognized, the leadership (or an important part of it) saw it as a threat."[32] Another possibility is that the current Chinese communist regime dominated by a corrupt power elite has lost its capacity to implement meaningful legal and political reform, even if it is willing to do so. Either way, when the slogans "stability over-riding everything" (稳定压倒一切) and "nipping destabilizing elements in the bud" (把不稳定因素消灭在萌芽状态) are put into effect, artificial "stability" is imposed by the Party-state at the expense of justice, reform, and progress, leading to more dangerous instability that Chinese sociologists call "social decay" (社会溃败) with serious symptoms such as structural corruption and a "situation beyond governance" (不可治理状态).[33]

Conclusion

The fact that the CCP rose to power through a violent revolution rather than a democratic election means a transition to constitutional democracy is the only viable way for the Party to ultimately make up for its lack of legitimacy. Charter 08 and the rights defense movement it tries to guide constitute a laudable attempt of the Chinese liberal force to seek constructive interaction with the communist Party-state and implement constitutional rights that the Party has promulgated in its quest for genuine legitimacy. The publication of Charter 08 would have been a welcoming step in the political development of the Chinese communist regime, had the latter decided to participate in the process of constructive interaction and political democratization rather than resist people's aspirations and demands. The CCP government does not have to live through one year after another in paranoia and panic over the next explosion of social instability.

While Chinese society is ready for the transition to constitutional democracy and Charter 08 provides a roadmap and platform for this process, the Chinese communist regime still follows its habitual thinking of blocking the transition, and risks plunging itself and China into an abyss of violence and turmoil. There is a viable way to achieve stability in contemporary China through institutional accommodation between conflicting social groups, as well as establishing rules and mechanisms for safeguarding citizen rights and for balancing legitimate interests. For the CCP to rejuvenate itself and maintain relevance, it has to abandon obsolete and discredited Leninism, which engenders the retrogression of the rule of law and market economy (as shown in the recent trend of the "advancing of the state economy and the retreat of the private economy"). Part of the CCP leadership may be intoxicated with Chinese economic achievement and the illusion of market Leninism, using economic success brought about by market reform to prove the "advantage" of communist monopoly of political power under a "market economy." However, in the final analysis, neither are the basic principles of market economy — such as private ownership and exchange based on equality and freedom — compatible with a Leninist "vanguard party" relying on political monopoly to advance its power and wealth, nor is the rule of law compatible with a Leninist Party-state, simply because the core of Leninism is "proletarian dictatorship," which, according to the classic definition by Lenin himself, means "nothing other than power totally unlimited by any laws and based directly on the use of violence."[34]

Chapter 7

Democracy, Charter 08, and China's Long Struggle for Dignity*

Man Yee Karen Lee

Introduction

2008 was as auspicious as it was ominous for China's national developments. The Olympics marked Beijing's long-awaited "coming-out" party and showcased its tremendous strengths to the world. But for Liu Xiaobo and fellow signatories of Charter 08,[1] a political manifesto released online on 10 December 2008, the subsequent crackdowns and imprisonment of Liu appeared to signal a turn for the worse for the country's democratic development. Still, China put on another spectacle in the 2010 Shanghai World Expo and proved yet again it could achieve all that without democracy.

Indeed, what is democracy for when a government has managed to pull hundreds of millions out of poverty in the space of three decades and secure the country's place as the second largest economy in the twenty-first century? Is there a preponderant human need that goes beyond sheer material wants for which some even dare to risk their lives? Does a nation have dignity if its people have none? These questions permeate John Fitzgerald's interesting paper on national dignity and individual dignity in China.[2] Despite a common assumption linking China's drive for national development and its people's aspirations for civil rights with a utilitarian pursuit of self-interest, Fitzgerald argues:

---

* An extensive version of this chapter, entitled "The Chinese People's Struggle for Democracy and China's Long Quest for Dignity," was published in Volume 27 (Spring 2012) of *Connecticut Journal of International Law*.

> We make too little allowance for the possibility that China pursues
> wealth and power for the sake of asserting national dignity, and
> that citizens demand rights, not in pursuit of liberty or happiness,
> but out of concern to preserve personal dignity.[3]

In light of Francis Fukuyama's thesis of "the struggle for recognition" in
The End of History and the Last Man,[4] Fitzgerald identifies the Greek term
thymos (θυμός), understood as "a propensity to feel self-esteem," as the
universal drive that makes people fight for democracy.[5] In the case of
China, Fitzgerald contrasts the notion of Chinese people "standing up"
at the People's Republic's founding in 1949 with "the felt experience of
a people reduced to jostling, crying and trading blows at home" during
the Cultural Revolution.[6] Today, the same nation is an indispensable
world power politically and economically. Its burgeoning middle-
class, however, are still jostling all the same with the authorities when
wishing to get to the bottom of their babies' illness after drinking
tainted milk formula,[7] or over the truth behind massive school col-
lapses during the deadly 2008 Sichuan earthquake.[8] While China as a
nation has, by many standards, stood up as a dignified superpower in
waiting, powerless individuals who dare to stand up for their share of
dignity back home languish precariously at the margins of society.[9]

Does China have national dignity if its people have no individual
dignity?[10] Liang Qichao (梁启超), a significant reformist thinker during
the Qing dynasty (清朝) famous for his "new citizenship" thesis, pow-
erfully wrote:

> The citizenry (*guomin*) [国民] is an assemblage of individual
> persons. The claims of the state (*guoquan*) [国权] are composed of
> the rights (*quanli*) [权利] of individuals. Therefore, the thoughts,
> feelings, and actions of a citizenry will never be obtainable without
> the thoughts, feelings, and actions of each individual member. That
> the people (*min*) [民] is strong means that the state is strong; that
> the people is weak means that [the] state is weak; that the people is
> rich means that the state is rich; that the people is poor means that
> the state is poor; that the people possesses rights means that the
> state possesses rights; and that the people is without shame means
> that the state is without shame.[11]

Building on Fitzgerald's idea, this chapter explores the notion that
Chinese people's quest for democracy embodies their ultimate quest
for dignity. Drawing on the defining events surrounding two of

China's foremost political dissidents, Liu Xiaobo and Wei Jingsheng (魏京生), I argue that their aspirations for democracy symbolize the people's wish to stand up against a state bent on maintaining stability at all cost. In Fukuyama's term, it showcases a "struggle for recognition" by those who jealously guard their dignity in the face of injustice.[12] How will this politics of dignity play out in China? In light of Premier Wen Jiabao's (温家宝) repeated speeches in 2010 linking dignity with political reforms,[13] this chapter also discusses the concept of dignity under Chinese constitutional order and traditional social ethos.

Charter 08 and the Idea of Dignity

The idea of dignity aroused great interests among China's intellectual circle in 2010. It all began with Premier Wen's widely reported aspirational remark on a number of occasions: "What we do is for people's happiness and dignity."[14] As a Chinese scholar pointed out, it was rather unusual for China's leaders to say that the government works for "people's dignity."[15] Elsewhere though, dignity is a *lingua franca* in contemporary rights and constitutional discourses. It has been a central ingredient in major international human rights treaties since the Universal Declaration of Human Rights (UDHR) in 1948,[16] but its history is much more ancient. Dignity (Latin: *dignitas hominis*) is a classical Western philosophical concept premised originally on human beings' unique relationship with divinity and later on their rational capacity and moral freedom.[17] As a rights concept, dignity first emerged in the 1944 Constitution of the International Labour Organization. It became one of the defining tones of human rights when Article 1 of the UDHR proclaimed: "All human beings are born free and equal in dignity and rights." Ever since, dignity has featured in many post-war constitutions — including that of India (1949), Germany (1949), Israel (1992), and South Africa (1996) — as a fundamental constitutional value. China's first Constitution in 1954 made no mention of dignity.[18] But its 1982 constitutional amendment saw the addition of a similar notion that in the Chinese language reads "personal dignity" or "personality dignity" (*renge zunyan*, 人格尊严). Article 38 of the 1982 Constitution says, "The personal dignity of citizens of the People's Republic of China is inviolable. Insult, libel, false charge or frame-up directed against citizens by any means is prohibited."[19] Hence, dignity is not a totally new idea in China's constitutional order, although its meaning in the Chinese context is subject to interpretation among academic circles.[20]

Dignity was also in the minds of Charter 08's drafters. Charter 08 mentions "dignity" (*ren de zunyan*, 人的尊严) altogether six times, but its meaning is more in line with that under the UDHR than the Chinese Constitution. In the foreword, it recites how the Chinese government's approach to modernization at the expense of universal values — freedom, equality, and human rights — has "destroyed" and "trampled" people's dignity. Most notably, the Communist Party's absolute grip over state powers and public resources has led to a series of human rights tragedies, from the 1957 Anti-Rightist Campaign through to the persecutions of ordinary citizens demanding fair treatment in recent times. In the second part entitled "Our Fundamental Principles," the Charter highlights the relationship between dignity and democracy by reiterating the basic values that are indispensable to political modernization. In emphasizing that "human rights are not bestowed by a state," the Charter adopts the language of the UDHR and declares "[e]very person is born with inherent dignity and freedom." It follows that the government should adhere to the principles of equality because every person has the same "integrity, dignity, and freedom." That not only goes for those in the majority but also the minorities. Along Abraham Lincoln's famous lines, the Charter declares that democracy is a means to make government truly "of the people, by the people, and for the people." In this connection, the third part of the Charter sets out nineteen policy recommendations that include the establishment of a Human Rights Committee tasked with defending people's rights and dignity.

Hence, Charter 08 expresses the close link between protecting dignity and attainment of freedom, equality, democracy, and rights for the people of China. That respecting dignity is seen as an end of state governance resonates with Immanuel Kant's moral treatise that human beings should treat each other as an end, never merely as means.[21] According to Kant, human beings have inherent dignity thanks to their inborn reason, free will, and ability to make and abide by moral decisions that affect others as well as themselves.[22] In this sense, human dignity is priceless. Here, Kant distinguished between things that possess a relative worth and those that possess an intrinsic worth. For example, while human inclinations such as desires for pleasure and "skill and diligence in work" have a relative price, "fidelity in promises and benevolence on principle" do not. The latter are essentially moral virtues for which alone "a rational being can be an end in itself". "Thus morality and humanity, so far as it is capable of morality, alone have dignity."[23]

Traces of Kant's idea can be found in Liu Xiaobo's thinking. In a 2006 article entitled "Changing the Regime by Changing Society,"[24] one of his six online articles that the Chinese court cited as evidence for his subversion charges in 2009,[25] Liu expresses the "uncompromising" nature of human dignity and what it means for the Chinese people. He says, although political persecution from a totalitarian regime may cause people to suffer economically and lose freedom, it cannot damage their social reputation or condemn them to social isolation. Simply put, "it cannot destroy their integrity, dignity or spirit." Hence, more ordinary citizens have emerged as "civic conscience" or "heroes of truth" who are willing to "defend themselves in the dock" in the belief of justice.[26] All the while, the trend of liberalization, democratization, and human rights has been spreading worldwide following the collapse of communist regimes in Eastern Europe. To Liu, this irreversible development and "the everlasting practice of non-violent resistance" bear testimony to "the spiritual aspect of human nature." What follows deserves quoting at length:

> Humans exist not only physically, but also spiritually, possessing a moral sense, the core of which is the dignity of being human. Our high regard for dignity is the natural source of our sense of justice. When a system or a country allows everyone to live with dignity, it can gain spontaneous approval from the people, which is how St. Thomas Aquinas understood political virtue: Virtuous good governance lies not only in maintaining order, but [even] more in establishing human dignity … The reason why the liberal system can gradually replace dictatorship, and the end of the Cold War can be seen as the End of History, lies in the fact that the former [liberal system] acknowledges and respects human dignity, while the latter [dictatorship] does not recognize human dignity and discredits it by dragging it in the dust.

Wei Jingsheng and the Fifth Modernization

A stubborn determination to live with dignity had driven another
man to start a democratic movement thirty years earlier. He was Wei
Jingsheng, whose nearly two decades of political imprisonment that
followed evokes memories of abject despair and unwavering hope. It
all began with his quest for liberty and democracy. It was two years
after the purging of the Gang of Four on the heels of Mao Zedong's
death. The Chinese people were recuperating from the ruins left by the
Cultural Revolution.[27] Petitioners of various causes began to emerge
in different cities, pleading for government redress.[28] Forums of
democracy mushroomed around the nation as reformist leader Deng
Xiaoping (邓小平) regained the helm as vice-chairman and vice-premier of the Chinese Communist Party (CCP). Hopes were high. It was
as if the democratic torch had finally arrived in China. Instead, Deng
urged fellow citizens to devote themselves in building the nation's
"Four Modernizations": agriculture, industry, national defense, and
science and technology.[29]

That failed to impress one compatriot. On 5 December 1978, at
Beijing's one-time Democracy Wall, Wei — a Red-Guard-turned-
liberal-writer — declared "the Fifth Modernization: Democracy,"[30] a
manifesto for China's democratization in which he announced, "We
want to be the masters of our own destiny." To Wei, democracy is the
ultimate modernization: "Democracy, freedom, and happiness for all
are our sole objectives in carrying out modernization. Without this fifth
modernization, all others are nothing more than a new promise."[31]

Having left his name and address on the Democracy Wall poster,
Wei was afterwards approached by interested readers who wanted "to
ascertain the real reason for the backwardness of Chinese society."[32]
Later, a few of them joined him in founding the journal *Exploration* (探
索). It became, in Andrew Nathan's words, "the boldest of the people's
journals" among at least fifty-five published in Beijing alone at the
time.[33] Wei's writings dominated the journal's first few issues, featuring
the topics "The Fifth Modernization" and "Human Rights, Equality,
and Democracy," as well as materials he had obtained from foreign
journalists about political persecutions in China. In the third issue,
there was a sensational report about the inside stories of *Qincheng* (秦

城), a political prison for top cadres that had kept his girlfriend's father for nearly twenty years.[34] The thorny issues that *Exploration* cared to expose also included mistreatments of petitioners by local authorities. In response to the municipal government's unfriendly attitude to political activities in Beijing, the journal minced no words in opining, "[S]ome bigwigs in the Peking Municipal CCP Committee are afraid that the people might be able truly to enjoy democracy."[35]

This newfound journalistic freedom as well as Wei's own did not last, however. A speech by Deng Xiaoping on 16 March 1979 marked the turn of the tide.[36] On 30 March, Deng again urged comrades to "uphold the four cardinal principles" by following the socialist road, the proletarian dictatorship, the Communist Party leadership, as well as Marxism-Leninism and Mao Zedong thought.[37] He denounced the activists as "trouble-makers" who misled people in the name of democracy, took advantage of social problems left by the Gang of Four, engaged in underground organizations, and conspired with forces both overseas and in Taiwan.[38] In a determined tone, he also declared the kind of democracy that China needed could only be socialist democracy, not bourgeois democracy.[39]

Deng's latest instructions immediately emboldened local cadres to begin cracking down on democracy walls and forums nationwide. Unfazed, Wei countered Deng's denouncement with a new poster at the Democracy Wall on 25 March 1979, entitled, "Do We Want Democracy or New Dictatorship?" In a matter of days, police arrested Wei and many of his *Exploration* staff. It not only spelt the end of the democratic movement but also the beginning of criminalization of political dissidents. In July 1979, the National People's Congress (NPC) enacted a series of criminal law including a provision on "counter-revolution," defined as actions undertaken "for the purpose of overthrowing the political power of the dictatorship of the proletariat and the socialist system and jeopardizing the People's Republic of China."[40] With the law in place, the government moved to convict Wei in October 1979 on charges of leaking state secrets and publishing counter-revolutionary statements and meted out a fifteen-year imprisonment term,[41] making him one of China's most persistent political prisoners for the next two decades.

Refusing to let physical confinement dampen his spirit, Wei kept on writing to Communist Party leaders demanding political reforms, to prison authorities complaining about his treatment, and to his family expressing his relentless aspirations.[42] Though most of the messages never reached his intended audience, his letters from prison spanning the period 1981 through to 1993 depict a political prisoner's continued struggle for recognition: of his presence and of his desire for democracy. To Fitzgerald, Wei's perseverance in speaking his mind was driven by a strong desire for the dignity of his and his fellow citizens.[43] His struggles are that of what Fukuyama once described as a man of *thymos* (θυμός), a self-respecting person whose pride turns into anger and shame when deprived of his sense of worth.[44] Wei is perhaps such a man. According to his own accounts, he had had no intent to take part in the Democracy Wall activism until the moment he felt his dignity was under attack.[45] It began with Deng's interview with an American reporter on 27 November 1978, in which the vice-premier, referring to the Democracy Wall, exhorted people to refrain from criticizing the central government and to "return to the factories" to contribute towards the four modernizations. Wall posters soon appeared, asking activists to "retreat" as Deng had spoken. Wei recalled the following comments from disheartened Beijing citizens,

> The Chinese are simply inept, and spineless. Look at it, having the freedom only for a couple of days, being able to speak out, now with a little directive from someone, they want to retreat. A bunch of spineless weaklings. Sigh, there is no hope for China.[46]

Profoundly saddened, Wei awoke to the democratic ideas and thoughts buried deep in his heart. He decided to utter them "with the primary motivation to prove to everyone, that not all Chinese were spineless"; hence, "the Fifth Modernization" the following day.

Democracy and the "Irrational" Quest for Dignity

It is this kind of *"ressentiment"* grounded in "personal indignation" that drives a person to struggle for "individual dignity and human rights," argues Fitzgerald.[47] And it is not necessarily about the utilitarian pursuit of a good life, personal liberty, or happiness. Instead, it is about the desire to preserve personal dignity, the power of which is enough to make people fight at huge personal cost. In Wei's case, he refused to be just another anonymous petitioner, as he publicized his identity at the Democracy Wall, prepared to face official vengeance and even shed blood. Asked later as to what made him step forward, he said, "[W]hich country has acquired democracy, freedom, and human rights without hard struggle, and shedding blood and sweat?"[48] Not wanting to see a good chance for speaking the truth squandered, he took the courage, believing "it was time for me to sacrifice." Such sentiment bucks the common wisdom of Hobbesian self-preservation but fits the mold of a "thymotic" man whose passion drives him to stake his life for a noble cause.[49]

The notion of *thymos* (θυμός) first appeared in Plato's *Republic*, in which Socrates observed the tripartite nature of the human soul: that of desire, reason, and *thymos* (translated as "the spirited element").[50] As Socrates explained, desire and reason are usually at work in influencing most human behaviors as basic as a craving for drink. When a person feels thirsty, the desiring part of the soul naturally urges him to drink while the reasoning part holds him back, for example, because drinking the particular substance would be bad for his health. Yet, without the third factor, the story of human behaviors is not complete. In this connection, Socrates likened the spirited element to our "'sense of honour', manifested in indignation," which usually sides with reason against desire but "cannot be identified with reason."[51] To highlight the presence of this "passionate element" that causes our anger and indignation, Socrates told the story of Leontius who was caught in a dilemma of whether to see or not to see the pile of executed human bodies lying in the open.[52] While wanting to take a look, Leontius at the same time despised his having such a desire and decided to turn away, only to have been overcome by desire to walk back and look in anger. According to Socrates, this is the classic case of a man whose desire forces him to defy his reason, cursing himself and feeling angry with this part of his nature that reasons against his craving: "It is like a struggle between two factions, in which indignation takes the side of reason."[53]

This passionate side of the soul is manifested in our sense of justice, as Socrates illustrated by the following example.[54] When a good-natured man believes he is in the wrong, he is often less inclined to be indignant at any ill treatment inflicted by the person he has offended — because his spirit recognizes it as just. On the contrary, if the man believes he has actually been wronged, his spirit is aroused to wage a war against the perceived injustice. It perseveres "until its gallant struggle has ended in success or death; or until the restraining voice of reason, like a shepherd calling off his dog, makes it relent."[55] Wei's long-time struggle in the prison cell epitomizes the relentless spirit of such a man. He continued his literary campaign for political reforms and struggled to compose himself, shedding no tear, as fellow political dissidents underwent persecutions one after the other. How did he manage to maintain himself for all these years as his comrades succumbed successively to the wear and tear of prison? Wei's reply was: "For your own actions, and even just for your own dignity, you would have to endure."[56] He firmly rejected the idea that those fellow prisoners who had committed suicide were mentally weak. Instead, they were strong people who had presaged their looming mental deterioration and decided to act. "Some of them wanted to avoid disgrace, to preserve the dignity of friends who remained alive, so they would rather terminate their own lives." For political dissidents like him, death was not the most horrible thing to happen, said Wei: "What we feared the most was the possibility of developing mental disorder, and losing our dignity, that would be the worst eventuality."

The quest for dignity in a democratic society has driven the likes of Liu and Wei to put aside their rightful reason and personal desire to risk their freedom and even lives. To Fukuyama, such "irrational" endeavors cannot be explained in pure economic terms,[57] for a human being is not simply a materialistic sort; he wants to be recognized for his existence. Citing G. W. F. Hegel's philosophical doctrine of the "struggle for recognition,"[58] Fukuyama argues that human beings, in addition to the physical needs that they share with animals, demand recognition of their status and dignity. "For only man is able to overcome his most basic animal instincts — chief among them his instinct for self-preservation — for the sake of higher, abstract principles and goals."[59] This struggle for recognition helps explain why people down the ages have continued to strive for liberty and democracy in the face of state suppression.[60] In the same way that desire and reason alone cannot explain certain acts of indignation, material prosperity and economic fortunes are not enough to satisfy the part of human nature that demands recognition of their rights and dignity.

In China, civic voices for political reform subsisted even after Deng Xiaoping spearheaded the Four Modernizations and led his people back to the fold of capitalism. When Wei decided to put up the Fifth Modernization in 1978, his concerns lay not in the state of economy but of democracy. As he lamented, however hopeful people once were of Deng's return to power, "the old political system so despised by the people remains unchanged, and the democracy and freedom they longed for has not even been mentioned."[61] He demanded that China needed true democracy. To him, that was when people were able to "choose representatives to manage affairs in accordance with their will and interests" and "have the power to replace these representatives at any time in order to prevent them from abusing their powers to oppress the people."[62] Thirty years down the official road to modernization, in a more sophisticated political manifesto named Charter 08, Liu and others began with the following observation of China's encounters with modernization over the past century:

> The Chinese people, who have endured human rights disasters and uncountable struggles across these same years, now include many who see clearly that freedom, equality, and human rights are universal values of humankind and that democracy and constitutional government are the fundamental framework for protecting these values. By departing from these values, the Chinese government's approach to "modernization" has proven disastrous.[63]

Dignity in Democratic and Constitutional Order

This depiction of democratic governance strikes a chord with constitutional jurists who believe that democracy requires the support of fundamental values as much as procedural mechanisms. Dignity is one of those values. Aharon Barak, former president of the Supreme Court of Israel, wrote that democracy "has its own internal morality, based on the dignity and equality of all human beings."[64] Hence, real democracy must lie in the "recognition of basic values and principles such as morality and justice." Insofar as human rights embody the soul of democracy, the right to dignity takes centre stage.[65] Barak's view of dignity is typically Kantian. As autonomous agents, human beings possess free will and free choice. Hence, "[h]uman dignity regards a human being as an end, not as a means to achieve the ends of others."[66]

Dignity as a fundamental ground of democracy was a doctrine promoted by the late American constitutional law expert Walter Murphy. In his seminal work *Constitutional Democracy*, he argued that human dignity necessitates democratic rule: "the great and equal dignity of all men and women — the fundamental moral value of most theories of democracy — requires that every citizen share in making the rules that he or she must obey."[67] This self-binding nature of democratic citizenship is rooted in free consent and human reason. In an earlier article on consent and political legitimacy, Murphy explained the human imperatives of democracy.[68] He said, our capacity to reason encompasses our need for moral autonomy and allows us to recognize the same capability and need of others.[69] It enables us to understand the undesirability of imposing our will on others as much as having others' will imposed on us. At the same time, our reason works to legitimize our own choices and oblige us to bear the ensuing consequences despite the potential risks. It follows that "no one has authority to impose choices" on us and to compromise our moral autonomy in deciding the kind of society and political regime that we aspire.[70] Hence, Murphy argued, to the extent that consent is the "ultimate legitimator" of democratic governance, it is fundamentally a reflection of human dignity based on "a capacity to reason, a need for moral autonomy, and an ability to make morally binding commitments."[71] In practice, a polity built on consent and justified by human dignity must have procedures for people to articulate their will, while at the same time be open to limiting the powers of the government as well as the civic majority.[72] This will entail, for example, giving each citizen "inalienable rights" to treatment as being equal in worth in relation to every other, freedom to physical privacy, and a reasonable level of material enjoyment.

Dignity and China's Political Reforms

If dignity is indeed a foundational value of democracy as Murphy understood, one may wish to anticipate the things to come in China after Premier Wen Jiabao's heavily publicized series of "dignity talks" when referring to political reforms in 2010. What was not as widely reported, perhaps, is that he had already referred to dignity when addressing an overseas audience at the University of Cambridge in February 2009 as part of his European visits.[73] At the beginning of his speech entitled "See China in the Light of Her Development," Wen said:

> The essence of China's reform and opening-up is to put people first and meet their ever growing material and cultural needs through releasing and developing productive forces. It aims to give everyone equal opportunities for all-round development. It aims to protect the democratic rights of the people and promote stability, harmony and prosperity across the land. And it aims to safeguard the dignity and freedom of everyone so that he or she may pursue happiness with ingenuity and hard work.

Prose of this kind would have been commonplace for leaders in liberal democracies where dignity is either written into the constitution or widely regarded as a fundamental value. The conspicuity of this very word in China's case probably lies in the fact that it was from a top leader in a country that remains a staunch adherent to one-party communist rule. Back home, Wen reportedly debuted his "dignity talk" at the State Council's Lunar New Year reception in February 2010 with the comment, "all the things we do is aimed at letting people live more happily and with more dignity."[74] Two weeks later, he invoked the term again in an online interview with Mainland netizens, saying, "Chinese citizens shall enjoy full freedom and rights within the framework of the Constitution and laws, which is key to the promotion of 'greater dignity' of the population."[75] As to what that "greater dignity" means, Wen referred to first, equality before the law, and second, meeting people's material and cultural needs, and facilitating freedom and full development of individuals — a view that echoes Murphy's.

If those words were not impressive enough, the Premier seemed to have struck a chord with his empathetic comrades as he was delivering the government's work report at the Eleventh NPC on 5 March 2010.[76] Having reviewed his government's performance in the past year, Wen highlighted the eight "Main Tasks for 2010." In the last task entitled "Working Hard to Build a Service-Oriented Government that the

People are Satisfied with," Wen emphatically mentioned dignity as he concluded a section teeming with expressions such as "democracy," "fairness and justice," and "public trust": "Everything we do we do to ensure that the people live a happier life with more dignity and to make our society fairer and more harmonious."

On the surface, this statement was no more than a modified version of his earlier statements on dignity. Yet, the fact that this report was in effect the Premier's policy address requiring approval from the politburo of the CCP has made his remarks somewhat interesting and appealing. One commentator called it "a signal of a fundamental, though also subtle, shift in Beijing's approach toward human rights."[77] For another, the enthusiasm was less reserved. "The Great Hall of the People burst into applauses upon Wen's remarks," recalled an academic present at the address.[78] The Premier's choice of words was seen to have marked a new beginning from an era dominated by economic developments. As that academic put it, "[t]he promise of 'greater dignity' shows that government is paying more attention to the development of Chinese citizens themselves now. It represented China's 'people-first' principle in the social and political arena." Such optimism aside, does Wen's self-proclaimed democratic manifesto really presage another coming-out party for China in embracing the universal value of human rights widely revered in the Western world?[79] What does dignity really mean in China?

Dignity in Chinese Constitution

A possible starting point is the constitutional framework within which the Premier has made those comments. As mentioned earlier, the word "dignity" first appeared in China's 1982 constitutional amendment. Article 38 reads, "The personal dignity of citizens of the People's Republic of China is inviolable. Insult, libel, false charge or frame-up directed against citizens by any means is prohibited." While "personal dignity" is not defined and, as mentioned, is subject to interpretation among Chinese academics, dignity in this context is linked with the idea of "moral personality," translated as *renge* (人格) in Chinese.[80] Hence, literally speaking, it appears that the Constitution confers dignity a relatively limited scope as far as protection of individual rights is concerned. Look at the nature of the acts prohibited under Article 38 and we may envisage the possible meaning of dignity under Chinese constitutional order. The prohibition of insult, libel, false charge, and frame-up against other citizens apparently points to a particular aspect of rights, i.e., the protection of one's reputation, self-esteem, and personal integrity. It allows dignity a much narrower room compared to the overarching status it is accorded under international law as well as in other constitutional regimes such as Germany and South Africa.

An explanation may lie in history. According to Chinese legal expert Lin Laifan (林来梵), the inclusion of "personal dignity" in the 1982 Constitution is generally seen as reflecting a national sense of abhorrence against the grievous personal abuses and violations perpetrated during the decade-long Cultural Revolution.[81] It was a sorry chapter of Chinese history that saw parents and children, teachers and students pitted against each other in a nationwide anti-capitalist frenzy.[82] Hence, Article 38 appears as a grim reminder of the distortions of humanity that the Chinese people had once collectively experienced — and it was predominantly against this historical background that Lin believes the notion "personal dignity" was invoked.[83] Taking this view and in light of the language of Article 38, it is therefore reasonable to infer that the right to "personal dignity" in the Chinese Constitution particularly refers to the protection of a person's rights to privacy, reputation, and personal integrity.[84]

Dignity and Truth in Chinese Social Ethos

This narrow interpretation does not take us very far unless we go back to the origin of dignity as a cultural and philosophical idea historically constructed. In any case, Premier Wen has apparently meant more than protecting reputation and privacy when using dignity to highlight his aspirations for political reforms. Then, what is dignity to Chinese society? To start with, it is submitted that "human dignity" was an idea that originated outside the Chinese belief system. According to legal philosopher Zhang Qianfan (张千帆), it was "neither explicitly mentioned in classical Confucian texts nor systematically explained by traditional interpretations."[85] But it is quite a different thing to say that Chinese culture rejects the concept. On the contrary, a reconstructed

version of Confucianism helps reveal the "dignity-laden" teachings of ancient sages — particularly Confucius (孔子) and Mencius
(孟子) — in a society where moral integrity and human relationships
were deeply treasured.[86] In this respect, while it is inaccurate to say
that Chinese culture is hostile to the idea of dignity, it is perhaps fair
to say that it perceives the concept in a different light compared to the
West. In any case, not only does dignity remain a contested idea,[87] it
also tends to yield different meanings across cultures and communities. As American political scientists Rhoda Howard and Jack Donnelly
once argued, "Conceptions of human dignity, in their social and political aspects, express particular understandings of the inner (moral)
nature and worth of the human person and his or her proper (political)
relations with society."[88] As opposed to being a correlate of Western
individualism against the collective, dignity in the Chinese (or more
broadly, East Asian) context is linked to a societal setting that is deeply
embedded in relations.

As a result of the traditional emphasis on collectivism, dignity in
Chinese culture essentially lies in relationships.[89] In Confucian times,
social order was premised on five cardinal relationships, i.e., "parent
and child, ruler and subject, husband and wife, old and young, and
friend and friend," around which all human activities revolved.[90] This
relational norm binds not only ties between family members but also
that between the emperor and his subjects as well as the emperor and
his ministers. Society was highly hierarchal and patriarchal, yet people
of all classes were believed to have possessed equal moral potential in
practicing humanity (*ren*, 仁) and becoming a "gentleman" (*junzi*, 君
子), a man of high moral standing deserving of respect and leading the
family, community and nation.[91]

In those days, filial piety was seen as the lifeblood of a harmonious family and socio-political order. But reverence to one's parents or
authority was never meant to be blind loyalty. This state of affairs was
best captured by a teaching on "reproof and remonstrance" in *Xiao Jing*
(孝经), a classic text on filial piety recording Confucius' dialogues with
one of his disciples, Zeng (曾子).[92] In Chapter XV, Zeng asked if simple
obedience could be regarded as filial piety. Confucius' reply epito-
mized the highest moral point where filial piety and good governance
coincide:

> Anciently, if the Son of Heaven had seven ministers who would remonstrate with him, although he had not right methods of government, he would not lose his possession of the kingdom. If the prince of a state had five such ministers, though his measures might be equally wrong, he would not lose his state. If a great officer had three, he would not, in a similar case, lose (the headship of) his clan. If an inferior officer had a friend who would remonstrate with him, a good name would not cease to be connected with his character. And the father who had a son that would remonstrate with him would not sink into the gulf of unrighteous deeds. Therefore when a case of unrighteous conduct is concerned, a son must by no means keep from remonstrating with his father, nor a minister from remonstrating with his ruler. Hence, since remonstrance is required in the case of unrighteous conduct, how can (simple) obedience to the orders of a father be accounted filial piety?

According to this, filial piety is no blind loyalty. Rather, a truly pious son is obliged to admonish unbecoming deeds even of his father, if he is to fulfill his duty to the family, just as a devoted minister is required to do so of his ruler for the sake of the kingdom. Hence, moral uprightness from the king down to the citizenry is the utmost harmony and dignity of the land. It is on the basis of this ethical order that man minds not just his own business.[93] His existence is necessarily shaped by his kindred, neighbors, and community; without them, life would be insignificant.[94] Hence, a man should value the wellbeing of others as his own and even be prepared to sacrifice self-interest for the sake of higher virtues. It was summed up in Mencius' famous saying that a virtuous person should forsake life for humanity if he could only choose one, just as he should give up "fish" to take the more precious "bear's palm."[95] This is the pursuit of a lifetime. Hence, a gentleman must persist in acting benevolently lest he should lose his personal honor and bring shame to his clan's name. "Thus, a Chinese individual acquires humanity (*ren*), and thereby attains dignity, through moral virtue attained from fostering harmony and stability in the family and community."[96]

From Dignity, Harmony, to Stability?

This brief sketch of classical Confucian moral teachings reveals the cultural backdrop against which the Chinese polity has been functioning for centuries. A society sustained by a culture of altruism, filial piety, and social harmony, by nature, provided limited room for ideas of personal interests and individual rights to take root.[97] Nevertheless, people's allegiance to the state was based on an understanding that the king and his ministers treat them like a benevolent father would do to his children. It became what Mencius espoused as "the people as fundamental" (minben, 民本) doctrine that still holds sway in China today.[98] This political philosophy and the pursuit of harmony appear to have underlain Premier Wen's conviction that the government's over-riding task is "to ensure that the people live a happier life with more dignity and to make our society fairer and more harmonious."[99]

What does a harmonious society mean in this context? For one, "harmony" is the defining theme of the Hu-Wen leadership officially endorsed by the CCP in 2006.[100] President Hu Jintao (胡锦涛) first set the tone when addressing major Party and provincial leaders at an event organized by the CCP Party School in 2005, saying, "The [CCP] and the central government have made it an important task to build a harmonious society" in the face of thorny challenges both domestically and internationally.[101] In elaboration, he continued:

> A harmonious society should feature democracy, the rule of law, equity, justice, sincerity, amity and vitality. Such a society will give full scope to people's talent and creativity, enable all the people to share the social wealth brought by reform and development, and forge an ever closer relationship between the people and government. These things will thus result in lasting stability and unity.

Buzzwords such as "democracy" aside, the ultimate concern of a harmonious society seems to lie in maintaining stability and unity. It resonates with comments Hu reportedly made two months before the arrest of Liu Xiaobo, that "Stability is the over-riding duty. Without stability, we will be able to achieve nothing and will lose all that we have already achieved."[102] The thesis "the need for stability over-whelms everything else" was a legacy of Deng Xiaoping, who first coined the term in February 1989 at the time when the student-led pro-democracy movement was simmering.[103] It has since become a popular motto for Chinese leaders after the official People's Daily featured an editorial bearing the same title on 4 June 1990, the first anniversary of the Tiananmen crackdown. Hu's predecessor Jiang Zemin (江泽民)

toed Deng's line in the Fifteenth CCP National Congress, declaring, "Without stability, nothing can be achieved"[104] — a line Hu has obviously borrowed.

There is no denying that political stability may well be a desirable factor for successful democratization.[105] Not only can democracy not healthily develop in unstable societies, it can also exasperate social disruptions when powers are suddenly up for grabs. One needs to look no further than some of the fledgling democracies in Asia — such as Indonesia and the Philippines — to see the destabilizing potential of democratization in politically unstable states rife with ethnic tensions and social unrests.[106] Richard Robison once described, "As in Russia, the rapid unraveling of state power left reformers exposed to the full force of oligarchic power and gangsters — this was the sort of civil society unleashed in Indonesia."[107] So it probably makes good sense for governments to strive to maintain a stable society for democratization to take place. In the same way, rights and democracy may not mean much to people who constantly worry when their next meal will come.[108] Countries that democratized at low levels of wealth, such as Cambodia and Nepal, remain relatively poor and backward despite the façade of electoral freedom,[109] hence Randall Peerenboom's positive evaluation of China's achievements of late:

> Most Chinese citizens are happy with their lives, optimistic about the future, and relatively satisfied with the government on the whole, largely because the government has been successful at maintaining stability and improving the living standards of most people.[110]

Conclusion

Livelihood is no doubt a fundamental issue for a population as vast as China's. Nevertheless, material prosperity alone cannot satisfy the "spirited" part of human nature that demands recognition of our status as rational beings. It cannot blind our sense of right and wrong in the face of blatant injustice and unfairness — for only human beings are capable of transcending basic animal instincts for the pursuit of higher values. Despite China's spectacular economic growth and infrastructure development, such has not stopped ordinary people who believe that truths are withheld and rights trampled from standing up for themselves and fellow citizens. It has not deterred people like Tan Zuoren (谭作人) (Sichuan earthquake activist) and Zhao Lianhai (赵连海) (father of victim of tainted baby milk scandal) from demanding justice in the face of official repression and oppression. Charges of subversion and disrupting social disorder and the accompanying incarceration might have stripped away their freedom, but not their sense of justice. In Liu Xiaobo's words, political persecutions of acts of civic conscience did nothing to destroy people's "integrity, dignity or spirit,"[111] for struggle is a distinct trait of human nature in the face of flagrant violations of dignity. As American anti-slavery activist Frederick Douglass once proclaimed, "If there is no struggle there is no progress."[112]

In any event, the "social harmony" that the Chinese government has been painstakingly trying to maintain may well be a "disguised sense of stability" — if all it means is "preemptive strike" against all dissents.[113] What is revealing is the rapid increase in the number of organized protests in the streets of China in recent years for all kinds of grievances, from land disputes[114] to protection of a local dialect.[115] In our Internet age, it is virtually impossible to clamp down on the dissemination of ideas, as revolutionary changes seen in much of the Arab world in 2011 have shown.[116] The seemingly perpetual double-digit economic growth cannot forever suppress a people's wish to achieve genuine harmony as embedded in the Chinese culture — to speak the truth for the sake of the people and the state. A nation does not have dignity if its people do not have the dignity to merely speak the truth for the sake of its present and future.

As Liu Xiaobo's counterpart Václav Havel — who co-authored then-Czechoslovakia's Charta 77 — wrote in 1978, "The essential aims of life are present naturally in every person. In everyone there is some longing for humanity's rightful dignity, for moral integrity, for free expression of being and a sense of transcendence over the world of existence."[117] In respect of the totalitarian era in which Havel and his comrades found themselves, Fukuyama has the following observation.[118] In communist Czechoslovakia where people risked their wellbeing by defying the authorities, many might have been lured into a "Faustian bargain" in exchange for a life of tranquility and prosperity. Those who refused to let go of their self-esteem chose to opt out and become professional dissidents. But it also meant forsaking their desiring part of human nature and embracing a life spent in "prison, mental institution, or exile," as Havel and others did.

The lives of Liu Xiaobo and Wei Jingsheng have depicted the tremendous lengths to which some professional dissidents in China could possibly go in defending the rights of themselves and others. In "I Have No Enemies," his final statement written two days before his sentence on 25 December 2009,[119] Liu recounted the years in which he endured constant surveillance, re-education through labor, imprisonments, and most regrettably, prolonged separation from his beloved wife of twenty years — merely for his political dissents. Yet he bore no hatred or regret, but strived to transcend his personal experiences and look forward to his country's change. With gratitude, he observed improvements in prison management and the courtesy he had received from judges and interrogators. Hence his optimism for a free China: "For there is no force that can put an end to the human quest for freedom, and China will in the end become a nation ruled by law, where human rights reign supreme."

Fukuyama said, "There is no democracy without democrats,"[120] individuals who care about dignity more than their own welfare. Liu's optimism would have been quixotic if not for his profound insights into the indomitable human quest for truth and freedom to speak the truth, the power of which could even drive a man "to walk in front of a tank or confront a line of soldiers."[121]

When will the day come for China? For all the reverberations it has created worldwide, Charter 08 is now a silenced cause at home. Yet, one may not reckon with success too easily when it comes to reforming a country as dynamic as China. In any event, it took nearly twenty years for its founding father Dr. Sun Yat-sen (孙逸仙/孙中山) to overthrow the Qing Dynasty in its twilight.[122] To Havel, there is always a silver lining in a reformer's tortuous path. When presenting a human rights award to Liu in absentia in March 2009, he reminded fellow freedom-fighters not to be too calculative about success, saying:

> [In] our experience, not reckoning with that did pay in the end, we found that it was possible to change the situation after all, and those who were mocked as being Don Quixotes, whose efforts

were never going to come to anything, may in the end and to general astonishment get their way. I think that is important. In a peculiar way, there is both despair and hope in this. On the one hand we do not know how things will end, and on the other, we know they may in fact end well.[123]

More and more Chinese individuals have resolved to stand up at home. And China as a nation will stand up as its people have spoken. No matter when the moment comes, the spirit of Charter 08 and the determination of a growing league of Chinese democrats will see China through.

Chapter 8
Charter 08 and Charta 77

East European Past as China's Future?

Michaela Kotyzova

After the release of Charter 08 on 10 December 2009, many comparisons have been made between this Chinese manifesto and the Czechoslovak Charta 77 (hereafter "Charta 77"). The connection between the two is obvious: Charter 08 makes a direct reference to Charta 77 and the relation between the two is in fact suggested by the very title of the Chinese document. In just about every report in the Western media about Charter 08, the connection with Charta 77 has been duly noted and pointed out.

However, the comparisons in these newspaper and magazine articles seldom venture beyond superficial declarations of the obvious, and very few have attempted to examine and analyze the relationship between the two charters in a detailed, systematic, and rigorous manner. There has been just one short academic paper dealing directly with this topic.[1] A few essays by East European scholars of modern China have approached the topic in a more roundabout way.[2] I am indebted to these works and used them as my point of departure.

Among other works relevant to the topic, I would like to mention Václav Havel's book-long interview with Karel Hvízďala, titled *Disturbing the Peace* in the English translation,[3] which to my mind offers probably the best summary of the political and the philosophical backgrounds of the Charta 77 movement in Czechoslovakia. Another worthy and thought-provoking source was two essays by Timothy Garton Ash, the pre-eminent scholar of democratic transition in Eastern Europe, published in *The New York Review of Books* on the occasion of the twentieth anniversary of the 1989 political upheaval.[4]

Rule of Law and One-Party Systems

The few authors who subjected the connection between the two charters to serious scrutiny typically proceed by listing the perceived similarities and differences between the two documents, their background, and their wider environment in terms of the political systems in Eastern Europe and contemporary China.

As we shall see below, all of these supposed differences and similarities seem rather relative. Especially on the East European side of the comparison, the supportive facts seem selective, and sometimes inaccurate. This would seem to reflect the reality that the situation in Eastern Europe as described in these comparisons is now, twenty years later, somewhat removed, and that many authors have not had direct experience with the circumstances then. On the Chinese side of the comparison, the arguments often fall short of the complexity of today's China, a complexity that defies simple characterization. In short, the argumentation used in these cases appears at the same time somewhat true and somewhat false.

Instead of these hasty comparisons, a more useful perspective to examine the connection between the two charters is based on a simple, theoretical question: can the insistence on the rule of law in a one-party system that is ultimately not based on this principle eventually undermine the system itself? This seems to be the crucial issue to consider when juxtaposing the two charters.

In other words, can a well-organized campaign by public intellectuals, political dissidents, and human rights defenders aiming to bring their governments to respect their own laws eventually prevail over the one-party political system? The implicit assumption in virtually all studies devoted to the Charta 77-Charter 08 comparison is that the former is one clear example of such a struggle being ultimately successful. I question this as unproven.

The assumption is obviously derived from the fact of the peaceful political transition in Eastern Europe in 1989, and specifically from the experience of the Czechoslovak Velvet Revolution. The Velvet Revolution has indeed been a spectacular example of a peaceful political change; whether this is a direct consequence of the Charta 77 movement is, however, far from clear. Such a revolution and the peaceful transition of Czechoslovakia from one-party rule to political pluralism in 1989 would hardly have been possible without the changes in the external environment of communist Czechoslovakia brought about by Gorbachev's "perestroika" in the Soviet Union. Ever since the Soviet occupation of 1968, the communist system in Czechoslovakia remained in place by sheer external force. Czechoslovakia was in fact reduced to the status of a colony, and without the support of the Soviet Red Army, its communist regime would most likely have collapsed decades before 1989.

It was not so much the Charta 77 movement that had finally brought down the government in 1989, but rather the unwillingness of Gorbachev's Russia to intervene once again militarily. This point of view would seem to be supported by the fact that the other East European communist countries had very different dissident movements of their own, yet they all collapsed at about the same time in 1989. The only East European regime that took a little longer, and ended much more violently, was Ceaușescu's Romania (and arguably, Hoxha's Albania and Milošević's Yugoslavia — exactly the countries that were far more independent from Soviet power than the rest of Eastern Europe).

Communist regimes in Eastern Europe had been, for the most part, on artificial life support for years before 1989, propped up only by the threat of overwhelming military force presented by the pre-Gorbachev Soviet Union. As soon as this external force ceased to present a veritable threat, the whole system collapsed like a deck of cards.

That is not to say that Charta 77 did not have a role to play in the democratic transition. However, this role was not so much in bringing about the fall of the system, but rather in creating parallel structures, and in a more abstract sense, a parallel public space, ready to take over from the one-party system once it duly collapsed. Charta 77 was not able by itself to bring down the Communist state, but it created the environment for a relatively smooth transition to a workable pluralistic system. In the twelve years before 1989, a whole community of dissident personalities with a proven track record was created to come into positions of influence immediately after these had been vacated by proponents of the previous regime. To realize the magnitude of these parallel structures, one only needs to look at neighboring Slovakia, which had almost exactly the same starting position as the Czech part of the country, but had far weaker oppositional dissident structures. After the collapse of communist power in Slovakia, the situation was markedly more chaotic in the power vacuum, which made it possible for a variety of obscure, post-communist politicians to come up and to slow down, or even sidetrack, the transition there.

The significance of Charta 77 therefore lies not in prevailing *against* the communist state, but rather in prevailing *after* the communist state. In other words, Charta 77 helped to keep alive a certain critical culture throughout the worst years of political nihilism, and prepared a pool of trusted personnel with a proven track record and credentials (one would almost be tempted to say that it prepared reliable "cadres") for the political transition after the regime's demise. This was by no means a small feat. It was in fact probably as important as the political turnaround itself.

If there is a significant role for Charter 08 to play, it might be somewhere in this area. Charter 08, like Charta 77, is built on the premise that, if the one-party communist state really is to uphold its own laws, it would ultimately have to change its nature into something closer to political pluralism, or else collapse. This seems to be a very viable strategy, basically calling the "bluff" of a one-party state: if the governing power is a lawful system, everybody needs to abide by the law and no special political interest can be above the law. This is the inherent communist state contradiction: it either is a lawful system or not. The problem is that this logical strategy would only seem to be able to go so far. Once the bluff is called, the communist state reverts to its basics. It stops pretending it is a lawful system and strikes down those who challenge its authority to rule. The communist state reverts to its repressive mode, which is exactly what happened in Czechoslovakia in the late 70s, and now history repeats itself in China. The one-party regime can only pretend to be tolerant when it is not challenged; once challenged, it strikes back. If the one-party communist system could be reformed by gradual development of the rule of law, it would probably had happened in one of the many different varieties of the system as witnessed throughout the world since the 1970s.

Charta 77 did not bring about the regime change in Czechoslovakia. It merely called the regime's bluff and paid dearly with years of heavy repression. At the same time, Charta 77 did play a role in keeping alive a political ideal throughout these dark years, and in bringing together people who identified with these ideals and who would be ready to come up once the political situation changed. The transformation itself, however, came from without rather than from within this movement.

Can Charter 08 play a similar role in the specifically Chinese environment, admittedly quite different from pre-1989 Czechoslovakia and Eastern Europe? The significance of Charta 77 did not lie only in the initial proclamation of January 1977; it became a movement complete with internal structure, procedures, and evolution.[5] Whether or not the Chinese Charter 08 can acquire any of these attributes is yet to be seen, and will probably very much depend on the similarities or differences between the two historical situations. Here, we can perhaps, with the above disclaimer in mind, revisit some of the more relevant analyses of these differences and similarities as presented by various authors.

Similarities and Differences

The main similarity between the two charters is their strict adherence to the rule of law. They place themselves within the constraints of the existing system, or rather, the part of it that is based on the rule of law. As stated before, this aspect of the system has the theoretical potential to undermine the other, that is, the political supremacy of the communist country, which amounts to a privileged political interest not bound by otherwise applicable rules and regulations. The Chartists do not attack this directly, except when demanding that the one crucial constitutional clause guaranteeing the privileged position of the communist party be abolished. For both charters, the main instrument for pursuing their cause is the relevant international human right treaties — the International Covenant on Civil and Political Rights (ICCPR) and the International Covenant on Economic, Social and Cultural Rights (ICESCR) — to which both the Czechoslovak and Chinese governments are signatories.[6] By signing these two treaties, both governments took upon themselves the commitment to protect and promote the rights stipulated in the covenants. Most of these rights have also been guaranteed in the respective constitutions of the Czechoslovak Socialist Republic and the People's Republic of China.

There is, however, a crucial difference between China today and Czechoslovakia in the late 70s in this particular respect. Czechoslovakia's Charta 77 movement was not so much relating itself to the international covenants on rights, but rather to the Helsinki Accords of 1976,[7] which among other things declared the right of citizen initiatives to monitor the human rights record in signatory countries. These clauses did not seem really relevant at the time of signing, but became a very potent instrument for Charta 77 to defend its activities vis-à-vis the state. It has also helped to focus international attention on the movement as well as on the plight of its activists. By suppressing the Charta 77 activists, the Czechoslovak government came into direct violation of its solemn international commitments made a few years earlier. This, of course, made it very difficult for Czechoslovak authorities to justify their repressive attitude towards the movement and also provided a legal basis for international endorsement support from among the West European signatories of the Helsinki Accords. From day one, there was a groundswell of support for Charta 77. It was meant to be released on 6 January 1977, but the petitioners were arrested on their way to file it with the Czechoslovak authorities. Already, on 7 January, the full text of the document was published in translations in four major West European dailies: *Frankfurter Allgemeine Zeitung*, *The Times*, *Le Monde*, and *Corriere della Sera*. Major American newspapers, *The New York Times* and *Washington Post*, joined in the chorus one day later with reports summarizing the document, and the full text was published in *The New York Times* on 27 January 1977.[8]

Because of the Helsinki Accords, Charta 77 was guaranteed international attention and support, especially in West European countries, since its beginning, and possibly even before. This seems rather different from Charter 08. The Chinese document has attracted worldwide interest, but publicity was nowhere as unanimously supportive. For example, the document was never published in full in any major European newspaper. In the US, the full text appeared in the *New York Review of Books*, an intellectual daily with significant impact among its select readership, but limited circulation. Many commentaries in the international media and on the Chinese Internet (whenever they lasted long enough to be noted) seemed distinctly more reserved,[9] and it seems that most observers have lost faith that there could appear an influential dissident movement inside China. The potential impact of Charter 08 has never been gauged in its own right: the significance of the document has, if at all, nearly always been considered within the framework of the obvious comparison with Charta 77 — just like in this chapter. This would in itself speak volumes about the difference in the international reception of the respective charters.

In this context, it is surprising that probably the most vocal support awarded to Charter 08 (before the Nobel Committee's historical decision in late 2010) came from the country of origin of the other charter, the Czech Republic. Václav Havel, one of the original drafters of Charta 77, came in support of the Chinese Charter with an op-ed piece published in the *Wall Street Journal* on 19 December 2008.[10] A few months later, Liu Xiaobo, the main drafter and proponent of Charter 08, was awarded the prestigious human rights award Homo Homini[11] by an influential Czech non-governmental organization (NGO), the People in Need Foundation. This award has definitely helped focus international attention again on the fate of Liu Xiaobo, but ironically, it has also reinforced the debate about the "similarities and differences" between the two countries.

Another perceived similarity between the two documents often cited in international media, and even some of the more thoughtful analyses, is the official response to the respective charters. Predictably, both the Czechoslovak government in 1977 and the Chinese government in 2008–09 reacted with an instinctive campaign of repression. Note, however, that the mode of repression has been quite different in China than in the old communist Czechoslovakia. This is partly to be explained by the different stages of development of the one-party system in both countries.

Czechoslovakia in the 70s was at the height of its totalitarian system. The new "normalization leadership" of Gustáv Husák was triumphant in its suppression of all dissenting voices after the Warsaw Pact invasion of 1968. In fact, the very emergence of Charta 77 was sparked by the outrage of the surviving dissident community at the authorities' attempt to extend the purges from the political into the cultural sphere. The dissent movement came together in solidarity when the rock-and-roll band Plastic People of the Universe (Plastic People)[12] was placed on trial for utterly non-political, albeit quite eccentric behavior.

As Václav Havel describes in his book, *Disturbing the Peace*, the Charta 77 movement stemmed from the realization among independent intellectuals that the Czechoslovak authorities were no longer content with persecuting their former opponents in the Prague Spring upheaval, but were now attacking any non-conformist behavior. The decimated civil society in Czechoslovakia reorganized itself in a self-defensive response to this frontal attack on its autonomy. By prosecuting a band of apolitical, albeit non-conformist musicians, Husák's regime simply went too far and crossed all unwritten red lines.

By contrast, today's post-totalitarian China seems largely beyond this stage of indiscriminate repression. Instead, the Chinese authorities are increasingly sophisticated in targeting just the few dissident voices, which the government considers potentially dangerous to its own survival. This cannot be taken for granted: the Chinese repressive apparatus can easily revert to the Mao-like type of mass persecution, as we have seen in the case of the Falun Gong. In most situations, however, China's internal security organs are much more selective and focused, and it is hard to imagine that a rock band like the Plastic People would cause much concern for the Chinese public security authorities today. In other words, an independently thinking autonomous Chinese individual today need not feel as threatened as the remnants of civil society in Czechoslovakia in the 70s. This has obvious implications for the domestic support for Charter 08 in China.

Whereas scores of Chartists went through prisons in communist Czechoslovakia, the Chinese security organs have so far only incarcerated one crucial individual, Liu Xiaobo. This one individual the security organs apparently consider very dangerous, belying those who denigrate Charter 08 as totally insignificant. Anne Marie Morris finds it curious that the Czechoslovak "government decided not to persecute the authors directly on the grounds of publishing the Charter, but rather on other claims of subversive behavior."[13] In fact this is hardly surprising, as there is little in either of the two charters for which anybody could be possibly prosecuted. A government cannot put people on trial for insisting on upholding the government's own laws. That would be just too arbitrary, even for a one-party regime. It would, in fact, be self-implicating on the part of the government involved, as it would clearly show that there is something fundamentally wrong with the legal system. This must be the reason the Chinese government appears to have had such difficulty in charging Liu Xiaobo with a specific crime. He was only formally charged half a year after detention, and his case went to the prosecutor almost a year after he was taken away by state security personnel.[14]

In connection with the official response in China and in Czechoslovakia, a distinction is often emphasized between the means of distribution of the two charters. Whereas Charta 77 had to rely on typewritten and mimeographed copies of the original document, in China's case there is the omnipresent Internet. According to Morris:

> Despite the government efforts to filter out Charter 08 from the Chinese cyber space, it is relatively easily available online. Despite Chinese government attempts to shut down any mention and discussion of the Charter from Chinese-accessible internet, there has been only limited success, and new blogs and sites pop up as soon as the government takes down others. A recent study found that the Chinese Google search engine has registered over 119,000 hits for the Chinese words for Charter 08.[15]

That is of course true, but again, these different distribution mechanisms are hardly relevant to either of the two charters' social impact. We have to admit that neither of the two charters is a very attractive or even readable document for mass consumption. By the very fact that each charter stays within the realm of its respective existing legal system, it does not strongly appeal to potential rebels and the disaffected. In fact, few in communist Czechoslovakia have actually read Charta 77, and fewer still can claim truly to relate to it. Those who have read it usually found it rather unappealing, and, especially the younger ones, oftentimes plain boring.

This did not stop many of these youth from signing the document eventually, but they would often identify more with its image, rather than its actual wording. This image ironically had been created to a large extent by the Czechoslovak government itself, which, in contrast with the Chinese government, organized in 1977 a widespread propaganda campaign against Charta 77 all across state-controlled media. The document was denounced viciously and unrelentingly in the press and on state TV and radio.

This propaganda overkill seriously backfired. Although few people actually read the text, nearly everyone was aware that there was something called Charta 77. The numerous sections of society disenchanted with the government naturally gravitated towards the document. Many decided to sign it long before having had a chance to read it, and, in some cases at least, without actually reading it. In short, by orchestrating the propaganda campaign, the government in effect declared war on Charta 77, an ideological fight many people were only too happy to take on.

In contrast, the Chinese government is trying to erase Charter 08 from the public sphere with minimum publicity. The few direct rebuttals were published in specialized inner-party journals like the *Qiushi* magazine (求是).[16] This approach seems to be a rather wise attitude by the government. Charter 08 may be available on the Internet, but relatively few people seemed aware of its existence outside a particular community of the usual suspects, at least before the awarding of the Nobel Prize to Liu Xiaobo. A blogger going by the name Youren laments the silencing of Charter 08 in these words:

> It [the government of China] has done an impressive job this time at downplaying and silencing the Charter. The lesson of 1989 is well learnt. The sad consequence of this is that today the vast majority of the Chinese population has no idea of the existence of the Charter 08. And I am not only speaking of the masses of peasants. A quick survey among my personal Shanghai friends, all of them with university education and speakers of at least one foreign language, gave discouraging results: Not a single one of them had even heard the term *"Lingba Xianzhang* (Charter 08)" one week after its publication.[17]

Morris finds that "the most distinct difference between the reality in China today and the reality of Czech Republic in 1977" is "the debate of the universality of human rights and the role of 'Chineseness' in implementing human rights."[18] According to her, the Chinese government was able to counter Charter 08 with an argument that "China and the West are founded on inherently different cultural understanding of human rights — Chinese culture, and thus its conception of human rights is based in ideas of the community and harmony, whereas the Western world's vision of rights is based on the individual."[19] In a revealing comment, she claims that:

> This point cannot and should not been taken lightly. The concept
> of harmony is finding more and more holding even in the western
> legal world, as globalization makes it difficult for court enforce-
> ment and disputes are pushed into mediation and negotiations
> more and more. China's impressive revelation of harmony in the
> 2008 Olympic Opening Ceremony was in itself an embodiment
> of the power, effectiveness and beauty of harmonious activity.
> Thousands of Chinese men and women worked themselves into
> visions of art during the ceremony, a symbol of the importance
> of working together and the reality that humans are not isolated
> individuals, but a community of people who benefit from a har-
> monious society.[20]

Here, the otherwise rather critical Morris seems to be falling for the
official Chinese propaganda. The Olympic Opening Ceremony was
viewed by many in China, including some signatories of Charter 08, as
an ultimate expression of "Fascist art."[21] Similarly, the concept of "harmonious society" (*hexie shehui*, 和谐社会) has been ridiculed all over the
Chinese Internet with the hilarious pun on "river crabs" (*he xie*, 河蟹).[22]
One only needs to spend a few days on the streets of Chinese cities
to understand that the notion that Chinese society after sixty years of
communism should be somehow more altruistic and less individualis-
tic than the West is totally misguided. If anything, the prevailing ethos
in daily interpersonal dealings seems more like "dog eats dog," rather
than any kind of harmony.

In any case, the Czechoslovak authorities have, in fact, presented
exactly the same line of argument in their propaganda war against
Charta 77. They, too, had argued that Communist Czechoslovakia
had developed its own concept of democracy ("socialist democracy")
and human rights, but they did not connect these supposedly unique
qualities with any notion of "Czechness": that would have been too
outlandish even for the propaganda machinery of that time. Rather,
they ascribed them to the different social and political establishment
in Czechoslovakia, and by extension, in all of Eastern Europe and the
Soviet Bloc.[23]

The difference with today's China lies not in the official position,
but rather the public's reception. In Czechoslovakia, a cultural relativ-
ist argument would be simply laughed off by the vast majority of the
population. In China, it appears, however, that many ordinary people

do take the government's line quite seriously. To a large extent, this reflects the different image of the two respective governments among their populations. Czechoslovakia had since 1968 been an occupied country, reduced to the status of a *de facto* colony, its government perceived by its citizens as little more than a colonial administration. This is obviously not the case with the Chinese government today. For all its faults, the Chinese government represents a sovereign power, and one aspiring to big-power status. After a century and half of weakness and foreign encroachment, many people in China credit their government with lifting the country from its former "semi-colonial" status, and leading it in its post-Mao rise on the world stage.

Here may lay the main difference between Eastern Europe of yesteryear, and China of today. Eastern Europe had been subject to foreign domination as part of the once powerful Soviet empire. The very existence of this post-war political arrangement was considered by most East Europeans as an aberration of history, a temporary result of conquest by foreign power that needed to be redressed. Many countries in Eastern Europe, Czechoslovakia foremost amongst them, also boasted their own proud pre-war tradition of a democratic and pluralistic political culture. The causes of political liberalization and national emancipation were seen as two sides of the same coin, inter-related processes that went arm in arm.

In China, on the other hand, the official propaganda has managed to a large extent to present these two causes as being in opposition to each other, and the fact that political democratization could actually weaken China as a rising power by threatening its political, ethnic, and social unity. Many have noted that nationalism tends to be the last bastion of communism. Nationalism, especially in countries that have suffered in their recent history at the hands of foreigners, is always the easiest instinct for any propagandist to play upon. The argument that democracy could somehow undermine China's rise and its future greatness is the most powerful weapon in the Communist Party's ideological arsenal.

In his thoughtful analyses of the demise of communism in Eastern Europe, Timothy Garton Ash has argued that the so-called "Velvet Revolution" (and the Color Revolution, which he sees as closely connected to the original Velvet Revolution) constituted a new kind of political change, a "revolution" in its pre-1789 sense. The word "revolution" denotes in its original etymology a return to some pre-existing natural social and political order;[24] it was only with the French Revolution that the term acquired its contemporary meaning of a violent political upheaval. In Ash's view, this notion of "revolution" as a violent, typically bloody, regime change had established itself for the two hundred years between the French Revolution of 1789 and the Velvet Revolution in Eastern Europe in 1989.

The Velvet Revolution was indeed very different from the political revolutions in the eighteenth, nineteenth, and twentieth centuries. In the prevailing current terminology, it might even be described as a "counter-revolution" — in essence annulling the previous post-1945 "revolutions." In 1989, Eastern Europe was indeed reverting to its past, more natural state of affairs before Soviet domination. The obvious question is whether the Velvet Revolution can possibly succeed in countries that do not have such "utopian" moments in their past to which to refer, or which do not recognize their past as something to which it is worth returning. In other words, in its democratic transition, Eastern Europe was largely only going back to a previous stage in its history; China, on the other hand, will have to move forward to something new, without a clear precedent.

Another oft-quoted comparison between the two charters concerns their collective authorship, supposedly diverse in the case of Charta 77, and "narrowly intellectual" in the case of Charter 08. Again, as Morris points out:

> [Charta 77] grew out of the most unlikely partnership: intellectuals and rockers. [Charta 77's] simplicity brought together writers and artists, Christians and atheists, laborers and clerks, old and young. Although Charter 08's creators formed a more homogenous group than [Charta 77's] authors, the reach of the internet has brought Charter 08 to a broad array of supporters.[25]

I would again find this comparison not very precise. Charta 77 indeed arose from "the most unlikely partnership between intellectuals and rockers," but although this original partnership provided the spark for Charta 77's conception, it did not extend to the actual authorship. The drafters were, just like the case of Charter 08, a rather narrow group of elite intellectuals like Václav Havel, Pavel Kohout, and Petr

Uhl. But the popular support for Charta 77 after its inception was substantial.

The prosecution of the rock band Plastic People was a significant event. The Czechoslovak apparatchiks probably thought that Plastic People would be easy to isolate and demonize before the general public. It was the political genius of Václav Havel and a few other intellectuals to realize that this seemingly marginal group of non-conformist youth in fact represented a whole new target, and an escalation of repression that would eventually hit the entire population. Unlike the previous purges which only targeted political opponents of the regime who were politically active in 1968, this persecuted a basically apolitical group of young people who only wanted to live their own lives and play their own music.

Havel realized that if the regime succeeded with this seemingly marginal trial, eventually all free independent expression would be silenced one by one. He organized a broad front of support for the band, which resulted in not just "the most unlikely partnership between intellectuals and rockers"[26] (who after all need not be so far apart from each other), but also one which extended to the exponents of the suppressed Prague Spring — in other words, the reform communists of 1968 who lost power after the Soviet invasion. Thus, as described by Václav Havel, you could see in the courtroom a long-haired non-conformist shaking hands and engaging in a lively discussion with a former communist apparatchik from the reform movement of 1968, something that would seem unthinkable before that very special event.

The broad solidarity among various disenchanted groups in Czech society may not have lasted for long, if it had not received another impetus from the Helsinki Accords of 1975. The agreement was perceived by many at the time of its signing as a major geopolitical triumph of Brezhnev's Soviet Union, which seemingly won through it official recognition for its territorial gains after World War II in Eastern Europe. Some even saw in the Helsinki Accords an international legitimization of the Soviet system as such. In fact, the Helsinki Accords, and specifically its third part devoted to "Co-operation in Humanitarian and Other Fields,"[27] proved in the long run to be a major element in bringing down the whole Soviet system. It provided justification and cover for independent civic groups to conduct unofficial monitoring of their governments' compliance with the document, and in effect, promoted independent advocacy for human rights in the signatory countries.

This was the second major impetus for the drafting of Charta 77 in the latter part of 1976. The drafting itself was done by a few dissident intellectuals like Václav Havel, Jan Patočka, Zdeněk Mlynář, Jiří Hájek, Pavel Kohout, and Petr Uhl. This was a diverse group in terms of political inclinations, but had little to do with the underground rock-and-roll subculture represented by the Plastic People.

The disenchanted, "underground" youth had very little to do with Charta 77's drafting and was only marginally involved in its further development, although it eventually did form a very substantial portion, if not the bulk, of Charta 77 signatories. Immediately after Charta 77's release in January 1977, the first wave of signatories mostly represented "the usual suspects": the few active dissident intellectuals and former politicians and public figures purged after the Russian Invasion of 1968. This pool of natural sympathizers with the document quickly dried out, and the following wave of new signatures mostly came from among the "underground," an alternative subculture of rebellious youth. This does not mean, however, that these young rebels would be directly involved in Charta 77's daily working, or even that they would identify with it very closely. Mostly, they would sign as a symbol of protest and because of Charta 77's origins in the solidarity movement with the Plastic People during their trial in 1976. The "underground" way of life and philosophical outlooks were in fact quite different from the Charta 77 spirit, with the "underground" youth of that time looking up more to Egon Bondy, rather than Václav Havel.

Bondy was a rather colorful figure of the Czech cultural underground ever since the 50s. He was a self-proclaimed Trotskyist and Maoist, one of the very few, if not the only one, in all of Eastern Europe. Naturally, his political opinions differed significantly from Václav Havel's and Charta 77's mainstream supporters. In fact, throughout the late 70s and 80s, there was something of a competition for the young generation's hearts and souls between Bondy and Havel.[28]

During this period, Bondy appeared to be winning this informal popularity contest. He was recognized as the "pope of the underground" and was hugely influential over the whole underground scene. It is now largely forgotten that Bondy had written all the lyrics for the Plastic People's first album release in Sweden in the late 70s, with a cover featuring portraits of Lenin and Mao.[29] This was an environment quite detached from that of the mainstream Chartists.

All through the 80s, Bondy was bitterly complaining that Charta 77 would not allow full participation by the underground youth. He managed to implant his argument upon some of the more impressionable youth, who would then try to fight for bigger representation in the Charta 77 decision-making process, which was indeed not very transparent or democratic. In the situation of constant and aggressive police surveillance and harassment, it would have been difficult for Charta 77 to maintain formal democratic processes such as voting or public debates and consultations, and its daily business was controlled by a small group of "spokespersons" (usually three) plus an informal body of its more prominent members. The underground culture was largely shut out from this process. From today's point of view, it is difficult to say whether this was by design or by default, given the conditions of clandestine work in a police state.

One way or another, the drafting and subsequent conduct of Charta 77 was driven, just like in the case of Charter 08, by a small group of elite intellectuals. Again, the oft-quoted argument that Charta 77 had more diverse authorship and participation than Charter 08 does not seem to hold up to closer scrutiny.

One powerful argument regarding the differences between Czechoslovakia and contemporary China concerns the very different path of economic development. In fact, China has probably escaped the "reverse domino effect" of international communism in the late 80s and early 90s exactly because it managed to fashion a total overhaul of its economic system. China joined the accelerated process of economic globalization after the end of the Cold War, leveraged its competitive advantages (first of all, cheap labor) and eventually positioned itself as the manufacturing base for global economy. Through this transformation, it recovered part of its shaken legitimacy after 1989, and also provided a whole new purpose for the society at large.[30]

In comparison, the 70s and 80s presented a period of economic "stagnation" in Eastern Europe. Therefore, the argument goes, the

Soviet Bloc governments were far less stable and more vulnerable to domestic unrest. This observation is real, but a little too sweeping and general. On closer scrutiny, there are many surprising partial similarities in this overall difference.

Many authors describe Husák's Czechoslovakia as an economic basket case. Morris claims that "[t]he government was failing to meet the basic daily needs of the general public."[31] That is not an accurate description of the actual situation. Part of Husák "normalization" social contract after 1968 was that people would not become involved in politics, but the government would take care of their basic livelihood. Thus, politics might have been controlled even more strictly in Czechoslovakia than in other East European countries, but the standard of living was relatively high in comparison. People were living in relative material comfort, as long as they were willing to put up with the political oppression.

From this point of view, Husák's Czechoslovakia was really not so dissimilar from post-Mao China. The difference is that people in Czechoslovakia could not get as far ahead as their Chinese counterparts of today. At the same time, few would have been left behind as drastically as what happens to millions in today's China. In other words, in terms of economic prosperity, material stratification in China appears as striking, if not more so, as its material progress. There were few super-rich in Husák's Czechoslovakia, but also few super-poor. China may be progressing much faster economically, but at the cost of glaring inequality.

Whether this makes China's situation more stable is unknown. One could also argue that China's breakneck development accompanied by rising stratification actually makes it more vulnerable to potential unrest. Unlike in Czechoslovakia, there are large underprivileged sections in Chinese society representing a potential source of destabilization. There is no connection between the underprivileged and the elite intellectuals behind Charter 08 (yet), but the history of the Solidarity Movement in Poland demonstrates that a potential link between the two is not beyond imagination. The different path of economic development in China may not necessarily make it less vulnerable to potential unrest.

Conclusion

The debate about Charta 77 and Charter 08 has so far mostly focused on the perceived differences and similarities in the two documents' respective social and political backgrounds. These are interesting discussions, but they sometimes tend to dwell on somewhat superficial observations. As we have seen, the "similarities" as well as "differences" can prove rather relative in closer scrutiny. The reality in both cases appears too complex for a straightforward, mechanical comparison.

Rather, this chapter offers a different perspective of looking at the linkage between the two documents. Instead of examining the often incomparable specific aspects of daily life and political backgrounds in both countries, it might make more sense to look at the broader philosophical approach of the two charters — which points out that the discrepancy between the supposed rule of law on one side and the special political interest on the other is indeed comparable in its similarity. This does not necessarily have to lead to the same result, simply because we cannot be sure if the *fait accompli* in Czechoslovakia — the demise of a one-party system and its replacement with a pluralistic democracy — has indeed been the result of this basic approach. Even after 1989, it remains unclear whether initiatives promoting the rule of law in one-party systems can be successful by themselves. Charter 08 may follow the same philosophical principle as Charta 77, but given the many different aspects in its domestic and international situation, the actual result could be different.

Beyond the basic broad approach, it does not make much sense to look at the supposed parallels unless we can embark on a much deeper and more comprehensive comparative study than has been the case till date. At the rather superficial level presented so far, apparent resemblances can easily turn into dissimilarities, and vice versa, under closer examination. As Martin Hala quotes the old Chinese philosopher Zhuangzi (庄子): "When you look at things from the point of difference, they appear distinct; whereas from the point of similarity, they would look the same."[32]

The common philosophical approach notwithstanding, there would indeed loom one fundamental difference between Eastern Europe before 1989 and today's China. The former was part of the Soviet empire. Czechoslovakia itself was occupied by Russian troops since 1968, and its government was in effect a colonial administration with virtually no legitimacy among its own population. This constituted the basic external situation in which all dissident movements in Eastern Europe operated. Domestic conditions could not be changed without first a change in the "mother country" — the Soviet Union. This was the fundamental restriction of such movements, but at the same time also their biggest potential — their respective governments were so compromised by collaboration with the occupying forces and their legitimacy so low vis-à-vis their own populations that once the outside force was gone or weakened, as happened under Gorbachev's reforms, there was little domestic opposition and few hindrances to the dissidents' eventual success, and the communist governments' collapse.

To borrow some Marxist dialectics, the basic internal situation may be the same in China and former Czechoslovakia — a political system based on the privileged special interest of one party, yet pretending to operate on the basis of universally applicable law. The external situation, however, is quite different: the Chinese government represents a sovereign power.

Describing dialectic materialism in his *Little Red Book*, Mao Zedong gives the example of an egg. It has the internal condition of becoming a chicken, but without proper external condition of incubation, it would not hatch. This would seem to bode ill for Charter 08. But then again, we know that the late Chairman was not always right in his predictions.

Part Three

Charter 08 and the Politics of *Weiquan* and *Weiwen*

Chapter 9
Challenging Authoritarianism through Law

Fu Hualing*

Introduction

The publication of Charter 08 and the subsequent prosecution of Liu Xiaobo symbolize two significant developments in China during the reform period. The first is the rising rights awareness among ordinary citizens and their determination to claim and assert their rights through political and legal channels. The bottom-up demand for rights from civil society originates from economic and social changes; it is also intentionally promoted by government-initiated legal reform. The second significant development is the stagnation of political and legal reform relative to social and economic changes, the political failure to provide an institutional solution to social and economic conflicts, and the incapacitation of legal institutions to protect rights that the law provides.

What we are witnessing is a dynamic process in which, on the one hand, a strong social force — spearheaded by the challenges posed by dissident intellectuals, *weiquan* (维权, rights defense) lawyers, and other citizen activists — grapples with and pushes forward the authoritarian system, and on the other, the system, in panic, pushes back and responds to the confrontation with enhanced violence and repressive-

* The author would like to thank the following people for commenting on earlier versions of this paper: Richard Cullen, D. W. Choy, Deborah Davis, Michael Dowdle, Stephen Mau, Eva Pils, and Lynn White. A slightly different version was published in Volume 6 (2011) of *National Taiwan University Law Review*.

ness. This chapter places the cases of Liu Xiaobo and Charter 08 in the context of this confrontational dynamics.

This chapter studies the role of lawyers in China's emerging contentious politics. It aims at broadly describing the origin, development, and limit of public interest lawyering and the legal and political implications of those developments to China's authoritarian system. The potentials and limit of legal reform in an authoritarian state is a fascinating issue.[1] Scholars and practitioners have argued whether legal reform can soften the edge of such a system and eventually liberalize it, or whether that would simply further entrench its rule.[2] This chapter attempts to contribute to this debate by examining the efforts of activist lawyers in China in mobilizing the law to protect and promote rights, and the implications of their legal activism on China's political and legal development.

Activist lawyers come in different shapes. This chapter refers to the politically moderate lawyers as "public interest lawyers," and their politically more challenging colleagues interchangeably as "*weiquan* lawyers," "rights lawyers," or "political lawyers."

This chapter is divided into five parts. Following this introduction, Part Two puts public interest litigation (PIL) in China into perspective by identifying the political and legal forces that promote or contain the development of PIL, arguing that the promotion of the rule of law and expansion of legal rights in China, even without corresponding changes in politics, have created strong incentives and limited opportunities for PIL. Part Three of this chapter identifies five changes in PIL in China over the past decade or so. These vary in pace and intensity, but are all visible and reinforce each other. There are significant developments in PIL in China and lawyers have become more demanding and challenging. Part Four discusses government responses to legal activism and the politics of PIL in China, arguing that the current pushback by the government in restricting aggressive public interest lawyering is, in part, a response to the growth of PIL in China in the past decade. Legal reform in China necessitates activism on the part of lawyers, but at the same time, political stagnation suffocates the very activism the rule of law reform demands. Part Five is the conclusion.

Political Lawyering in Context

The single golden thread that runs through the thirty-year reform in China is economic development through privatization, industrialization, and marketization.[3] Parallel to economic reform and in support of economic growth, political and legal reform has evolved in distinct stages, with different policy goals and priorities in each phase.

Political and legal reform started in the aftermath of the Cultural Revolution. There was, since the late 1970s and throughout the 1980s, a consensus between political elites and the masses that China desperately needed democratization and the rule of law. Reform in the first decade was defined by a consistent call for, and concerted effort to promote, the liberalization of thought and change in the political structure. There was first of all a decisive ideological shift from revolution to modernization, and the adaptation of legal rationality as the basis of the legitimacy of the Chinese Communist Party (hereafter "Party" or "CCP") to replace Maoist revolutionary ideology.[4] On top of that, political and legal institutions were redesigned to embrace democratic values and the rule of law.[5] In sum, the lack of these two elements within the ruling party was regarded as the cause of the Cultural Revolution, and ideological and institutional adaptation of democratic values was expected to improve political participation, enhance political accountability, and bring order and stability to political life.

There might be less understanding as to how the rule of law and democracy actually operated on the ground, and there was a high degree of idealization of what they could achieve, but there was nevertheless a strong political will to explore this potential. China at that time remained largely isolated from the world. Without confidence in its own political system and desperate to reach out for capital, technology and ideas, it was eager to learn and to adopt these Western ideas.

The reform was one led by the central government. It is important to note that the CCP, or at least a faction of it, was progressive and reform-minded: Deng Xiaoping (邓小平) led the open-door policy and was instrumental to the political emancipation in the early 1980s. His followers, including Hu Yaobang (胡耀邦) and Zhao Ziyang (赵紫阳), were the most liberal-minded politicians in that period. In the shadow of the government-led political reform, there was a consensus that the

CCP was making the correct choice and that citizens were supportive of its policies. For a brief moment, there was a healthy interaction between the state and the society in inching toward political openness despite the four core principles that were entrenched in the 1982 Constitution[6] and the occasional resistance from the conservative faction of the Party.

The political and legal reform in that period was groundbreaking in both breadth and depth. It was strongly associated with democratization and liberalization, with the Party initiating a series of reform policies to liberalize the congresses, to democratize village governance, to separate the judiciary from local CCP control, and, above all, to free the media.[7] The first stage of reform witnessed a vibrant discussion on the need for democracy within the ruling CCP, which eventually resulted in a violent confrontation between the liberal and conservative factions, and led to the crackdown and bloodshed in Tiananmen Square in 1989.[8]

The agenda for democratization and legal reform ended tragically then, and its path fundamentally changed. Although the incident dashed the hope of political liberalization and ended experimental programs on incremental democratization and institutional independence from excessive political control, it did not lead to the demise of the rule of law. After a short lapse, the rule of law was revived decisively under a different name.

Less than two years after the crackdown in Tiananmen, Deng Xiaoping, then China's paramount leader, made a historical tour to southern China in early 1992, in which he demanded the deepening of China's economic reform.[9] While the government had halted political reform and democratization, it was initiating a grand scale of economic liberalization, and along with it, the creation of a legal framework for market activities and legislative expansion of rights and freedoms in the personal, social, and economic spheres.[10] However, this development was characterized by the promotion of the rule of law without politics — the development of the rule of law and legal rights as an alternative to democratization.

This discourse on the relationship between law and economic development is a familiar one: market economy requires certainty, stability, and predictability for domestic players as well as foreign investors; and legal rules are necessary to establish a framework for economic transactions and to regulate the behavior of parties involved.[11] To achieve a market economy and ensure sustainable economic growth, the Party/state should respect and obey the rules of the market and the "invisible hand" of the market should replace the visible meddling of the government. Law is necessary to maintain such orderly market conditions and to reduce government intervention in economic activities.[12] After all, the market economy is commonly referred to as the "rule of law economy."

To be meaningful players in the reformed marketplace, citizens require a larger realm of rights and personal freedoms — including freedom to contract and engage in private business, and the right to private property — and laws in China reacted responsively to the increasing need for legal protection of these. Parallel to the expansion of economic freedom was the demand for rights and freedoms in the political sphere, including the freedom of conscience, religion, and expression.

The second stage witnessed the age of rights with a legislative exploration of legal rights. All this was accompanied by the landmark signing of the International Covenant on Civil and Political Rights (ICCPR) and the International Covenant on Economic, Social and Cultural Rights (ICESCR);[13] the CCP's endorsement of the rule of law; and the entrenchment of the rule of law and human rights in the constitutional amendments in 1999 and 2004 respectively.

A significant new development in the 1990s was administrative reform. Instead of democratization, the CCP promoted "administration according to law" as the central aim to compensate for the lack of political initiatives. The National People's Congress passed the landmark Administrative Litigation Law in 1989, which created a general power of judicial review of administrative acts. This was followed by the enactment of the State Compensation Law in 1994, the Law on Administrative Punishment in 1997, the Law on Administrative Reconsideration in 1999, the Law on Legislation in 1999, and the Law on Administrative Licensing in 2003. The administrative reform aimed to create a "thin version" of the rule of law in China: a law-abiding government with defined legal procedures and mechanisms of accountability and redress.[14] Through enhancing responsibility, reducing corruption, and more effective implementation of law, the CCP intended to use executive reform to capture the rising demand for rights and to contain social conflicts.[15]

China was fully integrated into the international community in the 1990s,[16] and this engagement became an additional force for promoting commercial rule of law in China. Economic reform in the age of globalization necessitated closer economic relations between China (as the world's factory) and its trading partners (where the markets are located). Economic interdependence also forced China to participate in, and to a lesser degree, comply with, international rules. China's accession to the World Trade Organization (WTO) became a further catalyst of legal reform in fostering commercial rule of law. Indeed, it has been pointed out that the Chinese government seized the opportunity to launch its own "WTO-plus" reforms to improve the quality of government service, such as increasing the predictability of administrative rules and the transparency of executive processes.[17] The increasing engagement with the global community has also placed a strong demand for accountability toward the international human rights regime into which China is integrating.

There has been tremendous growth on the supply side of the rule of law, as demonstrated in the acceleration of law-making activities, the increase in empowering legal provisions, the putting in place of facilitative legal procedures and mechanisms, and the enhancement of the institutional capacity of courts.[18]

More importantly, there is also a strong development on the demand side of the rule of law. A key indicator is the emergence of civil society forces in China characterized by the mushrooming of associations and non-governmental organizations (NGOs), along with a new wave of volunteerism, civic culture, and moral reasoning.[19] Within the context of cultural and institutional changes, there is also a growth in demand for rights and the rule of law. The social and economic changes characterized by migration, job layoffs, economic exploitation, or, more recently, land grabbing, have created tremendous stress and frustration in people's lives. These have been felt most strongly by the already vulnerable groups within society who are slowly, but gradually, stepping forward to air their grievances and demand their rights. In public forums, these groups — including migrant laborers; unpaid workers; abused wives; harassed women; demobilized soldiers; people suffering from hepatitis B, HIV/AIDS, and other diseases; and many others whose property and other rights may have been infringed upon — have all demanded remedies as provided by law for the injustice that they may have suffered.[20]

The thesis of rightful resistance, as developed by O'Brien and Li, captures well the demand for rights in China's emerging civil society. By rightful resistance, the authors refer to:

> [A] form of popular contention that operates near the boundary of authorized channels, employs the rhetoric and commitments of the powerful to curb the exercise of power, hinges on locating and exploiting divisions within the state, and relies on mobilizing support from the wider public.[21]

Rightful resistance thus consists of legally sanctioned actions taken to protect one's legal rights. In carrying out rightful resistance, the resisters strategically engage the state, exploit gaps within the state, and change the society.

Rightful resistance emerges because of the growth in political opportunities in China, broadly defined as the widening of gaps between the improved and increasing legal rights in law and policies (offered by the central authorities) and the violation of these rights in action (by the local governments). This "structural opening" provides the context for rightful resistance to develop. In addition, social groups' appreciation of the opportunity, as well as their willingness and ability to exploit the gap between law and practice is another important condition for rightful resistance. Because of improved transportation and communication, the penetration of mass media, and many other social and economic changes brought about by economic reform in China, citizens have become more aware of their rights and are prepared to assert and defend them.[22]

The demand for rights in society is rising. Netizens are engaging in online activism,[23] workers are taking to the streets,[24] citizens are organizing themselves through associations,[25] and petitioners have taken the law into their own hands. But there is a widening gap between the supply of legal rights and legal institutions and the demand for them, hence a resulting crisis in the channeling of all grievances into institutional channels. This has created a pressing need for lawyers and their services, and offers opportunities for lawyers and other intermediaries to improve access to justice and to make an effective connection between the world of conflict and the world of conflict resolution.[26]

Against this backdrop, China has witnessed a steady increase in law schools and student admissions, an expansion of legal aid services, and a growth in the number of partnership law firms and lawyers.[27] There has also been an important institutional change: the separation of the legal profession from direct government administration, and thus, the socialization of the profession. In 1996, the Chinese legislature passed the landmark Lawyers' Law, which changed the identity of Chinese lawyers from "state legal workers" on government payroll to private legal service providers.[28]

Critics are correct that lawyers are embedded in the political system, that the government can still control the legal profession as if it were government-owned, and that most lawyers try to maintain close ties with government officials in order to advance their legal careers.[29] At the same time, it is also true that some lawyers treasure their professional independence and have used the opportunity to be critical and challenging of state policies. Before this socialization of the legal profession, lawyers rarely brought cases concerning general public interest to court or attempted to make social changes through litigation. The institutional change provided by the Lawyers' Law creates some preliminary conditions for an independent legal profession based on civil society, and a space in which lawyers can raise policy issues through litigation and challenge the Party/state through law. China's corporatist state is active, and dominant, in shaping and meeting the demand for the rule of law in civil society; and lawyers, either working under the state, with the state, or against the state, are also channeling social problems to law, hence applying the law and challenging the state in this process.[30]

The Development of PIL[31]

The defining characteristic of PIL in China is the use of litigation by lawyers and other rights advocates as a strategy to protect a general interest that is larger than that of an individual case, and to effect policy changes through the legal process. Cases that are litigated thus reflect a general social concern which affects the interests of a wider group of people.

PIL in China is both focused on wider interests and — particularly, although not exclusively — concerned with the social and economic rights of a largely urban and consumer society, that is, the well-being of an emerging middle class. Through representative litigation, lawyers and other intermediaries in PIL focus on certain sets of social and economic problems, aiming at remedies that are politically permissible within China's authoritarian system and legally enforceable by its weak judiciary. Public interest lawyering is moderate in its political stance and typically insists on working within the system.

These ostensibly norm-setting and policy concerns distinguish PIL from legal aid in China, which is concerned primarily with the *individual* suffering of the poor, the powerless, and other vulnerable groups in society. PIL builds on but has elevated itself beyond the legal aid system. What sets public interest lawyers apart from others are the former's willingness and ability to stand out, speak out, and act out in addressing public policy issues through litigation.

On the other hand, however, the political moderation of public interest lawyers distinguishes themselves from their more critical and radical counterparts, who often have more public objectives of changing the political system and are ready to use more extreme measures to achieve them. Radical lawyers are willing to take on politically sensitive cases that the government regards as off-limits, ready to mobilize media and NGOs, and prepared to work with foreign entities. They are less confident in the system, although they demand that the system live up to its rhetoric.

Five trends can be identified in the development of PIL in China in the past decades. The first is its shift from spontaneous action to institutionalization. PIL began as unplanned responses by citizens who individually challenged monopoly enterprises and public authorities in court for their abusive activities and negligence. Many of the first-generation citizen activists, such as Wang Hai (王海)[32] and Qiu Jiandong (邱建东),[33] were themselves parties to a dispute in which they were treated unfairly by their adversaries. Through their suffering, they learnt the law and became experienced in using law and litigation to protect their own rights and the rights of others.

Lawyers entered the field at the same time, but played a less active role at the outset. Noticeably, major players in China's PIL community made their debut around 1995 to 1996.[34] The involvement of lawyers (along with law students and law professors) has led to the professionalization of PIL. Replacing citizen activists, lawyers have become the spokespersons of public interest and dominate the discourse on rights and remedies, pushing towards a more legalistic protection of rights. While lawyers take on essentially similar types of cases, with some exceptions, their approach is more refined and sophisticated when compared to the activists. Since 2000, lawyers and law students have instituted a series of lawsuits against various kinds of discrimination.[35]

Professionalization leads to institutionalization. Based on their training, stronger organizational clout, and specialist identity, lawyers have institutionalized PIL after the promulgation of the Lawyers' Law, and PIL in turn has become a convenient and useful tool which allows them to strategize and become more self-conscious of the efforts they are making and the consequences they wish to bring about. A successful rights practice generates the necessary fame and socio-economic capital for lawyers to institutionalize their practice by setting up their own specialist firms. This in turn creates and reinforces a collective identity among like-minded public interest lawyers, providing a meeting place and platform where they can exchange ideas, share experiences, and provide mutual support. Institutionalized PIL has become more specialized, with public interest lawyers providing specific legal services targeting particular groups in society.

The second trend is from passivity to aggressive defense. PIL in China has become more combative over the years, with few taboo topics. Lawyers are confident that if a matter can be converted into an issue of a legal right or a political argument can be framed in legal terms, then it is politically "doable." If a court accepts a case for litigation, then there is normally no longer any political concern. Such lawyers do not hesitate in applying for judicial review against powerful government departments to protect legal rights.

Procedurally, lawyers are asserting their independence in advancing legal arguments. The time when the government could dictate what lawyers could say in court has long gone. Moving beyond mere application of law, lawyers have challenged the illegality or unconstitutionality of local rules, administrative regulations, and other subsidiary legislation. Moreover, lawyers mobilize constitutional rights to protect individual rights from government or private infringement. In criminal cases where lawyers are most constrained, they routinely launch a not-guilty defense and argue aggressively for their clients even in the most politicized cases, including dissidents' trials.

The third development is from litigation to social networking, creating a support structure for public interest lawyering. Lawyers typically possess good organizing abilities, and once a case is filed in court, lawyers, journalists and other advocates who share the same interest cluster around that case, creating a moment of collective action. Consequently, what otherwise are sporadic, disorganized, and inconsistent voices of criticism become a co-ordinated alliance with well-defined common objectives.

There is a tacit partnership between the media and public interest lawyers.[36] The latter need reporters to publicize the case and their cause, seeking support in the court of public opinion with the hope of channeling this to influence judicial decision-making. Reporters, on the other hand, have a professional interest in getting inside stories and updates on recent developments. The reputation of reporters and the profitability of their organizations depend to a degree on access to news sources — and lawyers can often be reliable and interesting ones.

Public interest lawyers rely on information technology to maintain constant communication with one another. Many maintain a mailing list of reporters and have close relations with journalists from high-ranking newspapers or Xinhua News Agency, especially those who have the privilege of writing internal references.[37] Public interest lawyers also maintain personal blogs for uploading information and maintaining contact with supporters and comrades-in-arms. To handle breaking news, some rely on mobile phone messaging among themselves and their supporters.

The fourth trend is from using law as a shield to protect to a sword to attack. Lawyers conventionally react to government abuses,[38] and most of the public interest lawyers play a largely defensive role, representing people whose rights have been infringed upon or violated by the government and public authorities. Beyond this, lawyers have also started to use the law more proactively and tactically, and to exploit opportunities for legal action. Potential legal claims against the government and powerful groups abound. Activist lawyers can wait for clients passively as they traditionally do — or they can plan ahead, spotting legal opportunities (mostly a problematic government decision) and devising strategies (particularly by identifying a suitable plaintiff) to enhance the possibility of winning and maximizing the impact of a case.

During this shield-to-sword transition, public interest lawyers are taking the initiative in the litigation process, "calling the shots" in determining matters such as who is to speak to the press, when and how; or whether and how to settle with the defendant. In using law as a sword, lawyers have a pre-emptive instrument to prevent the violation of rights, particularly in the fields of labor rights, where workers are developing collective bargaining; religious rights, where religious groups (house churches, for example) retain the in-house services of lawyers or recruit believers with a legal background; and in environmental PIL, in which lawyers resort to courts to prevent possible environmental disasters.

The final trend is the shift from handling cases to advocating policy changes. Lawyers are faithful to the politics of rights and insist that court action can serve as a catalyst for policy change through education, mobilization, and participation. PIL generally produces greater value in political symbolism than in delivering tangible results for litigants.[39] Because of its moderate political objectives and tolerance of the official standpoint, it is most effective in promoting policy and legal changes that advance public interest.[40]

In litigating individual cases, lawyers have in mind legislative and policy reforms where applicable. While lawyers working on the rights of children, women, migrant workers, hepatitis B virus carriers, or issues of environmental pollution are handling their own cases, they also attempt to lobby the legislature, the court and the government for legislative changes whenever an opportunity arises. Moderate public interest lawyers are more successful in promoting policy or law reform because they work on less sensitive policy areas and are regarded as part of the establishment.

The Politics of *Weiquan* Lawyering

Public interest lawyers tend to be court-centric and use litigation as the primary strategy for policy advocacy, although they also realize the limit of court-based action and use the court as a springboard. *Prima facie*, it seems surprising that lawyers and citizen activists have chosen the courts to pursue certain rights within China's authoritarian system, especially where courts are timid and compliant, and the legal culture is said not to be receptive to litigation.

However, China's political and legal environment, in fact, makes litigation the most viable and effective tool in promoting legal changes. The popularity of PIL in China can be explained principally by the lack of alternative political institutions and processes where aggrieved citizens can claim their rights. In China's authoritarian system, political participation and competition for political power is prohibited or even criminalized, and representative institutions, such as local people's congress, while emerging, are intrinsically weak. Dispute resolution through political deliberation and participation is often blocked or simply not available. Courts, in these circumstances, provide an institutional forum to bring social issues to public attention.

Studies have shown that judicialization of politics within authoritarian regimes is a recognized phenomenon,[41] and that authoritarian regimes are known to use courts to resolve disputes, maintain legitimacy, and control local-level bureaucrats. Matters that can be more properly resolved politically in democracies find their way into the courts in authoritarian regimes. As Ellmann pointed out, lawyering and litigation may not be the best vehicle to achieve democratic objectives, and activist lawyers may choose to engage in direct political actions, where the circumstances permit.[42] Public interest lawyers elsewhere — including Hong Kong, Taiwan, South Korea, and South Africa — abandon their litigation strategy to engage in direct political competition and participation once a meaningful political channel is accessible.[43]

There are opportunities for litigation. Access to courts is a right and parties are entitled to bring a defendant to court to answer a complaint. The rhetoric of equality before the law is a powerful tool of political legitimation, in authoritarian regimes in particular. The Chinese state itself had been instrumental in promoting the use of litigation to settle disputes throughout the 1980s and 1990s. With little exaggeration, resorting to the courts to settle disputes was regarded as the symbol of the rule of law in action and a defining characteristic of modern citizenship in modern China.

There are also incentives for litigation. The judicial process is normally well structured and has a relatively higher degree of predictability, transparency, and publicity than the political (e.g., petition) and executive (e.g., agency review) processes. Compared with the latter two, the judicial process is better organized and appears to be more neutral and accountable. There is a higher expectation of fair play: parties know they are all bound by rules of procedure from which they cannot depart without proper justification. Judges in particular are more inclined to follow those rules to maintain legitimacy and credibility. As Hershkoff aptly puts it, "The very act of litigation affords a juridical space in which those who lack formal access to power become visible and find expression."[44]

Litigation is a cost-effective way to advance public interest and effect policy changes.[45] The cost to bring a claim to court is not prohibitive. Similarly, Hershkoff argues that, in the US context, "for marginalized groups, litigation sometimes offers the only, or least expensive, entry into political life at a given time."[46] With a valid claim, a plaintiff could bring the offending policy or practice to court, often without incurring excessive cost. As a result, courts become the meeting place to debate social injustice.

Without the opportunities to participate in political movements in China, lawyers are virtually forced to use the courts as the *only* platform to achieve their objectives. However, legal mobilization in an authoritarian state is intrinsically limited. The court may be relatively effective in delivering justice in ordinary cases and upholding the rule of law in certain areas: consumer protection or anti-discrimination lawsuits, for instance. Courts are, however, fundamentally limited in cases that are ostensibly political, with strong policy implications, or otherwise regarded as "sensitive." The long-held wishful thinking on the part of many public interest lawyers is to build the rule of law and constitutionalism in China without touching, or without touching directly, the core of the political system.

Rights promotion may develop a life of its own. The initial rights action took place at the margin of political power and was congruent to the government's agenda. On issues of certain social and economic interests, the state was more pluralistic and its response may vary depending on the perceived nature of a particular rights advocacy. By and large, claimants of a moderate nature could, through courts or other institutions, achieve some legal and political victories at the early stage of PIL without questioning and challenging the Party/state.

However, legal activism without politics can only carry public interest lawyers so far, and politically compliant lawyers can merely scratch at the surface in a wide range of cases. The law may be more effective in providing protection of rights situated at the margin of authoritarian politics, playing an ameliorative role in an otherwise harsh system, but given its close relations with politics (as the Party/state defines it), it would only be artificial to make a legal argument without touching upon the political power in those cases. Dedicated political lawyers, regardless of the types of rights they try to protect, would sooner or later confront a common, seemingly insurmountable barrier: not being able to advocate effectively without displaying an express agenda for political change.[47]

Lawyers become political, thus challenging, in different ways. Political lawyers have used the courts instrumentally as a forum for free speech. For some, this is a calculated and strategic decision. Discussion of sensitive topics, such as the Falun Gong (法轮功), is off-limits in the Chinese media because of tight political censorship; but court procedures provide a rare opportunity for lawyers and their clients to speak out legally and politically. If courts are the CCP's tools of dictatorship, lawyers are exercising their free speech right in the heart of the Party/state.

Defending the Falun Gong has become the hard core of radical lawyering in China. Lawyers not only rigorously fought for the rights of Falun Gong adherents to practice their religion on the ground of constitutional freedoms of conscience, speech, and religious belief; they moved one step further by praising the Falun Gong in open courts in front of prosecutors and security personnel. As these lawyers recalled, they put to the courts firmly that the Falun Gong not only strengthened human bodies and improved health, but also nurtured the soul and enhanced the nation's moral standard.[48] When Falun Gong lawyers fought hard and left no room for compromise with the system, they truly turned the trial of dissidents into a trial of the system.

Most lawyers are intimidated into silence, but there are a few who are defiant. Those who remain in the business of defending the Falun Gong and dissidents would have developed a thick skin and be immune from routine harassment by the government. They shouted back, banged tables, and reported judges to the authorities, complaining of any court irregularities; some even walked out of the trial in protest. The best weapon for lawyers is the ability to spot errors in the legal process, magnify them, and report offenders to the relevant competent authorities. In a way, lawyers are adopting the strategy of their clients to protect their own right of legal representation through petition — a process with which judges are highly concerned and are eager to avoid, if possible.

Even lawyers who are handling cases in policy areas that are tolerated by the government are no longer scratching at the surface and have started to approach the deeper structure. After bombarding enterprises and the government with discrimination lawsuits for a decade, lawyers and activists have started to plan similar suits against core state organs such as the police and the military, as well as to launch anti-discrimination actions based on ethnicity and religion.

Labor law is also advancing. In addition to bread-and-butter cases on behalf of the poor, some lawyers and activists are moving beyond defending the rights of individual workers and are starting to litigate for a more fundamental policy such as collective bargaining,[49] which would indirectly demand the authority to tolerate more meaningful and independent labor unions at the grassroots level and recognize the legal rights to take industrial action, including strikes.

Ultimately, challengers have the opportunity to face the Party/state directly and lawyers bring politics into the juridical space, upholding the supremacy of the Constitution with a clear agenda to tame the Party through law: the constitutionalism argument that was advanced in courts led to a simple conclusion that the CCP should not be supreme in court. Radical lawyers, through the legal process and a court trial, express their free political speech; humiliate compliant courts; and attack Party policies in a public forum, sending alarm to the CCP that some lawyers have turned against them.

What then is the role of lawyers in the eyes of the CCP? There could be two conceptually different ones. The traditional argument is that lawyers, through PIL, channel disputes to a legal institution through legal processes, so that sensitive and potentially politically explosive issues are isolated into individual cases. The rule of law is in essence a conservative project which serves to depoliticize disputes. Within this conceptual framework, lawyers and litigation deflect political contention, strengthen legal institutions, and help stabilize the existing political order. This is an appealing argument that has been accepted by the government and also the reason why the CCP has tolerated and supported PIL. After all, lawyers are mostly embedded in and support the existing political system.[50]

However, in the eyes of the CCP, circumstances have changed over the past decade. Citizens are now airing their grievances more aggressively to realize their interests, as the law promises. They organize unofficial associations; participate in informal rallies and demonstrations; and take industrial action, including strikes. These forms of resistance represent an emerging movement of civil disobedience and unrest. Citizens are demanding the CCP and government to live up to their commitments; if these fall too short for too long, aggrieved and frustrated citizens may start radicalizing and taking the law into their own hands. The government is well aware of this risk, knowing that serious politically motivated action can lead to politically motivated violence, including riots, property destruction, and killings. Fundamentally, people are more energized and are taking their grievances to the streets and to the court of public opinion, forcing the government to take the law more seriously.

Civil society organizations have grown and expanded, and are active outside government control. Women's groups, AIDS groups, homosexuality groups, anti-discrimination groups, and labor groups are organizing their constituents to promote their causes, with legal rights and lawyers playing a pivotal and instrumental role in the process. Those civil society organizations use information technology to co-ordinate their activities, mobilize support, advance their causes, and work closely with overseas donor agencies.

Alarmed by the social activism on different fronts, the Party retreated to its comfortable conservative zone. After 2003, rights discourse started to diminish and stability discourse came to the fore, and the "rights talk" which was popular in the 1990s was replaced by "harmony talk." The broad concept of the rule of law remains valid but is increasingly interpreted in the framework of socialist legal ideals. The defining characteristic of the current stage is the heightened alert to any sign of unrest and imbalance. While the CCP has prioritized stability in the past thirty years, stability now has a new meaning: it has become an end in itself.

At the same time, the CCP has become confident in its legitimacy and capacity to rule because of the economic success it has achieved so far. It is becoming increasingly impatient with a democratic process (which it regards as chaotic) and the rule of law (which it associates with inefficiency). Governance reform continues and anti-corruption efforts may have been enhanced, but the Party is clearly in charge of and hands-on in managing these changes, crowding out the constitutional process and legal institutions. The CCP has clearly pressed the "rewind" button and is rolling back the legal reform of the past decade. In this context, there is the clear danger that harmony is reduced to conformity and uniformity, while repression and brutality are equated with effectiveness and efficiency.

The concern of the CCP is that through *weiquan* lawyering and rights promotion, lawyers and other activists are mobilizing otherwise isolated victims and aggrieved citizens, drawing them together to pursue a common objective: to challenge the Party. In the particular case of Falun Gong, the perception is that, by legally representing the cult, lawyers may have willingly abandoned their professional identities and taken on a political role as its spokespersons.

The CCP concedes that there is inequality and injustice, and people who have suffered are entitled to legal remedies. But legal mobilization, as rights lawyers have envisaged and are practicing, is too interruptive to the political stability that is essential for the survival of the Party/state. Injustice, as widespread as it is, can only be brought to solution at a pace and according to a method with which the CCP is comfortable. Lawyers cannot be the representatives of the people's interests; only the Party can.

Watching these social forces charging forward, the political system stood firm and then pushed back. It first targeted rights lawyers in Beijing, where such activists cluster,[51] and in doing so, created a repressive environment. As with rights promotion, suppression of rights is also contagious. Such a move by a higher authority narrows the political space for all rights claims, because judges and others lower down the hierarchy pick up cues quickly and respond spontaneously. When Beijing tightened its control over rights lawyers, copycats at the local level followed the lead, and even introduced some add-ons of their own. Legal mobilization is a two-way street: while a successful mobilization in one case makes the next one easier, one instance of legal suppression makes the next one more straightforward as well. Within a repressive context, it is easy to make a repressive decision.

Conclusion

PIL has evolved over the past decade and has become more institutionalized, professionalized, and established in China. The practice is taking root. Lawyers are actively pursuing PIL, and the government encourages or tolerates its existence when the issues do not confront and challenge the legitimacy of the one-party state. From handling issues concerning fake and defective consumer goods, equality rights and non-discrimination, to religious freedom and the right to criticize the government, lawyers have traveled a long way on a tortuous road and continue to search for interesting cases. PIL has the potential to grow and develop further in China, especially in areas that are less politically challenging.

At the very beginning of China's legal development, there were many common grounds between the CCP and social forces, with the former taking the lead in opening up the political system and initiating constitutional changes. Lawyers and activists took moderate steps in correcting market and government failures in politically marginal areas, with the encouragement (or at least tolerance) of the CCP.

Initially, rights that were permitted to grow were narrowly defined civil law rights, starting with consumer rights and followed by the rights of children, women, disabled persons, and migrant workers. The government had been pushing for more legal rights and more effective legal protection of rights, but soon grew suspicious and began to suppress some of the rights advocacy it used to support. Once a legal case becomes a rallying point for otherwise isolated plaintiffs, law becomes a meeting point for aggrieved people, and lawyers become

organizers of social movements. It is then that the government withdraws its support and moves to limit the autonomy of the law and
lawyers. When the initial restriction fails to achieve its objective, the
CCP becomes repressive.

The current pace of political and institutional reform and improvement in China does not match civil society's expectation and demand.
Social and economic change has been so brutally drastic, and social and
economic conflicts so acute and fundamental that they are beyond the
grasp of existing legal norms and the capacities of legal institutions.
Both the people on the supply and demand sides are giving up on law
and resorting to something else outside the established legal process
and institutions altogether.

When public interest lawyers move forward from the periphery to
the core of the system, they risk backlashes. Facing an institutionalized
and aggressive PIL fraternity and its potential for organizing and mobilizing, the government perceives certain political risks that PIL may
bring about. As a result, it has become more antagonistic and repressive, seeing lawyers as leaders of an emerging social force that aims
at transformative politics. The fact that PIL is largely foreign-funded
gives an easy excuse for the government to link PIL in China to hostile
forces outside China, and to second-guess its ulterior motives for a
color revolution in China. In an authoritarian state, the line between
the permitted and the prohibited is blurred and unpredictable, even at
"normal" times. When the regime perceives an existential threat, this
line may vanish and legality may lose its hold on governance.

At this juncture, the Party/state has panicked at the emerging rights
movement and its social and legal mobilization, and the current system
is not able to contain and internalize societal demand. There is much
less room for consensus-building and for agreement between conflicting imperatives. While the regime may not have regarded any particular public interest or political lawyer, or any group of them, as the
vanguard of a new revolutionary force subverting the Party/state, they
are clearly seen as a part of a larger color revolution backed by hostile
international forces, with the potential of organizing broad social and
political mobilization against the regime — hence the current repressive episode.

Chapter 10
Popular Constitutionalism and the Constitutional Meaning of Charter 08

Michael W. Dowdle

Introduction

> When China's first Premier Zhou Enlai (周恩来) was asked in the mid-20th century for his opinion on the historical significance of the 1789 French Revolution, he is said to have replied: "It's too soon to tell." I've started to give the same answer when people ask me about Charter 08.[1]

Rebecca MacKinnon's above observation about the possible constitutional meaning of Charter 08 may well be accurate if one thinks of that meaning as lying exclusively in the degree to which Charter 08 does or does not foretell China's constitutional future. But meanings come in a variety of packages. In this chapter, we will see that Charter 08 may have a constitutional meaning that is not captured by the simple substance of its predictions.

The framework for this exploration will be that of what we will call "popular constitutionalism" — an often overlooked aspect of constitutionalism that is not captured in the form-focused analyses that tend to dominate American and comparative constitutional scholarship. In Part Two, we situate popular constitutionalism within the larger meaning of constitutionalism, before then exploring in Part Three what its particular attributes consist of. Part Four outlines how popular constitutionalism has manifested itself in China's post-Mao constitutional era, identifying in it a distinctive trajectory towards an increasingly juridified discourse. In Part Five, we locate Charter 08 in that trajectory, showing that while — as per MacKinnon — it probably does not resonate insofar as its particular constitutional prescriptions are concerned, it may nevertheless represent an important contribution to China's ability to imagine its constitutional future.

The Regulatory Constitution

A constitution is a collaborative phenomenon, one that arises out of the shared understandings of the polity. This may seem like a trite statement: after all, constitutions are commonly associated with popular empowerment vis-à-vis the state, particularly in the form of democracy. But it is often forgotten that the nature of this collaboration is much more difficult, complex, and nuanced than this term alone is able to capture. Democracy is the product of a constitution, not its progenitor: in a modern polity, it is the constitution that dictates the terms of democracy, and dictation is different from collaboration, at least in any sense of the word that would give constitutionalism meaning as a distinct form of government.[2]

Historically, the true innovation that drove the advent of modern constitutionalism was epistemic, not structural. Modern constitutionalism was borne out of a new understanding that emerged in Europe in the eighteenth century that political morality — questions of what constitutes good and bad, right and wrong, in the context of the state — was a form of knowledge, like rationality, that was understandable by all humans.[3] This was an idea that grew naturally out of the Enlightenment, which was driven by the belief that it was only through reason — a mental capacity that was innate to all humans — that truth, including political moral truths, could be established.[4]

Today, at least in the realm of politics, this presumption is so taken for granted that it is easy to forget just how radical and, more importantly, destabilizing it was in the eighteenth century.[5] For most of European existence, it was believed that only a small portion of the population had innate capacity to understand and evaluate issues of political morality.[6] This presumption was not simply the product of the self-serving justifications of the powerful for their power;[7] it enabled the perpetuation of society. For communities of any size, commands are critical components of social organization. But the question becomes: what gives someone the authority to issue such commands? The idea of democracy does not really help us here, because the particular procedures by which democracy is reified are subject to exactly the same critique: why those processes rather than others?[8]

The most chilling demonstration of the very real destructive implications of this new way of thinking was the French Revolution, and in particular, its collapse into the Terror. France was the epicenter of the Enlightenment and, as documented by Tocqueville, the Terror was in many ways the Enlightenment's ultimate culmination.[9] The Revolution was a direct product of the Enlightenment's demand that political authority should not be the exclusive purview of one class or type of person. But this ultimately ended up meaning that no one could establish the authority necessary to bring the revolution to a close, since no persons could establish why their word should prevail over someone else's simply by virtue of the fact that they were a part of a governmental institution.[10]

The modern notion of the constitution was the solution to this dilemma (one that, tellingly, the French revolutionaries expressly rejected during their descent into Terror). It did this by associating particular social meanings with particular political institutions (both organizations and procedures). For example, a germinal event in the development of modern constitutionalism is found in Edward Coke's characterization of the Crown — i.e., the King — as an abstract institution distinguished by certain responsibilities and roles, and not simply with a specific person.[11] This would later feed into the constitutional theories of Lord Bolingbroke,[12] whose ideas in turn would directly inspire Montesquieu's notion of "separation of powers." Such social meanings are by their very nature more or less universal within the society in which they resonate.[13] In this sense, they enjoy what Charles Collier has termed "intellectual authority" — authority that stems from their appeal to our own personal understanding of the world rather than from their source of origin.[14] Attaching this meaning to an institution bestows the associated authority on that institution, and thus converts that intellectual authority into institutional authority.

A good example of this in the context of present-day Anglo-American constitutionalism is that of rule of law. Law has a complex social meaning within the Anglo-American constitutional system. On the one hand, it refers to a collection of positivist norms whose authority comes from their source of origin — what Collier calls "institutional author-ity,"[15] in contrast to the above-defined "intellectual authority."[16] On the other hand, the law is also seen as expressing a particular view of the good.[17] Modern legal theory has been trying to resolve this conun-drum at least since Hart and Fuller locked horns in 1958.[18] In fact, this contradiction is irresolvable: in order to govern, or govern effectively, modern political-constitutional institutions need *both* intellectual authority — because of our presumptions that the demands of politi-cal morality cannot simply be dictated to us *ad verecundiam* from some outside authority[19] — and institutional authority — because at the end of the day, effective governance requires an ultimate decision-maker.[20]

Constitutionalism does not resolve this conflict — rather, it *regulates* it (in the homeostatic sense of the word)[21] by establishing a shared vocabulary (such as "law") so as to allow these two different episte-mologies to communicate with each other.[22] Perhaps the most influen-tial description of this constitutional-regulatory process at present is found in the legal interpretative models of Ronald Dworkin, who sees legal interpretation as a process of "balancing" "fit" — the positivist component of law — with "justice," its moral component.[23]

But the full range of the process of constitutional regulation is more complex than just this, because in performing such a balancing, con-stitutional regulation allows these separate regulatory components (fit and justice, or form and social meaning) to themselves evolve in response to each other.[24] Numerous studies have shown that our understanding of what constitutes justice, as a social meaning, is itself informed by the constitutional processes that are associated with it: for example, persons living in different constitutional systems have dif-ferent understandings of which procedures are "just" or not,[25] and of what the role of government is.[26] These understandings can change in response to constitutional or legal evolution.[27] In the United States, for example, suffrage was not originally considered a critical element of citizenship, but for practical reasons, it expanded throughout the nine-teenth century, largely spontaneously, as different political factions continually sought to add new social classes sympathetic to their politi-cal interests to the electoral rolls. It was this practical universalization of suffrage that led to the subsequent change in its social meaning, from that of a privilege due to the deserving to that of a right stemming from citizenship.[28]

It is here that the oft-neglected collaborative aspect of constitutional-ism referred to at the beginning of this section is found. Because social meaning is an ultimately spontaneous product of society, it cannot be produced via simple social engineering, by elite or legislative proclama-tion, or by being recorded in a document that someone in authority has chosen to entitle a "Constitution."[29] This is because we cannot choose what we believe; belief — meaning — is something that operates prior to *strategic* intentionality, and hence to strategic *manipulation*, either for good or bad, and either by ourselves or by some political or social elite.[30]

Social Meaning and "Popular Constitutionalism"

It is this social meaning component of constitutionalism that I intend to capture by the term "popular constitutionalism," and it is a critical element of constitutional survival. Constitutions are not simply imple-mented; they must propagate themselves across generations. As each new individual enters the constitutional terrain, she can only bring with her the ideas and understanding about the meaning and impor-tance of that terrain that she acquired earlier through society. In this sense, a particular constitutional structure — written or otherwise — cannot completely control its own meaning. Even where that meaning is grounded in text, that text must be interpreted, and that interpreta-tion can only be done by society itself if the constitution's meaning is to cross generations.

As described above, popular constitutionalism is thus identified by two features. First, it is characterized by the fact that its claims are based on intellectual rather than institutional authority. It does not appeal to law or other forms of institutional authority. It appeals to norms and understandings that are presumed to be innate to the polis, inde-pendent of codification in constitutional text or sanctification by the formal pronouncements of judicial or other political institutions. Note here that the focus is on the epistemology that underlies the claim, not on the source of the claim. Governmental officials and constitutional institutions can participate in popular constitutional discourse, to the extent that they appeal to intellectual sources of authority. At the same time, private individuals can speak to the institutional epistemology of constitutional form, such as when they present arguments founded on positive legal texts and formal institutional pronouncements.

Second, it is also identified by the fact that its terms both shape and *are shaped by* the institutional authority that comprises the formal constitutional system. The dialogue between the popular and formal component of constitutionalism is not unilateral. The possibility of popular constitutionalism is not negated by an observation of popular constitutionalism itself accepting as legitimate institutional arrangements of which it was previously critical. Indeed, since formal authority is as essential to constitutional survival as intellectual authority, some significant degree of institutionalist colonization of popular constitutional discourse is necessary for constitutional survival.

It is also not dependent upon the endorsement or projection of any particular set of symbols or values. We need to remember, in this light, that symbols and named "values" are ultimately just social constructs. As Robert Putnam famously demonstrated in his *Making Democracy Work*, a liberal understanding of the constitutional meaning of "individualism" is more-or-less the same as a republican understanding of the constitutional meaning of "communitarianism."[31] Even in the United States, which many regard as the *sine qua non* of Western constitutionalism, popular constitutionalism has often explored America's constitutional possibilities using symbologies that are non-democratic,[32] anti-legal,[33] and/or anti-liberal.[34]

We might also note that this dialogue need not necessarily be verbal. A classic demonstration of non-verbal articulations of popular constitutionalism was the "London Mob," a form of popular constitutional expression that emerged in England in the later part of the eighteenth century. Mobbing was a distinctive form of popular demonstration that, while threatening, nevertheless evinced a choreography that distinguished it from a simple riot. It was staged as a riot, but in fact featured very little actual violence, and what violence it did display was always against property, not against persons. Ceremony and ritual featured prominently. Acts of mobbing were clearly attached to particular political motives and concerns, most famously, those associated with the Crown's attempted persecution of John Wilkes in the late 1760s and early 1770s, and its efforts to impeach Queen Caroline in 1820. It articulated a consistent set of political and constitutional beliefs that would later become identified with England's working class. The English state acknowledged and frequently acquiesced to the constitutional meanings that this mobbing was being used to advance. In this way, this particular choreography evinced the distinctly dialogic nature of popular constitutionalism.[35]

Popular Constitutionalism in Post-Mao China

Once we know what to look for, we can see that China's present-day constitutional system actually evinces a robust history of popular constitutionalism. Indeed, the present system was itself born out of a popular constitutional moment — one that was triggered by the famous trial of Mao Zedong's wife, Jiang Qing (江青), for her role in the Cultural Revolution.[36]

The Trial of Jiang Qing

The Jiang Qing trial represented an effort by the leadership of the Chinese Communist Party (hereafter "CCP" or "Party") to distance the CCP from the ruinous Cultural Revolution. Jiang Qing was both Mao's wife and a leader of the Cultural Revolution in her own right. Recognizing the disastrous legacy of the Cultural Revolution, the CCP leadership put Jiang Qing and other Cultural Revolutionary leaders on trial for their role in the formation and execution of that ten-year event. These trials were intended to serve two goals: first, through these trials, the CCP sought to establish that the Cultural Revolution was the product of bad individuals within the Party acting on their own accord and not of the Party itself. Second, the CCP leadership also wanted to use these trials to demonstrate the return of "rule of law" to China's political system. Since the Cultural Revolution was notable for its express rejection of law-based governance, it was hoped this would further distance the new CCP leadership from the Cultural Revolution.

The trial of Jiang Qing was, of course, a show trial. Nevertheless, even as a show trial, its effectiveness was dependent on its ability to appeal to social meanings that operate outside of the court's or the Party's control: in this case, those of political responsibility and of the nature of the CCP's political-constitutional identity. For this reason, even though the Party was able to script the verdict of the Jiang Qing trial, it could not script its ultimate social meaning. Because of its symbolic purposes, the trial was televised nationally, and in order to give it some semblance of legitimacy, the judges had to at least let Jiang Qing speak. Jiang argued passionately that she was indeed a leader of the Cultural Revolution, and that in being so, she was clearly acting for the CCP (who had in fact authorized or acknowledged her leadership in numerous fora). Moreover, she was proud of her role in that movement, which she argued was a heroic effort to further the Party's long-stated political mission of transforming Chinese society. To the wider audience of China, Jiang's speech — and the particular social meanings she attached to the events of the Cultural Revolution —. was simply more compelling than that of the Party's prosecutors. True to script, Jiang was found guilty and effectively sentenced to life imprisonment. But the Party was also well aware that while it had won the battle in this regard, it had nevertheless lost the war: it could not deny its own institutional involvement in and responsibility for the Cultural Revolution.[37]

The Tiananmen Demonstrations and "Creeping Parliamentarianism"

Several years later, Peng Zhen (彭真), the leader of China's national parliament — the National People's Congress (NPC) — began promoting arguments very similar to those advanced by Jiang in her trial to advocate the development of a somewhat more autonomous parliamentary and constitutional structure. Like Jiang, he attributed the Cultural Revolution to innate limits in the Party's institutional capacities. He argued that a more autonomous NPC, in particular, could defend against the dangers of these limitations — and this argument was ultimately successful. The NPC began to gain autonomy and to assert the Constitution as a separate source of political authority independent of the Party.[38] With this, China's still fitful and tortuous exploration of what Andrew Nathan would later famously term its "constitutional option" was born.[39]

A significant discourse of popular constitutionalism can also be perceived in the aftermath of the Tiananmen Square demonstrations in the summer of 1989. The state's response to these demonstrations — a severe and, to some extent, still ongoing repression of elements associated with liberal civil society — is often portrayed as a retreat from constitutionalism. But in fact, Tiananmen also appears to have triggered or catalyzed recognizably "constitutional" developments on other institutional fronts. The NPC in particular had shown significant support for the demonstrators. After the suppression of that demonstration and its larger organizational elements, the NPC started taking up several of the principal concerns that larger society had associated sympathetically with that movement — most particularly those associated with corruption and abuse of power (e.g., the recurring delegate skepticism regarding the annual work reports of the Supreme People's Court; the delegate's independent amendment of the Criminal Law to remove a clause that gave absolute immunity to police who used force in the line of duty), political voice (e.g., the development of legislative hearings and delegate responsiveness to constituencies; NPC support for the development and expansion of rural village elections), and the promotion of labor interests (e.g., sustained delegate activism against trade liberalization). The NPC and its delegates enjoyed a surprising level of political autonomy in advancing these issues.[40]

Thus, while the organizational — or formal — aspects of the Tiananmen demonstrations were indeed repressed, some of the popular constitutional meanings established by these demonstrations were in fact able to embed themselves in evolutions in China's constitutional form. Notably, this quickening of parliamentary development was also accompanied by a significant deepening of what we might call China's "constitutional vocabulary." Parliamentary scholars in particular began associating particular parliamentary procedures with particular constitutional doctrines (such as delegate professionalization and public input into legislative drafting with "democracy"). This, in turn, appeared to shape the subsequent evolution of these practices. Delegate assertiveness, traditionally discouraged by the CCP, came to be equated with the parliament's constitutional supremacy, and in turn became increasingly tolerated. Public input into legislative drafting came to be associated with a parliament's distinctive representative function, and it too began developing rapidly.[41] It is also during this time that the vocabulary of rule of law embedded itself into Chinese constitutional discourse, and in particular came to be associated with a distinct juridical practice: that of suing the state through administrative litigation.

Many might dismiss as paradoxical a claim that significant seeds of popular constitutional discourse can be found embedded in China's severe social repressions of the Tiananmen demonstration, but such apparent paradoxes are in fact fairly common. Recall, for example, that the institutionalization of American constitutionalism via the American Constitution of 1787 was itself in many ways a "repressive" response to the democratic self-autonomy demands advanced by Western Massachusetts rebels in Shays' Rebellion of 1786–87.[42] Likewise, the defining intellectual codification of England's constitutional structure — that of A. V. Dicey — was inspired by a desire to counteract what he (and others of the aristocratic classes) regarded as the democratic radicalization of English politics during the eighteenth century.[43] Similar observations have been made about the constitutionalization of India in the 1940s and 1950s,[44] and late-colonial Hong Kong.[45]

We find this paradox counterintuitive because of the strong ideological association that has developed between constitutionalism and democracy, particularly in the United States. But in fact, it is really a logical consequence of the distinctly "regulatory" nature of constitutionalism. Remember that constitutionalism works by balancing institutional authority with social meaning. The establishment of an institutional structure, no matter how "democratic" we call it, is appealing precisely because it offers to constrain the (innately democratic) evolution of social meaning. As was well recognized in the late-eighteenth century in particular — by the Republican Revolutionaries in France,[46] as well as by the Anti-Federalists and "Democratic-Republican Societies" in the early United States[47] — when the idea of modern constitutionalism was still new enough to engender critical and even skeptical analysis even among enlightened and liberal political thinkers, a constitutional form's essential reliance on institutional rather than intellectual authority makes it an inherently repressive structure.[48] For this reason, it is in how this repression is exercised, in the possible presence of an often quiet and subtle discursiveness, and not in the fact of the repression *per se*, that the evolutionary trajectory (or lack thereof) of constitutionalism is actually evinced.[49]

Juridification

In China, the regulatory symbiosis between evolving constitutional structures and evolving popular social meanings of constitutionalism propagated into other social environments during the 1990s. Consider, along these lines, the evolving use during the 1990s of administrative litigation and other forms of "suing the state" — such as industrial dispute litigation. The popularity of such litigation did not seem to derive from calculations of chances of litigatory success. Rather, it appears to have stemmed in significant part from a growing popular feeling that such litigation could be used to promote constitutional meanings, independent of the state's formal handling (or even mishandling) of these cases, in much the same way as happened in the trial of Jiang Qing.[50] It is also interesting to note that through the 1990s and the first half of the 2000s at least, the Chinese state encouraged this dynamic — by actively supporting, for example, the development of legal aid programs that did in some cases facilitated the bringing of certain types of cases (such as industrial labor disputes against state-owned enterprises) that indeed catalyzed popular understandings of the nature of China's constitutionalism.[51]

Another related political forum in which popular constitutionalism began to manifest itself in the later 1990s was that of what we might broadly call the "petitions" (which includes both "petitions" as legally defined and other petition-like expressions, such as what Keith Hand translates as "constitutional proposals"[52]). A dramatic manifestation of this development famously occurred in 2003, when the Sun Zhigang (孙志刚) case triggered an especially visible expression of popular constitutionalism.[53] Sun was a 27-year-old graduate of Wuhan University who lived and worked in Guangzhou after graduation. Being of rural origin, he was mistaken for an "illegal" migrant by the Guangzhou police (rural immigrants need formal permission to reside in urban areas legally) and was taken into custody to be deported — or "repatriated" — to his home village. In fact, Sun was not illegally residing in Guangzhou; he simply had not been carrying evidence of his legal status when he was detained. When he complained of his detention, detention administrators had him severely beaten by other inmates. He eventually died from this assault. News of and sympathy for Sun's plight, and the state's involvement in his tragedy, spread rapidly over the Internet and even in the state controlled print media, and public anger began focusing in part on the constitutionality of the Custody and Repatriation (*shourong qiansong*, 收容遣送) system under which Sun had been detained.

Against this background, a number of lawyers and legal academics in China submitted several petitions (technically "proposals") to the NPC arguing that the Custody and Repatriation system was unconstitutional and needed to be reformed or abolished. Neither the NPC nor any other state institution officially responded to these petitions or their constitutional claims, but within two months of their tender, the state — in the form of the State Council — did in fact abolish the existing Custody and Repatriation regulations, and replace them with a system that did meet formal constitutional requirements and that at least formally alleviated some of the problems revealed by the Sun Zhigang case.

While the government never acknowledged the validity of the constitutional claims advanced by these proposals, the state press nevertheless both reported on and reprinted these proposals, and even celebrated them as important steps in China's constitutional evolution.[54] This, in turn, popularized the significance of petitioning as a means of expressing popular constitutional understandings. The Sun Zhigang petitions spawned a number of other petitions to the NPC, challenging a variety of laws and regulatory practices as being unconstitutional.[55]

The growing popular embrace of litigation and later of petitioning suggests a larger evolution within Chinese popular constitutional discourse over the past decade towards an increasingly juridified discourse — i.e., an increasing framing of popular constitutional discourse using the technical language of the state's own positive law. A particularly telling example of this evolution was the petition challenging the draft Property Law drafted and submitted by Gong Xiantian (巩献田) in 2006.[56] In contrast to other petitions evincing the more traditional legal-liberal perspective, Gong's challenge to the draft Property Law came from a Maoist-Marxist perspective. His leftist use of juridified popular constitutional discourse shows that the appeal of this kind of discourse has become quite broad-based — and is not limited to a particular ideology or political perspective.[57]

History suggests that this evolutionary trend towards juridified discourse could be of particular developmental significance. The emergence of such discourse can portend a marked effectiveness in shaping the evolution of constitutional form over the *longue durée*, even in non-democratic polities.[58] By causing popular constitutionalism to use the language of the state itself — i.e., law — to express popular constitutional meaning, juridification takes advantage of and thereby enhances a constitution's distinct regulatory functionality of linking social meanings (i.e., particular patterns of intellectual authority) to constitutional form (i.e., particular patterns of institutional authority). This suggests that the emergence of a more juridified popular constitutional discourse can and often has triggered long-term developmental trajectories associated with constitutional strengthening.

The Post-2005 Crackdown and the "Double Movement" of Popular Constitutionalism

Since around 2006, however, the Party-state has become increasingly antagonistic to juridified expressions of constitutionalism, particularly in the areas of public interest litigation. Many have read from this an overall retreat on the part of the Chinese state from rule of law and constitutionalism. How does this comport with the narrative developed above? Does it necessarily evince the closing — or disproving — of whatever popular constitutional promise China might have previously seemed to have, as many suggest?

As I have argued elsewhere, the dynamics of constitutional development, in China as everywhere, are too complex to allow for a definite or perhaps even meaningful prediction.[59] The most we can do is to map as best we can the details of possible trajectories. Regime collapse due to lack of regard for the universals of political liberalism is one such possible trajectory.[60] Another is that of a perpetual repression and cruelty inflicted by an all powerful one-party state intent on maintaining its power at any cost.[61] And of course, the Chinese leadership's ongoing crackdown on public interest litigation and constitutional challenge is consistent with both of these possibilities. But are these the only possible trajectories suggested by this suppression?

In thinking about these possibilities, we might first note that since 2003, China's political evolution has taken a decidedly populist turn

— reversing the more technocratic emphasis of Jiang Zemin's (江泽民) tenure.[62] This populism has emphasized using social and popular mobilization — rather than juridification — as the principal motors for policy implementation. We see this particularly prominently, for example, in the "Three Supremes" (三个至上) campaign.[63] Stemming from a speech given by Hu Jintao (胡锦涛) to the National Conference on Political-Legal Work in December of 2007, the "Three Supremes" has been interpreted as directing the courts to "regard as supreme the Party's cause, the people's interest and the Constitution and the laws" in that order — suggesting, in other words, that Party directives and the people's political interests should come before "the Constitution and the laws." In China's political cosmology, the Party has long been associated with populism, even by ordinary people, and Party mobilization has often been seen as an attractive alternative to more technocratic forms of legalist implementation.[64]

Related to this, there has also been a renewed emphasis on what is called the "*Ma Xiwu*" method of adjudication (马锡五审判方式), particularly for rural areas,[65] which emphasizes procedural informality and communal norms rather than formal law. It is applied generally to civil disputes, but is sometimes being used in minor criminal matters as well. Finally, we can also see this movement towards populism reflected in growing Chinese interest in the use of juries and "people's mediation."[66]

As described above, most contemporary comparative constitutional thinking emphasizes formal and legalist sources of authority, and for this reason, China's shift towards populism is commonly regarded as anathematic to constitutionalism. But as we also saw above, a constitution is really a regulatory bridging of both formal and populist epistemologies. In order to think about China's constitutional possibilities within the context of this movement towards populism, we need to examine it also from the perspective of a constitution's generally overlooked populist aspects, rather than simply from its more reflexively familiar, formalist aspects.

We might begin by noting that this shift to populism is not completely without its own justifications. Throughout the 1990s and into the early 2000s, the earlier regime of Jiang Zemin and Zhu Rongji (朱鎔基) had strongly favored legality and juridification as the principal tools of political and social development — but this also coincided with a perception of growing corruption, and with decreasing local responsiveness to the needs of the population, particularly in rural areas.[67] As early as the middle 1990s, NPC delegates — the principal source of political populism in China during the 1990s — started spontaneously censoring the judicial system for their failure to stem corruption, including corruption within the judiciary itself.[68] As the social problems of the modernist transition seemed to multiply, a growing popular nostalgia for pre-modern Maoism began to emerge as an appealing alternative to modernism and modernist legalization.[69] The populist policies of the Hu regime are thus not inconsistent with this larger evolution in China's social constitutional meaning. While they could be, they are not *necessarily* founded simply in naked efforts to re-establish Party-based totalitarianism.

The real question is whether this shift towards populism has had any significant resonance with and impact on evolving social meanings of the Constitution. Recall that constitutional regulation establishes a dialogue between the institutional and the intellectual aspects of constitutionalism. What we need to look for is whether this institutional shift towards populism has triggered corresponding evolutions in the social understandings of the normative meaning or demands of China's constitutional framework. There is evidence that it has.

An example of this is found in Stéphanie Balme's recent sociological studies of rural adjudication in China, particularly as it takes place in People's Tribunals, the lowest courts in China's judicial hierarchy.[70] As with other reports, Balme finds that these Tribunals engage in methods of adjudication that are consistent with the *Ma Xiwu* model described above. However, she also finds that judges are using this model to introduce into their adjudication distinctly constitutional sources of judicial interpretation that would otherwise be locked out of more formal litigatory processes by a judicial rule prohibiting citation to the Constitution in official court opinions. Balme's study suggests that the CCP's populist turn may in fact be opening new doors for the development of popular constitutionalism at the same time as it is trying to close existing ones.

We see a similar "double movement" in the ongoing evolution of Chinese civil society. As noted by long-time academic observer Shawn

Shieh,[71] the recent evolutionary trajectory of civil society in China has been "schizophrenic" — in the sense that "a rapidly developing civil society sector [is] coming head to head with a government that remains ambivalent and conflicted about how to deal with that growth."[72] China's populist turn has corresponded with an explosion in the establishment of what we might call "true" non-governmental organizations (NGOs) — "true" in this context meaning that these NGOs do indeed appear to be operating independently from governmental control.[73] By conservative estimates, China presently has over one million such NGOs, and this number has not been significantly affected by the recent political retrenchment, which has focused primarily on NGOs with foreign contacts.[74] On the one hand, the Chinese state has been working fervently to find ways of regulating the activities of these NGOs. On the other, it has also acknowledged becoming increasingly dependent on these NGOs for the delivery of public services, and indirectly, through this, for its own political legitimacy.[75] In this sense, Chinese NGOs are increasingly occupying what Ronald Burt famously called "structural holes" between state and society,[76] meaning that they provide a unique conduit of communication and connection between these two social spheres.[77] Occupation of a structural hole gives the occupier significant say over the development of social norms that govern the interaction between the spheres it connects[78] — a phenomenon that has been observed in China.[79] In this way, too, China's populist turn seems to be opening up new avenues for popular constitutional discourse at the same time as it is shutting down old ones.

Another example of a constitutionalist "double movement" corresponding to China's recent populist turn is seen in the emergence of a popular-demonstrative mode of political discourse expressed through public demonstration. China's populist turn has been marked by a large increase in public demonstrations.[80] At the same time, the Chinese also appear to be increasingly satisfied with the quality of their lives.[81] One possible explanation for this apparent contradiction is that growth in popular demonstrations is being triggered by raising social expectations rather than by deterioration in quality of life. Surprisingly, given the seemingly authoritarian trends in Chinese governance, a recent study by Yanqi Tong and Shaohua Lei found that:

[T]he Chinese government has tolerated most large-scale mass incidents and rarely applied force. Furthermore, the government has also accommodated close to 30 per cent of the large-scale mass incidents with economic compensation … While the authorities hardly ever admit to wrong doing or offer any apologies, they certainly correct their mistakes. Failed policies would be revoked or changed due to persistent social protests, such as the abolition of agricultural tax and the increase in retirement pension for [State-Owned Enterprises] retirees.[82]

This kind of regulatory response to large-scale public demonstrations in China parallels the English government's response to mobbing in the late eighteenth century, discussed earlier.

A similar double movement can be found taking place on China's Internet, as recently shown in studies by Guobin Yang:

Protest is … increasingly common on the Internet. I recently counted 60 major cases of online activism, ranging from extensive blogging to heavily trafficked forums to petitions, in 2009 and 2010 alone. Yet these protests are reformist, not revolutionary. They are usually local, centering on corrupt government officials and specific injustices against Chinese citizens, and the participants in different movements do not connect with one another, because the government forbids broad-based coalitions for large-scale social movements.[83]

Because of those political limits, protesters express modest and concrete goals rather than demand total change. And the plural nature of Chinese society means that citizens have sometimes conflicting interests, making it difficult to form any overarching oppositional ideology. In other words, the government allows a certain level of local unrest as long as it knows it can keep that activism from spreading.[84]

In each of these examples, we see China's move towards populism generating new pathways for popular constitutional meaning, even as it is closing down others. The emphasis on mediation and *Ma Xiwu* adjudication styles limits lawyer's capacity to promote evolutions in constitutional meaning, but allows rural citizens to do so. The increasing regulation of civil society restricts the scope of NGO participation in constitutional meaning, but increases the legitimacy of that participation. And at the same time that people's ability to propose new constitutional meanings through formal court litigation is being restricted,[85] their ability to promote constitutional meaning through mass demonstration seems to be increasing. In its effort to control popular voices on the Internet, the government has felt compelled to allow the proliferation of moderate popular interpretations, even as it cracks down on more radical or oppositional ones. All in all, this suggests that China's recent repression of more oppositional and litigatory forms of political activism has shifted but not shut down the discourse of China's ongoing constitutional evolution.[86]

To be clear, of course, identifying such double movements in China's recent constitutional evolution does not guarantee a successful constitutional development (however one might want to define success in such a context). As also noted above, this chapter is skeptical regarding our ability to accurately and authoritatively predict China's or anyone else's constitutional future. The best we can do is to look for possible, evolutionary pathways. The double movement described above simply suggests that there are a greater diversity of possibilities in China's constitutional future than are captured by more narrow and common foci on constitutional form alone.

Locating Charter 08 in China's Popular Constitutionalism

Having mapped out the history and trajectory of popular constitutionalism in China, we can now explore what Charter 08 means in this context. We begin by looking at some of the significant features of Charter 08 itself, and then examine how these fit in with the ongoing evolution of China's popular constitutional discourse.

Charter 08 as an Expression of Popular Constitutionalism

Charter 08 was promulgated on 10 December 2008. Its development was led by the prominent literary critic and political activist Liu Xiaobo. A veteran of the Tiananmen Square demonstrations of April and May 1989, Liu served as president of the Independent Chinese PEN Center from 2003 to 2007.[87] In 2004, Reporters Without Borders awarded him the *Fondation de France* prize for his efforts to promote press freedom in China.

Charter 08 is a political manifesto published on the sixtieth anniversary of the Universal Declaration of Human Rights. Both its name and its style were adapted from the famous Charta 77, a political manifesto issued in 1977 by a number of prominent Czech dissidents (including the internationally renowned Czech writer and future Nobel Peace Prize winner Václav Havel) that called on the then-authoritarian, Soviet-controlled Czech government to honor its stated constitutional and international treaty commitments — as a signatory to the Helsinki Accords, the International Covenant on Civil and Political Rights, and other international human rights instruments — to respect and protect the civil and political rights of its citizens.

Charter 08 is an expression of popular constitutionalism. It argued, *inter alia*, that the present constitutional system — i.e., the CCP's Party-state — had lost all legitimacy, and called for the drafting and implementation of a new constitution featuring multi-party elections, judicial review, and other structural features associated with liberal, or at least American, constitutionalism. In doing so, it appealed to popular understandings of constitutional meaning, not to the formal structure of the constitutional-legal system. In fact, it eschewed legalism and juridical argument, perhaps because Liu, like many other more ideologically oriented critic-activists in China, felt that by appealing to the state's existing norms, he would indirectly be legitimating the very system he was trying to end.[88]

To say that Charter 08 is an articulation of popular constitutionalism, however, is not to mean that it is necessarily one that reflects the understanding of the larger polity. Recall that popular constitutionalism describes a particular kind of political epistemology, not a particular ideology. Along these lines, to many, the degree to which Charter 08 resonates with the popular constitutional attitudes of the larger polity appears to be slight.[89] Of course, Chinese censorship and political oppression may have something to do with this, but this is not likely to be the whole, or even principal, explanation. For example, overseas Chinese websites and bulletin boards that are not censored by the Chinese government show little significant support for Charter 08 *as an articulation of constitutional principle* — even while many do support it as a public demonstration of popular constitutionalism *per se*.[90]

This lack of resonance may well have to do with the fact that the discourse of Charter 08 actually works against the larger popular constitutional trajectory towards increasingly juridified constitutional expression, as discussed above. Consider, along these lines, the analysis offered by Rebecca MacKinnon, Bernard L. Schwartz Senior Fellow at the New America Foundation in Washington, DC:

> Even among people who agreed with most or all of the Charter's content, many said they felt its impact would be limited because it has no practical component. As one 20-something person who works in publishing put it: "It's performance art. There is no practical strategy for how its goals can be achieved." ...
>
> Many felt that the first step is to build platforms that enable the Chinese people to engage in an informed discourse about their future so that concrete solutions and strategies for getting from A to B — or perhaps to some other Point C — can eventually emerge. The Internet is already facilitating a great deal of discourse, despite all the censorship, propaganda, nationalism, manipulation, and cyber-mob behavior. A more constructive discourse would be possible, many argue, if a law could be passed upholding the right of journalists to do their jobs. Thus some people are focusing on building professionalism and improving the quality of Chinese journalism, and trying to push for more media freedoms. Another step, which I heard from many people, was the need to build a stronger sense of citizenship throughout Chinese society: people need to take responsibility for the problems they see around them, and get in the habit of doing what they can to help improve whatever is in their power to improve, however small. Not to change the whole country right away, but to make small changes in their own communities. Efforts by Zhang Shihe aka "Tiger Temple" to raise money to help petitioners and vagrants in Beijing is one small example. Another better known example is the spontaneous relief effort that rose up around the Sichuan earthquake. Finally, there is the heroic work being done by China's growing group of rights-defense lawyers such as Xu Zhiyong [许志永], Teng Biao [滕彪], and Liu Xiaoyuan [刘晓源] who are doing what they can to educate the public about the rights they are already supposed to have under China's existing laws and constitution, and who are trying to advocate for the upholding of those rights.[91]

Liu Xiaobo as Thomas Paine: Towards a Popular Constitutional Meaning of Charter 08

Above, we noted that despite its possible failure to capture or articulate the political understandings of China's larger polity, Charter 08 must still be recognized as an act of popular constitutionalism. Popular constitutionalism describes a particular kind of political epistemology, not a particular ideology; it describes participation in a particular kind of discourse, not capacity to control the outcome of that discourse. Along these lines, we might note that both Charter 08 and Liu Xiaobo have received a good deal of support from among even those ordinary Chinese who disagree with the Charter's ideas. In evaluating the constitutional meaning of Charter 08, we have to look beyond the mere impact of its prescriptions.

Along these lines, there is a telling parallel between the constitutional meaning of Liu Xiaobo and Charter 08 in present-day China and that which Thomas Paine and his *The Rights of Man*[92] had for England's constitutional evolution during its early-industrial era (c. 1770–1830). There are significant similarities between China's present-day experiences with a possible popular constitutionalism and those of England some two centuries ago. Like China's today, England's early-industrial constitutional transformation proceeded out of a well-developed authoritarian institutional structure; it was gradualist and reformist rather than revolutionary; and it was a transformation that was triggered to considerable extent by changes in economic and industrial organization, and by rapid development in information technologies (namely rapid advances in printing press technology and a steep decline in the price of paper).[93] It witnessed an explosion of civil society (working-class) organization, which often expressed their constitutional understanding through the symbolic speech of popular movement (such as mobbing)[94] rather than through the more articulate formalisms of judicial endorsement.

It is in this English constitutional experience, rather than that of the United States, that the real possibilities of popular constitutionalism are best identified. In fact, it was in the context of this constitutional transformation that the term "popular constitutionalism" first appears in the English language.[95] There was no new constitutional text associated with this transformation, and the overall constitutional structure remained secure. What changed was the social meaning of the "constitution." Within a generation, the English constitution went from being Blackstone's "noble pile"[96] of elite political arcania into being a public vocabulary for the expression of political understandings and legitimacies.[97] This transition ultimately paved the way for the democratization of England's traditionally oligarchical Parliament and its ultimate transition to a democratic, "constitutional" monarchy in the later part of the nineteenth century.[98]

It was also a transformation that would take several generations to realize, one that traversed several waves of governmental resistance and oppression interspaced between periods of relative political accommodation. Along these lines, it was also a transformation which was criticized from within precisely for being reformist rather than revolutionary, and thus acquiescing to contemporary constitutional illegitimacies rather than confronting them directly.[99]

More than anywhere else, the confrontation between reform and revolt was crystallized by Thomas Paine in the publication of his peerless *The Rights of Man*. An insuppressible advocate for the Englishman's revolutionary option, Paine argued with inimitable passion, wit, and force that England's "ancient constitution" was not a constitution worthy of the name; that the English royalty and English aristocracy were tyrannical usurpers, plain and simple; and that reason and not tradition was the only source of political legitimacy in England. By some accounts, Paine's *The Rights of Man* was the most widely read publication in English history. Within a year of its initial publication, some 280,000 copies had been distributed in England, despite the fact that printing or distributing *The Rights of Man* was a crime punishable by fourteen years transportation to Australia.[100] It was an important catalyst for the explosion in English civic organization, spawning the formation of innumerable secret "corresponding societies" which sustained the radical movement during its infant years.[101]

But in the end, the English radical movement failed to pursue Paine's revolutionary option. Its turning point came in the trial for sedition of that movement's intellectual leader, Joseph Gerrard, in 1794. In his self-conducted defense, Gerrard — after much deliberation with radical colleagues — chose to associate the radical movement with a reformist rather than a revolutionary platform. He was nevertheless convicted, as he knew he would be, but his impassioned and elegant trial defense, particularly in the face of a clearly biased and hostile judge, captured popular imagination. In the end, it would be Gerrard, not Paine, who would identify the course of England's constitutional transformation.[102]

So, in the end, just as might be the case with Liu Xiaobo and Charter 08, Thomas Paine's revolutionary vision of English constitutionalism simply did not resonate with the evolving trajectory of English popular constitutional imagination. But that did not diminish his profound importance. In order to pursue a reformist trajectory of constitutional transformation, the English polity had to choose to pursue such a trajectory — and more than anyone else, it was Paine and *The Rights of Man* who made the choice between radical revolution and radical reform visible to England's emerging working-class polity. Without Paine, Gerrard's particular choice of defense would not have had the meaning and the appeal that it did, particularly insofar as the more conservative classes were concerned, because it could not have been framed against an alternative.[103] It seems a very real possibility that without Paine, the emergence of England's new popular constitutional consciousness during the 1790s would have been stillborn: consciousness is symbiotic on the awareness of choice; and it was Paine who ultimately brought this awareness into being.

And, it is proposed, herein lies the constitutional meaning of Liu Xiaobo and Charter 08 as well. Like that of Paine in the context of late-eighteenth century England, Liu and Charter 08's distinctly revolutionary vision of China's constitutional future and constitutional possibilities may not resonate with the evolving strands of popular constitutionalism they had sought to affect. But also like Paine, Liu and Charter 08 may well have catalyzed among the Chinese polity a much more concerted mapping of the choice between reform and revolution, a mapping that had previously operated primarily in the fringes of China's popular constitutional imagination. As noted by Rebecca MacKinnon:

> It has not been possible for the Chinese people to debate China's political future fully and openly.... Still, debates are happening. In spite of censorship, many people have managed to find their way to the document and many have managed to blog about why they

did or didn't sign Charter 08. Xujun Eberlein has a good summary of the wide gamut of opinions about the Charter that can be found around the Chinese-language internet. Even some people who agreed with the charter and were brave enough to sign it some-times felt the need to qualify their support.[104]

The above-mentioned Xujun Eberlein writes:

> On nearly every website I visited that discusses Charter 08, in English or Chinese, there are not only voices advocating and opposing, but also supporters raising constructive criticism and contenders issuing moral support (plus the usual white noises and meaningless vituperates). The issues that are at the center of argument include — by no means an exhaustive list — whether the ideas are too "Western," or the proposed democracy model suits China; whether the proposal for a "Federal Republic of China" makes sense, or it has gone too far; whether the wording in the Foreword is needlessly inflammatory; whether Taiwan's democ-racy is a good model for the mainland; whether the aim of the Charter is to agitate the government or have a practical impact.... If nothing else, "Charter 08" has stimulated a great discussion on China's future direction.[105]

No matter what direction China's popular constitutional evolution ultimately takes, the conceptual mapping of its possible trajectories triggered by Charter 08 is likely to be critical for propelling a meaning-ful movement into China's constitutional future.

Conclusion

Thomas Paine would become the defining figure of England's early industrial constitutional transformation, and The Rights of Man would become its defining literary expression, not because they made the critical choice of that transformation, but because they helped the English polity understand what the full range of their constitutional choices were. This could well be the ultimate constitutional legacy of Liu Xiaobo and Charter 08, as well. This is no mean accomplishment: in the incredibly complex and ultimately spontaneous world of consti-tutional regulation, this is really all anyone can ever really hope to do.

Chapter 11
Charter 08 and Violent Resistance

The Dark Side of the Chinese Weiquan *Movement*

Eva Pils*

Introduction

If, fantastically, an opinion poll on "Do you support Charter 08?" could be conducted in China today, its results would have to be read bearing in mind that you cannot look up "Charter 08" on the domestic Internet, and that any expression of support for it may result in state persecution. Attempts to measure the impact of or support for the Charter would therefore be inherently limited,[1] even though naturally, we will continue to ask ourselves how strong such support is.[2] Charter 08's significance lies not in its measurable impact or support but in its proposition of a peaceful kind of political change, a proposition that represents but one group within an increasingly diverse opposition to the current government. Charter 08 supporters face not only government repression, but also opposition from those who do not approve of its supporters' apparent advocacy of non-violence.

This chapter seeks to understand the perspective of those represented by the Charter, as well as some of the perspectives of those within the wider Chinese rights defense movement who do not consider themselves represented by it. It draws on a distinction often used by rights defenders themselves, namely that between "grassroots" and "elite" rights defense or *weiquan* (维权); but also urges recognition of the fact that an analysis of attitudes, ideals and social practices among rights

* Many thanks to Deborah Davis, Michael Dowdle, Fu Hualing, Swati Jhaveri, and Josh Rosenzweig for their comments.

defenders shows these groups to be mingling and interacting, rather than rigidly separate.[3] It is argued here that the Charter attempts to pose an enlightened alternative to the popular political opposition's and *weiquan* movement's darker sides, because its agenda is non-violent and non-vindictive. Its proposals are premised on values germane to a practice of adequate rights protection, but increasingly at risk of being sacrificed to public anger and destructiveness in China's volatile society, in which "rights defense" is not infrequently combined with support for strategies and policies inimical to the very idea of rights.

Like the distinction between "grassroots" and "elite," so too is the imagery of light and shadow used here complex and unstable — for the "darkness" attributed to parts of the "grassroots" movement contrasts starkly with the light, warmth, and transparency people in this movement apparently desire: "Sunshine Charity" (*Yangguang Gongyi*, 阳光公益) as the name of one of those "grassroots" groups may serve as a good illustration. The darkness in which much of *weiquan* is situated, on the other hand, is in many ways due to especially vicious state repression, and also affects "professional" or "elite" *weiquan*, in particular human rights lawyers.

In the following pages, I first explain the stagnation of constitutional change (or reform) as a result of the inherent contradictions within the current constitutional setup, the *weiquan* movement's early successes, and its current repression. Then I turn to examining attitudes of heightened enmity and vindictiveness among the grassroots *weiquan* movement. These can be understood as a consequence of repression, yet they also complement and enable some government practices of repression. Lastly I discuss how public figures in the *weiquan* movement, including some of the Charter's prominent signatories, view Chinese society's prospects for change, focusing not on views about the end goal, captured in the Charter itself, but on views about the way to get there.

Weiquan and Constitutionalism

Human rights lawyer and scholar Teng Biao (滕彪) once related how an older liberal exclaimed over why earlier generations of dissidents had not thought to use the law to challenge the state, the way "rights-defending" lawyers and activists do today. Teng's answer at the time was to point out that it was because *weiquan* only became possible after the legal system had developed sufficiently.[4] His account serves well to illustrate the changes the *weiquan* movement has brought to Chinese society. In the early 1980s, *weiquan* was not yet a popular concept or practice. Today, it is a popular, as well as a contested idea. For some, *weiquan* is now less a term indicating the use of "authoritatively" condoned rules and rights that can be found in many laws and regulations of the People's Republic of China (PRC),[5] and more a term indicating principled, rights-based opposition to the government, whether or not the government has "authoritatively" endorsed a particular right or principle.

If we look merely to the text of the PRC Constitution, we already see a document riven by complexity and contradiction. The PRC Constitution claims to uphold both supremacy of the law and supremacy of the Chinese Communist Party (Party). It seems to give liberties, and then take them away again. Because of these contradictory assertions, it was never a convenient document for constitutionalists — scholars, lawyers, public intellectuals, etc. — to work with. Compared to constitutions more unambiguously committed to protecting the freedom of speech, for instance, an analysis of its guarantee in the PRC Constitution will have to address the fact that it requires its citizens to "safeguard the security, honour and interests of the motherland" (Article 54, PRC Constitution).[6]

But constitutional text is not the greatest obstacle to constitutional rights protection. Institutional and political realities have further reduced the role of the Constitution because, as is well known, there is very little institutional space for challenging state conduct of any kind on the grounds that it violated the Constitution.[7] Some scholars have asserted that, therefore, the Constitution in a certain sense has no value. Donald Clarke has characterized the Constitution as in some ways an insignificant document.[8] Ling Bing (凌兵), commenting on Liu Xiaobo's conviction, argued that since the PRC "Constitution" — the text entitled "PRC Constitution" — was obviously not the real Constitution of China, it was simply wrong to assume that Chinese citizens did enjoy the freedoms the text entitled "Constitution" purported to guarantee.[9] Similarly, while the PRC's international law obligations to protect human rights are abstractly recognized,[10] officials of the Chinese legal system often pay no more attention to international law than to constitutional norms.

Chinese human rights lawyers have been forced to deal with the resulting institutional intransigence to rights-based arguments for years. They have again and again submitted criminal defense statements, petitions, suggestion letters, and public appeals referring to the Chinese people's constitutional and international-treaty-based rights.[11] Again and again they have failed to elicit even a response to these arguments from the authorities or — it is suspected — improve the lot of their clients by raising them, even though the presence of a lawyer has surely helped in other respects.

Yet, civil rights movements the world over have drawn force and momentum from much more than constitutional or international treaty texts and cases fought in courts of law. Even in jurisdictions in which constitutional arguments can enter the judicial process, the spirit of constitutionalism has always been to transcend and challenge constitutional text and insist on underlying moral values that give force and life to the written words, rather than the purported authority of constitutional text. In the United States, for instance, this has engendered a long and passionate debate on the justifications for and the point of civil disobedience. The Civil Rights movement relied on the US Constitution, of course; but its success was due in part to campaigns of civil disobedience that violated the "law" understood narrowly.[12] In Germany, to give another example, the Basic Law contains a provision recognizing the right of "everyone to resist anyone seeking to subvert the constitutional order." It thus tries to ensure, by "authoritatively" stating it, that no "authority" should be obeyed unless it commits to the values that Constitution articulates.[13] Both these examples point to the conclusion that, ultimately, constitutionalism must be understood as a moral political principle. It can be postulated, especially where constitutional rights are imperfectly protected, as a way of proposing political reform.

Many Chinese rights defenders are increasingly acting on this understanding. Aware that courtrooms are unlikely to accommodate their complaints and demands for better rights protection, they have gradually become more politically articulate. From petitions to change the custody and repatriation (*shourong qiansong*, 收容遣送)[14] and the *hukou* (户口, household registration) system[15] to public calls for China to ratify the International Covenant on Civil and Political Rights (ICCPR),[16] it is only a short though an important step to suggest the redrafting of a Constitution, as Charter 08 and other appeals before it have done.

As it has become more contested and acquired more edge, *weiquan* has also become an officially disapproved of activity in many contexts, and a censored term on the Chinese Internet. While they are wary of directly attacking the idea of rights, some in the judicial leadership, for instance, have criticized human rights defense as unduly focusing on individual problem cases and "politicizing them."[17] The forces of order represented by the Public Security Ministry, in turn, have suggested that *weiquan* activities by themselves pose a problem to the maintenance of stability (*weiwen*, 维稳).[18] It seems therefore fair to say that in recent years, the climate for actual rights-defending has got harsher, even as the ideas of rights-defending and human rights have become "vernacularized."[19] These changes are not accidental; they are due, in part, to the early successes of the rights defense movement, to the government's perceived need to suppress it with increasing viciousness, and to the deeply conflicting principles in China's constitutional and political framework.

In contrast to other jurisdictions, the Chinese state has not responded to such challenges reasonably, and instead treated them in several instances as potentially subversive.[20] It has persecuted not only dissidents, but also human rights lawyers and non-professional human rights defenders, as well as petitioners in their own causes. Human rights lawyers have suffered persecution with superficially "legal" and illegal means. A 2010 documentary about the fate of two lawyers who were disbarred ends with a brief summary of incidents of persecution of thirty-seven named human rights lawyers, in cases ranging from disbarment to imprisonment for subversion and other crimes, and torture.[21] The majority of the incidents mentioned occurred in the past two years. A wave of enforced disappearances and other measures affecting human rights lawyers and other human rights defenders between November 2010 and May 2011 indicated a worsening trend.[22]

The techniques of surveillance and control the state employs against *weiquan* lawyers and other rights defenders have made it necessary for them to study these techniques and find ways of evading them. Lawyers' daily lives are punctuated by encounters with the prying, interfering, and threatening police state. They are always conscious of the possibility (and sometimes likelihood) of being detained, abducted, or arrested. Petitioners and members of grassroots organizations have been driven even more deeply into a complex underground, as illustrated by reports from human rights organizations that the number of incidents in which citizens are illegally detained each year in black jails in Beijing alone is as high as ten thousand.[23] It is such illegal conduct on the part of the state that leads to *weiquan* groups adopting some of the forms and methods of criminal gangs, only it seems that they are gangs fighting for the rule of law against "law enforcement" authorities opposing it: that, at least, is the perspective many rights defenders have on *weiquan*, an expression that could also translate into "defense of power." The following sections discuss how difficult prolonged harassment makes it for grassroots *weiquan* groups to maintain a focus on genuine rights defense.

"If You Don't Give Me an Explanation, I'll Give You One": *Weiquan* and Violence

As was shown above, popular efforts to engage in *weiquan* cannot, firstly, be characterized as a civil rights movement in the sense familiar in Western countries, because the political-legal system in China does not provide the institutional channels needed for a civil rights movement. Nor, secondly, do they constitute a full-blown resistance movement, because they lack — and indeed generally try to avoid taking on — the forms and features of visibly organized resistance, out of fear of repression. These conditions shape contemporary grassroots rights defense, and in part explain what is described as its "dark" sides.

There are important commonalities and interaction between "grassroots" and more professional rights defense. Anecdotal evidence from conversations with petitioners suggests that many among the grassroots rights defenders and petitioners attribute their plight to the lack of rule of law and democracy, to which they often refer on their banners and "complaint garments" (*zhuangyi*, 状衣),[24] as well as in their shouted slogans[25] and open letters.[26] For petitioners, prolonged engagement in their own case will often lead to reflection on and discussion about the system that allows these cases to remain unaddressed. Thus, petitioners who have come to Beijing have increasingly organized themselves collectively and articulated more general political demands: by declaring solidarity with human rights lawyers;[27] by protesting injustice; by demanding better protection of the right to free speech, rule of law, and democratic reforms.

Like human rights lawyers, so too do petitioners suffer the consequences of prolonged life in the shadows of government repression; only it appears that the repressive measures they suffer involve more casual everyday violence than that borne by more established or "elite" lawyers and dissidents. Petitioners who have become the target of surveillance and repression live in fear and isolation from their original lives, be it in the provinces or in the capital, as it becomes difficult for them to return to these lives without risk to them or their relatives. In the places where they petition, many of them endure delays, detentions, threats, and verbal and physical abuses affecting themselves or people in their new environment (e.g. the "petitioning villages").[28] Detentions include "legal" forms such as administrative punishment and re-education through labor,[29] as well as extralegal forms such as black prisons[30] and psychiatric hospitals.[31]

The minds of some rights defenders and petitioners exposed to these measures become gradually closed to the possibility of peaceful and reasonable conflict resolution and attracted to illiberal political views; more easily so, it seems, than human rights lawyers, whose professional experience, and commitment to human rights defense on behalf of others may contribute to making them skeptical of violent resistance. Take, for example, those involved in land and housing disputes, such as are often the cause of petitioning. Thousands of such increasingly well-documented eviction processes in recent years have illustrated the variety of forms of protest and resistance by evictees. Their methods include the "illegal" display of slogans challenging the lawfulness of the eviction, refusing to move from their land or buildings, and physical confrontation with eviction teams. The use of violence in such disputes is common. Eviction teams use it to intimidate and remove evictees before any clashes can develop, and evictees engage in violence against themselves to protest, for instance, by self-immolation.[32] Some petitioners and grassroots rights defenders are thus driven into attitudes of anger and despair that make the promise of legality and constitutional values seem increasingly remote to them, even if their calls for rule of law remain sincere.

There is a growing number of informal groups established by grass-roots rights defenders for the purpose of helping other rights defenders and petitioners, even though many such groups are transient, always threatened by clampdowns. In 2009, for example, a group calling itself the "League of Chinese Victims [of Injustice]" (LCV) or "Chinese League of Yuanmin" (中国冤民大同盟) was founded. On its website, it describes itself as "a civil society initiative in Mainland China for the protection of fundamental lawful rights and interests," and that it "consists mainly of China's disenfranchised, dispossessed and under-privileged."[33] LCV tried, among other things, to bring cases against allegedly corrupt Shanghai government officials before courts of law in other countries.[34] Its actions, however, immediately brought trouble for its members, who were subjected to questionings, surveillance and threats.[35]

Another group is Sunshine Charity, or *Yangguang Gongyi*. In the fall of 2009, its Beijing protagonist and chief organizer and a few other founders obtained a "non-profit limited liability" company registration for the group.[36] From that time onward until about February 2010, they set up a system of volunteers who distributed food, clothes, and blankets to petitioners in Beijing, providing not just daily essentials but also psychological support to these people in need, and at the same time, in a very limited way, advertising their activities on websites and appealing for further volunteers to join their actions.[37] Again, it did not take long for the authorities to begin to pay attention to the group. According to author interviews with current and former members of the group, persecution took many different forms: from being told to discontinue their activities; to being "invited to tea" and threatened; to being abducted; taken back to their hometowns, and forced to write "guarantee letters" promising to discontinue their actions.[38] Even the group's modest efforts to distribute food were thwarted: unidentified individuals reportedly stole the small tricycle that was used to transport steamed buns and similar food items to the petitioners, and repeatedly damaged the wheels of the motorized wheelchair belonging to the disabled main organizer.

Sunshine Charity's main organizer related that between January and May 2010, he was detained three times, twice by the police and once by unidentified thugs who assaulted him in the street, dragged him away, kept him blindfolded for several days, and "warned" him to discontinue his activism before eventually releasing him in one of Beijing's rural counties. After this release in late April 2010, he remained largely under house arrest, allowed to leave home only on some occasions.[39] His partner reported receiving several "visits" from the police at her home as well as death threats by telephone; she barely escaped an attempt to detain her, by breaking loose from the persons who were holding her and barricading herself in her own flat in a residential complex on the outskirts of Beijing.[40] When the authorities were challenged to explain why Sunshine Charity was put under so much pressure, some of the group's members were reportedly told that "the objects of your charity [i.e. the petitioners] aren't the right ones."[41] Under pressure from the authorities and their thug helpers, the group has now been all but disbanded.

Experiences of intimidation, violence, and terror such as those described above discourage victims and witnesses from placing any further hopes in the legal system. Victims' attitudes are also affected by the fact that abductors and tormentors, while deporting themselves like thugs, declare themselves to be part of the government or dispatched by the government, even though they do not specify which department, according to reports by group members.[42] Because of the methods employed by the police and other persons entrusted with *weiwen*, the state takes on a rather thug-like appearance for organizers of rights defense activities, however complex or tenuous the actual connection between the thugs in question and public security authorities may be. They come to see themselves in a relationship of fundamental hostility with the public security forces and forces of "stability preservation."[43]

> Let us learn from Model Yang Jia (杨佳)!
> Who feared no evil, who refused to acknowledge the Party,
> Who forgot neither love nor hatred,
> Who killed the policemen with a butcher's knife,
> Who killed the policemen with a butcher's knife.[44]

This is the first verse of a song celebrating Yang Jia, a jobless young man turned petitioner who in July 2008 stabbed six Shanghai police officers to death, in an apparent act of revenge after the police and other authorities had treated him and his mother in what he thought was a highly unfair way. He was swiftly tried and executed in a flawed criminal justice process.[45] To the police who asked him why he had committed the killings, Yang had reportedly said, "If you don't give me an explanation, I'll give you one."[46] This phrase became instantly famous among rights defenders, who passed it on and commented on it via the Internet.

In a 2010 online "leak" of what was purported to be a transcript of a police interrogation of Yang Jia shortly after the brutal killings, Yang reportedly also said this:

> I have always been a simple person, but you have twice framed me and made me end up in this police station, and for no other purpose one can think of than getting at my money. If even a person like me can't escape misfortune at your hands, what kind of person can? Today your evil government has no scruples to extort the people, because it so badly needs money; it needs a lot of money to feed a lot of you dog-like, slavish officials. You call this "preserving stability"? Sooner or later there will come a day when the Chinese people will finish you monsters[47] — a clean killing of all of you.[48]

Whether or not Yang Jia actually spoke these words is in a sense less significant than the great popular fascination to which it testifies. No one talking to petitioners and grassroots activists could be mistaken about the appeal of Yang Jia's legend to some of them. He is both a victim and a hero, personifying a daring many who feel they share his desperation do not have. His story speaks to the disillusionment and despair of many petitioners and grassroots rights defenders. It has also attracted much comment and controversy from intellectuals, as is discussed below. Its significance has been further deepened, and the truth of what happened to him been recorded so far as possible, in the famous artist Ai Weiwei's (艾未未) documentary film, *A Lonely Person* (*Yige Gupi de Ren*, 一个孤僻的人).[49]

Moreover Yang Jia's story keeps being re-enacted. In June 2010, when a person in the provincial city of Yongzhou (永州) went on a shooting rampage in a courtroom, killing four judges of the court and then himself, petitioners immediately converged upon the court building and feted him as someone who had dared to stand up to the authorities.[50]

In sum, grassroots *weiquan* is prone to vindictiveness, and those who engage in it live in some degree of fear due to the at-times intense repression they suffer. Grassroots activism thus has a tendency to helpless, self-destructive violence; it often lives in darkness, in large measure produced by state persecution and oppression. Yet despite the aspirations of Sunshine Charity and other groups to overcome it, many attitudes and methods adopted by them only serve to perpetuate the existing, fundamentally violent relationship between *weiquan* and the state, as I shall further argue.

Logics of Punishment and Revenge at Government and Grassroots Levels

If authoritarian governments believe that they need to suppress dissidence in order to maintain their existence, they do not — and cannot — require the criminal process to demonstrate the correctness of this perception. What convictions like those of Liu Xiaobo indicate, instead, is that the authoritarian system of governance creates its own instability concerns by making hypothetical predictions: if we had not locked him up, Liu Xiaobo would have gone on to do worse things. If we had not scared others by punishing him, Charter 08 would have become a more widely distributed document and more people would have signed it; this, ultimately, would have resulted in harm or "social instability." The pithy reasoning of Liu Xiaobo's verdict and nigh impossibility of successful defenses against subversion charges discussed in Rosenzweig and Mo's contributions to this volume[51] illustrate that the hypothetical logic at play here is virtually closed to critical challenges.

This kind of reasoning is also why picking Liu Xiaobo out of a potential group of persons involved in the launch of Charter 08 seemed somewhat arbitrary to some observers: while Liu was an extremely prominent critic and important supporter, others, it was observed at the time, had made no less a contribution to the drafting of the Charter. But then, from the stability-obsessed perspective of the state, the question whether Liu was "the most guilty person" and therefore the right person to single out for harsh punishment would not be an important or even sensible question to ask. The circumstances suggest that he was not strictly speaking punished for something he did but rather became an instrument of political (social) stability maintenance, of vindictive symbolism on the part of the state. For not only did his conduct harm no one in the sense of the liberal harm principle, and was Charter 08 merely the expression of political ideas and demands — not only did punishing Liu Xiaobo amount to rejecting any possible liberal justification of criminal punishment.[52] As has been argued more widely for criminal trials in China, Liu Xiaobo's trial was also conducted on an effective presumption of guilt.[53]

To the extent that a presumption of guilt reigns also in ordinary criminal justice processes, the state, in its current practices of criminal punishment, licenses itself to punish on suspicion, rather than conviction, of wrongdoing. Or to put it differently, it arrogates the power to decide who merits punishment, without meaningful and decent legal constraints. The trial process becomes a bureaucratic procedure without the function of deciding *whether* the defendant deserves any punishment;[54] and in the case of petitioners and grassroots activists, it is supplemented by the use of black jails, psychiatric *ankang* (安康) hospitals and similar institutions.[55] This ultimately guilt-indifferent attitude contrasts starkly with liberal (utilitarian) conceptions of criminal punishment; with the idea that punishment is only justified when there is evidence of harm done to others, and with retributivist conceptions based on a genuine conviction of moral wrongdoing severe enough to merit criminal punishment. So there is an important similarity between the kind of repression prominent dissidents and ordinary *weiquan* activists and petitioners locked up in black jails may suffer: they are "guilty" before having had a chance to defend themselves.

The political leadership's decision to pay more heed to popular opinion in adjudicating cases is in keeping with the approach to criminal punishment exhibited in the case of Liu Xiaobo. Judicial populism is deeply problematic. Among other things, letting public opinion play a role in deciding cases potentially compromises the principle that punishment ought to be a response to crimes in fact committed, and that punishment should be proportionate to guilt.[56] If the effects of a particular criminal court decision on the wider public are to determine the content of that decision, criminal adjudication is reduced to a mere form of "social management" (*shehui guanli*, 社会管理). The case of Liu Xiaobo is an example illustrating the same basic principle. While the verdict against him was not motivated by a desire to placate public opinion, it was motivated by a desire to manage that opinion. A prominent intellectual and perceived state enemy, Liu Xiaobo "needed" to be criminally punished not because he was guilty of wrongdoing but because a criminal conviction was needed to send a signal to wider society. The verdict against Liu Xiaobo was therefore vindictive rather than retributive; it was necessary to make it clear that the challenge he and others had launched against the state would not be tolerated, and that the state would "strike back".

In their general vindictiveness and language of enmity the government and some elements of grassroots opposition complement and reinforce each other. Much of the popular anger directed at the government seems to be genuinely, albeit illiberally motivated by feelings of revenge against hated, corrupt officials. Some grassroots rights defenders see the government, or that part of it which they consider directly responsible for its repression, as enemies, and they seek help from higher authorities in fighting their enemy. As one petitioner put it matter-of-factly in a conversation, "petitioners feel hatred toward all the officials from their own local government, because they are the cause of their misery. Of course they want these officials to come to grief."[57]

As the petitioning process drags on, some petitioners come to focus less on the goal of protecting their own rights and instead turn to the more feasible aim of getting officials punished for their alleged misdeeds. Thus, in the summer of 2009 hundreds of petitioners descended angrily on Peking University Law School to demand an explanation from a professor of that university, who had characterized petitioners as "over 99.9 percent mentally ill."[58] They were in part motivated by the knowledge that officials from their hometowns would be given demerits if they turned up, as it meant that petitioners from these officials' jurisdiction had caused "instability" at the gate of the university.[59] Petitioners frequently speak as if by achieving an official's criminal conviction they had "scored" a victory in battle.

Reflecting such attitudes, a civil society group named "China Citizen Supervision Network" (中国舆论监督网) has made it its main goal to campaign for the punishment of corrupt officials. Among other actions, this group has reportedly published on its domestic website open letters from citizens asking for the death penalty to be carried out,[60] and pressurized the authorities to enforce sentences against corrupt officials.[61] In an interview, its founder Li Xinde (李新德) states as his goal to "make those corrupt elements tremble with fear," and emphasizes the importance of "becoming one with the masses, immersing oneself in the masses."

"Mass-line" criminal justice — the form of justice propagated by the Chinese Communist Party in its early decades[62] — however, is notoriously erratic. Among its more recent examples is the anti-mafia campaign carried out by Bo Xilai (薄熙来), the Party Secretary of Chongqing (重庆).[63] In his campaign of "chanting red slogans and striking black" (*changhong dahei*, 唱红打黑) (i.e. striking mafia groups), criminal procedure requirements have been largely set aside, and there have been allegations of torture and other grievous violations of procedural and substantive justice. In a well-reported case against alleged "mafia" members, lawyer Li Zhuang (李庄), arguing that his client Gong Gangmo (龚刚模), the principal co-defendant in one of the most widely reported criminal cases in the context of the Chongqing campaign, had been tortured, was himself convicted of the crime of instigating his client to present false evidence.[64] Li's colleague, lawyer Zhu Mingyong (朱明勇), bravely published credible evidence of torture against another co-defendant in the same case.[65] But even so he could not save this co-defendant's life. There is ample evidence of the high popularity of the Chongqing "striking black" campaign;[66] the wider public, to some extent fuelled by celebratory government comments on the successes of the campaign, does not appear greatly disturbed by the possibility that defendants' rights could have been violated. It sees Bo Xilai as a champion of its anger against corruption and organized crime, just as it also celebrated Yang Jia, the police killer, as a hero of the common people.

Liu Xiaobo wrote, commenting on the Yang Jia case:

> I do not deny that there is a natural right to resistance against government violence. Especially in situations where all legal channels of rights defense have already been blocked off, and where the victim has unsuccessfully exhausted all his resources and energy on obtaining protection of their rights through the law, the victim

has a right to violent resistance. But even in the Chinese system and within the constraints of Chinese society, I do not endorse ineligible forms of resistance to government violence. To assess the justice of individuals using violent resistance we must first of all distinguish between passive [reactive] violence and active violence, and secondly we must distinguish violence directed against the system and violence for the purpose of revenge, and lastly we must differentiate in accordance with the objective effects of violent resistance. If violence was used actively and out of a motive of individual revenge and if it results in loss of life on both sides — if it results in a no-win situation of "both jade and stone getting crushed" — that does not deserve to be called justice....

Justice after Yang Jia's manner is ... at most a form of "primeval justice." The popular opinion praising Yang Jia makes me think of many "strong guys" who were forced onto the path toward "the Liang Mountain."[67] Assuming that historically, autocratic Chinese rulers have all practiced the art of managing the populace according to a logic of "if we don't kill [criminals] it will not satisfy the people's anger," then hero worship for Yang Jia reflects a vengeful popular mindset of "if we do not kill bad officials, the people cannot be happy."[68]

When petitioners and other members of the popular, grassroots opposition to government become attracted to the Bo Xilai style of anti-corruption campaign or to Yang Jia-style "justice," they abandon the goals of constitutionalism, genuine rule of law, and individual rights protection. Their actions only serve to stabilize a relationship of enmity and potential violence between the state and its citizens. Supporters of Charter 08 propose non-violence but, as the following discussion shows, come up against considerable controversy about whether non-violence is possible.

Breaking Out of the Violent-Vindictive Cycle: The Program of Charter 08

Charter 08 presents an "enlightened" liberal program for political change in China. Its call for a new Constitution indicates that its drafters — liberal intellectuals seeking to realize constitutional government — have abandoned the hope of achieving this goal through reliance on existing legal institutions.

> As ... conflicts and crises grow ever more intense, and as the ruling
> elite continues with impunity to crush and to strip away the rights
> of citizens to freedom, to property, and to the pursuit of happi-
> ness, we see the powerless in our society — the vulnerable groups,
> the people who have been suppressed and monitored, who have
> suffered cruelty and even torture, and who have had no adequate
> avenues for their protests, no courts to hear their pleas — becoming
> more militant and raising the possibility of a violent conflict of dis-
> astrous proportions. The decline of the current system has reached
> the point where change is no longer optional.[69]

Charter 08 asks for an end to one-party rule and the introduction
of a democratic system in the mold of Western liberal democracies,
a system that will protect human rights and (better) protect private
property. This can only be achieved, the Charter asserts, after a review
of the past one hundred years of efforts to implement constitutional
government in China,[70] through a new Constitution for China (the
People's Republic). This new Constitution will get rid of the internal
tensions and inadequacies of the current one. The Charter ends with
nineteen detailed and concrete suggestions, including the creation of a
national Human Rights Committee, national Constitutional Court, and
a federal system of governance.

From the perspective of the present discussion, it is particularly
interesting to see how the Charter proposes that China should deal
with past government crimes and with historic injustice. Most importantly, the Charter rejects the retributivist, vindictive mold. It recommends a practice of criminal justice based on liberal principles and the
protection of human rights (proposition no. 6), and the establishment
of institutions apparently modeled on the idea of truth and reconciliation and transitional justice, aimed at rehabilitating and compensation
to the politically persecuted such as prisoners of conscience, and "the
victims who suffered political persecution during past political movements as well as their families" (proposition no. 19).[71]

But we cannot help noting that in looking to the future, the Charter
does not propose immediate steps to be taken by anyone in particular. Its proposals of constitutional reform, separation of powers, and
the creation of a constitutional court, to mention a few, appear to
be directed at the — at present — intransigent and hostile government. Its call upon other citizens "who feel a similar sense of crisis,

responsibility, and mission, whether they are inside the government or not, and regardless of their social status" to "set aside small differences to embrace the broad goals of this citizens' movement"[72] is not a call for any kind of specific action.

And looking to the past, the section on transitional justice focuses on "prisoners of conscience" and "political prisoners"; it focuses on "political movements" that brought about political persecution. In that sense it probably reflects the experience of its drafters. It does not particularly dwell on the experience of the many more ordinary citizens who have not been designated as dissidents by the state yet suffered injustice, for instance, from ordinary official corruption, and who are seeking justice in more mundane, less clearly political cases. Yet doing justice in those mundane cases would surely be important in any future legal and political order for China, not least because as the Charter notes, it is one of the major grievances concerning the current political and legal system that this system is incapable of protecting citizens against official corruption and miscarriages of justice. In suggesting a judicial process based on liberal principles and articulating the need for reconciliation, Charter 08 indicates a general direction for how to address these cases without yet providing much guidance on how to achieve such an enormous task.

In conversations on the problem of violent tendencies within the Chinese *weiquan* movement, especially its grassroots, scholars and lawyers may point out that people who appear to endorse violence often do so "merely" online or on paper; their support of violent retaliatory action is not necessarily "for real".[73] But of course, no one will deny the complexity of attitudes to violence in Chinese society today, or deny that support for violence is a problem to be contemplated. Many among Charter 08's prominent current protagonists as well as other liberal scholars have addressed the problem of the insurgent, violence-leaning mood engendered by long-term exposure to repression and indignity, expressions of which we have encountered in the previous section of this chapter.

In his comment on the Yang Jia case, Liu Xiaobo also wrote:

> So far as a genuine change of a social system is concerned, choosing violent revolution not only carries too high a price, it also inevitably results in the opposite of freedom. Therefore, violence in exchange

for violence has already become an outdated way of achieving a change of the political power, whereas non-political transition both satisfies the legitimacy standards of human civilization, and is also in accordance with a principle of beneficial social change ... Even assuming for the sake of argument that the people could violently overthrow the Communist Party, this would be followed by massive cleanup under the bayonets. The violence-prone climate in China today is preparing a rich social soil for such a cleanup.[74]

Other public intellectuals such as Cui Weiping (崔卫平),[75] He Weifang (贺卫方),[76] Teng Biao,[77] Xiao Han (萧瀚),[78] Xu Youyu (徐友渔), and Xu Zhiyong (许志永)[79] have joined in this advocacy of non-violent struggle; and human rights defenders such as Wang Lihong (王荔蕻) of Beijing agree:

I feel we need to push this society forward. Part of that change needs to happen offline. And those of us who do take it offline must remain civil and rational. Actual growth of civil society needs everyone involved to go through a process of learning this, such as with the riots in Tibet in March 2008 and Xinjiang in July 2009. It's possible, and this is just speculation, that there might be no violence at the beginning — this was the experience leading up to 4 June 1989: A lot of those army vehicles that got burnt, it was students who did it; and then they can say you were smashing and burning things, and then they can suppress you for having done that. So we don't want to go down that road, partly because we believe in non-violence. There is no power in violence. It is not just that citizens alone can't win a violent fight, but even if they could, this is the dynastic cycle we were in for thousands of years. And we feel that this dynastic cycle should end with our generation.[80]

But against a background of general agreement, there still is much controversy about the viability of non-violent resistance effecting real change. According to Xu Youyu, the cycle of extreme violence practiced during the Land Reform, the Great Leap Forward, the Cultural Revolution, and other movements was broken by the 1989 June Fourth protests — an exemplary, albeit unsuccessful, event of non-violent resistance. Xu believes that in the intervening twenty years, Chinese citizens have had far more opportunities to improve their understanding of non-violence.[81] China, if this is true, is ready for a non-violent transition.

Yet other scholars, for instance Xiao Han, are skeptical. Xiao argues that China has only managed to move from an initial "equality of slaves" in the first three decades of the PRC to "wealth disparity and great unfairness in the distribution of power and rights" in the past three decades. While in past decades, non-violent ideas belonging to the Western as well as China's own moral and political tradition have been revived to some extent, he argues that the Chinese have in some ways retained a fundamentally violent conception of political governance. This is due to the fact, he argues, that the government itself has not abandoned its own practices of power abuse and violence.[82] Therefore, Xiao Han believes that Charter 08, while praiseworthy in its goals, has no chance of achieving its stated goal of non-violent and peaceful constitutional change.[83]

Informal discussion within the *weiquan* movement is taking skepticism about non-violence much further, as can be gleaned from the following excerpts from an online discussion. Defenders of the non-violence principle are struggling. Xu Zhiyong's comment that:

> The central significance of non-violence is that it minimizes the price for social change … China must need to undergo transformation toward democracy, and the question is only how high the price to be paid will be … The core of non-violence is love; and that rests on faith, faith that everyone is a person and fellow human being, with a heart that has two sides, a good side and a weak side. We must trust in the power of love, only love can vanquish evil and give us hope.[84]

is countered by "Lawyer Online":

> The central significance of non-violence is that it minimizes the price for social change — anything you get will come at some cost, and I'm afraid that if you get something at low cost its quality can't be guaranteed. Too little blood is shed actively and too much passively. The fruit of passive bloodshed is autocracy, that of active bloodshed, democracy.[85]

Teng Biao's warning that violence could spiral out of control:

> Through the practice of *weiquan* and moral activism we can build up a healthy civil society force, and once our strength has reached a certain level, the government will have no choice but to sit down and negotiate with us. What I am afraid of is that even before this

> spirit of non-violence comes to guide political transition, the hatred
> and contradictions accumulated in society might get out of hand.

meets with Wang Xiaoyang's (王晓阳) comment that the responsibility
for such a development would lie with the government:

> We should be clear about one basic condition: The power to decide
> whether China can go down a path of non-violence, of improve-
> ment, lies with the government, not with ordinary people. From
> what things look like at the moment, the government is not set to
> introduce improvements [of its own accord].[86]

These brief excerpts may help to illustrate the degree of controversy
surrounding the issue of political change in China to date. Of course,
they do not provide any insight into the question of *how much* support
there is for violence or non-violence, respectively.

Charter 08, with its simple proposition that "change is no longer
optional," leaves open the question of how to achieve change. There
is no other option for a document written so clearly in the spirit of
peaceful transition, but directed at so nervously intolerant, so increasingly repressive a government as the current Chinese one. In apparent
recognition of the great challenge this situation presents to rights activists, the scholar and activist Xu Zhiyong commented:

> There is no limit to the price. We might lose our freedom; we might
> lose everything at any time. But to say that there is no limit to the
> price is not to say that we are seeking senseless sacrifice, it means
> that only if there is no limit can we have force. Simply put, we can
> only persevere with being peaceful if we do not fear anything.[87]

Conclusion

This chapter has argued that rights defense based on liberal notions
such as rights and constitutionalism remains an important concern
among petitioners and grassroots activists, but that there is also a clear
trend away from these goals toward vengefulness and endorsement of
violence. Many *weiquan* activists from various walks of life have been
subjected to great cruelty, and most of them are living in the dark
shadows that the state's attitude to *weiquan* has cast over them.

Against this background, the goals articulated in Charter 08, based on ideals of non-violent resistance, transitional justice, and constitutionalism are challenged in two ways: by the authorities who reject reasonable proposals for change, as well as by those in the "grassroots" opposition who have come to focus on their enmity toward the political establishment. For his own person, Liu Xiaobo provided a perfect illustration of the liberal and conciliatory attitude of the program of Charter 08 when, at the end of his trial, he titled his concluding remarks, "I have no enemies."[88] The scholar Xiao Han reminds us of the Confucian roots of this idea in the saying of Mengzi (孟子), "the benevolent person has no enemies."[89] But many in the *weiquan* movement are clearly finding it difficult to be benevolent, as they are faced with a state that seems anything but.

Chapter 12
The Politics of Liu Xiaobo's Trial

Willy Wo-Lap Lam

Introduction

The conferment of the Nobel Peace Prize on Liu Xiaobo caused a big stir within the Chinese dissident community and around the world. Thorbjørn Jagland, the Norwegian Nobel Committee Chairman, said Liu was a symbol for the fight for human rights in China and the government should expect that its policies would face more scrutiny. "China has become a big power in economic terms as well as political terms, and it is normal that big powers should be under criticism," Jagland said.[1] While liberal intellectuals and non-governmental organization (NGO) activists in China said they were encouraged by the award, the seminal event will unlikely have any impact on the Chinese Communist Party's (hereafter "CCP" or "Party") policies on ideological and political issues in the near term. Beijing's first reaction to the announcement was to arrest several dissidents who dared hold a celebration party — and to put Liu Xiaobo's wife, Liu Xia, under house arrest.[2] Particularly since the topsy-turvy year of 2008 — which witnessed the Olympics, and massive riots in Tibet and neighboring provinces — the priority of the administration under President Hu Jintao (胡锦涛) has been to preserve stability, which means neutralizing "troublemakers" ranging from dissidents to separatists.

This chapter looks at the political significance behind the Liu Xiaobo phenomenon, especially the messages that the Beijing authorities want to send to intellectuals as well as ordinary Chinese through the eleven-year jail term meted out to the country's best-known dissident. While in the past two years, the CCP leadership seems to be experimenting with more tolerant and conciliatory measures regarding groups ranging from laborers to Uighurs, relaxation of its policy toward dissent seems unlikely. The no-holds-barred expansion of what critics call the country's police-state apparatus will be examined. Also analyzed will be the rightist — or conservative — turn that official ideology has taken as President Hu raises slogans such as the "Sinicization of Marxism" (马克思主义中国化). The chapter will end by evaluating the possibilities of liberalization in the foreseeable future.

Political Significance behind the Harsh Treatment of Liu Xiaobo: Ensuring the CCP's "Perennial Ruling Party" Status

Ridding the Opposition of Its Most Charismatic — and Dangerous — Figure

To understand the significance of the heavy sentence slapped on Liu, it is instructive to look at the high regard with which the charismatic former professor is held among liberal intellectuals in general. The Changchun (长春) native is learned in both Chinese and Western thought: he has written cogent analyses about the ideas of major democratic theorists in both China and the West. Liu's advocacy of non-violence — and his profession of not harboring any hatred even to his jailers — have invited comparisons with Nelson Mandela and even Gandhi.[3] The bespectacled, chain-smoking intellectual also has the image of a Mr. Clean, which is important given the fact that numerous dissidents both at home and abroad have been mired in scandals involving money and other matters. At fifty-four, Liu is deemed a key figure who has ample appeal to — and can serve as a link among — various generations within China's dissident movement, which include the "Democracy Wall" activists of 1978 and 1979, student protesters of 1989, and members of the short-lived China Democracy Party (CDP) of the 1990s.[4]

Striking down Liu demonstrates the CCP's determination to "nip instability in the bud." Also in the late 2000s, several globally known human-rights lawyers and NGO activists who could form the nexus of an opposition movement, such as Hu Jia (胡佳) and Gao Zhisheng (高智晟), were detained or subjected to severe harassment.[5] It is true that despite the "kill the chicken to scare the monkey" tactic, hundreds of intellectuals will continue to use disparate means to press for genuine political reform. Yet, it may take time for China's severely outgunned dissidents to pull themselves together after Liu's arrest, and it will be particularly difficult for radical intellectuals to nurture a leader with Liu's credentials and effectiveness. The failure of the CDP to regroup after most of its leaders were incarcerated seems to have given the Beijing leadership confidence that the entire dissident movement would enter a prolonged period of low tide after Liu's disappearance from the scene.[6]

Dealing a frontal blow to Liu and the Charter 08 Movement is also Beijing's answer to the challenge of the "color revolution." The Charter 08 campaign was modeled after the Czech Charta 77 campaign launched by now-famous European dissidents such as former president Václev Havel.[7] Since the start of the Solidarity Movement in Poland in the early 1980s, CCP leaders including Deng Xiaoping (邓小平) had warned about the copycat impact of liberalization movements in authoritarian regimes. During the December 1986 student protests (seen as a precursor of the 1989 democracy movement), Deng warned against the "Polish disease" spreading to China.[8] In the 2000s, the Hu Jintao leadership became nervous about a series of so-called velvet or color revolutions that took place in Georgia, the Ukraine, and Kyrgyzstan from 2003 to 2005. Beijing's reading was that pro-West opposition groups in these small countries were able to seize power thanks to profuse support from US government agencies and NGOs. Hu issued numerous internal edicts warning that political movements akin to the color revolutions must never be allowed in China. Chinese NGOs with links to the West were placed on watch lists or subjected to harassment.[9]

Clipping the Wings of Internet-Enabled Opposition Movements

The CCP considers the Internet as posing a big threat to one-party authoritarian rule. 400 million Chinese netizens — a majority of whom are young and relatively highly educated — see the Internet and related new media as a cheap, convenient, and cool way to express themselves. And while it is a mistake to assume that most netizens are politically motivated, the Internet has proved a potent weapon for Chinese who want to freely air their opinions about social, economic, and political events. This is despite the fact that the multi-billion yuan Great Firewall of China has been largely effective in weeding out "poisonous weeds" from the Net.[10]

According to Minister of Public Security Meng Jianzhu (孟建柱), "the Net has become a principal vehicle for anti-Chinese forces [in the West]." Meng claimed that anti-Chinese forces used the Internet to "perpetrate infiltration and sabotage" by means including playing up inner contradictions in Chinese society. The Party-and-state apparatus has since 2008 been devoting gargantuan resources to building an anti-subversion system to counter Net-based sabotage[11] (see the following section). Throughout 2010, the authorities launched a well-publicized campaign to mop up manifestations of the "three vulgarities" — "vulgar, cheap and kitsch" forms of art and entertainment — particularly on TV and the Internet.[12] While, as in previous campaigns, the butt of the commissars seemed to be gross commercialization and pornography, this "new culture movement" was geared toward bowdlerizing politically incorrect materials in the media and in cyberspace.

Before its website was closed down by Net police in early 2009, the Charter 08 Movement managed to collect some twenty thousand signatures from within China. Apart from intellectuals and professionals, those who signed included workers and housewives in towns and townships far away from the prosperous eastern coast.[13] There had, of course, been earlier attempts by various advocacy groups to use the Internet to launch political movements. For example, various nationalistic groups successfully used the Net to organize huge anti-Japanese and anti-French demonstrations in 2005 and 2008 respectively. The "patriotic" NGOs, however, enjoyed government acquiescence if not patronage.[14] The severe punishment meted out to Liu was meant as a clear warning to other dissidents not to use the new media to make "subversive" propaganda against central authorities.

Stopping "Foreign Interference" in China's Domestic Affairs

Despite the fast-growing authority of the quasi-superpower, Liu's case elicited a lot of attention from international government leaders, and in particular, influential intellectuals and opinion-makers in the West. Salman Rushdie, Umberto Eco, and Margaret Atwood were among three hundred writers and academics who called on Beijing to unconditionally release Liu. A dozen-odd representatives from Western embassies attended Liu's show-trial in December 2009. Gregory May, first secretary with the American Embassy in Beijing in charge of human rights, read out a statement to the effect that "we continue to call on the government of China to release him immediately."[15]

Liu's arrest was almost immediately followed by a rash of nominations of the dissident for the Nobel Peace Prize for 2010. Among those who put forward Liu's name were Václev Havel and Herta Müller, the Romanian-German novelist who won the Nobel Prize for Literature in 2009 for her uncompromising portrayal of life under Romanian Communist dictatorship. A couple of weeks before the announcement of the prize, Havel, former Czech dissident Dana Nemcova, and the Bishop of Prague Václav Malý wrote an emotional op-ed in the *New York Times* calling on the award to be given to Liu. Indeed, back in October 2009, a *Foreign Policy* magazine article of October 2009 entitled "Nobel Peace Prize Also-Rans" cited Liu Xiaobo as one of seven outstanding world figures "who never won the prize, but should have."[16]

By thumbing their nose at global opinion, Beijing wants to convince the Western world once and for all that the CCP leadership will brook no foreign intervention in such sensitive issues as human rights. In fact, in what could be construed as an example of interfering in the domestic affairs of other countries, Beijing has in the past few years been putting unsubtle pressure on Norwegian authorities to ensure that no Nobel Peace Prize be awarded to Chinese dissidents such as Hu Jia and the Tiananmen Mothers. Nobel Institute Director Geir Lundestad revealed in September 2010 that earlier in the year, Vice-Foreign Minister in charge of European Affairs Fu Ying (傅瑩) had told him in the summer that an award for Liu could "be seen as an unfriendly act" against China.[17] There is of course, the double irony that the Peace Prize is awarded by the Nobel Peace Prize Committee (NPPC), which is an NGO and not a government agency. And while senior members of the NPPC usually consist of retired officials and public figures in Norway, it is an NGO that does not do the bidding of the Norwegian government.[18]

Limited Reconciliation — But Not with the Dissidents

Beijing's policy toward Liu Xiaobo and fellow dissidents will be put into better perspective if we examine a series of apparently auspicious initiatives the CCP leadership has taken to deal with increasingly sharp contradictions among the nation's disparate classes and interest blocs. There were signs from early 2010 that the Hu Jintao administration might adopt a policy of at least partial reconciliation toward disaffected sectors. The latter include workers and migrant laborers, Uighurs in Xinjiang, as well as Party members who are sympathetic with the ideals of liberal icons Hu Yaobang (胡耀邦) and Zhao Ziyang (赵紫阳). While, as of this writing, the authorities have offered nothing concrete to substantiate these placatory gestures, Beijing seems to have demonstrated a degree of willingness to replace traditional strong-armed tactics with a softer and more flexible approach. The jury is out as to whether the CCP leadership is genuinely committed to reconciliation. Yet it is important to point out that Beijing has shown no evidence of changing its scorched-earth policy toward the likes of Liu and his colleagues.

Limited Reconciliation on the Socio-Economic Front

The CCP leadership's new emphasis on "distributive justice" — or how national wealth should be divvied up — beginning early 2010 has been cited as evidence that it is ready to take measures to defuse increasingly ferocious social tension. Premier Wen Jiabao (温家宝) pledged at the March plenary session of the National People's Congress (NPC) that his cabinet will strive to let all Chinese have a more equitable share of the economic pie. "Let equality and justice shine brighter than the sun," he said. "Let the people live with more dignity." This was followed by President Hu's pledge during his speech marking Labor Day 2010 that "workers should be able to work with dignity."[19]

Particularly after the rash of labor unrest that hit a number of big-name foreign-invested companies such as Japan's Honda and Taiwan's Foxconn in the spring, Beijing and local administrations have adopted placatory measures. A few dozen cities raised their minimum wages by at least 25 percent; lowest-level monthly wages in big cities ranging from Shenzhen to Shanghai went up to slightly more than 1,000 yuan.[20] More significantly, some leeway was given to collective action by labor representatives, and in many cases, even outside the framework of the All-China Federation of Trade Unions (中华全国总工会, ACFTU), China's Party-run labor organization. Senior officials as well as the state media have for the first time voiced support for collective bargaining — or, in official parlance, "determining salaries through collective consultation" (集体协商) — as a means through which workers can get higher wages.

"Collective consultation," of course, is not collective bargaining (集体谈判). Rather, cadres from the ACFTU branch of a certain factory negotiate a "collective [salary] contract" with the bosses. There is minimal participation by ordinary workers.[21] Yet in light of the rapid spread of labor troubles, individual branches of the official union are amenable to, on a case-by-case basis, allowing workers to join ACFTU cadres in collective consultation sessions with employers for fixing salaries and benefits. Geoffrey Crothall of the Hong Kong-based China Labour Bulletin said that "some local-level ACFTU branches are all too aware of the need for worker involvement and consultation if these 'collective contracts' are to have any value at all."[22] Also notable is the fact that several mainstream papers seemed supportive of freer rein to be given to labor organizations. The state-run *Global Times* noted that the labor incidents exposed "the embarrassing lack of a worker's union that would serve as a collective wage bargaining channel."[23]

There are also indications that the lot of the estimated 150 million migrant workers in urban areas might be improved. This is despite the fact that Beijing has refused to abolish the much-maligned *hukou* (户口) (or residence permit) system, which relegates rural laborers in the cities to second-class citizenship. For example, medical and education benefits of migrant workers — and their children — in selective cities have been augmented. Individual areas such as Chongqing have laid out plans for giving permanent residence status to migrant workers. In other regions, authorities have made it easier for rural laborers to join the ACFTU, thus ensuring that they are entitled to rights such as minimum wages.[24]

Rehabilitation of the Reputations of the CCP's Former Liberal Chiefs

Of more relevance to Beijing's attitude toward dissidents — and political reform in general — are signs that the CCP leadership might take a more tolerant stance toward democracy movements of the 1980s. Consider Wen Jiabao's 15 April 2010 tribute to the late Hu Yaobang — who was sacked by patriarch Deng Xiaoping in 1987 for failing to deal harshly with free-thinking intellectuals — which was published in *People's Daily*. In his article, Wen saluted Hu's "superior working style of being totally devoted to the suffering of the masses." The premier, who worked under Hu from 1985 to 1987, also praised his former boss's "lofty morality and openness [of character]."[25] Premier Wen's eulogy of Hu attracted attention also because the liberal Party leader's death twenty-one years earlier was the immediate cause of student protests that ended in the bloody Tiananmen Square crackdown. The article led to speculation that the CCP leadership might consider reintroducing reforms associated with Hu — and even reappraising the verdict on the June Fourth massacre. The day the article appeared, some twenty thousand Chinese posted comments on SINA.com, a popular web portal. Many hailed the piece as a "positive development" in the direction of liberalization.[26]

Three months after Wen's essay on Hu Yaobang, the iconoclast monthly *Yanhuang Chunqiu* (炎黄春秋), which specializes in recent CCP history, published an article praising Zhao Ziyang's work in Sichuan. The piece, entitled "Exploration in Sichuan: Early Reforms in China," was written by former Communist Party secretary of Sichuan, Yang Rudai (杨汝岱). Yang, who had worked under Zhao, extolled the late Party chief's achievements in "thought liberation" when the latter was Sichuan Party boss in the late 1970s. "Comrade Zhao Ziyang repeatedly emphasized the need to reform fossilized and half-fossilized thinking," Yang wrote. He added that Zhao had seconded Hu Yaobang's famous thought-liberation movement, and that his rule in Sichuan was highly affirmed by Deng.[27] Apart from Yang, other Zhao followers, especially former vice-premier Tian Jiyun (田纪云), have written articles testifying to the late Party chief's contributions to the reform initiative.[28]

The big question is, of course, whether the Hu-Wen leadership is committed to a reappraisal of the official June Fourth verdict. More significantly, does the appearance of a series of articles on Hu Yaobang and Zhao Ziyang mean the CCP has become more conciliatory toward avant-garde intellectuals, if not full-fledged dissidents? Du Daozheng (杜导正), a former Zhao aide and one of the founders of *Yanhuang Chunqiu*, said in mid-2010 that Party authorities had become "slightly more practical, tolerant, and democratic." Du said he had heard nothing about a possible reappraisal of either the historical position of Zhao Ziyang or the June Fourth massacre. Yet, the veteran Party member said he and his friends were "optimistic" about Beijing's willingness to face up to the reality of 1989.[29]

There is, however, no credible evidence that the Hu-Wen team will initiate a substantially new policy toward liberal intellectuals in the last two years of their term. Yang Jisheng (杨继绳), a former Xinhua News Agency editor and biographer of the late Zhao Ziyang, said Wen's eulogy of Hu Yaobang could "not be interpreted as a harbinger for the return of reforms."[30] Moreover, the decision to partially rehabilitate Hu Yaobang's reputation had already been made by President Hu and his Politburo Standing Committee (PBSC) colleagues in early 2005. On the late leader's ninetieth birthday in November of that year, the CCP held a commemorative meeting at the Great Hall of the People in which Hu Yaobang posthumously received praise for his contribution to the Party and country.[31]

Limited Efforts at Reconciliation in Xinjiang

By mid-2010, there were signs that Beijing might fine-tune its policy toward ethnic minorities. In April that year, the hard-line "Emperor of Xinjiang," Wang Lequan (王乐泉), was replaced as Party secretary of the Xinjiang Autonomous Region (XAR) by Hunan Party boss Zhang Chunxian (张春贤), who is deemed a moderate and pragmatist. The removal of Wang, who had been the top official in Xinjiang since 1995, was taken as an indication that the Hu Jintao leadership might want to turn a new page in Beijing's policy toward the Uighurs. At a session devoted to Xinjiang policies, the Politburo vowed to "promote harmonious relations among masses of different nationalities and different religions, and to consolidate and develop harmony and stability in Xinjiang society."[32] There were hopes that new Party boss Zhang might eventually revise some of Wang's draconian policies against ethnic minorities. These included suppressing Uighur identity and cracking down hard on Uighur intellectuals who demand that XAR officials vouchsafe to Uighurs the degree of autonomy in cultural and religious matters that are guaranteed by the Chinese Constitution.[33]

The official media has heaped praise on Zhang's work in Xinjiang, particularly his close-to-the-people style. The China News Service described his marathon, town hall-style meetings with ordinary Xinjiang folks as the "Zhang hurricane." Zhang was particularly credited with not avoiding hot potatoes. In a mid-2010 speech, he admitted that the 5 July 2009 incident, in which up to 200 residents in Urumqi were killed during a spate of rioting by Uighurs, had dealt a blow to relations between Han Chinese and Uighurs. "Feelings among the nationalities need to be repaired so as to revive the bondage among brothers," he said. "We need to seek truth from facts and to face the facts squarely," the Party boss said, adding that Party and government cadres would "work with enthusiasm, seriousness and diligence" on reconciling differences between Han Chinese and Uighurs. After having worked in Xinjiang for seventy days, Zhang told the Chinese media in July that Beijing's policy in the XAR "must get out of the cycle of toughness alternating with softness."[34]

As of late 2010, however, there was no conclusive evidence that the Hu leadership would tamper with its iron-fisted suppression of "splittists" and other dissident elements among underground Uighur groups. Top priority is being placed on buttressing military and security forces in the XAR. The public security budget for Xinjiang in 2010 was set at 2.89 billion yuan, up 88 percent from that of the previous year.[35] In 2010, law enforcement officers proved their mettle in the run-up to the first anniversary of the July 5th riots, when a dozen or so "terrorists" were arrested. In accordance with the nature of a "strike hard" campaign (yanda, 严打), many of the suspects detained in late 2009 and 2010 were given hefty sentences after abbreviated trials.[36]

Moreover, the policy of Sinicization — facilitating the migration of more Han Chinese businessmen, technicians, and laborers to the XAR

— has received a big boost. In April, Party secretaries and other top officials from cities and provinces including Beijing, Guangdong (广东), Liaoning (辽宁), Jiangxi (江西), and Zhejiang (浙江) visited Xinjiang under the banner of "assisting Xinjiang in economic [construction], providing Xinjiang with cadres and talents, and helping educate Xinjiang [residents]." A record number of state-run and private businesses from these eastern and central regions were also set to substantially boost their investments in Xinjiang that year.[37] Given that Uighurs are already outnumbered by Han Chinese in Xinjiang, the influx of more businessmen and laborers from other provinces will serve to consolidate Beijing's control over the restive region.

Beefing up the Control Mechanisms

Most indicative of the CCP leadership's hardened stance toward dissidents and other "agents of instability" is an array of initiatives to beef up the already formidable control mechanisms under the CCP Central Commission on Political and Legal Affairs (CCPLA). Headed by PBSC member Zhou Yongkang (周永康), the CCPLA is responsible for maintaining law and order — and crushing challenges to the Party's monopoly on power. The commission has direct control over the *gongjianfa* (公检法) apparatus, a reference to the police, the prosecutor's offices, and the courts.[38] The year 2008 — which witnessed the Tibetan riots, the Olympics, and the Charter 08 Movement — can be considered a watershed regarding the no-holds-barred expansion of China's police state apparatus. New offices and mechanisms have been established to, in Deng Xiaoping's words, "snuff out the seeds of instability at the embryonic stage." The extent of the beefed-up police state apparatus can be gauged by the fact that the NPC in early 2010 approved outlays worth 514 billion yuan for public security departments for the year, almost as big as the People's Liberation Army budget of 532 billion yuan. The regional Chinese media disclosed that the *weiwen* (维稳, uphold stability) budget for 2010 in provinces and cities including Liaoning, Guangdong, Beijing, and Suzhou (苏州) had jumped at least 15 percent over that of 2009.[39]

The Ministry of State Security (MSS) and Ministry of Public Security (MPS) have since 2008 been putting together a new nationwide network

to counter what the official media call "the redoubled threats of separatism, infiltration and subversion" and to stop the leakage of state
secrets. This was revealed in a late 2009 meeting of senior state security
personnel in Tianjin (天津), a port and industrial hub just outside
Beijing.[40] Firstly, big and medium-sized cities are setting up Leading
Groups on State Security (LGSS) to be headed by municipal Party secretaries. According to MSS Minister Geng Huichang (耿惠昌), the LGSS
are "erecting a people's defense frontline to protect national security."
"We must win the 'people's warfare' in safeguarding national security
and ensuring socio-political stability under new conditions," Geng
said.[41]

The majority of municipal-and county-level administrations are
also establishing Offices to Maintain Social Stability and to Rectify
Law and Order (OMSS). In rich coastal cities, such outfits are being
set up in every district and even every major street. According to an
MSS circular, these bi-brother units are charged with ferreting out
"anti-CCP elements" and "snuffing all destabilizing forces in the bud."
The circular called upon OMSS to boost investigative and surveillance
work at the grassroots level, so as to "get a firm grip on the activities
of hostile forces within and outside China." The document specifically
fingered subversion and sabotage allegedly perpetrated by foreign
NGOs as well as religious organizations. Local social security networks
were also called upon to foster socio-political harmony by defusing
"contradictions" between the masses and government departments.
This was, the circular said, to "prevent hostile elements from foment-
ing chaos by inflaming hot-button issues" in Chinese society.[42]

The LGSS and social stability offices are latest additions to an already
labyrinthine state security apparatus that employs several million full-
time police and spies, in addition to many more part-time informants.
The police chief of Kailu County (开鲁县), Inner Mongolia, boasted in
early 2010 that he was able to recruit 12,093 of his county's 400,000 inhab-
itants — or roughly one in 33 — as part-time informants. Municipalities
nationwide were asked to emulate how Beijing mobilized more than
1.5 million vigilantes and informants to safeguard security during the
Olympic Games of August 2008 and celebrations marking the sixtieth
birthday of the People's Republic of China in October 2009.[43] Moreover,
police and MSS agents in increasing numbers of cities were conducting

regular training and operations in conjunction with private security staff employed by factories and universities. Beijing never publishes its state security budgets. Yet aggressive recruitment of college graduates — particularly those who are conversant in information technology and foreign languages — by OMSS nationwide testifies to the fact that the CCP has earmarked unprecedented resources to keep itself in power.[44]

According to MPS Minister Meng Jianzhu, Beijing's goal is to construct a *fangkong* (防控, prevention and control) grid that is "multi-dimensional, all-weather, and foolproof." Writing in the CCP theoretical journal *Seeking Truth* (求是), Meng referred to several layers of such anti-infiltration and anti-subversion networks: those based in streets and districts of cities as well as communities; internal security and anti-sabotage units in every government office, college, and commercial firm; CCTV and surveillance grids especially in big cities; co-ordination networks among security-related units in each province and region; and Internet-policing facilities. For example, two million surveillance cameras were installed in the prosperous Pearl River Delta, and Internet police units in provincial and municipal public security departments were given more funding and resources to erect firewalls and to track down "subversive" websites.[45] Meng also called upon police officers to boost co-operation with high-tech companies. "We should make good use of the fruits of [domestic] IT research and development so as to provide our prevention-and-control system with strong technological support," Meng said in late 2009.[46]

At the same time, the politicization of the judiciary has been exacerbated, particularly since a CCPLA official and former police officer Wang Shengjun (王胜俊) became President of the Supreme People's Court in March 2008. Wang, who never attended law school, vowed repeatedly to boost CCP leadership over "judicial work" so that the courts could do a better job of implementing Party goals such as maintaining stability. In a controversial speech that year, Wang called for the "consolidation of Party construction" in courts of all levels. "We must safeguard the Party's absolute leadership over the work of courts," Wang said. "We must ensure that Party organizations [in courts] will fulfill their functions as leadership cores and as fortresses in combating [destabilizing forces]."[47] The Chinese chief justice has also indicated that "a major criterion for assessing and testing the juridical and implementation functions of the people's courts" would be whether they could "promote social harmony."[48] In the tradition of the *gongjianfa* apparatus, of course, promoting harmony is tantamount to locking away undesirable elements who are undermining the regime.

The Conservative Turn in Party Ideology

The Hu administration has presided over a remarkable turn toward conservatism in the last few years of its tenure. Even as the Chinese economy is further being integrated with the international marketplace, the Party is looking inwards to its Marxist roots with the purpose of preserving its "perennial ruling party status." This "rightist" development was anticipated in Party Chief Hu Jintao's speech in December 2008 marking the thirtieth anniversary of the inauguration of the era of reform and the open door. Hu said the CCP was committed to "hoisting high the great flag of socialism with Chinese characteristics and to pushing forward the Sincization of Marxism." The Party of seventy-six million members would uphold the "Four Cardinal Principles" of Marxism, Leninism, Maoism, as well as absolute Party leadership. Moreover, the supremo noted, the CCP would boost its ability "to guard against changes [to a capitalist system] and to withstand risks," particularly socio-political instability.[49]

At the Fourth Party Central Committee Plenum in September 2009, Hu reiterated that the CCP would "push ahead with the Sinicization of Marxism and rendering Marxism contemporary and popular."[50] Just what is the meaning of the "Sinicization of Marxism," a slogan first issued by Mao Zedong in the 1930s? It simply means that, firstly, China would not adopt "Western" ideals about democracy and human rights; and secondly, the authorities would pull out all the stops to uphold "democratic dictatorship of the proletariat," which is another term for crushing real and potential challenges to the CCP's stranglehold on power. Thus in his December 2008 address, Hu delivered a stern warning to the relatively liberal cadres in the CCP: "We shall never take the deviant path of changing the flag and standard [of the Party]." Indeed, while the sixty-eight-year-old leader made *pro forma* reference to "implementing democratic elections, democratic decision-making and democratic supervision" as well as safeguarding the people's "right to know, to take part in politics, to express themselves and to exercise supervision," his real message was that Beijing "would never copy the political system and model of the West."[51]

While China seems to be an increasingly cosmopolitan and globalized society that is ready to embrace the multifarious challenges of the twenty-first century, the CCP's sole preoccupation remains preserving the political status quo — and its own undisputed authority. One of Hu's oft-repeated messages is that "stability is the Party's overriding task, because nothing can be accomplished without stability." Citing the well-known Chinese proverb *ju'an siwei* (居安思危, beware of dangers in the midst of comfort and plenty), the General Secretary has repeatedly raised the specter of the Party being thrown out of power. Talking about the CCP's ruling-party status, Hu warned in speeches made in 2008 and 2009: "What we possessed in the past doesn't necessarily belong to us now; what we possess now may not be ours forever."[52]

Cadres responsible for ideology and the media are sparing no efforts to push forward President Hu's slogans about "Sinicizing and popularizing Marxism" as a means to safeguarding socio-political stability and to buttressing national cohesiveness. This has rendered the possibility of accommodating liberal opinions — even those sponsored by the most moderate dissidents — very remote. At an early 2010 forum on "Promoting Popular Contemporary Chinese Marxism," Director of the CCP Propaganda Department Liu Yunshan (刘云山) urged cadres to "deeply grasp the laws of Marxist development, and to better arm the entire Party — and educate the people — with the theoretical system of Chinese socialism." "We must take hold of the people through better [use of] the latest fruits of the Sinicization of Marxism," said Liu, a conservative commissar who is also a member of the CCP Politburo.[53]

Ideologues and propagandists have also been waging a campaign that is focused on "distinguishing four boundaries." In a nutshell, Party commissars are demanding that China's intellectuals, particularly college teachers and students, make clear-cut distinctions between four sets of values. They are Marxism versus anti-Marxism; a mixed economy led by Chinese-style public ownership on the one hand, and an economic order dominated by either private capital or total state

ownership on the other; democracy under socialism with Chinese characteristics versus Western capitalist democracy; and socialist thoughts
and culture on the one hand, and feudal and corrupt capitalist ideas
and culture on the other. According to ideologue Li Xiaochun (李孝
纯), "Party members and cadres must sharpen their political sensitivity
and their ability in political discrimination." "We must bolster [our]
ideological defense line through self-consciously drawing a demarcation between Marxism and anti-Marxism," he said. Moreover, in a
paper on differentiating socialist and capitalist democracy, the Chinese
Academy of Social Sciences' Center on Socialist Systems pointed out
that Western democracy was no more than "the game of the rich" and
"democracy of the pocket book." The piece concluded that the quintes-
sence of Chinese democracy must remain "democratic people's dictatorship" — and not Western-style democracy.[54]

Also militating against ideological diversity — and the ideal of
a more pluralistic social and cultural milieu — is the CCP's zealous
propagation of nationalism. While Communist Youth League Clique
leaders and princelings such as Bo Xilai (薄熙来) may disagree on
the extent of the revival of Maoist norms, there is a strong consensus
among all factions that they should do whatever it takes to promote
nationalism so as to foster cohesiveness among 1.3 billion Chinese.
(Cadres and the official media usually use the milder — and less controversial — term "patriotism" to convey quintessentially nationalistic
sentiments.) This partly explains the enormous resources that the CCP
leadership has lavished on prestigious mega-projects that will gal-
vanize national pride. They include the 2008 Summer Olympics; the
military parade marking the sixtieth anniversary of the founding of the
People's Republic of China on 1 October 2009; and the Shanghai Expo
of 2010. Propaganda czar Liu has repeatedly urged Party and government units handling ideology, culture, and the media to "raise the
level of patriotism, enhance the nationalistic spirit, and crystallize the
strength of the people." "Patriotism is an emblem that will unify [all
sectors and races], a gargantuan spiritual force that will propel Chinese
society toward ceaseless development and progress," he said.[55] In
2007, the CCP authorities revived a comprehensive set of "Principles
on Implementing Patriotic Education," which was first issued in 1994.
The "Principles" called upon not only schools and media units but

also enterprises and social organizations to nurture patriotism among students, workers, and members of all social sectors.[56] It goes without saying that the premium put on nationalism will result in less tolerance for free-thinking intellectuals, who are often suspected of colluding with "anti-Chinese foreign forces" in undermining CCP rule.

With the Eighteenth Party Congress just two years away, PBSC members and other senior cadres were in 2010 preoccupied with sustaining socio-political stability — and paving the way for the elevation of faction affiliates into the new Central Committee and Politburo. It is significant that in early 2007, Premier Wen, deemed the Politburo's most liberal member, ignited hopes in many quarters when he heaped praises on certain "universal values and institutions." Wen indicated on two public occasions that "values such as science, democracy, a [fair] legal system, freedom and human rights are not the monopoly of capitalist [countries]," but "universal values that should be pursued by all mankind." Wen's message was that it was appropriate for socialist China to at least experiment with some of these international norms.[57] The pendulum, however, had by mid-2008 swung to the other side. Crypto-Maoist commissars began assailing the concept of "universal values" as so many "sugar-coated bullets" to lure China to morph into a capitalist nation via "peaceful evolution." For instance, Chinese Academy of Social Sciences President Chen Kuiyuan (陈奎元) stated in late 2008 that "we must establish self-respect and confidence in our own people." "We must not engage in blind worship [of the West] and we must not extol Western values such as so-called universal values," said the ultra-conservative ideologue.[58]

Conclusion: Slim Possibilities for Liberation in the Foreseeable Future

The persecution of Charter 08 dissidents continued well into 2010. In late June, one of the first signers of the petition, Sichuan-based writer Liu Xianbin (刘贤斌) was picked up by state security in the city of Suining (遂宁市). His relatives were told that he had been criminally detained on suspicion of "inciting subversion of state power." While Liu (not related to Liu Xiaobo) was being questioned, fourteen policemen searched his home and confiscated two hard drives, two USBs, books, bank books, and printed materials.[59] It seems unlikely that the Nobel Prize for Liu will have any impact on the CCP leadership's stringent treatment of dissidents and "Westernized" intellectuals.

By mid-2010, preparations for the Eighteenth Party Congress were well underway, and stability had become an even more important consideration as the heads of different CCP factions started focusing on delicate — and potentially treacherous — personnel-related maneuvers and horse-trading. Moreover, Party cadres seem convinced that if enough resources are invested in boosting the security apparatus, destabilizing forces can be put at bay. The city of Lianjiang (廉江市), Guangdong was cited as an example of how "stability can be bought." In 2009, the city lavished 31 million-odd yuan on boosting police forces, including setting up a "Flying Tiger" squad to handle contingencies such as riots. The *weiwen* budget that year was equal to the entire sum of such expenditures over the 2003–2008 period. On average, each Lianjiang citizen had to spend thirty-eight thousand yuan a year on maintaining law and order.[60] Party Secretary Xu Shun (许顺) was happy with the results. Citing the fact that there was not a single "mass incident" in 2010, he said in August that year that "the facts show that stability can be bought," and that "we must be willing to spend big on maintaining stability." Xu's remarks drew sharp rebukes from several Chinese media. For example, commentator Yin Yuzhi (银玉芝) of the popular *Qianlong* website (千龙网) said "'using money to buy stability' was tantamount to quashing thirst with drinking poison."[61] Such criticisms, however, have not affected the Party leadership's commitment to this draconian strategy.

In theory, of course, the CCP has not given up reconciliation as a means of defusing contradictions within the country's increasingly polarized groupings. In mid-2010, the NPC passed the country's first "People's Mediation Law," which lays down the framework for the resolution of disputes between the people and government units of different levels. The official China News Service commented that this was an attempt by the authorities to "solidly construct the 'first line of defense' regarding social contradictions." As of late 2009, some 823,000 grassroots "people's mediation organizations" had been set up all over the country. In the five years ending 2009, such units had reportedly resolved 20 million cases of altercations among the people as well as disputes between the people and the government.[62]

There seems little question, however, that official attempts at "reconciliation" remain a "top-down" way of imposing a solution on disputes, not genuine efforts to listen to the voices of the people. This is evident from the hard-line steps authorities of various levels have taken to root out *shangfang* (上访), or the age-old practice of "lower-class" citizens with grievances presenting their petitions to provincial capitals and Beijing. Until the "Olympic year" of 2008, it was common to find hundreds of thousands of petitioners — as well as alleged victims of injustices of different kinds — congregating in the capital demanding from various Party and government offices that their cases be heard.[63] From 2009 onwards, central authorities seemed to have acquiesced in brutal tactics adopted by regional administrations to prevent petitioners from reaching Beijing. Even the official media have reported about so-called "security companies" employed by local governments to abduct petitioners, who are often illegally detained in "black jails." It was apparently due to such extra-legal activities that the number of petitioners dropped by 2.7 percent in 2009 compared to that of 2008.[64]

While it is not within the scope of this chapter to discuss the political views of the Fifth-Generation Leadership, which is due to take over the helm at the Eighteenth CCP Congress set for late 2012, it is instructive to examine the orientation of Vice-President Xi Jinping (习近平). Xi, fifty-seven, who is expected to succeed Hu as CCP General Secretary and state president, has closely toed the orthodox Party line. Many of Xi's statements on ideology and statecraft were made in his capacity as President of the Central Party School (CPS), the CCP's training ground for rising stars. Xi has repeatedly urged CPS students to "insist upon the synthesis between the basic principles of Marxism on the one hand, and China's concrete realities and contemporary characteristics on the other." Xi emphasized in a 2009 talk on grooming young cadres that utmost emphasis must be put on "strengthening education on political loyalty … education about Party discipline and education about resisting corruption and *fangbian* (防变, preventing changes)." *Fangbian* is CCP jargon for the possibility of the Marxist party degenerating into a "vassal of capitalism." Xi particularly urged leading cadres to "firm up their political cultivation, and to boost the resoluteness of their political beliefs, the principled nature of their political stance, the sensitivity of their [ability in] political discrimination, and the reliability of their political loyalty."[65] Can such a leader be counted upon to reignite the flames of liberalization?

For well-known Tsinghua University (清华大学) sociologist Sun Liping (孙立平), social stability can only be attained by the "institutionalization of the expression of vested interests," or ways and means whereby representatives of interest blocs and groupings can freely air their points of views. At least among Beijing's intellectual circles, Sun saw a "gradual consensus toward institutionalization, the formation of institutions and mechanisms for resolving social contradictions and conflicts."[66] Beijing, however, obviously does not see things this way. The fate of Liu Xiaobo and his colleagues shows that it may take a long time before CCP authorities will take the necessary steps to begin a dialogue with dissidents, let along share power with members of the opposition.

Chapter 13
The Political Meaning of the Crime of "Subverting State Power"*

Teng Biao

> The moment you try to understand your country, you have already started down a path of crime.
>
> — Ai Weiwei (艾未未) [1]

After it established itself as the ruling power in 1949, the Chinese Communist Party (hereafter "Communist Party" or "Party") immediately launched a movement to detect and repress counter-revolutionaries. In July 1950, the Government Administration Council and the Supreme People's Court jointly issued the Regulation Concerning the Suppression of Counter-revolutionary Activities and in February 1951, the Central People's Government promulgated the Regulation on Punishing Counter-revolutionaries. By the end of the "Great Cultural Revolution," the practice of criminalizing "counter-revolution" had not only become entrenched in the law; it was also an important part of political and social life.

In the 1979 Criminal Law of the People's Republic of China, twenty counter-revolutionary crimes were set out in Chapter One of the division containing provisions on specific crimes.[2] Among these, Article 90 defined the crime of counter-revolution as "any act committed with the aim of overthrowing the political power of the dictatorship of the proletariat and the socialist system, and endangering the People's Republic of China." The 1997 Criminal Law of the People's Republic of China abolished the designation "crimes of counter-revolution" and replaced it with "crimes of endangering national security." This, at the

---

* This article was originally written in Chinese and translated into English by Eva Pils.

time, was thought of as progress, both conceptually and practically. At least in form, it seemed to free the Criminal Law from its old ideological shackles; this liberation seemed to be in line with the political changes occurring domestically, as well as with international trends. Article 105 of the 1997 Criminal Law stipulates in its first subsection that:

> Among those who organize, plot or carry out the scheme of subverting the State power or overthrowing the socialist system, the ringleaders and others who commit major crimes shall be sentenced to life imprisonment or fixed-term imprisonment of not less than 10 years; those who take an active part in it shall be sentenced to fixed-term imprisonment of not less than three years but not more than 10 years; and other participants shall be sentenced to fixed-term imprisonment of not more than three years, criminal detention, public surveillance or deprivation of political rights.

In its second subsection, Article 105 provides that:

> Whoever incites others by spreading rumors or slanders or any other means to subvert the State power or overthrow the socialist system shall be sentenced to fixed-term imprisonment of not more than five years, criminal detention, public surveillance or deprivation of political rights; and ringleaders and others who commit major crimes shall be sentenced to fixed-term imprisonment of not less than five years.[3]

These two provisions define "subversion" and "incitement to subversion." The present chapter focuses on the political background and meaning of these two variants of the crime of subversion.[4]

Deprivation of the Right to Effect a Lawful Change of Government

In modern democracies, the government is responsible toward the people, and the constitution safeguards the people's freedom of association, a freedom that naturally includes the freedom to form political associations to ensure that popular demands can find expression through different political parties. Each political party gets the chance to participate in political decision-making by competing in elections; and it is through elections, through the media, non-governmental organizations (NGOs), and various other mechanisms that citizens can constrain and supervise the exercise of public power. Thus, changes of the ruling party and of political leaders can be effected in a peaceful and lawful manner. While there is room for improvement in Western democracies, the opportunity peacefully to change the government satisfies a minimum standard of modern political civilization that has not yet been met in China.

From 1949, the Communist Party established itself as a typical totalitarian and communist political power in China. Basing its control upon the use of violence and terror as well as ideology, and launching wave after wave of political movements, it trampled on citizens' basic human rights and human dignity. Not only was there no space for civil society, but also the individual's right to privacy and freedom of belief and thought were nonexistent.[5] The Communist Party's monopolization of political power, as well as its control of thought and expression were taken to an extreme degree. Any word or act opposing the Communist Party or the government, opposing the official ideology, or opposing individual leaders' words or acts could all lead to a person being branded a "counter-revolutionary." Indeed, there were also examples of people who were loyal to the idea of Communism and to individual leaders, but who were so labeled nevertheless.

After the end of the Great Cultural Revolution, a change in the form of governance occurred. Class struggle, in particular, and other rigid ideological doctrines were abandoned, along with the planned economy, while elements of competitive market economy were introduced. This did lead to great social and political changes — but the Communist Party never changed its monopoly on political power, and China remained strictly a one-party state. Just as the 1954, 1975, and 1978 Constitutions had done before, so, too, did the 1982 Constitution enshrine the Communist Party's leading role, and this turned the provision concerning the freedom of association in Article 35 of the Constitution into an empty clause, not to say a trap ensnaring those who sought to rely on it. The inherent contradiction in the Chinese Constitution is that the fundamental rights and freedoms of citizens set out in its second chapter cannot be realized under the power structure established by its other chapters. The right peacefully to change their government cannot even be sensibly discussed in such conditions. And yet in fact, the right to revolution that is mentioned by

Locke[6] and in the American Declaration of Independence is also articulated in some Marxist theorists' works,[7] while parts of the Preamble of the Constitution [of the People's Republic of China], draw on the "revolutionary history" of the Communist Party. Only, by establishing totalitarian political rule in the name of "perpetual revolution," the Communist Party actually ended all possibility of revolution. Yet, according to Arendt, "the goal of revolution has always been and will always be freedom."[8] So the Communist Party's "revolution" has in fact only been a false revolution, or a counter-revolution.

It is this kind of political system, a system that robs the people of the right to elect their own government and of the right to wage revolution, that has created the crimes of "counter-revolution" and of "subversion of state power."[9] The very fact that it uses the "crime of subversion of state power" to punish dissidents shows that this political power lacks legitimacy; this very fact already shows that this political power ought to be changed. Legitimacy means that a political system deserves to be accepted. Historically, different kinds of system have enjoyed legitimacy, but for governments in our time, their only legitimate source of legality is approval by the people, gained through a system of elections. Since the totalitarian system rests on the use of violence and ideology, it is incapable of obtaining people's genuine approval. After the totalitarian ruler dies and the totalitarian system he built falls apart, those in power have no choice but to introduce reforms in order to alleviate the ensuing crisis of governance and regain legitimacy by acquiring merit in the eyes of the ruled. But even if they can achieve a situation in which basic human rights are protected and living standards are continuously rising, such rulers will at best attain "justification" of their rule; they can never attain "legitimacy."[10] How much worse, then, are the chances for a reform that only promotes the economy and does not make any progress at all in the area of politics! Through such a process, not only will basic rights not be protected but social and economic problems will also become more and more serious: in particular, issues of collusion between officials and businesspeople, rising wealth disparity, and environmental degradation.[11]

Even democratic elections can only superficially be seen as a source of legitimacy. The true source of legitimacy is freedom of expression. The Party-state system lacks legitimacy from its very beginnings, because there are neither elections nor popular approval to legitimize it. In order to maintain political control/rule, the system must repress the people's efforts to fight for democracy and freedom. It must take away or restrict the right to elections; suppress non-official media and carry out "prior restraint" censorship; impose restrictions on collective demonstrations; and suppress civil society NGOs. It must use the state security apparatus as well as domestic security squads belonging to the police to control thought, and bring the administration of justice and education under Party control. Viewed from this angle, the crime of "subversion of state power" is a repressive instrument used by the Party which is the last means save for the use of military force.

Civil Resistance under Post-Totalitarianism/ Neo-Totalitarianism

The translation and distribution of *Havel's Collected Works* in Mainland China made a mark in contemporary China's intellectual history. Even though the book was not openly on sale, copies were widely distributed in private and on the Internet, and thus Havel's thought came to influence many civil society intellectuals. Havel had used the concept of post-totalitarianism to provide an incisive analysis of the social psyche and people's conduct in Czechoslovakia; and because post-1989 China greatly resembled this situation, Chinese intellectuals drew great hope from Havel. The immediate reason that Havel's books could not be published in China was that the translator refused to omit the lengthy foreword written for the Chinese edition of this book by Li Shenzhi (李慎之),[12] entitled "The Power of the Powerless and Anti-Political Politics — Life Philosophy in a Post-Totalitarian Age" (无权者的权力和反政治的政治——后极权主义时代的人生哲学). Li believed that China was also in a situation of post-totalitarianism, and many other scholars agreed with this.[13]

Ben Xu (徐贲)[14] believes that from 1949 onward until the end of the Cultural Revolution, the Chinese political system closely resembled the original model of totalitarian government. From the end of the Cultural Revolution until the brutal repression of the students' movement in 1989, it reflected a post-totalitarian model, whereas the political system after 1989 reflected a "neo-totalitarian" model: in parting with post-totalitarianism, it reverted to original totalitarianism for help, but was still unable fully to return to Stalinism. According to Xu:

> Thus this system generated features drawing on original totalitarianism but also retained some features of the post-totalitarian era; and in addition, it developed some historically new features. [The Communist Party] fell into a state of unprecedented existential fear concerning its prospects as a ruling power; a state that it had never experienced before. This gave rise to a very defensive mindset and meant that whenever there was the slightest attack it became afraid of a "demise of Party and state." As a result, [the Party] has no confidence in "positive guidance". Its exercise of political power has gradually reverted to traditional methods, such as for instance reinforcing its plainclothes police contingents and relying on them to carry out comprehensive infiltration and surveillance; further strengthening its totalitarian organization and propaganda apparatus, and controlling the media, public opinion and expression within civil society even more severely, etc. Without any doubt, these [recent] measures represent a regression from post-totalitarianism back toward totalitarianism.[15]

"Neo-totalitarianism" may also be understood as a mere result of post-totalitarianism's transformation. The political prospects of this system await further analysis.[16]

Whichever of these concepts one uses, it is clear that compared to the Mao Zedong era, Chinese society after 1989 developed a multitude of subtle and complex new features.

With a gradual reduction of ideological jargon, the government has been forced to invent language taken from elsewhere to deal with social changes. But whether it is "Three Represents" (三个代表)[17] or "Harmonious Society" (和谐社会)[18] or "Scientific Development Perspective" (科学发展观),[19] none of these slogans can command genuine respect. In fact, not only do the people show zero enthusiasm for the slogans of the government, but even government and Party officials have also stopped believing in these rigid dogmata. The government's language has even become the substance of ridicule, parody, and spoofs in popular verses, jokes, video clips, etc. People who enter the Party do so out of personal interest, and the status attached to being a Party member cannot compare to what it once was. The Communist Party has thus become a for-profit group lacking in self-confidence; it is an organization for mutual benefit endowed with special powers; and it no longer has anything to do with ideological attitudes. It has hijacked the state's power to make policies and has thus become a crucial obstacle to political transition.

Through policies that liberalized the economy, a superficial kind of prosperity was achieved and living standards were improved. But the repression of the democratic movement by means of the 1989 massacre and the ensuing great reckoning and purge made everyone first afraid, and then later unwilling to engage too much in political questions. The political movement, its leaders, and its ideology lost their deified status. People had opportunities to make money, and under the influence of consumer greed, sensory stimulation, and the mediocrity of mass culture, they indulged in self-intoxication. Now, consumerism and vulgarity have pervaded the whole of society.

In his book *The Malady of Cynicism — Contemporary China's Mental Crisis* (犬儒病——当代中国的精神危机), Hu Ping (胡平) analyzes the causes and manifestations of this "illness" that has affected intellectuals and the general public:

> Totalitarian rule is founded on people's fanaticism, and consolidated through widespread terror. However, neither fanaticism nor terror is long-lasting. Therefore ultimately, totalitarianism comes to rely on despondency and apathy amongst the people to stay in existence.
>
> Fear is not cynicism; it is only a bridge leading to cynicism. ... The admission and knowledge of fear would necessarily push us toward the stance of dissidents and opponents, even if we kept our dissident views locked in our hearts. But precisely because a proper understanding of fear stimulates one's conscience, because it can lead to an awakening and revolting of conscience, the majority of people will try to avoid fear. They will avert their faces and pretend not to see, pretend that such-and-such a matter does not exist, and prefer to leave their consciences in a state of confusion. This is what is called "hard-to-attain confusion."[20]

Attaining this "confusion" actually requires the ability to engage in "double-think" as described in George Orwell's *1984*. "Double-think" is not an easily acquired skill, but an indispensable survival technique for people under totalitarianism. In "Civic Virtues and Civic

Responsibilities in the Post-Totalitarian Age" (后极权时代的公民美德
与公民责任), I once wrote that:

> Shying from sublimity, mocking sincerity, disdaining ideals, vili-
> fying heroes, deconstructing morality, questioning humanity, dis-
> secting meanings, and denying faith are the characteristics of the
> post-totalitarian mentality in China. Apathy and lack of empathy,
> vulgar enjoyment without reverence, forgetful contentedness,
> "clever" self-preservation, servility and submissiveness, blind
> belief and blind obedience, all of these become everyone's life
> philosophy.[21]

And only against this background can we fully understand the unique-
ness of political prisoners — prisoners of conscience convicted of
crimes of "subverting state power." They are outstanding individuals
belonging to a tiny minority of people who do not want to go against
their own conscience, who do not want to shirk their civic responsibilities, who dare to push for political change and break political taboos.

Modern means of communication and the Internet have gradually
widened spaces for civil society. The emergence of the Internet has
presented an enormous challenge to the Communist Party. On the one
hand, it must, for the sake of economic growth and promotion of its
own political interests, go with the wave of globalization, accede to
the World Trade Organization, hold the Olympic Games and World
Expo, and thus cannot possibly isolate itself from the Internet. On the
other hand, if it wants to maintain the current political system, it must
repress speech and the free flow of information, use Internet blocks and
take down website content, and engage in prior restraint and *ex post
facto* censorship at all times. And yet it is virtually impossible to control
the Internet in the way traditional media could be. There is no way of
banning and removing "sensitive news" or "politically opposed essays"
completely. With Freegate, Ultrasurf, and similar tools for scaling the
Great Firewall, as well as new media and new forms of Internet communication — such as Twitter, Facebook, Skype, e-mail list software,
online chat groups, discussion forums based on membership participation — news can now spread even more rapidly and conveniently than
before, and has become more difficult to block. Modern technology has
thus brought a certain measure of informational freedom. Add to this
economic progress as well as widening spaces and increased capacities

for civil society activism — all this has very greatly strengthened exchange among and association of "people power" elements. Genuine NGOs have begun to emerge, as have activists engaged in popular movements, human rights lawyers, citizen journalists, independent writers, and rights defenders: and those belonging to the opposition within the establishment are progressively reinforcing each other and becoming united.

Clashes between officials and citizens have become increasingly common, intense, and publicly known. Because the authoritarian one-party system does not allow for the existence of any organized opposition force, it lacks effective checks on the power of the government, and systemic corruption becomes more and more serious. Because collusion between officials and businesspeople distorts the market, monopolies held by elites of wealth and power allow them to make enormous profits, and paths for upward mobility from the lower to the higher strata of society are increasingly blocked off. The disparity between rich and poor is already very striking: China's Gini coefficient has already reached a level internationally considered alarming, and there is palpable discontent with unfairness in society.[22]

Because the administration of justice is not independent, new miscarriages of justice are occurring every day: for instance, large scale human rights violations occur as a consequence of land expropriations, building demolitions, and relocation of original residents. In addition, because the right to vote has been virtually taken away or denied, the right to assemble and demonstrate severely restricted, the media controlled, and "letters and visits" (*xinfang*, 信访) as an avenue to redress have become basically ineffective, it is harder for public anger to find an outlet, and "mass incidents" are becoming more common and acerbic.[23]

On the other hand, the general public is increasingly aware of the law and increasingly rights-conscious, and there is a rising potential for resistance [to illegal government action] among the general public. A liberal-minded force of human rights lawyers, rights defenders, citizen journalists, independent writers, and Internet and traditional media users is playing an increasingly important role in this area. The creation of the slogan "ruling the country in accordance with law" and the writing of "human rights" into the Constitution meant that "rule of law" and "human rights" attained a certain measure of formal legal recognition. Clashes between ordinary people and officials that used to be brought under control, silenced, and violently suppressed are now increasingly reported and have thus entered public awareness.

The post-1989 "Chinese model" can be said to have achieved economic development at the cost of weak human rights protection, collusion between officials and businesspeople, rising disparity between the rich and the poor, and environmental destruction. It has led to confusion among the people through control of the media, ideological propaganda, and consumerism, and to acquiescence among intellectuals through criminalization of speech on the one hand, and bribes and payoffs on the other. "Mass incidents" have been handled by the use of violence as *ultima ratio*. Calls for democratization from within the system have been stemmed temporarily with *ad hoc* measures. China today is an extraordinarily complex system; in the areas of politics, intellectual life, culture, etc., there are concurrent, seemingly contradictory trends. Against this background, the scope, methods, and current position of popular resistance are necessarily somewhat different from what they used to be.[24]

The Risks of Resistance

In historical comparison, the likelihood of being convicted and sentenced to imprisonment for "inciting subversion of state power" has slightly decreased. An article similarly critical of the Party or government leadership that would have landed you in jail in the 1980s may now be safe to write.[25] Because frontline activists are tirelessly engaged in probing the boundaries and breaking taboos, spaces for speech are continuously widening in society, and the authorities are forced to become more tolerant too. Formerly, dissidents were frequently convicted and sentenced to imprisonment for writing one or two such articles, or for signing an open letter; nowadays, this is fairly unlikely to happen, although it certainly still cannot be ruled out. If everyone who had written articles criticizing the Communist Party were sent to jail, it would be hard to fathom the number and range of persons affected. To use Charter 08 as an example, among its signatories are retired former high officials, well-known dissidents, university professors, journalists, lawyers, civil servants, peasants, workers, and students: the signatories come from vastly different groups in society. Criminally convicting all the signatories — or even just the 303 initiators and first signatories — of the Charter would already far exceed the authorities' capacity.

Compared to before, those who have been sent to prison for "inciting subversion of state power" are likely to be sentenced to shorter terms of imprisonment. During the era of "the crime of counter-revolution," dissidents were frequently sentenced to ten years or more, with many sentenced to life imprisonment or given the death sentence.[26] From 1999, the number of cases with a sentence of ten years or longer decreased, and there were more cases with a sentence of five years or less.[27] Broadly speaking, then, the costs of engaging in democracy activism and political dissent have decreased, while the number of people able to overcome fear has increased, as has, very clearly, the number of those who participate in activism and dissent. This is in part due to the point discussed in the following section.

Changes in Resistance Methods and Strengthened Ties between Resistance Activists and Ordinary People

The democracy activists of the 1980s more often formed political associations, used political slogans and declarations, wrote proposals for constitutional amendments, and signed open letters calling for political reform and the release of political prisoners. These pro-democracy pioneers were sentenced to long prison terms under the name of counter-revolutionary crimes, or were banned from the country and forced to go into exile. They made very great sacrifices, as well as significant contributions to the promotion of political opening in China. But these political ideals and political slogans lacked a direct connection with ordinary people's lives and interests, because social conditions were not ripe yet. In the wake of further dissemination of democratic ideas in society, the rise in Internet usage, the emergence of human rights lawyers as a group, and the growth of independent NGOs, it became possible for the citizen rights defense movement to connect to people's interests through participation in individual cases and promotion of public interest litigation. Many dissidents were aware of this and actively joined this form of resistance.[28] Even though the government tried hard to block any information about political prisoners, as a consequence of the incessant rise in the number of persons whose fundamental rights had been violated and of the rapid dissemination of information through the Internet, the influence of those involved in resistance among ordinary people was also on the rise.[29]

Even though some dissidents are still mainly calling for the formation of a political opposition party, there is growing popular consensus that the time is not yet ripe,[30] and that work of the following kinds is more practical and effective: protecting human rights and freedom of speech and religion; promoting the participation of independent candidates in basic-level elections through individual cases; encouraging the perfection of civil society organizations through NGOs; providing skills training for rights defenders; as well as fostering connections and integration between rights defenders in various places. The vast majority of persons convicted and sentenced to prison under Article 105 of the Criminal Law have engaged in human rights work and independent writing, not in the establishment of a political organization opposed to the Party or other organizations of a political nature.

Widening of the Circle of Persons Engaged in Resistance

With expanding social space and decreasing costs of engagement in dissidence, there has been a gradual rise in activism. Consequently, the range of persons convicted of "subversion of state power" has also widened. As Guo Guoting (郭国汀) puts it:

> Subversion and inciting subversion have become two crimes that serve as readily available tools for the Chinese Communist Party to incarcerate democracy activists for their speech as they please; it is a set of chains fastened around the people's neck. All kinds of people have been ensnared by this crime: some have been convicted because they took video footage of schools collapsed in the Sichuan Earthquake and posted it online; some because they put forth the slogan "We Want Human Rights Not the Olympics"; some because they engaged in environmental activism and voiced support for Tibetans; some because they proposed the protection of the rights of workers and peasants; some because they called for democracy and constitutional government; some because they called for support for the Dalai Lama's request for Tibetan

independence and autonomy; some because they published texts heralding democracy; some because they drafted a Charter; some because they published online articles commemorating June Fourth; some because they published appeals in the form of open letters; some because they formed a democratic party; some because they published articles satirizing Deng Xiaoping [邓小平], Jiang Zemin [江泽民], or Hu Jintao [胡锦涛]; some because they spoke the truth about Falun Gong [法轮功] adherents; some because they criticized the Four Basic Principles [四个基本原则], the Three Represents, the Communist Party, or the politicized administration of justice in online texts; some because they wrote essays criticizing and exposing corrupt officials, causing their downfall; some because they published open letters to [Hu Jintao (胡锦涛) and Wen Jiabao (温家宝)] asking for political reform and requesting an end to the persecution of Falun Gong; some because they proposed separation of powers and a multi-party system; some because they used Mao Zedong songs to criticize Jiang Zemin's corruption; some because they wrote critical commentaries about politics and current affairs; some because they wrote letters to Voice of America; and some even because, themselves suffering from mental disability, they were instigated by others to post anti-government slogans. But the majority amongst them has been wrongfully convicted due to essays on political and current affairs published online. Not one among them was convicted because they proposed a violent overturn of the Chinese government; even less is there anyone who actually engaged in violence. The victims [of this law] have come in all kinds of social roles; there have been professors, lawyers, authors, scholars, journalists, teachers, officials, businessmen, editors, democracy movement activists, dissidents, religious believers, workers, peasants, urban residents, and students.[31]

Stability Preservation Work in New Forms

The domestic security squad police officers[32] and state security officers[33] are no longer loyal guards of Communist Party ideology. Mostly, their attitude is one of "obeying orders," "needing to put food on the table," and "not letting anyone mess things up." Due to a widening of social spaces; ever-increasing pluralism of thought and opinion; and the fact that "subversion of state power" and "inciting subversion of state power" lack conceptual clarity, are hard to delineate, and are enforced using inconsistent criteria,[34] the fates of those dealt with under Article 105 of the Criminal Law are vastly different. For quantitatively and qualitatively similar writings, some are heavily punished, while others are punished more lightly. The factors taken into consideration include how well known or influential the defendant is, his attitude, his status, his family situation, international and domestic pressure to help him, and the mindsets of officials concerned. Some authors write biting criticisms of the government yet remain safe and undisturbed, or merely receive some warnings from the police, while other authors are criminally punished because of one open letter, a small number of essays, or even just an e-mail. Some are arrested on suspicion of "inciting subversion of state power" but ultimately sent to re-education through labor, or the charges against them are dropped after they have been released on bail.[35] Some are clearly imprisoned for political reasons but convicted of "illegal business operation."[36] Sentences for dissident national minorities are clearly heavier, and more of them are sentenced (far more than is known to the outside world, or than the outside world reports on or appeals about); moreover, in those cases there is even less of a show of adhering to criminal procedure rules.[37] Some regions are more tolerant toward dissidents; others are harsher.[38]

That different people receive different treatment reflects the subtlety and complexity of the political scene under neo-totalitarianism. On the one hand, the authorities are unable to seize everybody who is in opposition, and are not even able to set down consistent criteria of application of the law as to who ought to be detained or criminally convicted. Instead, they must take all kinds of extralegal factors into consideration in handling individual cases. On the other hand, the logic of this system requires them to keep seizing, trying, and imprisoning its political opponents in order to reaffirm its political legitimacy and to maintain deterrence, create a climate of fear, and intimidate other activists and potential opponents.

Another often overlooked and so far under-researched problem is that domestic security squad police and state security apparatuses, of course, have their own motives for consuming, misappropriating, and applying for more funds for "stability preservation." They and the members of the political opposition (as "targets of stability preservation") come to live in a subtle relationship of symbiosis. Without targets of stability preservation, domestic security squad police and state security would have no work achievements to claim, and these officials could therefore not benefit from the stability preservation budgets. That, surely, constitutes a difference to the bygone era of "counter-revolutionary crimes."[39]

The Crime of Subverting State Power and Prospects for China's Political Transition

If we consider law in practice as opposed to merely statutory texts, it is clear that all the vast majority of those who have been labeled with this crime have been to express their political views. "Subverting state power" has become a kind of "political crime" and "inciting subversion of state power" a kind of "thought crime." This clearly violates both China's Constitution and international treaties. China's current system still clearly preserves some features of a totalitarian system, and this kind of system still needs to be able to label some people as having "subverted state power." It must at all times investigate, identify, and punish "dangerous" and "subversive elements": all persons who have independence and dignity, dare to speak the truth, and dare to change the political system may be identified as "subversives" at any point.

But in the era of post-totalitarianism, as a result of the secularization and vulgarization of society, ideology and leadership have long been "exorcised." Among the public, cold indifference has replaced a sense of fear about politics, cynicism has come to replace fanaticism; and the language of rule of law has become widely popular. Partly due to an increasing diversification of interests, there is a certain degree of pluralism of political and moral viewpoints and values. As a further consequence, the authorities are no longer able to plunge the whole of society into crazy political movements at will. They can no longer deploy all the tools for influencing public opinion to brand someone as an "anti-government element" and to instill hatred and abhorrence of "criminal subversives" in the populace.

At the international level, due to reasons such as anti-terror efforts, the North Korea problem, cross-border trade, global warming, the financial crisis, and political short-sightedness, Western countries are focusing less attention and exerting less pressure on China's human rights problems. But the October 2010 award of the Nobel Peace Prize to Liu Xiaobo, who had been convicted of "inciting subversion of state power" and sentenced to eleven years' imprisonment, can be regarded as an expression of skepticism on the part of the Western countries toward the legitimacy of China's rulers. It also became an occasion for the international community to pay renewed attention to human rights and democratization in China. The third wave of global democratization, the trend toward democratization brought about by the color revolutions, and the interest and support coming from international human rights organizations have been a great encouragement to Chinese democracy activists.

Yet the promotion of political changes in China will depend mainly on domestic support. In that context, those who have been labeled with the crime of "subversion of state power" or who stand a chance of being labeled with it are at the frontline of resistance; they are the ones who are best able to challenge the existing system. Spurred by their conscience and sense of social responsibility, these citizens hope for political change; they hope for a system that will respect individual dignity and freedom.[40] So they establish opposition parties or other political groups and underground publishing houses, sign open letters, call for political change, criticize the current situation, expose corruption, distribute leaflets, publicize the truth, protect fundamental rights, organize peaceful protests, and so on. These actions put enormous pressure on the Communist Party authorities; they represent an indispensable part of the force for political change. Surrounded by a general cynical attitude of "resistance is useless," these citizens, through their practical actions and their suffering, show the people the force of human conscience, the force of truth, and that it is possible to dispel fear and take action. Without them, the survival of civil society NGOs would be even harder. Without them, now not-so-progressive essays and actions would be the most progressive ones, and their protagonists would be the ones thrown into prison. Without them, the fasting movement in support of Liu Xianbin (刘贤斌)[41] and Chen Guangcheng (陈光诚)[42] would have difficulties continuing. Kang Xiaoguang (康晓光) believes that China has become a "society without politics";[43] in reality, there has been no interruption of genuine popular politics, only popular politics has for a long time been concealed, insulted, locked up, and forcibly forgotten. In this long and cruel era of suppression, through tears and pain behind and outside iron bars, humanity has been upheld, moral principles proved, political skills honed, experience gained, and common understandings reached. All these have helped prepare the ground for a future democracy. Surely, "you can destroy the flowers but you cannot prevent spring."

China's per capita GDP has already surpassed US$3,000. It is generally thought that this has an important influence on the economic, social, and political structure. Transition does not occur when citizens are in extreme poverty and totally deprived of their rights; it occurs more easily when the economy has developed up to a certain point, when civil society spaces have opened, when there is an awakening of rights consciousness, and when the ability to resist is gradually increasing. Observers of China may gradually realize that China is on the eve of a massive change. Without any doubt, the values of the current political prisoners and heroic prisoners of conscience will be confirmed by history. China must ultimately realize freedom of the press, general elections, and a multi-party system. But while it has not done so yet, the post-totalitarian Chinese system will continue to send the most courageous, most conscientious, and most historically responsible and outstanding citizens of this society to prison under the name of "subverting state power" and "inciting subversion of state power."

Appendix: Charter 08*

9 December 2008

I. Preamble

This year marks 100 years since China's [first] Constitution,[1] the 60th anniversary of the promulgation of the Universal Declaration of Human Rights, the 30th anniversary of the birth of the Democracy Wall, and the 10th year since the Chinese government signed the International Covenant on Civil and Political Rights. Having experienced a prolonged period of human rights disasters and challenging and tortuous struggles, the awakening Chinese citizens are becoming increasingly aware that freedom, equality, and human rights are universal values shared by all humankind, and that democracy, republicanism, and constitutional government make up the basic institutional framework of modern politics. A "modernization" bereft of these universal values and this basic political framework is a disastrous process that deprives people of their rights, rots away their humanity, and destroys their dignity. Where is China headed in the 21st century? Will it continue with this "modernization" under authoritarian rule, or will it endorse universal values, join the mainstream civilization, and build a democratic form of government? This is an unavoidable decision.

The tremendous historic changes of the mid-19th century exposed the decay of the traditional Chinese autocratic system and set the stage for the greatest transformation China had seen in several thousand

---

* Reprinted with permission. Translation by Human Rights in China. The full text of the translation is available at Human Rights in China, *Freedom of Expression on Trial in China* (*China Rights Forum*, No. 1 of 2010), <http://www.hrichina.org/crf/article/3203>.

years. The Self-Strengthening Movement [1861–1895] sought improvements in China's technical capability by acquiring manufacturing techniques, scientific knowledge, and military technologies from the West; China's defeat in the first Sino-Japanese War [1894–1895] once again exposed the obsolescence of its system; the Hundred Days' Reform [1898] touched upon the area of institutional innovation, but ended in failure due to cruel suppression by the die-hard faction [at the Qing court]. The Xinhai Revolution [1911], on the surface, buried the imperial system that had lasted for more than 2,000 years and established Asia's first republic. But, because of the particular historical circumstances of internal and external troubles, the republican system of government was short lived, and autocracy made a comeback.

The failure of technical imitation and institutional renewal prompted deep reflection among our countrymen on the root cause of China's cultural sickness, and the ensuing May Fourth [1919] and New Culture Movements [1915–1921] under the banner of "science and democracy." But the course of China's political democratization was forcibly cut short due to frequent civil wars and foreign invasion. The process of a constitutional government began again after China's victory in the War of Resistance against Japan [1937–1945], but the outcome of the civil war between the Nationalists and the Communists plunged China into the abyss of modern-day totalitarianism. The "New China" established in 1949 is a "people's republic" in name, but in reality it is a "party domain." The ruling party monopolizes all the political, economic, and social resources. It has created a string of human rights disasters, such as the Anti-Rightist Campaign, the Great Leap Forward, the Cultural Revolution, June Fourth, and the suppression of unofficial religious activities and the rights defense movement, causing tens of millions of deaths, and exacting a disastrous price from both the people and the country.

The "Reform and Opening Up" of the late 20th century extricated China from the pervasive poverty and absolute totalitarianism of the Mao Zedong era, and substantially increased private wealth and the standard of living of the common people. Individual economic freedom and social privileges were partially restored, a civil society began to grow, and calls for human rights and political freedom among the people increased by the day. Those in power, while implementing economic reforms aimed at marketization and privatization, also began to shift from a position of rejecting human rights to one of gradually recognizing them. In 1997 and 1998, the Chinese government signed two important international human rights treaties.[2] In 2004, the National People's Congress amended the Constitution to add that "[the State] respects and guarantees human rights." And this year, the government has promised to formulate and implement a "National Human Rights Action Plan." But so far, this political progress has largely remained on paper: there are laws, but there is no rule of law; there is a constitution, but no constitutional government; this is still the political reality that is obvious to all. The ruling elite continues to insist on its authoritarian grip on power, rejecting political reform. This has caused official corruption, difficulty in establishing rule of law, the absence of human rights, moral bankruptcy, social polarization, abnormal economic development, destruction of both the natural and cultural environment, no institutionalized protection of citizens' rights to freedom, property, and the pursuit of happiness, the constant accumulation of all kinds of social conflicts, and the continuous surge of resentment. In particular, the intensification of antagonism between the government and the people, and the dramatic increase in mass incidents, indicate a catastrophic loss of control in the making, suggesting that the backwardness of the current system has reached a point where change must occur.

II. Our Fundamental Concepts

At this historical juncture that will decide the future destiny of China, it is necessary to reflect on the modernization process of the past hundred and some years and reaffirm the following concepts:

Freedom: Freedom is at the core of universal values. The rights of speech, publication, belief, assembly, association, movement, to strike, and to march and demonstrate are all the concrete expressions of freedom. Where freedom does not flourish, there is no modern civilization to speak of.

Human Rights: Human rights are not bestowed by a state; they are inherent rights enjoyed by every person. Guaranteeing human rights is both the most important objective of a government and the foundation of the legitimacy of its public authority; it is also the intrinsic requirement of the policy of "putting people first." China's successive political disasters have all been closely related to the disregard for human rights by the ruling establishment. People are the mainstay of a nation; a nation serves its people; government exists for the people.

Equality: The integrity, dignity, and freedom of every individual, regardless of social status, occupation, gender, economic circumstances, ethnicity, skin color, religion, or political belief, are equal. The principles of equality before the law for each and every person and equality in social, economic, cultural, and political rights of all citizens must be implemented.

Republicanism: Republicanism is "joint governing by all, peaceful coexistence," that is, the separation of powers for checks and balances and the balance of interests; that is, a community comprising many diverse interests, different social groups, and a plurality of cultures and faiths, seeking to peacefully handle public affairs on the basis of equal participation, fair competition, and joint discussion.

Democracy: The most fundamental meaning is that sovereignty resides in the people and the government elected by the people. Democracy has the following basic characteristics: (1) The legitimacy of political power comes from the people; the source of political power is the people. (2) Political control is exercised through choices made by the people. (3) Citizens enjoy the genuine right to vote; officials in key positions at all levels of government must be the product of elections at regular intervals. (4) Respect the decisions of the majority while protecting the basic human rights of the minority. In a word, democracy is the modern public instrument for creating a government "of the people, by the people, and for the people."

Constitutionalism: Constitutionalism is the principle of guaranteeing basic freedoms and rights of citizens as defined by the constitution through legal provisions and the rule of law, restricting and defining the boundaries of government power and conduct, and providing appropriate institutional capability to carry this out. In China, the era of imperial power is long gone, never to return; in the world at large, the authoritarian system is on the wane; citizens ought to become the true masters of their states. The fundamental way out for China lies only in dispelling the subservient notion of reliance on "enlightened rulers" and "upright officials," promoting public consciousness of rights as fundamental and participation as a duty, and putting into practice freedom, engaging in democracy, and respecting the law.

III. Our Basic Positions

Thus, in the spirit of responsible and constructive citizens, we put forth the following specific positions regarding various aspects of state administration, citizens' rights and interests, and social development:

1. Constitutional Amendment: Based on the aforementioned values and concepts, amend the Constitution, deleting clauses in the current Constitution that are not in conformity with the principle that sovereignty resides in the people, so that the Constitution can truly become a document that guarantees human rights and allows for the exercise of public power, and become the enforceable supreme law that no individual, group, or party can violate, establishing the foundation of the legal authority for democratizing China.

2. Separation of Powers and Checks and Balances: Construct a modern government that separates powers and maintains checks and balances among them, that guarantees the separation of legislative, judicial, and executive powers. Establish the principle of statutory administration and responsible government to prevent excessive expansion of executive power; government should be responsible to taxpayers; establish the system of separation of powers and checks and balances between the central and local governments; the central power must be clearly defined and mandated by the Constitution, and the localities must exercise full autonomy.

3. Legislative Democracy: Legislative bodies at all levels should be created through direct elections; maintain the principle of fairness and justice in making law; and implement legislative democracy.

4. Judicial Independence: The judiciary should transcend partisanship, be free from any interference, exercise judicial independence, and guarantee judicial fairness; it should establish a constitutional court and a system to investigate violations of the Constitution, and uphold the authority of the Constitution. Abolish as soon as possible the Party's Committees of Political and Legislative Affairs at all levels that seriously endanger the country's rule of law. Prevent private use of public instruments.

5. Public Use of Public Instruments: Bring the armed forces under state control. Military personnel should render loyalty to the Constitution and to the country. Political party organizations should withdraw from the armed forces; raise the professional standards of the armed forces. All public employees including the police should maintain political neutrality. Abolish discrimination in hiring of public employees based on party affiliation; there should be equality in hiring regardless of party affiliation.

6. Human Rights Guarantees: Guarantee human rights in earnest; protect human dignity. Set up a Commission on Human Rights, responsible to the highest organ of popular will, to prevent government abuse of public authority and violations of human rights, and, especially, to guarantee the personal freedom of citizens. No one shall suffer illegal arrest, detention, subpoena, interrogation, or punishment. Abolish the reeducation through labor system.

7. Election of Public Officials: Fully implement the system of democratic elections to realize equal voting rights based on "one person, one vote." Systematically and gradually implement direct elections of administrative heads at all levels. Regular elections based on free competition and citizen participation in elections for legal public office are inalienable basic human rights.

8. Urban-Rural Equality: Abolish the current urban-rural two-tier household registration system to realize the constitutional right of equality before the law for all citizens and guarantee the citizens' right to move freely.

9. Freedom of Association: Guarantee citizens' right to freedom of association. Change the current system of registration upon approval for community groups to a system of record-keeping. Lift the ban on political parties. Regulate party activities according to the Constitution and law; abolish the privilege of one-party monopoly on power; establish the principles of freedom of activities of political parties and fair competition for political parties; normalize and legally regulate party politics.

10. Freedom of Assembly: Freedoms to peacefully assemble, march, demonstrate, and express [opinions] are citizens' fundamental freedoms stipulated by the Constitution; they should not be subject to illegal interference and unconstitutional restrictions by the ruling party and the government.

11. Freedom of Expression: Realize the freedom of speech, freedom to publish, and academic freedom; guarantee the citizens' right to know and right to supervise [public institutions]. Enact a "News Law" and a "Publishing Law," lift the ban on reporting, repeal the "crime of inciting subversion of state power" clause in the current Criminal Law, and put an end to punishing speech as a crime.

12. Freedom of Religion: Guarantee freedom of religion and freedom of belief, and implement separation of religion and state so that activities involving religion and faith are not subjected to government interference. Examine and repeal administrative statutes, administrative rules, and local statutes that restrict or deprive citizens of religious freedom; ban management of religious activities by administrative legislation. Abolish the system that requires that religious groups (and including places of worship) obtain prior approval of their legal status in order to register, and replace it with a system of record-keeping that requires no scrutiny.

13. Civic Education: Abolish political education and political examinations that are heavy on ideology and serve the one-party rule. Popularize civic education based on universal values and civil rights, establish civic consciousness, and advocate civic virtues that serve society.

14. Property Protection: Establish and protect private property rights, and implement a system based on a free and open market economy; guarantee entrepreneurial freedom, and eliminate administrative monopolies; set up a Committee for the Management of State-Owned Property, responsible to the highest organ of popular will; launch reform of property rights in a legal and orderly fashion, and clarify the ownership of property rights and those responsible; launch a new land movement, advance land privatization, and guarantee in earnest the land property rights of citizens, particularly the farmers.

15. Fiscal Reform: Democratize public finances and guarantee taxpayers' rights. Set up the structure and operational mechanism of a public finance system with clearly defined authority and responsibilities, and establish a rational and effective system of decentralized financial authority among various levels of government; carry out a major reform of the tax system, so as to reduce tax rates, simplify the tax system, and equalize the tax burden. Administrative departments may not increase taxes or create new taxes at will without sanction by society obtained through a public elective process and resolution by organs of popular will. Pass property rights reform to diversify and introduce competition mechanisms into the market; lower the threshold for entry into the financial field and create conditions for the development of privately-owned financial enterprises, and fully energize the financial system.

16. Social Security: Establish a social security system that covers all citizens and provides them with basic security in education, medical care, care for the elderly, and employment.

17. Environmental Protection: Protect the ecological environment, promote sustainable development, and take responsibility for future generations and all humanity; clarify and impose the appropriate responsibilities that state and government officials at all levels must take to this end; promote participation and oversight by civil society groups in environmental protection.

18. Federal Republic: Take part in maintaining regional peace and development with an attitude of equality and fairness, and create an image of a responsible great power. Protect the free systems of Hong Kong and Macau. On the premise of freedom and democracy, seek a reconciliation plan for the mainland and Taiwan through equal negotiations and cooperative interaction. Wisely explore possible paths and institutional blueprints for the common prosperity of all ethnic groups, and establish the Federal Republic of China under the framework of a democratic and constitutional government.

19. Transitional Justice: Restore the reputation of and give state compensation to individuals, as well as their families, who suffered political persecution during past political movements; release all political prisoners and prisoners of conscience; release all people convicted for their beliefs; establish a Commission for Truth Investigation to find the truth of historical events, determine responsibility, and uphold justice; seek social reconciliation on this foundation.

IV. Conclusion

China, as a great nation of the world, one of the five permanent members of the United Nations Security Council, and a member of the Human Rights Council, ought to make its own contribution to peace for humankind and progress in human rights. Regrettably, however, of all the great nations of the world today, China alone still clings to an authoritarian way of life and has, as a result, created an unbroken chain of human rights disasters and social crises, held back the development of the Chinese people, and hindered the progress of human civilization. This situation must change! We cannot put off political democratization reforms any longer. Therefore, in the civic spirit of daring to take action, we are issuing Charter 08. We hope that all Chinese citizens who share this sense of crisis, responsibility, and mission, whether officials or common people and regardless of social background, will put aside our differences to seek common ground and come to take an active part in this citizens' movement, to promote the great transformation of Chinese society together, so that we can soon establish a free, democratic, and constitutional nation, fulfilling the aspirations and dreams that our countrymen have been pursuing tirelessly for more than a hundred years.

Notes

Introduction

1. Samuel Huntington, *The Third Wave: Democratization in the Late Twentieth Century* (Norman: University of Oklahoma Press, 1991).
2. "China Overtakes Japan as World's Second-Biggest Economy," BBC, 14 February 2011, <http://www.bbc.co.uk/news/business-12427321>.
3. Andrew Nathan, "Authoritarian Resilience," *Journal of Democracy* 14 (2003): 6–17; Minxin Pei, *China's Trapped Transition: The Limits of Developmental Autocracy* (Cambridge, Mass: Harvard University Press, 2006).
4. Dali L. Yang, *Remaking the Chinese Leviathan: Market Transition and the Politics of Governance in China* (Stanford, California: Stanford University Press, 2004).
5. Teresa Wright, *Accepting Authoritarianism: State-Society Relations in China's Reform Era* (Stanford, California: Stanford University Press, 2010).
6. Randall Peerenboom, *China's Long March toward the Rule of Law* (Cambridge: Cambridge University Press, 2002).
7. Tom Ginsburg and Tamir Moustafa, *Rule by Law: The Politics of Courts in Authoritarian Regimes* (Cambridge: Cambridge University Press, 2008).
8. Despite the fact that he succeeded Jiang Zemin (江泽民) in 2002, Hu Jintao (胡锦涛) had been designated by Deng Xiaoping (邓小平) in 1992.
9. "Chinese Charter 08 Signatories Awarded Homo Homini, Speeches by Vaclav Havel, Xu Youyu, and Cui Weiping," Laogai Research Foundation, <http://www.laogai.it/?p=8060>.
10. Interview with Zhang Zuhua (张祖桦), January 2009.
11. "Wen Makes Accountability Pledge," *South China Morning Post*, 28 August 2010.
12. Liang Chen, "Exclusive: Ai Weiwei Breaks His Silence," *Global Times*, 9 August 2011, <http://www.globaltimes.cn/NEWS/tabid/99/articleType/ArticleView/articleId/670150/Exclusive-Ai-Weiwei-breaks-his-silence.aspx>.

13. Xia Yong (ed.), *Zouxiang Quanli de Shidai: Zhongguo Gongmin Quanli Fazhan Yanjiu* [Toward an Age of Rights: A Perspective of the Civil Rights Development in China] (Beijing: China University of Politics and Science Press, 1999).
14. Kevin J. O'Brien and Lianjiang Li, *Rightful Resistance in Rural China* (Cambridge: Cambridge University Press, 2006).

Chapter 1 Is Jail the Only Place Where One Can "Live in Truth"?

1. "2010 Nobel Peace Prize a Disgrace," *Global Times*, 9 October 2010, <http://opinion.globaltimes.cn/editorial/2010–10/580091.html>.
2. Zhou Duo (周舵) was then the head of the Stone Research Center, Gao Xin (高新) was a professor at Beijing Normal University (北京师范大学), and Hou Dejian (侯德健) was a Taiwanese singer who chose to settle down in the PRC at the beginning of the 1980s.
3. These articles have been republished and translated into English in *China Rights Forum* 2010, no. 1, <http://www.hrichina.org/crf/issue/2010.01>.
4. Liu Xiaobo's Final Statement, "China's Endless Literary Inquisition" (trans. David Kelly), *The Guardian*, 11 February 2010, <http://www.guardian.co.uk/commentisfree/2010/feb/11/china-liu-xiaobo-free-speech>.
5. After the publication of his article "Crisis! The New Era Literature is in Crisis!" (published in *Shenzhen Qingnian Bao* [Shenzhen Youth Post] on 3 October 1986), Liu Xiaobo was called "black horse". "Scar literature" (伤痕文学) refers to the novels and short stories which were published in the late 1970s and the 1980s which recalled the sufferings of the Chinese people under Mao's political campaigns. The name comes from a short story entitled "*Shanghen*" [伤痕, The Scar] by Liu Xinwu (刘心武), which was published on 11 August 1978 in the *Guangming Ribao* [Guangming Daily].
6. In 1981, a movement against "bourgeois liberalization" was launched to criticize Bai Hua's (白桦) *Kulian* [苦恋, Unrequited Love].
7. "Crisis!" (note 5). During the Jinshan conference on contemporary literature organized by Wang Meng in October 1986, many writers, especially Cong Weixi (丛维熙), lashed out at this iconoclast.
8. They made their poems known in the unofficial journal *Jintian* [今天, Today], created by Bei Dao (北岛) and Mang Ke (芒克) in 1978.
9. One of the most famous exponents of this school is Ah Cheng (阿城), who had been a member of *Jintian*, a group which had become famous during the Democracy Wall in 1979. He was the target of Liu's criticism.
10. Geremie Barmé, "Confession, Redemption, and Death: Liu Xiaobo and the Protest Movement of 1989," *China Heritage Quarterly* 17 (March 2009), <http://www.chinaheritagequarterly.org/017/features/ConfessionRedemptionDeath.pdf>.

11. The most famous liberal intellectual who denounced Liu's radicalism was the philosopher Li Zehou (李泽厚).

12. Barmé, "Confession, Redemption, and Death" (note 10).

13. Liu Xiaobo, "The National Pride of the Slave: On the Recent Wave of Nationalism in China," *Kaifang* [Open Magazine] (November 1994), translated in *China Perspectives* 11 (May–June 1997): 30.

14. "We Must Resolutely Oppose the Turmoil," *People's Daily*, 26 April 1989. This editorial, which was inspired by a declaration by Deng Xiaoping labeled the student movement a "turmoil," which opened the way to repression.

15. Liu Xiaobo, "Réhabilitation! La pire tragédie de la Chine moderne," Mimeeographed text published in J.-Ph.Béja, M.Bonnin, A.Peyraube, *Le tremblement de terre de Pékin*, Paris, Gallimard, Au vif du sujet, 205, translated from the leaflet published in *Tiananmen* (Taipei: Lianjing Press, 1989), 277.

16. Barmé, "Confession, Redemption, and Death" (note 10).

17. See Liu Xiaobo's Final Statement, "China's Endless Literary Inquisition" (note 4).

18. Liu Xiaobo, "Subverting the System Based on Lie with the Truth," — Speech for the prize reception of the Democratic Education Foundation (*Minzhu Jiaoyu Jijinhui*) — *Zhengming* [Chengming Magazine] 308 (June 2003): 47–9.

19. "June 2nd Hunger Strike Proclamation," in Zhang Jingyu, *Ziyou zhi Xue, Minzhu zhi Hua* [The Blood of Freedom, the Flowers of Democracy] (Taipei: National Chengchi University, International Relations Research Center, 1989), 426–31.

20. See for example, Wang Zhao, "Grabbing Liu Xiaobo's Black Hand," *Beijing Ribao* [Beijing Daily], 24 June 1989, cited in Barmé, "Confession, Redemption, and Death" (note 10).

21. Liu, "Subverting the System Based on Lie with the Truth," 47 (note 18).

22. Liu Xiaobo, "An Eternally Precious Record in My Heart," *Zhengming* [Chengming Magazine] 296 (June 2002): 37.

23. Such as political scientist Yan Jiaqi (严家祺), who went into exile after the movement. Author's conversation with Liu Xiaobo, September 2005.

24. Liu, "An Eternally Precious Record in My Heart" (note 22).

25. Li Zehou and Liu Zaifu, *Gaobie Geming* [Farewell to Revolution] (Hong Kong: Cosmos Books, 1996).

26. Liu Xiaobo, "The Governance Crisis Engendered by Reform," *Zhengming* [Chengming Magazine] 340 (February 2006): 32.

27. Liu, "An Eternally Precious Record in My Heart" (note 22).

28. Liu Xiaobo, "Reform in China: The Role of Civil Society," *Social Research* 73, no. 1 (2006): 121–38.

29. Liu, "The Governance Crisis Engendered by Reform" (note 26).

30. Liu, "An Eternally Precious Record in My Heart," 36–8 (note 22).
31. Liu Xiaobo, "The Philosophy of the Pig," *Dongxiang* [The Trend Magazine] 181 (September 2000): 29–36.
32. Ibid.
33. Liu Xiaobo, "The Unofficial Opposition's Poverty," *Minzhu Zhongguo* [Democratic China] 6 (2002): 8.
34. Liu Xiaobo, "The Post-Totalitarian Epoch Spiritual Landscape" (on file with author).
35. Liu, "The Philosophy of the Pig," 34 (note 31).
36. Liu, "The Unofficial Opposition's Poverty," 1 (note 33).
37. Liu and Du were netizens who were arrested for having expressed critical opinions online.
38. Jiang was an army doctor who denounced the attitude of the authorities during the SARS outbreak in 2003.
39. Liu, "Reform in China: The Role of Civil Society," 129 (note 28).
40. His article "Further Questions about Child Slavery in China's Kilns" is one of the six texts cited in the verdict against him as evidence of his crime of "incitement to subversion." The full text of this article in Chinese is available at <http://www.hrichina.org/cn/node/3505/3201>.
41. Liu Xiaobo, "Lettre ouverte à Jerry Yang, Président de Yahoo, au sujet de l'affaire Shi Tao," translated in *Esprit*, January 2006.
42. Author's conversation with Liu Xia, Beijing, March 2010.
43. Author's conversation with Liu Xiaobo, January 2000.
44. "Hu Jiwei and Other Old Party Members Ask Justice for Liu Xiaobo," *Duli Zhongwen Bihui* [Independent Chinese PEN Center], 17 January 2010, <http://chinesepen.org/Article/sxsy/201001/Article_20100117004353.shtml>.
45. Liu Xiaobo, *Weilai de Ziyou Zhongguo Zai Minjian* [The Future Free China Lies in the Unofficial] (Washington DC: Laogai Foundation, 2005).
46. Liu Xia noted that the generally auspicious figure eight was always bad for Liu Xiaobo as he was taken to *laojiao* (re-education through labor) on October 8, and this time on December 8.
47. "Signatories of Charter 08: We Share the Responsibility with Liu Xiaobo," a letter signed by 165 persons, 12 October 2009. It was sent to the author by a signatory.
48. "Liu Xiaobo Has No Regrets despite Paying a Heavy Price for His Ideals," *South China Morning Post*, 31 January 2010.

Chapter 2 The Sky Is Falling

1. Wang Qisheng, "Revolution and Counterrevolution: Interactions among Three Leading Chinese Political Parties in the 1920s," *Lishi Yanjiu* [Historical Research] 297 (2004): 101–5.

2. See Liu Hengwen, "Revolution/Counterrevolution: The Nationalist Party's Legal Arguments during the Nanjing Nationalist Government Period," in Wang Pengxiang (ed.), *2008 Falü Sixiang yu Shehui Bianqian* [Legal Thought and Social Change, 2008] (Taipei: Institutum Iurisprudentiae, Academia Sinica, 2008), 255–304.

3. *Zhonghua Suwei'ai Gongheguo Chengzhi Fan'geming Tiaoli* (1934) [Regulations of the Chinese Soviet Republic for the Punishment of Counter-Revolutionaries (1934)].

4. *Zhonghua Renmin Gongheguo Chengzhi Fan'geming Tiaoli* (1951) [Regulations of the People's Republic of China for the Punishment of Counter-Revolutionaries (1951)].

5. Article 90, *Zhonghua Renmin Gongheguo Xingfa* (1979) [Criminal Law of the People's Republic of China (1979)] [hereafter "Criminal Law (1979)"].

6. Article 102, Criminal Law (1979). See also Fu Hualing, "Sedition and Political Dissidence: Towards Legitimate Dissent in China?," *Hong Kong Law Journal* 26 (1996): 210–33.

7. Li Chun and Wang Shangxin, *Zhongguo Xingfa Xiuding de Beijing yu Shiyong* [Background and Application of Revision to the Chinese Criminal Law] (Beijing: Law Press, 1998), 100.

8. Chen Xingliang, *Xin Jiu Xingfa Bijiao Yanjiu: Fei, Gai, Li* [Comparative Research between the New and Old Criminal Laws: Abolition, Revision, and Establishment] (Beijing: Press of Chinese People's Public Security University, 1998), 11–2.

9. Ibid.

10. Ibid., 12.

11. Ibid.

12. In practice, however, this distinction soon broke down with the launch of the campaign against Falun Gong, as the rhetoric in this campaign has frequently invoked the group's alleged threat to national security. Primary responsibility for investigating the activities of this and other alleged cults formally rests with the "domestic security protection" police, the same unit responsible for investigating most crimes involving state security. See Gu Fusheng et al., *Xin Shiqi Gongan Paichusuo Gongzuo Quanshu* [Encyclopedia of Public Security Police Station Work in the New Era] (Beijing: Press of the Chinese People's Public Security University, 2005), 546–7.

13. In fact, one can even argue that there have been several individuals convicted of counter-revolution even since 1997, as courts continued to cite the 1979 code's espionage provisions — which underwent the most change in the revision process — to convict people like Wang Bingzhang (王炳章), Chan Yu-lam (陈瑜琳), and Yang Jianli (杨建利).

14. Articles 14–16, *Zhonghua Renmin Gongheguo Xingfa* (1997) [Criminal Law of the People's Republic of China (1997)] [hereafter "Criminal Law (1997)"].

15. See Fu, "Sedition and Political Dissidence" (note 6).

16. Yu Zhigang, *Weihai Guojia Anquan Zui* [The Crime of Endangering State Security] (Beijing: Press of the Chinese People's Public Security University, 1999), 209.

17. United Nations Working Group on Arbitrary Detention, "Visit to the People's Republic of China" (1998), UN Doc. E/CN.4/1998/44/Add.2, para. 45.

18. Article 56, Criminal Law (1997).

19. Article 54, Criminal Law (1997); Article 288, *Gongan Jiguan Banli Xingshi Anjian Chengxu Guiding* (1998) [Procedural Regulations for the Handling of Criminal Cases by Public Security Organs (1998)].

20. Article 61, Criminal Law (1997).

21. *Zhonghua Renmin Gongheguo Xianfa Xiuzheng'an* [Amendment to the Constitution of the People's Republic of China], 14 March 2004.

22. See Otto Malmgren, "Fragile Constitutionalism in China" (31 August 2010), Social Science Research Network (SSRN), <http://papers.ssrn.com/sol3/papers.cfm?abstract_id=1978169>.

23. See, for example, The Dui Hua Foundation, "Supreme People's Court 'Work Report' Indicates More Trials, Heavier Sentences for Endangering State Security in 2009," *Dui Hua Human Rights Journal*, 20 July 2010, <http://www.duihuahrjournal.org/2010/07/supreme-peoples-court-work-report.html> (accessed 21 December 2010).

24. This does not count a handful of individuals reported to have been sent to "re-education through labor" facilities for inciting subversion or individuals initially suspected of inciting subversion but ultimately released without punishment or convicted of different crimes.

25. See the typology of security threats set out in Fu Hualing, "Responses to Terrorism in China", chap. 14 in Victor V. Ramraj et al. (eds), *Global Anti-Terrorism Law and Policy (Second Edition)* (Cambridge University Press, 2012).

26. Public Security Record Compiling Office of the Dongshan District Public Security Sub-bureau, Guangzhou City Public Security Bureau, *Guangzhou Shi Gonganju Dongshan Gongan Zhi: 1991–2000* [Guangzhou Public Security Bureau Dongshan Public Security Records: 1991–2000] (Guangzhou: n.p., 2002), 214; The Dui Hua Foundation, *Dialogue* 10 (Winter 2003): 7.

27. "Man Jailed for Toilet Graffiti Attack on Chinese Government," Agence France-Presse, 9 June 1999.

28. Wang Jun et al., *Jianli Gongan Zhi* [Jianli Public Security Records] (Jianli County, Hubei: n.p., 2000), 109; "China Sentences 18-Year-Old to One Year in Prison for Subversion," Deutsche Presse-Agentur, 8 October 1999.

29. The Dui Hua Foundation, *Selection of Cases from the Criminal Law, Occasional Publications of The Dui Hua Foundation* 18, April 2005, 13.

30. China Internet Network Information Center, "The Internet Timeline of China 1997–2000," 26 June 2005, <http://www.cnnic.net.cn/html/

Dir/2003/12/12/2001.htm> (accessed 10 December 2010); "450 Million Chinese Use Internet," *China Daily*, available at Xinhua News Agency, 31 December 2010, <http://news.xinhuanet.com/english2010/china/2010–12/31/c_13671684.htm> (accessed 6 January 2011).

31. Chan Yee Hon, "Subversion Charge Laid Over E-mail Addresses," *South China Morning Post*, 30 July 1998, 7.

32. First Instance Criminal Verdict No. 49 (2001) of the Chengdu Intermediate People's Court Criminal Tribunal, Sichuan Province, 22 February 2003, <http://www.xs.gd.cn/ws/16863.html> (accessed 18 January 2011).

33. See, respectively, First Instance Criminal Verdict No. 36 (2000) of the Baotou Intermediate People's Court Criminal Tribunal, 18 July 2000 (on file with author); The Dui Hua Foundation, *Selection of Cases from the Criminal Law, Occasional Publications of The Dui Hua Foundation* 16, September 2004, 29; and National Judges College, *Zhongguo Shenpan Anli Yaolan: 2002 Nian Xingshi Shenpan Anli Juan* [Overview of Sentenced Cases in China: Sentenced Criminal Case Volume, 2002] (Beijing: Press of Renmin University of China, 2003), 123–6.

34. First Instance Criminal Verdict No. 2226 (2003) of the Beijing First Intermediate People's Court Criminal Tribunal, 12 September 2003, available at Human Rights in China, <http://www.hrichina.org/public/PDFs/PressReleases/Wang-Xiaoning-27Apr06.Judgment.pdf> (accessed 7 January 2011).

35. First Instance Criminal Verdict No. 49 (2000) of the Shijiazhuang Intermediate People's Court Criminal Tribunal, 22 November 2000 (on file with author).

36. For discussion of more recent cases involving the controversial use of criminal defamation charges to punish critics of local government officials, see Joshua Rosenzweig, "China's Battle over the Right to Criticize," *Far Eastern Economic Review* (May 2009): 12–5.

37. Unless otherwise noted, the discussion of the prosecution's case against Liu is drawn from Indictment No. 247 of the Beijing People's Procuratorate, First Division, 10 December 2009 (on file with author). Passages of the texts cited in the indictment have been translated by Human Rights in China, "What Constitutes Liu Xiaobo's 'Incitement to Subvert State Power'?," 23 December 2009, <http://www.hrichina.org/public/contents/press?Revision_id=172690&item_id=172669> (accessed 28 December 2010).

38. From the translation by Perry Link, "China's Charter 08," *New York Review of Books* 56, no. 1 (15 January 2009): 54–6.

39. Unless otherwise noted, the following discussion of Liu's defense is based on Shang Baojun and Ding Xikui, "Defense Statement in the Trial of First Instance Alleging Inciting Subversion of State Power by Liu Xiaobo," 23 December 2009 (on file with author).

40. There is no shortage of these kinds of statements, as one can see in Xiao Shu, *Lishi de Xiansheng: Ban ge Shiji Qian de Zhuangyan Chengnuo* [Herald of History: The Solemn Promise Half a Century Ago] (Shantou: Shantou University Press, 1999).

41. Mo Shaoping and Lü Xi, "Defense Statement in the Trial of Second Instance Alleging Inciting Subversion of State Power by Du Daobin," 21 July 2004 (on file with author).

42. Ibid.

43. Mao Zedong, "Speech before Enlarged Session of the Central Committee," 30 January 1962, Xinhuanet, <http://news.xinhuanet.com/ziliao/2005–01/26/content_2510714.htm> (accessed 5 May 2010).

44. The others, according to Article 19 of the ICCPR, are protection of the rights and reputations of others, public order (*ordre public*), public health, or public morals, provided that any restrictions are legally based and necessary to achieve those aims.

45. Principle 1.3., The Johannesburg Principles on National Security, Freedom of Expression and Access to Information (adopted 1 October 1995) [hereafter "Johannesburg Principles"], <http://www.article19.org/pdfs/standards/joburgprinciples.pdf> (accessed 25 April 2010).

46. Principle 2(b), Johannesburg Principles.

47. Principle 6, Johannesburg Principles.

48. See, for example, Mo Shaoping and Wang Gang, "Defense Statement in the First Instance Trial Alleging Inciting Subversion of State Power by Jiang Qisheng," 1 November 1999 (on file with author).

49. Fu Kexin, "Defense Statement in the Inciting Subversion Case of He Depu," 14 October 2003 (on file with author).

50. See, for example, Kevin J. O'Brien & Lianjiang Li, *Rightful Resistance in Rural China* (Cambridge: Cambridge University Press, 2006); and Eva Pils, "Asking the Tiger for His Skin: Rights Activism in China," *Fordham International Law Journal* 30 (2007): 1209–87.

51. First Instance Criminal Verdict No. 3901 (2009) of the Beijing Number One Intermediate People's Court, 25 December 2009, <http://www.chinagfw.org/2009/12/blog-post_5696.html> (accessed 26 April 2010).

52. First Instance Criminal Verdict No. 49 (2001) of the Chengdu Intermediate People's Court Criminal Tribunal, 22 February 2003, available at US Congressional-Executive Commission on China, <http://www.cecc.gov/pages/virtualAcad/exp/exphuangqidecision.php> (accessed 7 January 2011).

53. First Instance Criminal Verdict No. 170 (2003) of the Shijiazhuang Intermediate People's Court Criminal Tribunal, 10 September 2003, <http://www.chinagfw.org/2007/06/blog-post_8779.html> (accessed 20 April 2010).

54. See, for example, "Welcoming the Sixteenth Party Congress of a Ruling Party that Promotes Democracy 'In Step with the Times'," appendix to "Prominent Beijing Dissident He Depu was Arrested by the Police," *Dacankao* [VIP Reference] 1734 (6 November 2002), <http://www.bignews.org/20021106.txt> (accessed 5 May 2010). This open letter to the Party leadership was drafted by Zhao Changqing (赵常青) and Ouyang Yi (欧阳懿) (both of whom were subsequently convicted of inciting subversion) and signed by 192 political activists from throughout China.

55. Du Daobin et al., "We are Willing to Go to Jail with Liu Di," *Dajiyuan* [The Epoch Times], 30 September 2003, <http://www.epochtimes.com/gb/3/9/30/n385043.htm> (accessed 27 April 2010). See also Philip P. Pan, "A Trip Through China's Twilight Zone," *Washington Post*, 18 December 2004, A1.

56. See Keith J. Hand, "Citizens Engage the Constitution: The Sun Zhigang Incident and Constitutional Review Proposals in the People's Republic of China," chap. 13 in Stéphanie Balme & Michael W. Dowdle (eds.), *Building Constitutionalism in China* (New York: Palgrave Macmillan, 2009).

57. Li Jianqiang et al., "Proposal to Abolish or Revise the Crime of 'Inciting Subversion of State Power'," *Beijing zhi Chun* [Beijing Spring] 123 (August 2003) <http://beijingspring.com/bj2/2003/200/2003718213211.htm> (accessed 29 April 2010).

58. Article 57, *Zhonghua Renmin Gongheguo Xingshi Susongfa* (1996) [Criminal Procedure Law of the People's Republic of China (1996)]. See also Article 97, *Gongan Jiguan Banli Xingshi Anjian Chengxu Guiding* [Provisions of the Public Security Organs on the Procedure for Handling Criminal Cases].

59. For further discussion, see Yang Wangnian, "Examination of Several Issues Concerning Residential Surveillance," *Falü Kexue* (*Xibei Zhengfa Daxue Xuebao*) [Science of Law (Northwest University of Political Science and Law)] 114 (2001): 116–21.

60. *Zuigao Renmin Fayuan Guanyu Yifa Jianshi Juzhu Qijian Kefou Zhedi Xingqi Wenti de Pifu* [Reply of the Supreme People's Court Concerning whether a Sentence May Be Reduced Following Residential Surveillance in Accordance with the Law], 18 December 1984, <http://china.findlaw.cn/susong/qiangzhicuoshi/jianshijizhu/194.html> (accessed 7 January 2011).

61. See, respectively, Mo and Wang, "Defense Statement in the First Instance Trial Alleging Inciting Subversion of State Power by Jiang Qisheng" (note 48); Mo Shaoping and Ding Xikui, "Defense Statement in the First Instance Trial Alleging Inciting Subversion of State Power by Lü Gengsong," 22 January 2008, available at *Boxun*, <http://www.peacehall.com/news/gb/china/2008/01/200801242248.shtml> (accessed 22 April 2010); Mo Shaoping, "Defense Statement in the First Instance Trial Alleging Inciting Subversion by Zhang Lin," 21 June 2005, <http://www.chinagfw.org/2007/06/blog-

post_1152.html> (accessed 28 April 2010); Li Fangping, "Defense Statement Prepared in the Case Alleging Inciting Subversion of State Power by Hu Jia," 18 March 2008, <http://www.chinagfw.org/2008/10/blog-post_24.html> (accessed 19 April 2010).

62. First Instance Criminal Verdict No. 20 (2004) of the Xiaogan Intermediate People's Court Criminal Tribunal, 11 June 2004 (on file with author).

63. "Du Daobin Remanded to Custody for Violating Provisions of Monitoring during His Suspended Sentence," 22 July 2008, *Jingchu Wang* [The official website of the Hubei Government], <http://news.cnhubei.com/xwhbyw/jcwycyw/200807/t381291.shtml> (accessed 5 May 2010).

64. See Paul Mooney, "Beijing's Mafia Justice for Lawyer They Won't Lock Up but Can't Set Free," *South China Morning Post*, 13 June 2010, 12; "Beijing Court Withdraws Probation on Ex-Lawyer Convicted of Overthrowing State," Xinhuanet, 16 December 2011, <http://news.xinhuanet.com/english/china/2011-12/16/c_131311157.htm> (accessed 17 December 2011).

65. Li Jianqiang, "Defense Statement in the Inciting Subversion of State Power Case against Guo Qizhen," 12 September 2006, <http://www.penchinese.com/wipc/2006sep/013GQZ2.htm> (accessed 21 April 2010).

66. Ibid.

67. Li, "Defense Statement Prepared in the Case Alleging Inciting Subversion of State Power by Hu Jia" (note 61).

68. Li Jianqiang, "Defense Statement in the Inciting Subversion of State Power Case Against Li Yuanlong," 19 April 2006, <http://www.chinagfw.org/2007/06/blog-post_967.html> (accessed 8 April 2010).

69. Li, "Defense Statement in the Inciting Subversion of State Power Case against Guo Qizhen" (note 65).

70. Zheng Yongjun, "Defense Statement in the Inciting Subversion of State Power Case Against An Jun," 24 November 1999, available at *Dajiyuan* [The Epoch Times], <http://www.dajiyuan.com/gb/6/7/7/n1377026.htm> (accessed 19 April 2010).

71. Mo and Wang, "Defense Statement in the First Instance Trial Alleging Inciting Subversion of State Power by Jiang Qisheng" (note 48).

72. See First Instance Criminal Verdict No. 3901 (2009) of the Beijing Number One Intermediate People's Court (note 51). See also First Instance Criminal Verdict No. 967 (2008) of the Beijing First Intermediate People's Court Criminal Tribunal, 3 April 2008, <http://www.bullogger.com/blogs/zswgsdd/archives/306896.aspx> (accessed 7 January 2011).

73. See, for example, Articles 12 and 13, *Zuigao Renmin Fayuan Guanyu Shenli Feifa Chubanwu Xingshi Anjian Juti Yingyong Falü Ruogan Wenti de Jieshi* (1998) [Interpretation of the Supreme People's Court on Several Questions Concerning the Concrete Application of Law in Adjudicating Criminal Cases Involving Illegal Publications (1998)].

74. For an early articulation, see Zhang Shizhao's 24 April 1933 defense statement in the proceedings against Chen Duxiu, collected in Wang Junxi (ed.), *Zhang Shizhao Quanji* [Collections of Zhang Shizhao's Writings] (Shanghai: Wenhui Press, 2000), Vol. 7, 146–53.
75. Shang Baojun and Ding Xikui, "Defense Statement in Second Instance Trial of Inciting Subversion of State Power by Liu Xiaobo," 28 January 2010, <http://www.chinesepen.org/Article/yzzjwyh/201002/Article_20100216150610.shtml> (accessed 26 April 2010).
76. Yu, *Weihai Guojia Anquan Zui*, 207 (note 16).

Chapter 3 Criminal Defense in Sensitive Cases

1. The Chinese Communist Party (CCP) should represent 1) the advanced productive forces in society; 2) advanced modern culture; and 3) the interests of the vast majority of the people. The principle was formulated and promoted during the second term of Jiang Zemin (江泽民) as the general secretary of the CCP.
2. The provisions were jointly issued by the Supreme People's Court, Supreme People's Procuratorate, the Ministry of Public Security, the Ministry of State Security, the Ministry of Justice, and the Legislative Affairs Commission of the Standing Committee of the National People's Congress on 19 January 1998.
3. Article 96 of the Criminal Procedure Law provides that:

    After the criminal suspect is interrogated by an investigation organ for the first time or from the day on which compulsory measures are adopted against him, he may appoint a lawyer to provide him with legal advice and to file petitions and complaints on his behalf.

4. Article 36 of the Six Departments Provisions provides that:

    According to Article 150 of the Criminal Procedure Law, when a people's procuratorate initiates a public prosecution, it should transfer the duplicates or photos of all the major evidence of the facts of the crime to the people's court.

5. Article 42 of the Criminal Procedure Law provides that the seven categories of evidence are:

    (1) material evidence and documentary evidence;
    (2) testimony of witnesses;
    (3) statements of victims;
    (4) statements and exculpations of criminal suspects or defendants;
    (5) expert conclusions;
    (6) records of inquests and examination; and
    (7) audio-visual materials.

Chapter 4 Breaking through the Obstacles of Political Isolation and Discrimination

1. [Editors' note:] Liu Xiaobo was detained on 8 December 2008, the day before Charter 08 was published online.
2. [Editors' note:] Liu's brother and brother-in-law were allowed to attend the trial, but his wife Liu Xia was not, the official reason being that Liu Xia had been a prosecution witness. Among those denied access to the trial were many friends and supporters, as well as foreign diplomats and journalists affiliated with overseas media.
3. [Editors' note:] Xinhua News Agency is the official press agency of the Chinese government. It was founded in 1931 as the "Red China News Agency."
4. [Editors' note:] On 7 January 2010, Liu Xia wrote to former President of the Czech Republic and playwright Václav Havel, actor Pavel Landovský, and the Bishop of Prague, Václav Malý, thanking them for their 6 January 2010 letter to President Hu Jintao in support of her husband, other signatories to Charter 08, and the Charter itself. For the full text of the letter in Chinese, accompanied by a press release of the Independent Chinese PEN, see <http://www.peacehall.com/news/gb/china/2010/01/201001080001.shtml>. For the text of Havel, Landovský, and Malý's letter in English, see <http://vaclavhavel.cz/showtrans.php?cat=pr&val=98_pr.html&typ=HTML> [hereafter "Letter by Havel, Landovský and Malý"].
5. [Editors' note:] "Four Elements" (*silei fenzi*, 四类分子, or *hei silei*, 黑四类) included landlords, rich peasants, counter-revolutionaries, and bad elements. "Five Elements" or "Five Categories of Black Elements" (*hei wulei*, 黑五类) included landlords, rich peasants, counter-revolutionaries, bad elements, and rightists. "If a person had his status listed as [one of the five elements] then he himself, his family members and descendants would be labeled [as belonging to] 'the five categories of black elements'." Gucheng Li, *A Glossary of Political Terms of the People's Republic of China* (Hong Kong: The Chinese University Press, 1995), 150.
6. [Editors' note:] "In Chinese mythology, *niugui sheshen* (牛鬼蛇神) were evil spirits who took human shapes to perform evil tricks, but when unmasked, reverted to their ghostly forms. The term '*niugui sheshen*' was popularised by Mao when he used it in a speech in 1957: 'All erroneous ideas, all poisonous weeds, all *niugui sheshen* must be subjected to criticism; in no circumstances must they be allowed to spread unchecked.'" Ji Fengyuan, *Linguistic Engineering: Language and Politics in Mao's China* (Honolulu: University of Hawai'i Press, 2004), 195.
7. [Editors' note:] That is, the evening after the day of the trial, and the eve of the announcement of his verdict.

8.   [Editors' note:] The Tweet for Qian Liqun read: "I don't necessarily agree with all of Liu Xiaobo's views and methods, but that's beside the point; Liu Xiaobo is a peaceful and rational critic and to incarcerate him for this is a sign of weakness, one very difficult to accept." Cui Weiping, "Intellectuals' Views on Liu Xiaobo's Sentence," 19 October 2010, <http://www.bullogger.com/blogs/cuiweiping/archives/367777.aspx>.

9.   [Editors' note:] The Tweet for Mang Ke read: "Poet Mang Ke considers himself to be 'very good friends with Xiaobo, we were always happy when together. I have never considered him to have done anything wrong.' When he heard what had happened to Xiaobo he said, 'I wish he were alright again tomorrow.'" Ibid.

10. [Editors' note:] The Tweet for Tang Xiaodu read: "A friend of Liu Xiaobo's from the eighties, poetry critic Tang Xiaodu recalls that back then Liu Xiaobo, despite knowing Liu Zaifu (刘再复) very well, pretended not to know him! But he [Tang] also said that he felt more and more in agreement with Liu Xiaobo's thought as it had developed in recent years, and that he felt Liu had become increasingly solid. In China's current environment Liu Xiaobo exhibited the deservingness and rationality of Chinese intellectuals." Ibid.

11. [Editors' note:] The Tweet for Sun Jin read: "Xiaobo is clever and sensitive and has been a very good, conscientious friend. But it seems as though he had been placing too much confidence in the correctness of his personal ethical conscience." Ibid.

12. [Editors' note:] All the Tweets were later preserved at Cui Weiping's blog. Ibid.

13. [Editors' note:] 140 Chinese characters are capable of expressing much more than 140 letters using the Roman alphabet in a Western language.

14. *Analects of Confucius* 17: 9. The original Chinese text reads: "诗，可以兴，可以观，可以群，可以怨。"

15. [Editors' note:] Cui Weiping also contributed her own view in a Tweet: "Cui Weiping's view: (1) Charter 08 is within the framework of the current Constitution; (2) When people are no longer afraid, there will no longer be any point in incarcerating Liu Xiaobo; (3) This was the verdict of a religious tribunal. How can a person be held criminally liable for their thoughts? (Scholar of literature)" Cui, "Intellectuals' Views on Liu Xiaobo's Sentence" (note 8).

16. [Editors' note:] For a brief introduction of these two documentary films, see, for example, Wang Wo "Noise," *Jingxiang Zhongguo* [sinoreel.com], 24 December 2007, <http://sinoreel.com/index.php?mid=articles&document_srl=118>; "Torment," *21 Shiji Wang* [21cbh.com], 28 July 2010, <http://www.21cbh.com/HTML/2010–7-28/4NMDAwMDE4OTE4Ng.html>.

17. [Editors' note:] Cui, "Intellectuals' Views on Liu Xiaobo's Sentence" (note 8).

18. [Editors' note:] For a brief introduction to this 1958 film by Wang Ping, see "An Electric Wave that Will Never Fade Away," *Baidu Baike* [Baidu Encyclopedia], <http://baike.baidu.com/view/195131.htm>.

19. For the original Tweets, see Cui, "Intellectuals' Views on Liu Xiaobo's Sentence" (note 8). For a translation of some of the Tweets, see John Kennedy, "Cui Weiping Tweets Elite Views on Liu Xiaobo," 30 December 2009, <http://globalvoicesonline.org/2009/12/29/china-cui-weiping-tweets-elite-views-on-liu-xiaobo>. Note that since 140 Chinese characters are capable of expressing more than 140 letters using the Roman alphabet, the Tweets reproduced here in English translation are quite long.

20. Qin Hui, historian, professor, Department of History, School of Humanities and Social Sciences, Tsinghua University. Original Tweet: 秦晖的看法：现在还搞因言治罪那一套，真是太可悲了。我不是宪章的签名者，但我懂得"不赞成你的观点，但坚决捍卫你发表观点的权利"的道理，我坚决反对对刘晓波搞文字狱。（历史学学者）

21. Xu Youyu, philosopher, researcher, Institute of Philosophy, Chinese Academy of Social Sciences. Original Tweet: 徐友渔的看法：宣判刘晓波，罪名中有零八宪章。宪章重申联合国人权宣言，因此此判是对人类大家庭公认的文明准则的挑战，也是对中国现存宪法的挑战，因为该宪法载明了中国公民的言论自由。说到底，是对中国人民和人类良知的挑战。（哲学学者）

22. Zhang Yihe, writer, formerly researcher, Institute of Traditional Chinese Opera, China Art Academy Graduate School. Original Tweet: 章诒和的看法：1968年，我以现行反革命罪，判处有期徒刑20年；2009年，刘晓波以煽动颠覆国家政权罪，判处有期徒刑11年。我们都是因言获罪，前后相距四十一载。这种状况不得不使人怀疑：我们的制度，到底改善了多少？我们的社会，究竟进步了没有？（作家）

23. Yuan Weishi, historian, formerly professor at the Department of Philosophy of Sun Yat-Sen University. Original Tweet: 袁伟时的看法：二十一世纪了，还以言获罪，侵犯公民权利，亵渎文明，又一次往中国脸上擦黑！当局认定的罪犯刘晓波成了众人心目中的英雄，鸿沟如此巨大，执政者如何面对？（历史学学者）

24. Yu Yingshi, historian, professor emeritus of East Asian Studies and History, Princeton University. Original Tweet: 余英时的看法：1989以来，刘晓波先后入狱三次。这次竟将长至11年。但他入狱，一次比一次光荣，这次最光荣。中国史上恰好有一个光辉先例，那便是一千年来受人尊敬的范仲淹，一生"先天下之忧而忧，后天下之乐而乐"。他在政府猛烈批评朝政，主张"宁鸣而死，不默而生"。他一生被贬放三次。一次送行，朋友们说："此行极光。"第二次大家说："此行亦光。"最后一次说："此行尤光。"他笑答道："仲淹前后三光矣。"这便是今天我们的刘晓波。（历史学学者）

25. Fan Zhongyan (989–1052), a prominent official, literary figure, and outspoken government critic of the Northern Song Dynasty (北宋).

26. He Weifang, legal scholar, professor, Peking University Law School. Original Tweet: 贺卫方的看法：不久前，某海外传媒来电采访，问我对于 Mr. Hsiao-po Liu的十一年之罚的看法。我没有好气地说："我欲无言。"对方问："难道说你不觉得十一年太重？"我反问："难道说判三年就适当了么？对于根本无罪者，一天都太重，一天之罚都是冤狱。再说，你真以为他会在牢里服满十一年？"（法学学者）

27. Guo Yuhua, sociologist, professor, Department of Sociology, School of Humanities and Social Sciences, Tsinghua University. Original Tweet: 郭于华的看法：08县长表达的是公民最基本和正当的权利要求，而且提倡以温和改良的方式推进社会进步，道出常识何罪之有？即使说的全然不对，也不可以因言获罪。判刘晓波有罪才是真正的颠覆国家政权（合法性）之罪，而且是对社会良知和人类文明的挑战。（社会学学者）

28. Wang Xiaoyu, historian, professor, Institute of Critical Culture Studies, Tongji University. Original Tweet: 王晓渔的看法：我不会翻墙，没有在大陆媒体上看到报道。我坚信一个手无寸铁的书生因为几篇文章将在铁窗之内度过11年，是少数敌对势力制造的谣言。一个伟大、光荣、正确的国家，怎么可能允许这种违反法治的事情发生呢？希望广大善良的不明真相的群众，睁开眼睛，明辨是非，不要被谣言迷惑。（历史学学者）

29. Zhang Yiwu, professor of Literature, Department of Chinese Language and Literature, Peking University. Original Tweet: 与张颐武通了电话，他表示此前不知道刘晓波被判的事情，他的注意力主要在别的地方，比如小沈阳。崔解释只是想听听周围人们的反应，他说"一点反应也没有"。

30. Zhang Lifan, historian, director, China Charity Federation. Original Tweet: 章立凡的看法：1.宪政民主是庄严的历史承诺，也是通过社会和解维系执政合法性的救赎通道。今年圣诞节，权力的傲慢与偏见再度堵死通道。2.历史上一再失信，当前经济、政治改革和法制建设全面倒退，社会冲突无解。3.丧失现实判断力，开历史倒车自杀。尽管我不热爱革命，但已确认脑残无救。（历史学学者）

31. Ai Xiaoming, professor of Literature, Department of Chinese Language and Literature, Sun Yat-sen University. Original Tweet: 艾晓明的看法：在为自由设置的铁蒺藜前，刘晓波以血肉之躯突进；十一年的判决，要活埋自由思考的精神。沉默就是容忍、合谋、戕害良知、断送希望，让子孙万代苟活于谎言。对不起，可能根本没有万代，我们早已自我了断。中国人，不说实话、至死不说直到喑哑，怎与那诞生了《卡廷》、《窃听风暴》等艺术作品的民族共存？（文学教授）

32. [Editors' note] *Katyń*, a 2007 Polish film by Andrzej Wajda about a mass killing of Polish officers and citizens ordered by Soviet authorities in 1940.

33. *The Lives of Others* [*Das Leben Der Anderen*], a 2006 German film by Florian Henckel von Donnersmarck about the German Democratic Republic's (East Germany's) secret police, the *Stasi*.

34. Bei Dao, poet, professor of Humanities, Centre for East Asian Studies, The Chinese University of Hong Kong. Original Tweet: 北岛的看法：因言治罪，让人再次感到一个古老帝国的阴影。我想起三十年前的一次类似的审

判。我们是否能走出这帝国的阴影？让我感动的是刘晓波和刘霞之间的爱情，他们的爱远远超越了那自以为主宰他人命运的人的恨。（诗人）

35. Xu Xiao, writer, editor of *Jintian* [Today] poetry periodical. Original Tweet: 徐晓：晓波开庭之前，我对国保的警察说：如果因为《08宪章》而审判刘晓波，如果因为起诉书中所说的理由而重判刘晓波，作为宪章的签署者之一，请把我也抓进监狱。（作家）

36. Hu Yong, media studies scholar, associate professor, School of Media and Communication Studies, Peking University. Original Tweet: 胡泳的看法：第一，我们离文革、反右、反胡风很近；第二，我们离文明世界很远，仍然是一个野蛮国度。呼吁取消《刑法》第105条第2款这一臭名昭著的恶法，它既延续79年刑法反革命罪的思维，也延续中国古代的文字狱。（新闻学学者）

37. Wang Lixiong, writer. Wang's works include *Huang Huo* [Yellow Peril] (1991); *Wo de Xiyu, Ni de Dongtu* [My Western Regions, Your East Turkestan] (2007); and *Tianzang: Xizang de Mingyun* [Sky Burial: The Fate of Tibet] (2009). Original Tweet: 王力雄的看法：希望这11年中会有其他的变化。对刘晓波和所有政治犯最有效的支持，是尽快改变这个社会，解放所有的人。（作家）

38. Zhang Sizhi, famous first-generation criminal defense lawyer of the People's Republic of China, Wu Luan & Zhao Yan Law Firm. Original Tweet: 张思之的看法：读刘案，问苍天：伟大、光荣、正确的政党，许诺国人言者无罪，实施宪政，申明"言信、行果"，信誓旦旦，何以化为花言巧语，唯余空言？也曾宣示信奉人民民主，四大自由，何以在在违反？无奈之余，敢向为大众争民主而甘愿牺牲个人自由的志士表达我心中礼赞！（律师）

39. [Attributed to] Václav Havel, former President of the Czech Republic. Original Tweet: 哈维尔的看法：当公民按照自己的意志、通过自己的知识和良知采取行动时，当公民和平地相互结社、讨论和表达他们对社会将来发展的关心与观点时，根本就不存在颠覆国家安全。相反，当一个国家的公民不被允许自由地采取行动、结社、思考与表达时，这个国家未来的财富和精神就会被破坏。

40. [Editors' note:] Cui Weiping apparently excerpted this from the 6 January 2010 letter to President Hu Jintao by Václav Havel, actor Pavel Landovský, and Bishop of Prague Václav Malý. See Letter by Havel, Landovský, and Malý (note 4).

41. Hu Xingdou, economist, professor, Beijing University of Science and Technology. 胡星斗的看法：对于刘案，我已经在多个采访时说了：中国已经开始以言治罪，突破了文明国家甚至威权国家的底线了。无论中国经济多么辉煌，中国其实还是个野蛮国家，经济辉煌也只是特权腐败的畸形经济泡沫，希特勒的经济也辉煌过，斯大林的经济也辉煌过，结果呢还是举世唾弃。他们在围剿言论的时候，民心已经丧失。（经济学学者）

42. Liu Zaifu, literature scholar, formerly director, Institute of Literature, Chinese Academy of Social Sciences. Original Tweet: 刘再复的看法：刘晓

波在《美人赠我蒙汗药》这本书中骂我是"理论沙皇"（这之前又多次批评我是国家主义者等），但是今天，我这个"沙皇"要说一句话：我反对任何以言治罪的行为，包括以言治晓波的行为。（文学理论家）

43. This is a book written by Liu Xiaobo (pen name: Laoxia) and Wang Shuo. Wang Shuo and Laoxia, *Meiren Zeng Wo Menghanyao* [*A Beauty Drugged Me*] (Wuhan: Changjiang Literary Press, 2000).

44. Mao Yushi, economist, president, Unirule Institute (Beijing). Original Tweet: 茅于轼的看法：听几位党内的老同志说，党的二大、七大都提过联邦共和的说法。即使党的二大和七大没有提出过联邦共和的说法，难道刘晓波提出来就不可以吗？我们这个社会要不断进步，就要有新思想。（经济学家）

45. Zhang Boshu, formerly researcher, Institute of Philosophy, Chinese Academy of Social Sciences. Original Tweet: 张博树的看法：重判刘晓波，在司法意义上是一件非常荒唐的事情，是因言治罪的典型。这件事发生在21世纪的中国，是我们这个民族的耻辱。从转型意义上看，这个判决反倒使零八宪章更加彰显于天下，而且塑造了一位反对派英雄。不管零八宪章文本上还有什么可以讨论的地方，不管晓波作为具体的个人可能有什么弱点、不足，这些都已经不重要。重要的是转型正在因为这个判决形成某种新的布局，而且具有了新的道义力量。宣判者正在被宣判。这大概是那些决定重判刘晓波的人始料不及的。（哲学学者）

46. Wang Yi, researcher, Institute of Philosophy, Chinese Academy of Social Sciences. Original Tweet: 王毅的看法：我过去常常希望能够说服自己：中国历史上的专制包袱太重、又有种种现实国情的难处，所以我们作"蚁民"、"屁民"的，应该尽量体恤执政者在制度进步上的一步三回头，充分理解中国走上法治宪政道路不可能是一日之功。但现在这个判决说明，我们善以待人还应该有个底线，这就是你执政者在法治进步这件事上总要有一点儿起码的真诚，你不能一方面向全世界承诺《公民权利和政治权利国际公约》、流着鼻涕眼泪说民主人权如何如何体现了人类文明的进步，但同时你做的还是当年对付遇罗克、张志新、林昭的那一套。（历史学者）

Chapter 5 Boundaries of Tolerance

1. Xia Dongmei, "Peace Prize a Political Farce," *China Daily*, 11 December 2010, <http://www.chinadaily.com.cn/opinion/2010–12/11/content_11686473.htm> (accessed 15 December 2010).

2. A translation of the full text of the Charter is available in Perry Link (trans.), "China's Charter 08," *New York Review of Books* 56, no. 1 (15 January 2009), <http://www.nybooks.com/articles/archives/2009/jan/15/chinas-charter-08/> (accessed 17 November 2010). See also Pitman B. Potter, "4 June and Charter 08: Approaches to Remonstrance," *China Information* 25, no. 2 (July 2011): 121–38.

3. Link (trans.), "China's Charter 08," ibid.

4. The Action Plan was completed in 2009. See State Council Information Office, *National Human Rights Action Plan of China (2009–2010)*, China.org. cn, <http://www.china.org.cn/archive/2009–04/13/content_17595407.htm> (accessed 7 December 2010).

5. Link (trans.), "China's Charter 08" (note 2).

6. Feng Chongyi, "Charter 08 Framer Liu Xiaobo Awarded Nobel Peace Prize. The Troubled History and Future of Chinese Liberalism," *The Asia-Pacific Journal: Japan Focus* 41 (11 October 2010), <http://japanfocus.org/-Feng-Chongyi/3427> (accessed 7 December 2010).

7. See, for example, Feng Chongyi, "Democrats within the Chinese Communist Party since 1989," *Journal of Contemporary China* 17, no. 57 (November 2008): 673–88; Feng Chongyi, "The Chinese Liberal Camp in Post June-4th China," *China Perspectives* 2009, no. 2 (2009): 30–41.

8. State Council Information Office, *Building of Political Democracy in China*, October 2005, China.org.cn, <http://www.china.org.cn/english/features/book/145877.htm> (accessed 12 March 2012).

9. See, for example, Will Kymlicka, *Liberalism, Community and Culture* (Oxford: Clarendon Press, 1991); Robert A. Packenham, *Liberal America and the Third World* (Princeton: Princeton University Press, 1971).

10. "NPC Standing Committee Discusses Deletion of the 'Four Freedoms'," *Selections from World Broadcasts* FE/6398/BII/1, 18 April 1980.

11. State Council Information Office, *Building of Political Democracy in China* (note 8).

12. See, for example, "The Carter Center Report on China's Elections August 1–August 7, 2000," <http://www.cartercenter.org/documents/540.html> (accessed 12 March 2012).

13. See, for example, Pitman B. Potter, "China's Peripheries: Challenges of Central Governance and Local Autonomy," in Diana Lary (ed.), *China at the Borders* (Vancouver: UBC Press, 2007); Pitman B. Potter, "Selective Adaptation and Institutional Capacity: Perspectives on Human Rights in China," *International Journal* 61, no. 2 (2006): 389–410.

14. State Council Information Office, *China's Efforts and Achievements in Promoting the Rule of Law*, 28 February 2008 (on file with authors).

15. See, for example, Pitman B. Potter, "International and Domestic Selective Adaptation: The Case of Charter 08," in Penelope Nicholson and John Gillespie (eds.), *Law and Development and the Global Discourses of Legal Transfers* (Cambridge University Press, forthcoming 2012).

16. Article 51, PRC Constitution; "Professor: Rule of Law, Human Rights Strike Deep Roots in China," *China View*, 11 February 2009 (on file with authors).

17. See generally, Björn A. Gustaffson, Li Shi, and Terry Sicular (eds.), *Inequality and Public Policy in China* (Cambridge: Cambridge University Press, 2008).

18. State Council Information Office, *Building of Political Democracy in China* (note 8).

19. See, for example, Murray Scot Tanner, *The Politics of Law-Making in Post-Mao China: Institutions, Processes, and Democratic Prospects* (Oxford: Oxford University Press, 1998).

20. Preamble and Article 1, PRC Constitution.

21. See, for example, Kenneth G. Lieberthal and David M. Lampton, "Introduction: The 'Fragmented Authoritarianism' Model and Its Implications," in Kenneth G. Lieberthal and David M. Lampton (eds.), *Bureaucracy, Politics and Decision Making in Post-Mao China* (Berkeley, CA: University of California Press, 1992), 1–30.

22. Zheng Yongnian, *Defacto Federalism: Reforms and Dynamics of Central-Local Relations* (Hackensack, NJ: World Scientific, 2007); Sean M. Dougherty and Robert H. McGuckin, "Federalism and the Impetus for Reform in China," *China Law and Practice* 15, no. 4 (2002): 30–4; Michael Davis, "The Case for Chinese Federalism," *Journal of Democracy* 10, no. 2 (1999): 124–37.

23. Article 67, PRC Constitution.

24. Debates over the Property Law of the PRC are an example. See Wang Zhaoguo, "Explanation on the Draft Property Law of the People's Republic of China" (Delivered at the Fifth Session of the Tenth National People's Congress, 8 March 2007), *People's Daily*, <http://English.people.com.cn/200703/08/print20070308_355491.html> (accessed 12 March 2012).

25. Cf. State Council Information Office, *China's Efforts and Achievements in Promoting the Rule of Law* (note 14).

26. Article 126, PRC Constitution.

27. See Zou Keyuan, "Administrative Reform and Rule of Law," *Copenhagen Journal of Asian Studies* 24 (2006): 5–32; Administrative Charges Research Group, "Administrative Charges: Current Problems and Future Solutions," in Li Lin (ed.), *The China Legal Development Yearbook*, vol. 3 (2008) (Leiden: Brill, 2009), 145–63.

28. See "Administrative Detention," in Congressional-Executive Commission on China (ed.), *Annual Report 2006*, Section V, <http://www.cecc.gov/pages/annualRpt/annualRpt06/RightsofCriminalSuspects.php#admindetb> (accessed 23 November 2010).

29. For an assessment of the state of the *hukou* system, see Kam Wing Chan and Will Buckingham, "Is China Abolishing the *Hukou* System?" *The China Quarterly* 195 (2008): 582–606. See also Congressional-Executive Commission on China, "China's Household Registration System: Sustained Reform Needed to Protect China's Rural Migrants," 7 October 2005, <http://www.cecc.gov/pages/news/hukou.php> (accessed 23 November 2010).

30. State Council Information Office, "China's Progress in Human Rights in 2004," April 2005, <http://english.gov.cn/official/2005-07/28/content_18115.htm> (accessed 23 November 2010).

31. "Property Rights Law of the PRC," *China Economic News, Supplement* (16 March 2007), 9–10.

32. "Minister of Finance Jin Renqing Gives Detailed Interpretation of Two Major Amendments to the Individual Income Tax Law," Xinhuanet, 24 August 2005, available at Chinalawinfo.com (on file with authors). These measures expanded the scope of the 2001 provisions on tax enforcement for high-income individuals. See "Notice of the State Administration of Taxation on Further Strengthening the Administration of Collection of Individual Income Tax from High-Income Individuals" (1 June 2001) and "Law of the PRC to Administer the Levy and Collection of Taxes and Detailed Rules for the Implementation of the Law of the People's Republic of China to Administer the Levying and Collection of Taxes" (4 August 1993).

33. A law on social assistance has long been on the NPC's legislative agenda, with a draft released for comment in 2008. See "Notice on Public Consultation of the Social Assistance Law of the People's Republic of China (Draft for Consultation)," 15 August 2008, <http://www.gov.cn/gzdt/2008–08/15/content_1072843.htm> (accessed 20 October 2010). Other major initiatives in this area include the Labor Contract Law regime and new proposals on public access to health care. See Geoff Dyer, "China's Labor Law Raises US Concerns," *Financial Times*, 2 May 2007, and "China Passes New Medical Reform Plan," *China View*, 21 January 2009 (on file with authors).

34. Decision of the State Council on Achieving a Scientific Conception of Development and Strengthening Environmental Protection (3 December 2005).

35. Pitman B. Potter, *Law, Policy, and Practice on China's Periphery* (Oxford; New York: Routledge, 2011); Pitman B. Potter, "Governance of China's Periphery: Balancing Local Autonomy and National Unity," *Columbia Journal of Asian Law* 19, no. 1 (Spring–Fall 2005): 293–322.

36. Michel Bonnin, "The Chinese Communist Party and June 4th," *China Perspectives* 2009, no. 2 (2009): 52–61.

37. Irish Peace Society, "Reconciliation, Central Component of Conflict Transformation" (on file with authors).

38. This was suggested shortly after the publication of Charter 08, in Pitman B. Potter, "Charter 08: An Opportunity for Legal and Political Reform?," *Asia Pacific Bulletin* 306 (15 April 2009), <http://www.asiapacific.ca/sites/default/files/filefield/306Charter08.pdf> (accessed 19 November 2010).

39. "What Attention Will Be Paid to Wen Jiabao's Shenzhen Speech," *Caixinwang* [Finance News Network], 28 August 2010 (on file with authors); Justin Li, "Political Reform in China: Wen Will It Happen and Hu Will Lead It?" *East Asia Forum*, 19 September 2010, <http://www.eastasiaforum.org/2010/09/19/political-reform-in-china-wen-would-it-happen-and-hu-will-lead-it/> (accessed 19 November 2010); Malcolm Moore, "Wen Jiabao Promises Political Reform for China," *The Telegraph*, 4 October 2010,

<http://www.telegraph.co.uk/news/worldnews/asia/china/8040534/Wen-Jiabao-promises-political-reform-for-China.html> (accessed 17 November 2010).

40. Chris Buckley, "China Premier Wen Calls for Political Reform: Report," Reuters, 22 August 2010, <http://www.reuters.com/article/idUSTRE67L0AL20100822> (accessed 19 November 2010).

41. Link (trans.), "China's Charter 08" (note 2).

42. This comment echoes remarks Wen made in May 2008 during a visit at China University of Political Science and Law (中国政法大学) to the effect that implementation of law must be fair (*gongping*, 公平) and that having a legal system (*fazhi*, 法制) was not the same as having rule of law (*fazhi*, 法治). See "Wen Jiabao Speaks with University Students about the Rule of Law," *Fazhi Wang* [Legal System Net], 4 December 2009, <http://www.legaldaily.com.cn/bm/content/2009–12/04/content_1191558.htm> (accessed 20 October 2010). These remarks compare favorably with the statement in Charter 08 that "The political reality, which is plain for anyone to see, is that China has many laws but no rule of law; it has a constitution but no constitutional government". See Link (trans.), "China's Charter 08" (note 2).

43. "Transcript of Interview with Chinese Premier Wen Jiabao," CNN World, 29 September 2008 (on file with authors).

44. "Complete Transcript of Wen Jiabao Promoting Political Reform in Special CNN Interview: Rain and Wind Will Not Block Me until I Die or Retire," China Digital Times, 9 October 2010; "Fareed Zakaria GPS: Interview with Wen Jiabao," CNN <http://transcripts.cnn.com/TRANSCRIPTS/1010/03/fzgps.01.html> (accessed 22 November 2010). See also Han Yonghong, "Wen Jiabao: The People's Demand for Democracy and Freedom is Irresistible," China Digital Times, 8 October 2010.

45. John Garnaut, "Reform Struggle Hits China's Front Page," *The Age*, 16 October 2010, <http://www.theage.com.au/world/reform-struggle-hits-chinas-front-page-20101015–16nix.html> (accessed 19 November 2010); Moore, "Wen Jiabao Promises Political Reform in China" (note 39).

46. Link (trans.), "China's Charter 08" (note 2).

47. Feng, "Democrats within the Chinese Communist Party since 1989" (note 7).

48. "Original Text of Open Letter to the NPC Standing Committee Demanding Freedom of the Press and Expression," China Digital Times, 14 October 2010; David Bandurski, "Open Letter from Party Elders Calls for Free Speech," China Media Project, 12 October 2010, <http://cmp.hku.hk/2010/10/13/8035/> (accessed 19 November 2010).

49. Link (trans.), "China's Charter 08" (note 2).

50. Xiao Shu, "Is Anyone Really Secure in China?," China Media Project, 5 November 2010, <http://cmp.hku.hk/2010/11/01/8426/> (accessed 17 November 2010).

51. "Latest Directives from the Ministry of Truth, October 9–19, 2010," China Digital Times, 19 October 2010, <http://chinadigitaltimes.net/2010/10/latest-directives-from-the-ministry-of-truth-october-9–19–2010/> (accessed 19 November 2010).

52. The series, penned by Zheng Qingyuan (郑青原), was published in *Renmin Ribao* [People's Daily] under the title "On Vigorously Grasping the Historical Opportunity and Comprehensively Building a Moderately Prosperous Society." The three individual articles are: "In the Age of Accomplishment, Go All Out to Achieve Promise," 21 October 2010, <http://opinion.people.com.cn/GB/40604/13007462.html>; "Rely on Speeding up Transformation of Economic Development Styles to Win the Future," 25 October 2010, <http://opinion.people.com.cn/GB/40604/13034080.html>; "Grasping Political Aspects of Positively and Appropriately Promoting Reform of the Political System," 27 October 2010, <http://opinion.people.com.cn/GB/40604/13056137.html> (all three articles accessed November 2010).

53. "Full text of Communiqué of the Fifth Plenum of the 17th CPC Central Committee," Xinhuanet, 18 October 2010, <http://news.xinhuanet.com/english2010/china/2010–10/18/c_13563388.htm> (accessed 19 November 2010).

54. Chinese Human Rights Defenders (CHRD), *Annual Report on the Situation of Human Rights Defenders in China (2009)*, <http://www.ldh-france.org/IMG/pdf/Rapport_2009_Human_Rights_Defenders.pdf> (accessed 9 December 2010).

55. "Beijing University Law School Requires Students to Boycott 'Charter 08'," China Digital Times, 30 January 2009.

56. According to Feng, "Charter 08 Framer Liu Xiaobo Awarded Nobel Peace Prize," (note 6).

57. CHRD, *Annual Report (2009)* (note 54).

58. See the website of Charter 08, <http://www.2008xianzhang.info> (accessed 22 September 2010).

59. See Beijing No. 1 Intermediate People's Court Criminal Case Verdict No. 3901, 2009, full text published in *Ming Bao* [Mingpao Daily], 26 December 2009.

60. Ariana Eunjung Cha, "In China, a Grass-Roots Rebellion: Rights Manifesto Slowly Gains Ground Despite Government Efforts to Quash It," *Washington Post*, 29 January 2009, A1.

61. "Guangzhou Man Distributes Charter 08 around City," China Human Rights Briefing (9–15 March 2010) (on file with authors).

62. Liu Xiaobo, "I Have No Enemies: My Final Statement" (23 December 2009), *Foreign Policy*, 8 October 2010, <http://www.foreignpolicy.com/articles/2010/10/08/i_have_no_enemies> (accessed 23 November 2010).

63. "Beijing Blasts Nobel Peace Prize Meddling," *People's Daily*, 9 October 2010, <http://english.peopledaily.com.cn/90001/90776/90882/7160366.html> (accessed 10 October 2010).
64. Ibid.; Nicholas Bequelin, "The Prize China Didn't Want to Win," *Foreign Policy*, 6 October 2010, <http://www.foreignpolicy.com/articles/2010/10/06/the_prize_china_doesn_t_want_to_win> (accessed 23 November 2010).
65. "Activists Condemn Anti-Liu Crackdown," Agence France-Presse, 18 October 2010; Jerome Cohen and Eva Pils, "Empty Chairs in Oslo Speak Volumes," *The Wall Street Journal*, 11 November 2010, <http://www.freedom-now.org/wp-content/uploads/2010/11/Liu-WSJ-Op-Ed-by-Jerome-A-Cohen-and-Eva-Pils-11.11.10.pdf> (accessed 23 November 2010).
66. Perry Link, "At the Nobel Ceremony: Liu Xiaobo's Empty Chair," *New York Review of Books* blog, 13 December 2010, <http://www.nybooks.com/blogs/nyrblog/2010/dec/13/nobel-peace-prize-ceremony-liu-xiaobo/> (accessed 15 December 2010). For an insightful commentary on the impact of the empty chair, see Jeffrey Wasserstrom, "Liu Xiaobo and Three Noble Nobel Winners," *The Huffington Post*, 10 December 2010, <http://www.huffingtonpost.com/jeffrey-wasserstrom/liu-xiaobo-and-3-past-nob_b_795183.html> (accessed 15 December 2010).
67. Michael Warner, *Publics and Counterpublics* (New York: Zone Books, 2002), 67.
68. Guobin Yang and Craig Calhoun, "Media, Civil Society, and the Rise of a Green Public Sphere in China," *China Information* 21, no. 2 (2007): 211–36.
69. Jürgen Habermas, "The Public Sphere," in Steven Seidman (ed.), *Jürgen Habermas on Society and Politics: A Reader* (Boston: Beacon Press, 1989).
70. For example, Nancy Fraser, *Justice Interruptus: Critical Reflections on the "Postsocialist" Condition* (New York: Routledge, 1997). Habermas later revised his conception in response to his critics. See also Yang and Calhoun, "Media, Civil Society, and the Rise of a Green Public Sphere in China," 213 (note 68).
71. Timothy Cheek, "Pluralized Publics of Contemporary Chinese Intellectuals: Party, Profession, and 'The Public', " Paper presented for the conference *Chinese Visions on a Planetary Scale*, Monash University, 15–27 August 2007, 18.
72. Sophia Woodman, "Human Rights as 'Foreign Affairs': China's Reporting under Human Rights Treaties," *Hong Kong Law Journal* 35, Part 1 (2005): 179–203.
73. See various chapters of Peter Ho and Richard Louis Edmonds (eds.), *China's Embedded Activism: Opportunities and Constraints of a Social Movement* (Oxford; New York: Routledge, 2008).
74. Peter Ho and Richard Louis Edmonds, "Perspectives of Time and Change: Rethinking Green Environmental Activism in China," in ibid., 220.

75. Jiangang Zhu and Peter Ho, "Not Against the State, Just Protecting Residents' Interests: An Urban Movement in a Shanghai Neighborhood," in Ho and Edmonds (eds.), *China's Embedded Activism* (note 73).
76. Ibid; Kevin J. O'Brien and Lianjiang Li, *Rightful Resistance in Rural China* (Cambridge: Cambridge University Press, 2006).
77. Yang and Calhoun, "Media, Civil Society, and the Rise of a Green Public Sphere in China" (note 68).
78. Gloria Davies, "Habermas in China: Theory as Catalyst," *The China Journal* 57 (January 2007): 61–85.
79. Xueliang Ding, "Institutional Amphibiousness and the Transition from Communism: The Case of China," *British Journal of Political Science* 24, no. 3 (1994): 293–318.
80. Peter Ho, "Embedded Activism and Political Change in a Semiauthoritarian Context," *China Information* 21, no. 2 (2007): 187–210.
81. Carl F. Minzner, "Riots and Cover-Ups: Counterproductive Control of Local Agents in China," *University of Pennsylvania Journal of International Law* 31, no. 1 (Fall 2009): 54–123; Carl F. Minzner, "Xinfang: An Alternative to Formal Chinese Legal Institutions," *Stanford Journal of International Law* 42 (2006): 103–79.
82. For a recent example, see Sharon LaFraniere and Dan Levin, "Assertive Chinese Held in Mental Wards," *The New York Times*, 11 November 2010.
83. See, for example, CHRD, "Silencing Complaints: Human Rights Abuses against Petitioners in China," 8 January 2008 (on file with authors).
84. Feng, "Democrats within the Chinese Communist Party since 1989," 683 (note 7).
85. Flora Sapio, *Sovereign Power and the Law in China* (Leiden: Brill, 2010), 245.
86. The scope of the deprivation of political rights envisaged under Article 54 of the PRC Criminal Law is broad, indicating that those so deprived may not exercise the rights to vote and stand as a candidate for election; the rights to freedom of expression, publication, assembly, association, march, and demonstration; and that they may not hold positions in state organs, and may not have leadership roles in state companies and enterprises, public service organizations, or "people's organizations."
87. These offenses are contained in Chapter I of the PRC Criminal Law.
88. Article 56, PRC Criminal Law
89. Article 57, PRC Criminal Law.
90. We are indebted to Tim Cheek for suggesting this term.
91. Mao Zedong, "On the Correct Handling of Contradictions among the People," in Roderick MacFarquhar, Timothy Cheek, and Eugene Wu (eds.), *The Secret Speeches of Chairman Mao: From the Hundred Flowers to the Great Leap Forward* (Cambridge, MA: Harvard University Press, 1989), 131–90.

92. For a recent example, see Wen Hai, "Why Has 'Correctly Handling Contradictions among the People' Been Written into the Communiqué of the Fifth Plenum?," *Renmin Wang* [People's Daily website], 22 October 2010, <http://opinion.people.com.cn/GB/13019983.html> (accessed 22 November 2010).
93. Hualing Fu and Richard Cullen, "National Security Law in China," *Columbia Journal of International Law* 34 (1996): 449–68.
94. Bonnin, "The Chinese Communist Party and June 4th" (note 36).
95. Feng, "Charter 08 Framer Liu Xiaobo Awarded Nobel Peace Prize" (note 6).
96. See Beijing No. 1 Intermediate People's Court Criminal Case Verdict No. 3901, 2009 (note 59).
97. CHRD, "Lawyer for Liu Xiaobo Submits Formal Request Demanding Details of Activist's Detention," 11 February 2009.
98. Peter Foster, "China Upholds 11-Year Sentence for Dissident Liu Xiaobo," *The Daily Telegraph*, 11 February 2010.
99. Zhu and Ho, "Not Against the State" (note 75).
100. CHRD, "Silencing Complaints" (note 83).
101. Sophia Woodman, *Local Citizenship and Socialized Governance: Linking Citizens and the State in Rural and Urban Tianjin China*, PhD dissertation, October 2011, available at <https://circle.ubc.ca/handle/2429/38485> (accessed 12 March 2012).
102. Jean-Philippe Béja, "Editorial: Don't Forget June 4th," *China Perspectives* 2009, no. 2 (2009): 2–3.
103. See, for example, Nick Young, "Liu Xiaobo Wins Nobel, Reform Loses," *The Guardian*, 8 October 2010, <http://www.guardian.co.uk/commentis free/2010/oct/08/liu-xiaobo-china> (accessed 12 March 2012).
104. O'Brien and Li, *Rightful Resistance in Rural China*, 50–66 (note 76).
105. See, for example, Young, "Liu Xiaobo Wins Nobel" (note 103).
106. Liu, "I Have No Enemies" (note 62).
107. See Roderick MacFarquhar, *The Origins of the Cultural Revolution*, vol. 1 (London: Columbia University Press, 1974).
108. See Peng Zhen, "Several Questions on the Socialist Legal System," *Hongqi* [Red Flag] 1979, no. 11 (2 November 1979): 3.
109. Feng, "Democrats within the Chinese Communist Party since 1989" (note 7).
110. Link (trans.), "China's Charter 08" (note 2).

Chapter 6 The Threat of Charter 08

1. There are two slightly different versions of the text available in English. One was provided by Perry Link, whose translation was based on a draft version of the original text and published in *The New York Times Book*

Review 56, no. 1 (15 January 2009). The other translation, based on the finalized version of the original text and with the list of 303 signatories, was provided by Human Rights in China and is available at <http://www. hrichina.org/crf/article/3203>, which also provides a link to the Chinese text in both full and simplified Chinese characters.

2. Feng Chongyi, "Charter 08, the Troubled History and Future of Chinese Liberalism," *The Asia-Pacific Journal: Japan Focus* 2 (11 January 2010): 1–10.

3. Benjamin Schwartz, *In Search of Wealth and Power: Yen Fu and the West* (Cambridge: Harvard University Press, 1964); Hao Chang, *Liang Chi-chao and Intellectual Tradition in China, 1890–1907* (Cambridge: Harvard University Press, 1971); Feng Chongyi, "The Return of Liberalism and Social Democracy: Breaking Through the Barriers of State Socialism, Nationalism, and Cynicism in Contemporary China," *Issues & Studies* 39, no. 3 (September 2003): 1–31.

4. Chow Tse-tsung, *The May Fourth Movement: Intellectual Revolution in Modern China* (Cambridge, Mass.: Harvard University Press, 1960); Vera Schwarcz, *The Chinese Enlightenment: Intellectuals and the Legacy of the May Fourth Movement of 1919* (Berkeley: University of California Press, 1986); and Feng Chongyi, *Luosu yu Zhongguo* [Bertrand Russell and China] (Beijing: Sanlian Bookstore, 1994).

5. Jerome B. Grieder, *Hu Shih and the Chinese Renaissance: Liberalism in the Chinese Revolution, 1917–1937* (Cambridge: Harvard University Press, 1970); Roger B. Jeans (ed.), *Roads Not Taken: The Struggle of Opposition Parties in Twentieth-Century China* (Boulder: Westview Press, 1992).

6. Nicholas D. Kristof, "China Sees 'Market-Leninism' as Way to Future," *The New York Times*, 6 September 1993.

7. Feng Chongyi, "The Liberal Camp in Post-June 4th China," *China Perspectives* 2009, no. 2 (2009): 30–42.

8. Similarly, when Jiang Qisheng (江棋生) took the draft of Charter 08 to consult Xu Liangying (许良英), a prominent liberal who was expelled from the CCP after the June Fourth massacre in 1989, Xu's first reaction was to warn that the document would send its organizers to jail. See Jiang Qisheng, "Two Episodes about My Association with Charter 08," in Li Xiaorong and Zhang Zuhua (eds.), *Lingba Xianzhang* [Charter 08] (Hong Kong: Open Books, 2009), 16.

9. Xiao Han, "Concerns about Charter 08," in Li and Zhang (eds.), *Lingba Xianzhang*, 109–14 (note 8).

10. Qin Hui, "What China Needs More Urgently Are Debates on Democracy and a Fresh Enlightenment," in Li and Zhang (eds.), *Lingba Xianzhang*, 138–44 (note 8).

11. Diane Xiaodong Liu et al., "Second Letter to the Nobel Peace Prize Committee from Overseas Chinese Concerned with Chinese Democracy," *Liusi Tianwang* [64tianwang.com], 4 October 2010, <http://64tianwang.com/

bencandy.php?fid-13-id-6545-page-1.htm>; "Senior Chinese Dissident Criticizes Liu Nobel," Khaleej Times Online, 8 October 2010, <http://www. khaleejtimes.com/DisplayArticle08.asp?xfile=data/international/2010/ October/international_October330.xml&section=international>.

12. Liu Xiaobo, "I Have No Enemies: My Final Statement" (trans. David Kelly), 23 December 2009, <http://chinadigitaltimes.net/2010/02/ liu-xiaobo-i-have-no-enemies-my-final-statement/>.

13. Wen Jiabao, "Some Issues with Regard to the Historical Tasks during the Initial Stage of Socialism and Foreign Policies of Our Country," Xinhuanet, 26 February 2007, <http://news.xinhuanet.com/politics/2007–02/26/content_ 5775212.htm>; "Premier Wen Jiabao's Reply to Questions of Chinese and Foreign Journalists," Renminwang [The Website of People's Daily], 13 March 2009, <http://news.xhby.net/system/2009/03/13/010460240.shtml>; "Chinese Premier Wen Jiabao Speaks Exclusively to CNN's Fareed Zakaria," News on News, 24 September 2010, <http://www.newsonnews. net/cnn/4697-chinese-premier-wen-jiabao-speaks-exclusively-to-cnn-s-fareed-zakaria.html>.

14. Chen Kuiyuan, "Speech at the Working Forum of the Chinese Academy of Social Sciences," Zhongguo Shehui Kexue Yuan Yuan Bao [Journal of the Chinese Academy of Social Sciences], 2 September 2008, 1.

15. Jia Qinglin, "Raise High the Great Banner of Socialism with Chinese Characteristics and Uninterruptedly Advance the Cause of People's Political Consultative Conference," Qiushi [Seeking Truth] 2009, no. 1 <http://theory.people.com.cn/GB/49169/49171/8687469.html>.

16. Wu Bangguo, "Never Practice the Multiparty Rule by Turns," Zhongguo Xuanju yu Zhili Wang [China Elections & Governance], <http://www.china-elections.org/newsinfo.asp?newsid=144868>.

17. Feng Chongyi, "The Rights Defence Movement, Rights Defence Lawyers and Prospects for Constitutional Democracy in China," Cosmopolitan Civil Societies: An Interdisciplinary Journal 1, no. 3 (2009): 150–69.

18. Yu Jianrong, Dangdai Nongmin de Weiquan Douzheng: Hunan Hengyang Kaocha [Rights Defense Struggles of Contemporary Peasants: An Investigation into Hunan's Hengyang] (Beijing: Chinese Culture Press, 2007).

19. Kevin J. O'Brien and Lianjiang Li, Rightful Resistance in Rural China (Cambridge: Cambridge University Press, 2006).

20. Wang Yi, "2003: The Origins and Practices of the 'New Civil Rights Movement'," Guancha [Observation], 19 December 2003; Fan Yafeng, "The Politics of Rights Defense" (on file with author); Teng Biao, "Whither the Rights Defense Movement in China" (on file with author).

21. Qiu Feng, "The Year of New Rights Movement," Xinwen Zhoukan [News Weekly] 161 (2003): 52–3; Hu Ping, "Reflections on Rights Defense Movement in 2003," <http://www.bjzc.org/bjs/bc/129/03.txt>; Xian Jianglin,

"The First Year of Rights and Institutional Rights Defence" (on file with author).

22. Tony Carnes, "China's New Legal Eagles: Evangelical Lawyers Spur Civil Rights Movement Forward," *Christianity Today* (September 2006): 106–10.

23. Ji Shuoming and Wang Jianmin, "Rights Defense Lawyers in China: The Vanguard of the Rule of Law," *Yazhou Zhoukan* [Asia Weekly], 25 December 2005; Hu Ping, "Rights Defense Lawyers: Heroes of Our Times" (on file with author); Stacy Mosher and Patrick Poon (eds.), *A Sword and a Shield: China's Human Rights Lawyers* (Hong Kong: China Human Rights Lawyers Concern Group, 2009).

24. Teng Biao, "Whither the Rights Defense Movement in China" (note 20); Joseph Kahn, "Rivals on Legal Tightrope Seek to Expand Freedoms in China," *The New York Times*, 25 February 2007, <http://www.nytimes.com/2007/02/25/world/asia/25china.html?ref=josephkahn>; Guo Guoting, "On Defense of Political Cases" (on file with author).

25. Fan Yafeng, "The Politics of Rights Defense" (note 20); Fan Yafeng, "Harmonious Stability and Crisis of Emergency Politics: On the Middle-Way Model in the Rights Defense Movement and Transition to Constitutional Democracy," <http://21ccom.net/articles/zgyj/xzmj/article_201001204485.html>; Fan Yafeng, "From Rights Defense by Religious Groups to Middle-Way Model of Rights Defense," *Gongfa Pinglun* [Comments on Public Law], 14 March 2010, <http://www.gongfa.org/html/gongfazhuanti/minquanyuweiquan/20100314/1004.html>.

26. Ruth Cherrington, *China's Students: The Struggle for Democracy* (London: Routledge, 1991); Merle Goldman, *Sowing the Seeds of Democracy in China: Political Reform in the Deng Xiaoping Era* (Cambridge: Harvard University Press, 1994).

27. Feng Jian et al., "A Proposal for Overcoming Economic Difficulties and Making a Breakthrough in Reform," *Zhongguo Xuanju yu Zhili Wang* [China Elections & Governance], <http://www.chinaelections.org/NewsInfo.asp?NewsID=143773>.

28. Li Rui et al., "Carry Out Article 35 of the Constitution, Eliminate the Mechanism of Prior Approval, Honor the Commitment of the Freedom of Speech and Press: An Open Letter to the Standing Committee of the National People's Congress," *Redian Xinwen Wang* [www.hotnewsnet.com], 13 October 2010, <http://www.hotnewsnet.com/a/muhou/20101013/227098.html>. Premier Wen seems to have caused deep concern among his colleagues in the Politburo by repeatedly calling for democratic reform and declaring in his interview on CNN that "I believe I and all the Chinese people have such a conviction that China will make continuous progress, and the people's wishes for and needs for democracy and freedom are irresistible … I will not fall in spite of the strong wind and harsh rain, and I will not yield until the last day of my life."

29. Guoguang Wu, "China in 2009: Muddling through Crises," *Asian Survey* 50, no. 1 (2010): 25–39.
30. "Xu Zhiyong's Open Constitution Initiative Has Stopped Operating," Danwei, 17 July 2009, <http://www.danwei.org/breaking_news/xu_zhiyongs_open_constitution.php>.
31. Jerome A. Cohen, "China's Hollow 'Rule of Law'," CNN Opinion, <http://articles.cnn.com/2009–12-31/opinion/cohen.china.dissidents_1_liu-xiaobo-legal-system-china-s-communist?_s=PM:OPINION>; Jiang Ping, "The Rule of Law in China Is in the Stage of Major Retrogression," *Gongfa Pinglun Wang Luntan* [Forum of Comments on Public Law], 24 February 2010, <http://www.gongfa.org/bbs/redirect.php?tid=4037&goto=lastpost>.
32. Eva Pils, "Dislocation of the Chinese Human Rights Movement," in Mosher and Poon (eds.), *A Sword and a Shield*, 141 (note 23).
33. Sun Liping, "The Biggest Threat to China Is not Social Turmoil but Social Decay," China Digital Times, <http://chinadigitaltimes.net/2009/03/sun-liping-孙立平-the-biggest-threat-to-china-is-not-social-turmoil-but-social-decay/>; Social Development Research Group, Tsinghua University Department of Sociology, "New Thinking on *Weiwen*: Long-Term Social Stability via Institutionalized Expression of Interests," *Nanfang Zhoumo* [Southern Weekend], 14 April 2010, <http://www.infzm.com/content/43853>.
34. Vladimir Lenin, "The Proletarian Revolution and Renegade Kautsky," *Liening Xuanji* [Selected Works of Lenin] (Beijing: People's Press, 1972), vol. 3, 623.

Chapter 7 Democracy, Charter 08, and China's Long Struggle for Dignity

1. For the full text of Charter 08 in Chinese, see <http://www.dw-world.de/dw/article/0,,5064734,00.html> (accessed 11 February 2011). For its English translation, see Perry Link (trans.), "China's Charter 08," *New York Review of Books* 56, no. 1 (15 January 2009): 54–6, <http://www.nybooks.com/articles/archives/2009/jan/15/chinas-charter-08/> (accessed 20 May 2010).
2. John Fitzgerald, "China and the Quest for Dignity," *National Interest* 55 (1999): 47.
3. Ibid., 48.
4. Francis Fukuyama, *The End of History and the Last Man* (New York: Free Press, 1992).
5. Fitzgerald, "China and the Quest for Dignity," 48 (note 2).
6. Ibid., 49.
7. See "China Jails Tainted Milk Activist Zhao Lianhai," BBC News, 10 November 2010, <http://www.bbc.co.uk/news/world-asia-pacific-1172 4323> (accessed 28 January 2011).

8. See Sky Canaves, "China Sentences Earthquake Activist," *Wall Street Journal*, 10 February 2010, <http://online.wsj.com/article/NA_WSJ_PUB:SB 10001424052748704820904575054824114074304.html> (accessed 28 January 2011).

9. See John Garnaut, "Chinese Petitioners End up in 'Black Jails'," *Sydney Morning Herald*, 13 November 2009, <http://www.smh.com.au/world/ chinese-petitioners-end-up-in-black-jails-20091112-icgp.html> (accessed 7 February 2011).

10. In a fundamental sense, the answer is in the negative. See Dali L. Yang, "China's Long March to Freedom," *Journal of Democracy* 18, no. 3 (2007): 62.

11. Peter Zarrow, "Citizenship in China and the West," in Joshua A. Fogel & Peter G. Zarrow (eds.), *Imagining the People: Chinese Intellectuals and the Concept of Citizenship, 1890–1920* (New York: M.E. Sharpe, 1997), 20.

12. Fukuyama, *The End of History and the Last Man*, 135 (note 4).

13. See Jian Junbo, "Wen Pursues the Right to Dignity," *Asia Times Online*, 16 March 2010, <http://www.atimes.com/atimes/China/LC16Ad01.html> (accessed 17 January 2011).

14. Ibid. This issue will be discussed in the latter part of this chapter.

15. Ibid.

16. Apart from being a fundamental value under the UDHR, dignity features prominently in the International Covenant on Civil and Political Rights 1966 (ICCPR) and the International Covenant on Economic, Social, and Cultural Rights 1966 (ICESCR).

17. See my discussions in Man Yee Karen Lee, *Equality, Dignity, and Same-Sex Marriage: A Rights Disagreement in Democratic Societies* (Leiden: Martinus Nijhoff Publishers, 2010).

18. The Chinese and English texts of the 1954 Constitution are available at <http://e-chaupak.net/database/chicon/1954/1954bilingual.htm-a> (accessed 9 February 2011).

19. See the Constitution of the People's Republic of China, <http://english. people.com.cn/constitution/constitution.html>.

20. Among Chinese legal academics, views differ as to whether "personal dignity" under the Chinese Constitution bears the same wide meaning as "human dignity" understood in the West. On the other hand, while they generally agree that "personal dignity" entails a specific right, opinions range from it being a narrow right protecting only one's image, privacy, reputation, and personal integrity, to a more generous interpretation that it is capable of covering all the rights associated with a human being. See Benny Y.T. Tai & Man Yee Karen Lee, "The Discourse on 'Human Dignity' in the Constitution of the People's Republic of China," *Xianggang Shehui Kexue Xuebao* [Hong Kong Journal of Social Sciences] 38 (2010): 59.

21. Immanuel Kant, *Foundations of the Metaphysics of Morals with Critical Essays* (trans. Lewis White Beck, ed. Robert Paul Wolff) (Indianapolis: Bobbs-Merrill Education Publishing, 1969), 59.

22. Ibid., 59–61.

23. Ibid., 60.

24. Liu Xiaobo, "Changing the Regime by Changing Society" (trans. J. Latourelle), Human Rights in China, <http://www.hrichina.org/crf/article/3200> (accessed 30 December 2010).

25. "Liu Xiaobo Appeal Defense Statement" (trans. Human Rights in China), 28 January 2010, Human Rights in China, <http://www.hrichina.org/content/363> (accessed 30 December 2010).

26. See Mary E. Gallagher, "Mobilizing the Law in China: 'Informed Disenchantment' and the Development of Legal Consciousness," *Law & Society Review* 40, no. 4 (2006): 783.

27. Andrew J. Nathan, *Chinese Democracy* (New York: Alfred A. Knopf, 1985), 6–16.

28. Ibid., 26–30.

29. See Deng Xiaoping, *Selected Works of Deng Xiaoping (1975–1982)* (Beijing: Foreign Languages Press, 1984), 145–51.

30. Nathan, *Chinese Democracy*, 10 and 22 (note 27).

31. "Wei Jingsheng: The Fifth Modernization — Democracy, 1978" (trans. Kristina Torgeson), in Wm. Theodore de Bary & Richard Lufrano (eds.), *Sources of Chinese Tradition: From 1600 through the 20ᵗʰ Century*, vol. 2 (New York: Columbia University Press, 2000), 497–500.

32. Nathan, *Chinese Democracy*, 22 (note 27).

33. Ibid.

34. Ibid., 23.

35. Ibid., 32.

36. Ibid.; see also John A. Lent, "Freedom of Press in East Asia," *Human Rights Quarterly* 3, no. 4 (1981): 138–9.

37. See Deng, *Selected Works of Deng Xiaoping*, 172 (note 29 above).

38. Ibid., 181–2.

39. Ibid., 183.

40. Nathan, *Chinese Democracy*, 34 (note 27).

41. Lent, "Freedom of Press in East Asia," 139 (note 36).

42. Wei Jingsheng, *The Courage to Stand Alone: Letters from Prison and Other Writings* (ed. and trans. Kristina M. Torgeson) (New York: Penguin Books, 1998).

43. Fitzgerald, "China and the Quest for Dignity," 56 (note 2).

44. Fukuyama, *The End of History and the Last Man*, xvi-xvii (note 4).

45. See "A CND Interview with Wei Jingsheng — Part I," China News Digest, 15 January 1998, <http://museums.cnd.org/CND-Global/CND-Global.98.1st/CND-Global.98–01–14.html> (accessed 6 January 2011).

46. Ibid.
47. Fitzgerald, "China and the Quest for Dignity," 48 (note 2).
48. See "A CND Interview with Wei Jingsheng — Part I" (note 45).
49. Fukuyama, *The End of History and the Last Man*, 180 (note 4).
50. Plato, *The Republic of Plato* (trans. Francis MacDonald Cornford) (London: Oxford University Press, 1945), Ch XIII, 129–38.
51. Ibid., 130.
52. Ibid., 137.
53. Ibid.
54. Ibid., 137–8.
55. Ibid., 138.
56. "A CND Interview with Wei Jingsheng — Part II," China News Digest, 20 January 1998, <http://www.cnd.org/CND-Global/CND-Global.98.1st/ CND-Global.98–01–19.html> (accessed 6 January 2011).
57. Fukuyama, *The End of History and the Last Man*, xvi (note 4).
58. G. W. F. Hegel, *Phenomenology of Spirit* (trans. A. V. Miller) (Oxford: Oxford University Press, 1977), 111–9.
59. Fukuyama, *The End of History and the Last Man*, xvi (note 4).
60. Ibid., xviii.
61. See "Wei Jingsheng: The Fifth Modernization" (note 31).
62. Ibid.
63. See Link (trans.), "China's Charter 08" (note 1).
64. Aharon Barak, "The Supreme Court 2001 Term: Foreword: A Judge on Judging: The Role of a Supreme Court in a Democracy," *Harvard Law Review* 116 (2002): 39.
65. Ibid., 42 and 44.
66. Ibid., 45.
67. Walter F. Murphy, *Constitutional Democracy: Creating and Maintaining a Just Political Order* (Baltimore: Johns Hopkins University Press, 2007), 6.
68. Walter F. Murphy, "Consent and Constitutional Change," in James O'Reilly (ed.), *Human Rights and Constitutional Law: Essays in Honour of Brian Walsh* (Dublin: Round Hall Press, 1992), 123–46.
69. Ibid., 141.
70. Ibid., 142.
71. Ibid.
72. Ibid., 143.
73. For the full text of the speech, see "Premier Wen Jiabao Delivers an Emotional Speech at University of Cambridge," Website of the Ministry of Foreign Affairs of the People's Republic of China, <http://www.mfa.gov. cn/eng/zxxx/t535283.htm>.
74. "China Acts to Safeguard 'Dignity' of Its Citizens," *China Daily*, 8 March 2010, <http://www.chinadaily.com.cn/china/2010–03/08/content_9556285. htm> (accessed 18 January 2011).

75. Meng Na, Miao Xiaojuan, and Wang Cong, "Bracing for 'Most Complicated' Year, Premier Web Chat Focuses on Domestic Challenges," Xinhua News Agency, 27 February 2010, <http://news.xinhuanet.com/english2010/china/2010–02/27/c_13191054.htm> (accessed 17 January 2011).

76. See Report on the Work of the Government delivered by Premier Wen Jiabao at the Third Session of the Eleventh National People's Congress on 5 March 2010 and adopted on 14 March 2010, <http://www.china-daily.com.cn/china/2010npc/2010–03/15/content_9593380.htm> [hereafter "Government Work Report 2010"].

77. Jian Junbo, "Wen Pursues the Right to Dignity" (note 13).

78. See "China Acts to Safeguard 'Dignity'" (note 74).

79. Yu Jie (余杰), a famous liberal critic in China, calls Wen "China's Best Actor" (中国影帝) in talking the talk but not walking the walk. See "China's Best Actor Wen Jiabao, Chapter 5," Deutsche Welle, <http://www.dw-world.de/dw/article/0,,6098436,00.html> (accessed 11 February 2011).

80. Qianfan Zhang, "The Idea of Human Dignity in Classical Chinese Philosophy: A Reconstruction of Confucianism," Journal of Chinese Philosophy 27, no. 3 (2000): 305.

81. Lin Laifan, "Human Dignity and Personal Dignity: On Interpretation Scheme of No. 38 of the PRC Constitution," Zhejiang Shehui Kexue [Zhejiang Social Sciences] 3 (2008): 48.

82. David E. Christensen, "Breaking the Deadlock: Toward a Socialist-Confucianist Concept of Human Rights for China," Michigan Journal of International Law 13 (1992): 505.

83. Lin, "Human Dignity and Personal Dignity," 50 (note 81).

84. Nevertheless, Lin argues that one may be able to grasp the wider meaning of "personal dignity" under Article 38 if one goes beyond the "original legislative intent" approach and explores the normative content inherent in the provision, in light of changing constitutional norms both domestically and internationally. Ibid., 50–3.

85. Zhang, "The Idea of Human Dignity in Classical Chinese Philosophy," 301 (note 80).

86. Ibid., 300–1.

87. Lee, Equality, Dignity, and Same-Sex Marriage (note 17).

88. Rhoda E. Howard & Jack Donnelly, "Human Dignity, Human Rights, And Political Regimes," American Political Science Review 80, no. 3 (1986): 802.

89. Christensen, "Breaking the Deadlock," 489 (note 82).

90. As according to a Confucian classic, Chung Yung [中庸, The Doctrine of the Mean] (trans. James Legge), 20:8, <http://www.truthbook.com/index.cfm?linkID=1656> (accessed 10 May 2011).

91. Christensen, "Breaking the Deadlock" (note 82).

92. "Filial Piety in Relation to Reproof and Remonstrance," chap. 15 in Xiao Jing [孝经] (trans. James Legge), <http://ctext.org/xiao-jing/filial-piety-in-relation-to-reproof> (accessed 10 May 2011).

93. Confucius, *The Analects* [论语] (trans. D. C. Lau) (Harmondsworth: Penguin Books, 1979), 18:6.
94. Wenxiang Gong, "The Legacy of Confucian Culture in Maoist China," *Social Science Journal* 26, no. 4 (1989): 365.
95. *Mencius* [孟子] (trans. D. C. Lau) (Harmondsworth: Penguin Books, 1970), 6A:10.
96. Christensen, "Breaking the Deadlock," 491 (note 82).
97. Ibid., 494.
98. *Mencius*, 7B:14 (note 95).
99. See Government Work Report 2010 (note 76).
100. Maureen Fan, "China's Party Leadership Declares New Priority: 'Harmonious Society'," *Washington Post*, 12 October 2006, <http://www.washingtonpost.com/wp-dyn/content/article/2006/10/11/AR2006101101610.html> (accessed 25 January 2011).
101. "Building Harmonious Society Crucial for China's Progress: Hu," Xinhua News Agency, 27 June 2005, <http://english.peopledaily.com.cn/200506/27/eng20050627_192495.html> (accessed 25 January 2011).
102. Mark O'Neill, "Hu Jintao Takes Personal Charge of Fight Against Charter 08," *Asia Sentinel*, 7 January 2009, <http://www.asiasentinel.com/index.php?option=com_content&task=view&id=1650&Itemid=171&limit=1&limitstart=0> (accessed 12 August 2010).
103. Henry Yuhuai He, *Dictionary of the Political Thought of the People's Republic of China* (New York: M.E. Sharpe, 2001), 471–2.
104. Ibid., 472.
105. See Randall Peerenboom, *China Modernizes: Threat to the West or Model for the Rest?* (Oxford: Oxford University Press, 2007), 252.
106. Ibid., 236–9.
107. Richard Robison, "What Sort of Democracy? Predatory and Neo-Liberal Agendas in Indonesia," in Catarina Kinnvall & Kristina Jönsson (eds.), *Globalization and Democratization in Asia: The Construction of Identity* (London: Routledge, 2002), 103.
108. Christensen, "Breaking the Deadlock," 511–2 (note 82).
109. Peerenboom, *China Modernizes*, 236, 240–2 (note 105).
110. Ibid., 255.
111. See Liu, "Changing the Regime by Changing Society" (note 24).
112. See Frederick Douglass, "The Significance of Emancipation in the West Indies," speech delivered at Canandaigua, New York, 3 August 1857, <http://www.iefd.org/manifestos/significance_of_emancipation.php> (accessed 12 February 2011).
113. Ralph Hua, "China's Arsenal of Political Persecution: A Double-Edged Sword," *Pace International Law Review Online Companion* 2, no. 4 (2010): 7 and 23. To China, stability comes at a premium. It was reported that "more than 500 billion yuan" was spent on "ensuring social stability" in 2009

alone. See "Tide of Discontent Rises Against Abuse of Power," *South China Morning Post*, 2 December 2010.

114. "Thousands in Five-Day China Demo: Report," *Sydney Morning Herald*, 20 July 2010, <http://news.smh.com.au/breaking-news-world/thousands-in-fiveday-china-demo-report-20100720–10i3b.html> (accessed 16 February 2011).

115. Tania Branigan, "Protesters Gather in Guangzhou to Protect Cantonese Language," *The Guardian*, 25 July 2010, <http://www.guardian.co.uk/world/2010/jul/25/protesters-guangzhou-protect-cantonese> (accessed 16 February 2011).

116. The Chinese are not totally spared from those ideas, as the so-called "Jasmine Revolution," named after the political uprisings in the Arab world, has quietly found its way in some Chinese cities. See "Hundreds Join 'Jasmine Revolution'," *South China Morning Post*, 21 February 2011.

117. Václav Havel, "The Power of the Powerless," in Jan Vladislav (ed.), *Václav Havel: Living in Truth: 22 Essays Published on the Occasion of the Award of the Erasmus Prize to Václav Havel* (London: Faber & Faber, 1987), 54.

118. Fukuyama, *The End of History and the Last Man*, 169 (note 4).

119. Liu Xiaobo, "I Have No Enemies" (23 December 2009), *Foreign Policy*, 8 October 2010, <http://www.foreignpolicy.com/articles/2010/10/08/i_have_no_enemies> (accessed 26 January 2011).

120. Fukuyama, *The End of History and the Last Man*, 134 (note 4).

121. Ibid., 180.

122. Jonathan D. Spence, "Sun Yat-sen," *Time 100* 154, no. 7/8 (23–30 August 1999), <http://www-cgi.cnn.com/ASIANOW/time/asia/magazine/1999/990823/sun_yat_sen1.html> (accessed 3 September 2010).

123. Li Xiaorong, "Václav Havel Honors a Chinese Prisoner," *New York Review of Books* 57 (30 April 2009), <http://www.nybooks.com/articles/archives/2009/apr/30/vaclav-havel-honors-a-chinese-prisoner/> (accessed 26 August 2010).

Chapter 8 Charter 08 and Charta 77

1. Anne Marie Morris, "Will Charter 08 Follow the Same Trajectory as Charter 77?" (Unpublished thesis), 29 June 2009, <http://works.bepress.com/cgi/viewcontent.cgi?article=1001&context=annemariemorris> (accessed 20 December 2010).

2. Martin Hala, "China through Zhuangzi's Third Eye," Eurozine, <http://www.eurozine.com/articles/2009–06-03-hala-en.html> (accessed 20 December 2010).

3. Václav Havel, *Disturbing the Peace: A Conversation with Karel Hvížďala* (trans. Paul Wilson) (New York: Knopf, 1990).

4. Timothy Garton Ash, "Velvet Revolution: The Prospects," *The New York Review of Books* 56, no. 19 (3 December 2009), <http://www.nybooks.com/articles/archives/2009/dec/03/velvet-revolution-the-prospects/>.

5. *Informace o Chartě 77* [Bibliography of Charta 77 documents in 1978–1990] (Praha: 1998). See also <http://libpro.cts.cuni.cz/publ_infoch.htm> (accessed 20 December 2010).

6. For reference, see <http://www2.ohchr.org/english/law/ccpr.htm> (accessed 20 December 2010).

7. "Prohlášení Charty 77", 28 March 2005, <http://www.sds.cz/view.php?cisloclanku=2005032801> (accessed 20 December 2010).

8. Prof. Vilém Prečan, Dr. Svetlana Savranskaya, and Thomas Blanton (eds.), *Charter 77 after 30 Years* (trans. Derek Paton), National Security Archive Electronic Briefing Book No. 213, <http://www.gwu.edu/~nsarchiv/NSAEBB/NSAEBB213/index.htm> (accessed 20 December 2010).

9. For an exhaustive overview of media coverage of and responses to Charter 08, see China Digital Times — Tag: Charter 08, <http://chinadigitaltimes.net/china/charter-08/> (accessed 20 December 2010).

10. Václav Havel, "China's Human-Rights Activists Need Support," *Wall Street Journal*, 19 December 2008, <http://online.wsj.com/article/SB122964944665820499.html> (accessed 20 December 2010).

11. "Chinese Charter 08 Signatories Awarded Homo Homini, Speeches by Vaclav Havel, Xu Youyu and Cui Weiping," Laogai: Research Foundation Italia Onlus, 13 March 2009, <http://www.laogai.it/?p=8060> (accessed 20 December 2010). See also <http://www.oneworld.cz> (accessed 20 December 2010).

12. See the official website of the Plastic People of the Universe, <http://plastic-people.eu/>; <http://www.kandl.cz/plasticpeople/main.aspx> (accessed 20 December 2010).

13. Morris, "Will Charter 8 Follow the Same Trajectory as Charter 77?," 6 (note 1).

14. Keith Bradsher, "China Moves to Bring Dissident to Trial," *New York Times*, 9 December 2009, <http://www.nytimes.com/2009/12/10/world/asia/10china.html?_r=1&ref=asia> (accessed 20 December 2010).

15. Morris, "Will Charter 8 Follow the Same Trajectory as Charter 77?," 16 (note 1).

16. Rebecca MacKinnon, "What does Charter 08 mean? Too soon to tell…," RConversation, 20 January 2009, <http://rconversation.blogs.com/rconversation/2009/01/what-does-charter-08-mean-too-soon-to-tell.html> (accessed 20 December 2010).

17. Morris, "Will Charter 8 Follow the Same Trajectory as Charter 77?," 24 (note 1).

18. Ibid., 18.

19. Ibid., 19.

20. Ibid.
21. "Zhang Yimou and State Aesthetics," China Digital Times, 6 August 2008, <http://chinadigitaltimes.net/2008/08/zhang-yimou-and-state-aesthetics/> (accessed December 2010).
22. "'Grass-Mud Horse' (草泥马) — Netizens React to Censors," China Digital Times, 31 March 2009, <http://chinadigitaltimes.net/2009/03/grass-mud-horse-netizens-react-to-censors-with-photo/> (accessed 20 December 2010).
23. See, for instance, "Ztroskotanci a samozvanci", Rudé Právo, January 1977, <http://www.totalita.cz/texty/ch77_ztr.php> (accessed 20 December 2010).
24. Ash, "Velvet Revolution" (note 4).
25. Morris, "Will Charter 08 Follow the Same Trajectory as Charter 77?," 12 (note 1).
26. Ibid.
27. Conference on Security and Co-operation in Europe Final Act (Helsinki 1975), <http://www.osce.org/mc/39501> (accessed 20 December 2010).
28. For more information on Egon Bondy, see <http://ebondy.sweb.cz/> (accessed 20 December 2010); Kent Hunt, "Egon Bondy," The Guardian, 20 April 2007, <http://www.guardian.co.uk/news/2007/apr/20/guardianobituaries.obituaries>.
29. For details on Plastic People and the Czech underground, see note 12.
30. Hala, "China through Zhuangzi's Third Eye" (note 2).
31. Morris, "Will Charter 08 Follow the Same Trajectory as Charter 77?," 13 (note 1).
32. Hala, "China through Zhuangzi's Third Eye" (note 2).

Chapter 9 Challenging Authoritarianism through Law

1. Tom Ginsburg and Tamir Moustafa, Rule by Law: The Politics of Courts in Authoritarian Regimes (New York: Cambridge University Press, 2008).
2. See, for example, Thomas Carothers, "The 'Sequencing' Fallacy," Journal of Democracy 18, no. 1(2007): 12–27; Malcolm MacLaren, "'Sequentialism' or 'Gradualism'? On the Transition to Democracy and the Rule of Law," National Center of Competence in Research: Challenges to Democracy in the 21st Century, Working Paper No. 38 (October 2009), <http://www.nccr-democracy.uzh.ch/publications/workingpaper/pdf/wp38.pdf> (accessed 29 May 2010); Randall Peerenboom, "Rule of Law, Democracy and the Sequencing Debate: Lessons from China and Vietnam," Social Science Research Network (SSRN) (10 August 2009), <http://papers.ssrn.com/sol3/papers.cfm?abstract_id=1447051> (accessed 31 May 2010).
3. Loren Brandt and Thomas G. Rawski (eds.), China's Great Economic Transformation (Cambridge: Cambridge University Press, 2008).
4. Richard Baum, Burying Mao: Chinese Politics in the Age of Deng Xiaoping (Princeton: Princeton University Press, 1994); Harry Harding, China's

Second Revolution: Reform after Mao (Washington: Brookings Institution Press, 1987); Frederick C. Teiwes, *Leadership, Legitimacy and Conflict in China: From a Charismatic Mao to the Politics of Succession* (London: Macmillan, 1984).

5. Albert H. Y. Chen, *An Introduction to the Legal System of the People's Republic of China* (Hong Kong: LexisNexis, 2004); Randall Peerenboom, *China's Long March toward Rule of Law* (Cambridge: Cambridge University Press, 2002).

6. These are: the principle of upholding the socialist path; the principle of upholding the people's democratic dictatorship; the principle of upholding the leadership of the CCP; and the principle of upholding Marxist-Leninist-Mao Zedong thought. The principles are entrenched in the Preamble of the Constitution.

7. Andrew J. Nathan, *Chinese Democracy* (New York: Knopf, 1985); Kelvin J. O'Brien and Lianjiang Li, "Accommodating 'Democracy' in a One-Party State: Introducing Village Elections in China," *The China Quarterly* 162 (2001): 465–89; Chin-Chuan Lee, *China's Media, Media's China* (Boulder, Colorado: Westview Press, 1994).

8. Tony Saich (ed.), *The Chinese People's Movement: Perspectives on Spring 1989* (Armonk, N.Y.: M. E. Sharpe, 1990).

9. Barry Naughton, "A Political Economy of China's Economic Transition," chap. 4 in Brandt and Rawski (eds.), *China's Great Economic Transformation* (note 3).

10. Donald C. Clarke, "China: Creating a Legal System for a Market Economy," George Washington University Law School Public Law Research Paper No. 396 (report prepared for the Asian Development Bank, 2007), SSRN, <http://papers.ssrn.com/sol3/papers.cfm?abstract_id=1097587> (accessed 5 October 2010).

11. For a critical review of the literature on law and development in the China-specific context, see Donald Clarke, Peter Murrell, and Susan Whiting, "The Role of Law in China's Economic Development," chap. 11 in Brandt and Rawski (eds.), *China's Great Economic Transformation* (note 3); Donald C. Clarke, "Economic Development and the Rights Hypothesis: The China Problem," *American Journal of Comparative Law* 51 (2003): 89–111.

12. For discussion on law and economic development in the Chinese context, see Albert H. Y. Chen, "Rational Law, Economic Development and the Case of China," *Social & Legal Studies* 8 (1999): 97–120. See also Clarke, "China" (note 10).

13. China signed the ICESCR and ICCPR in October 1997 and October 1998 respectively. However, while the former was ratified in February 2001, the latter has not yet been ratified.

14. For a discussion of the concept of "thin" rule of law in the Chinese context, see Peerenboom, *China's Long March* (note 5).

15. Zheng Ge, "Toward Regulatory Neutrality in a Party-State? A Review of Administrative Law Reforms in China," chap. 5 in John Gillespie and

Albert H. Y. Chen (eds.), *Legal Reforms in China and Vietnam: A Comparison of Asian Communist Regimes* (New York: Routledge, 2010); Albert H. Y. Chen, "Toward a Legal Enlightenment: Discussions in Contemporary China on the Rule of Law," *UCLA Pacific Basin Law Journal* 17 (1999): 125–65.

16. Lee Branstetter and Nicholas R. Lardy, "China's Embrace of Globalization," chap. 16 in Brandt and Rawski (eds.), *China's Great Economic Transformation* (note 3).

17. Sarah Biddulph, "China's Accession to the WTO: Legal System Transparency and Administrative Reform," chap. 10 in Sylvia Ostry, Alan S. Alexandroff and Rafael Gomez (eds.), *China and the Long March to Global Trade: The Accession of China to the World Trade Organization* (London: Routledge, 2002).

18. See Chen, *Introduction to the Legal System*, and Peerenboom, *China's Long March* (note 5).

19. Yunxiang Yan, "The Good Samaritan's New Trouble: A Study of the Changing Moral Landscape in Contemporary China," *Social Anthropology* 17, no. 1 (2009): 9–24.

20. For the literature on civil society demand for rights, see Peter Hays Gries and Stanley Rosen (eds.), *Chinese Politics: State, Society and the Market* (New York: Routledge, 2010); Mary Gallagher, "Mobilizing the Law in China: 'Informed Disenchantment' and the Development of Legal Consciousness," *Law & Society Review* 40, no. 4 (2006): 783–816; Mi Shih, "Legal Geographies — Governing through Law: Rights-Based Conflicts and Property Development in Shanghai," *Urban Geography* 31, no. 7 (2010): 973–87; Keith J. Hand, "Using Law for a Righteous Purpose: The Sun Zhigang Incident and Evolving Forms of Citizen Action in the People's Republic of China," *Columbia Journal of Transnational Law* 45 (2006): 114–95.

21. Kevin J. O'Brien and Lianjiang Li, *Rightful Resistance in Rural China* (Cambridge: Cambridge University Press, 2006), 2.

22. Ibid.

23. Guobin Yang, *The Power of the Internet in China: Citizen Activism Online* (New York: Columbia University Press, 2009).

24. Ching Kwan Lee, *Against the Law: Labor Protests in China's Rustbelt and Sunbelt* (Berkeley: University of California Press, 2007).

25. Jonathan Unger (ed.), *Associations and the Chinese State: Contested Spaces* (Armonk, N.Y.: M.E. Sharpe, 2008); Gries and Rosen (eds.) *Chinese Politics* (note 20).

26. Eva Pils, "Asking the Tiger for His Skin: Rights Activism in China," *Fordham International Law Journal* 30 (2007): 1209–87.

27. Zhu Jingwen (ed.), *Zhongguo Falü Fazhan Baogao: Shujuku he Zhibiao Tixi* [Report on Chinese Law Development: Database and Indicators] (Beijing: Press of Renmin University of China, 2007).

28. Chen, *Introduction to the Legal System* (note 5).

29. Ethan Michelson, "Lawyers, Political Embeddedness, and Institutional Continuity in China's Transition from Socialism," *American Journal of Sociology* 113, no. 2 (2007): 352–414.

30. Richard Croucher and Lilian Miles, "Chinese Migrant Worker Representation and Institutional Change: Social or Centralist Corporatism?," *Asian Journal of Comparative Law* 5, no.1 (2010): Article 4.

31. For an extended discussion of this issue, see Fu Hualing and Richard Cullen, "The Development of Public Interest Litigation in China," chap. 2 in Po Jen Yap and Holning Lau (eds.), *Public Interest Litigation in Asia* (New York: Routledge, 2011).

32. "A Dialogue with 'Rights Fighter' Wang Hai," *Dongbei Xinwen Wang* [Northeast News Net], 12 March 2006, available at *Wangyi* [Neteast], <http://news.163.com/06/0312/07/2C0DUHOT0001124T.html> (accessed 8 August 2009); "Information Related to Wang Hai's Fighting against Fake Goods (1995–1997)," *Wangyi* [Neteast], 14 March 2006, <http://news.163.com/06/0314/15/2C6ELB970001126S.html> (accessed 8 August 2009).

33. Lin Xinghua, Chen Yu, and Wang Changfeng, "Is It Worthwhile to Initiate the 'One Dollar and Twenty Cents' Lawsuit'," *Jingji Ribao* [Economic Daily], 30 January 1996, 1.

34. For example, veteran PIL lawyer for women's rights Guo Jianmei (郭建梅), took up this role after participating in the 1995 World Women's Conference hosted in Beijing; labor lawyer Zhou Litai (周立太) brought his first lawsuit in Longgang, Shenzhen in 1996; and PIL lawyer specializing in labor rights and children's rights Tong Lihua (佟丽华) also started his PIL practice in Beijing in the mid-1990s. See, for example, "Guo Jianmei: The Colorful Life of Public Interest Litigation," *Renmin Zhengxie Bao* [News of the People's Political Consultative Conference], 14 April 2009, available at *Funü Guancha Wang* [Women's Watch-China] (on file with author); "Public Interest Lawyer Guo Jianmei: Helping the Weak to Move Forward," *Zhongguo Wang* [china.org.cn], 17 March 2009, available at *Renmin Wang* [People's Daily website], <http://finance.people.com.cn/BIG5/70392/8985423.html> (accessed 3 August 2009); "Zhou Litai: Zhou Litai who Finally Walks through from the Struggle," *Longbo Wang* [aweb.com.cn], 24 November 2007, <http://news.aweb.com.cn/2007/11/24/117200711241636340.html> (accessed 17 June 2009); Luo Xiao, "Tong Lihua: The Greatest Happiness Is to Feel the Existence of Justice," *Zhiye* [Occupation] 13 (2007): 34–5; Sha Lei, "Tong Lihua: Defender of the Weak," *Zhongguanchun* [Zhongguanchun Magazine] 10 (2008): 118–20.

35. For discussions of these cases, see, for example Zhou Wei, *Fan Qishi Fa Yanjiu: Lifa, Lilun yu Anli* [Study on Anti-Discriminative Law: Legislation, Theory and Cases] (Beijing: Law Press, 2008).

36. Benjamin L. Liebman, "China's Courts: Restricted Reform," *The China Quarterly* 191 (2007): 633–4.

37. Internal reference refers to internal reports on controversial issues prepared by journalists for senior government leaders.
38. Terence C. Halliday, Lucien Karpik, and Malcolm M. Feeley, "The Legal Complex and Struggles for Political Liberalism," chap. 1 in Terence C. Halliday, Lucien Karpik, and Malcolm M. Feeley (eds.), *Fighting for Political Freedom: Comparative Studies of the Legal Complex and Political Liberalism* (Oxford: Hart Publishing, 2007).
39. Stéphanie Balme and Michael W. Dowdle (eds.), *Building Constitutionalism in China* (New York: Palgrave Macmillan, 2009).
40. Andrew Mertha, "Society in the State: China's Nondemocratic Political Pluralization," chap. 3 in Gries and Rosen (eds.) *Chinese Politics* (note 20); Samantha Keech-Marx, "Airing Dirty Laundry in Public: Anti-Domestic Violence Activism in Beijing," chap. 7 in Unger (ed.), *Associations and the Chinese State* (note 25).
41. Ginsburg and Moustafa (eds.), *Rule by Law* (note 1).
42. Stephen Ellmann, "Cause Lawyering in the Third World," chap. 12 in Austin Sarat and Stuart Scheingold (eds.), *Cause Lawyering: Political Commitments and Professional Responsibilities* (New York: Oxford University Press, 1998).
43. Waikeung Tam, "Political Transition and the Rise of Cause Lawyering: The Case of Hong Kong," *Law & Social Inquiry* 35 (2010): 663–87; Patricia A. Goedde, "From Dissidents to Institution-Builders: The Transformation of Public Interest Lawyers in South Korea," *East Asia Law Review* 4, no. 1 (2009): 63–89.
44. Helen Hershkoff, "Public Interest Litigation: Selected Issues and Examples," <http://siteresources.worldbank.org/INTLAWJUSTINST/Resources/PublicInterestLitigation%5B1%5D.pdf> (accessed 11 October 2010), 9.
45. Tom Ginsburg, *Judicial Review in New Democracies: Constitutional Courts in Asian Cases* (Cambridge: Cambridge University Press, 2003).
46. Hershokff, "Public Interest Litigation," 14 (note 44).
47. Fu Hualing and Richard Cullen, "Climbing the *Weiquan* Ladder: A Radicalizing Process for Rights-Protection Lawyers," *The China Quarterly* 205 (2011): 40–59.
48. Interviews with *weiquan* lawyers, Hong Kong, September 2009.
49. See, for example, Zhang Wei, Cheng Lida, Huang Ying, "Over 20,000 Labor Disputes Solved Last Year, Shenzhen Trade Confederation Puts Great Effort in Defending Labor Rights," *Nanfang Ribao* [Southern Daily], 9 January 2008, available at China Labour Bulletin, <http://www.china-labour.org.hk/chi/node/1300188/print> (accessed 10 November 2009); Huang Biao, "Bus Crew Stops Hundreds of Buses, Labor Rights Lawyers to be Involved in Collective Bargaining," available at the website of Guangdong Laowei Law Firm, 21 October 2008 (on file with author).

50. Michelson, "Lawyers, Political Embeddedness, and Institutional Continuity" (note 29); Sida Liu and Terence C. Halliday, "Political Liberalism and Political Embeddedness: Understanding Politics in the Work of Chinese Criminal Defense Lawyers," *Law & Society Review* 45 (2011): 831–66.

51. For example, it was reported that in June 2009, almost twenty rights lawyers in China — the majority of whom were based in Beijing — had failed the justice bureaus' compulsory annual review for lawyers and hence could not renew their practice licences in time. The Beijing Justice Bureau revoked the licences of two Beijing lawyers, Tang Jitian (唐吉田) and Liu Wei (刘巍). For details of this incident, see, for example, "Chinese Rights Defense Lawyers under All-out Attack by the Authorities," Human Rights in China, 4 June 2009, <http://www.hrichina.org/content/300> (accessed 10 October 2010).

Chapter 10 Popular Constitutionalism and the Constitutional Meaning of Charter 08

1. Rebecca MacKinnon, "What Does Charter 08 Mean? Too Soon to Tell ...," RConversation, 20 January 2009, <http://rconversation.blogs.com/rconversation/2009/01/what-does-charter-08-mean-too-soon-to-tell.html>.

2. See generally, Martin Loughlin and Neil Walker (eds.), *The Paradox of Constitutionalism: Constituent Power and Constitutional Form* (Oxford: Oxford University Press, 2007).

3. See, for example, Anne M. Cohler, Basia C. Miller, and Harold S. Stone (trans. and eds.) *Montesquieu: The Spirit of the Laws* (Cambridge: Cambridge University Press, 1989), xliv; Alexander Hamilton, "No. 1: General Introduction," in Alexander Hamilton, James Madison, and John Jay, *The Federalist Papers* (ed. Clinton Rossiter) (New York: Penguin Putnam, 1961), 27; Thomas Paine, "The Rights of Man," reprinted in Thomas Paine, *Common Sense, The Rights of Man, and Other Essential Writings* (New York: Classic House Books, 2009), 62–289.

4. See also Michael Dowdle, "Of 'Socialism' and 'Socialist' Constitutional Transformations in China and Vietnam," in John Gillespie and Pip Nicholson (eds.), *Asian Socialism and Legal Change: The Dynamics of Vietnamese and Chinese Reform* (Canberra: Asia Pacific Press, 2004), 21–44. Cf. Peter Gay, *The Enlightenment: An Interpretation* (*Vol. 2: The Science of Freedom*) (New York: W. W. Norton, 1996).

5. See, for example, Alexis de Tocqueville, *The Old Regime and the Revolution* (eds. François Furet and Françoise Mélonio, trans. Alan S. Kahan) (Chicago: University of Chicago Press, 1998), 198.

6. See, for example, William Blackstone, *Commentaries on the Laws of England* (1765), IV: 443; Edmund Burke, *Reflections on the French Revolution* (New York: Dutton, 1955).

7. Gordon S. Wood, *The Radicalism of the American Revolution* (New York: A. A. Knopf, 1991), 11–95.

8. Loughlin and Walker, *Paradox of Constitutionalism* (note 2).

9. Tocqueville, *The Old Regime and the Revolution* (note 5).

10. Lynn Hunt, *Politics, Culture, and Class in the French Revolution* (Berkeley: University of California Press, 1984), 48–9; Simon Schama, *Citizens: A Chronicle of the French Revolution* (New York: Random House, 1990), 579–80, 860.

11. J. G. A. Pocock, *The Ancient Constitution and the Feudal Law: A Study of English Historical Thought in the Seventeenth Century* (Cambridge: Cambridge University Press, 1957), 30–55.

12. See, for example, Henry Bolingbroke, "The Idea of a Patriot King," in David Armitage (ed.), *Bolingbroke: Political Writings, Perspectives on Political Parties: Classic Readings* (Cambridge: Cambridge University Press, 1997), 217–94. See also, William D. Liddle, "'A Patriot King, or None': Lord Bolingbroke and the American Renunciation of George III," *The Journal of American History* 65 (1979): 951–70. See generally, Isaac Kramnick, *Bolingbroke and His Circle: The Politics of Nostalgia in the Age of Walpole* (Cambridge, MA: Harvard University Press, 1968).

13. Cf. Peter L. Berger and Thomas Luckmann, *The Social Construction of Reality: A Treatise in the Sociology of Knowledge* (Garden City, New York: Anchor Books, 1966).

14. Charles Collier, "Intellectual Authority and Institutional Authority," *Inquiry: An Interdisciplinary Journal of Philosophy* 35, no. 2 (1992): 145–81.

15. Ibid.

16. See, for example, H. L. A Hart, *The Concept of Law* (2nd edition) (Oxford: Clarendon Press, 1994); Hans Kelsen, *General Theory of Law and State* (trans. Anders Wedberg) (Cambridge, MA.: Harvard University Press, 1945).

17. Lon L. Fuller, *The Morality of Law* (rev. edition) (New Haven: Yale University Press, 1977); Ronald Dworkin, *Law's Empire* (Cambridge, MA: Belknap Press, 1986).

18. H. L. A. Hart, "Positivism and the Separation of Law and Morals," *Harvard Law Review* 71, no. 4 (1958): 593–629; Lon L. Fuller, "Positivism and Fidelity to Law — A Reply to Professor Hart," *Harvard Law Review* 71, no. 4 (1958): 630–72.

19. See, for example, Norman Daniels, *Justice and Justification: Reflective Equilibrium in Theory and Practice* (Cambridge: Cambridge University Press, 1996).

20. See, for example, Martin Shapiro and Alec Stone Sweet, *On Law, Politics, and Judicialization* (Oxford: Oxford University Press, 2002), 55–89; cf. Edward Rubin, "The Myth of Non-Bureaucratic Accountability and the Anti-Administrative Impulse," in Michael W. Dowdle (ed.), *Public Accountability: Designs, Dilemmas and Experiences* (Cambridge: Cambridge University Press, 2006), 52–82.

21. See, for example, Hugh Collins, *Regulating Contracts* (New York: Oxford University Press, 1999); Gunther Teubner, "Substantive and Reflexive Elements in Modern Law," *Law & Society Review* 17, no. 2 (1983): 239–85.

22. See also Gunther Teubner, "How the Law Thinks: Toward a Constructivist Epistemology of Law," *Law & Society Review* 23, no. 5 (1989): 727–57.

23. Dworkin, *Law's Empire* (note 17).

24. See, for example, Shapiro and Stone Sweet, *On Law, Politics, and Judicialization*, 55–89 (note 20).

25. See, for example, Oscar G. Chase, *Law, Culture, and Ritual: Disputing Systems in Cross-Cultural Context* (New York: New York University Press, 2005); Michael Asimow, "Popular Culture and the American Adversarial Ideology," in Michael Freeman (ed.), *Law and Popular Culture* (Oxford: Oxford University Press, 2005), 606–37.

26. See, for example, Ronald Inglehart, *Modernization and Postmodernization: Cultural, Economic, and Political Change in 43 Societies* (Princeton: Princeton University Press, 1977).

27. Ibid. See, for example, Wood, *Radicalism of the American Revolution* (note 7).

28. Alexander Keyssar, *The Right to Vote: The Contested History of Democracy in the United States* (New York: Basic Books, 2000).

29. Lawrence Lessig, "The Regulation of Social Meaning," *University of Chicago Law Review* 62, no. 3 (Summer 1995): 943–1045; *Planned Parenthood of Southeastern Pennsylvania et al. v. Casey, Governor of Pennsylvania et al.*, 505 U.S. 833 (1992).

30. Peter Jones, "Bearing the Consequences of Belief," *Journal of Political Philosophy* 2 (March 1994): 24–43. Cf. Berger and Luckmann, *The Social Construction of Reality* (note 13).

31. Robert D. Putnam and Robert Leonardi and Raffaella Y. Nanetti, *Making Democracy Work: Civic Traditions in Modern Italy* (Princeton: Princeton University Press, 1993), 86–91.

32. See, for example, Lawrence G. Sager, "The Incorrigible Constitution," *New York University Law Review* 65 (1990): 893–961. See also Robert H. Wiebe, *The Search for Order, 1877–1920* (New York: Hill and Wang, 1967).

33. See, for example, Hannah Arendt, *On Revolution* (London: Penguin, 1963).

34. See, for example, Michael J. Sandel, *Liberalism and the Limits of Justice* (Cambridge: Cambridge University Press, 1982). See also Wiebe, *The Search for Order* (note 32).

35. Robert Shoemaker, *The London Mob: Violence and Disorder in Eighteenth-Century England* (London: Hambledon and London, 2004); E. P. Thompson, *The Making of the English Working Class* (London: Penguin Books, 1980).

36. See generally, Michael W. Dowdle, "Beyond 'Judicial Power': Courts and Constitutionalism in Modern China," in Stéphanie Balme and Michael W. Dowdle (eds.), *Building Constitutionalism in China* (New York: Palgrave Macmillan, 2009), 199–217.

37. See also Ross Terrill, *Madame Mao: The White-Boned Demon* (rev. ed.) (Palo Alto: Stanford University Press, 1999), 333–47.

38. Michael W. Dowdle, "The Constitutional Development and Operations of the National People's Congress," *Columbia Journal of Asian Law* 11, no. 1 (1997): 21–25.

39. Andrew J. Nathan, "China's Constitutional Option," *Journal of Democracy* 7, no. 4 (1996): 43–57.

40. Dowdle, "Constitutional Development and Operations" (note 38); Murray Scot Tanner, *The Politics of Lawmaking in China: Institutions, Processes, and Democratic Prospects* (Oxford: Clarendon Press, 1999). See also Michael W. Dowdle, "Of Parliaments, Pragmatism, and the Dynamics of Constitutional Development: The Curious Case of China," *New York University Journal of International Law and Politics* 35 (2002): 1–200.

41. See generally, Dowdle, "Constitutional Development and Operations" (note 38); Dowdle, "Of Parliaments" (note 40); Michael W. Dowdle, "Public Accountability in Alien Terrain: Exploring for Constitutional Accountability in the People's Republic of China," in Dowdle (ed.), *Public Accountability*, 329–57 (note 20).

42. Michael Lienesch, "Reinterpreting Rebellion: The Influence of Shays's Rebellion on American Political Thought," in Robert A. Gross (ed.), *In Debt to Shays: The Bicentennial of an Agrarian Rebellion* (Charlottesville: University Press of Virginia, 1993), 161–82.

43. David Schneiderman, "A. V. Dicey, Lord Watson, and the Law of the Canadian Constitution in the Late Nineteenth Century," *Law and History Review* 16 (1998): 495–526.

44. Uday S. Mehta, "Indian Constitutionalism: The Social and the Political Vision," in Niraja Gopal Jayal and Pratap Bhanu Mehta (eds.), *The Oxford Companion to Politics in India* (Oxford: Oxford University Press, 2010), 15–27.

45. Carol Jones, "Politics Postponed: Law as a Substitute for Politics in Hong Kong and China," in Kanishka Jayasuriya (ed.), *Law, Capitalism and Powers in Asia: The Rule of Law and Legal Institutions* (London: Routledge, 1999), 38–57. See also Michael W. Dowdle, "Constitutionalism in the Shadow of the Common Law: The Dysfunctional Interpretive Politics of Article 8 of the Hong Kong Basic Law," in Hualing Fu, Lison Harris and Simon N. M. Young (eds.), *Interpreting Hong Kong's Basic Law: The Struggle for Coherence* (Hong Kong: Palgrave Macmillan, 2007), 55–76.

46. Hunt, *Politics, Culture, and Class* (note 10).

47. Jason A. Frank, *Constituent Moments: Enacting the People in Postrevolutionary America* (Durham, NC: Duke University Press, 2010).

48. Loughlin and Walker, *Paradox of Constitutionalism* (note 2); Arendt, *On Revolution*, 160 (note 33).

49. See, for example, Andrzej Rapaczynski, "Constitutional Politics in Poland: A Report on the Constitutional Committee of the Polish Parliament," *University of Chicago Law Review* 58, no. 2 (1991): 595–98.

50. Kevin J. O'Brien and Lianjiang Li, "Suing the Local State: Administrative Litigation in Rural China," *The China Journal* 51 (2004): 75–96; Mary E. Gallagher, "Mobilizing the Law in China: 'Informed Disenchantment' and the Development of Legal Consciousness," *Law & Society Review* 40 (2006): 783–813; David Kelly, "Public Intellectuals and Citizen Movements in China in the Hu-Wen Era," *Pacific Affairs* 79 (2006): 198–201; Jianrong Yu, "A Framework for Analyzing the Rights Protection Movement of Today's Peasants," *Shehuixue Yanjiu* [Studies of Sociology] 2 (2004): 49–55.

51. Gallagher, "Mobilizing the Law in China" (note 50); Fu Hualing, "Access to Justice and Constitutionalism in China," in Balme and Dowdle (eds.), *Building Constitutionalism in China*, 163–78 (note 36).

52. Keith J. Hand, "Citizens Engage the Constitution: The Sun Zhigang Incident and Constitutional Review Proposals in the People's Republic of China," in Balme and Dowdle (eds.), *Building Constitutionalism in China*, 221–2 (note 36).

53. See generally, ibid.

54. Ibid., 231–2.

55. Ibid., 232–9.

56. Matthew S. Erie, "China's (Post-)Socialist Property Rights Regime: Assessing the Impact of the Property Law on Illegal Land Takings," *Hong Kong Law Journal* 37 (2007): 919–49.

57. See also Liu Yiqing and Zhang Qinde (eds.), *Gong Xiantian Xuanfeng Shilu* [Records of the Gong Xiantian Storm] (Beijing: China Finance and Economic Press, 2007).

58. Jon Elster, "Deliberation and Constitution Making," in Jon Elster (ed.), *Deliberative Democracy* (Cambridge: Cambridge University Press, 1998), 97–122. See, for example, E. P. Thompson, *Whigs and Hunters: The Origin of the Black Act* (London: Penguin, 1977). Cf. Bronwen Morgan, *Social Citizenship and the Shadow of Competition: The Bureaucratic Politics of Regulatory Justification* (Aldershot: Ashgate, 2003), 215–25.

59. Dowdle, "Of Parliaments," 194–7 (note 40).

60. See, for example, Gordon G. Chang, *The Coming Collapse of China* (New York: Random House, 2001).

61. See, for example, Minxin Pei, *China's Trapped Transition: The Limits of Developmental Autocracy* (Cambridge, MA: Harvard University Press, 2008).

62. Li He, "China's New Left," *East Asian Policy* 1, no. 1 (2009): 30–7; Cheng Li, "One Party, Two Factions: Chinese Bipartisanship in the Making?," paper presented at the Conference on "Chinese Leadership, Politics, and Policy" (Washington, DC: Carnegie Endowment for International Peace, 2 November 2005), <http://www.carnegieendowment.org/files/li.pdf>;

Bruce J. Dickson, "Populist Authoritarianism: The Future of the Chinese Communist Party," paper presented at the Conference on "Chinese Leadership, Politics, and Policy" (Washington, DC: Carnegie Endowment for International Peace, 2 November 2005), <http://www.carnegieendowment.org/files/Dickson.pdf>.

63. Jerome A. Cohen, "Body Blow for the Judiciary," *South China Morning Post*, 18 October 2008; Donald C. Clarke, "He Weifang versus China's Legal Establishment on the 'Three Supremes'," China Law Prof Blog, 12 August 2009, <http://lawprofessors.typepad.com/china_law_prof_blog/2009/08/he-weifang-versus-chinas-legal-establishment-on-the-three-supremes.html>.

64. Zhu Suli, "'Judicial Politics' as State-Building," in Balme and Dowdle (eds.), *Building Constitutionalism in China*, 23–36 (note 36).

65. Fan Yu, "A Brief Analysis of the Ma Xiwu Trial Mode," *Chinese Sociology and Anthropology* 41, no. 2 (Winter 2008–09): 78–91.

66. Jerome A. Cohen, "The Jury's Out," *South China Morning Post*, 16 March 2011.

67. Yu Jianrong, "Social Conflict in Rural China," *China Security* 3, no. 2 (2007): 2–17. See, for example, Ching Kwan Lee, *Against the Law: Labor Protests in China's Rustbelt and Sunbelt* (Berkeley: University of California Press, 2007).

68. Dowdle, "Constitutional Development and Operations" (note 38).

69. Wang Hui, *The End of the Revolution: China and the Limits of Modernity* (New York: Verso Books, 2009); Cheng Li, "China's Team of Rivals," *Foreign Policy* (Mar/Apr 2009): 88–93.

70. Stéphanie Balme, "Ordinary Justice and Popular Constitutionalism in China," in Balme and Dowdle (eds.), *Building Constitutionalism in China*, 179–97 (note 36).

71. Shawn Shieh, "Regulating NGOs: Why the Schizophrenic Year for NGOs in 2010? (Part I)," NGOs in China: A Blog about Developments in the Nongovernmental, Nonprofit, Charitable Sector in China, 7 February 2011, <http://ngochina.blogspot.com/2011/02/regulating-ngos-why-schizophrenic-year.html>.

72. Shawn Shieh, "Regulating NGOs: Why the Schizophrenic Year for NGOs in 2010? (Part II)," NGOs in China: A Blog about Developments in the Nongovernmental, Nonprofit, Charitable Sector in China, 9 February 2011, <http://ngochina.blogspot.com/2011/02/regulating-ngos-why-schizophrenic-year_09.html>.

73. Guosheng Deng, "The Hidden Rules Governing China's Unregistered NGOs: Management and Consequences," *The China Review* 10 (2010): 183–206.

74. Ibid., 202–3.

75. Karla W. Simon, "Two Steps Forward, One Step Back — Developments in the Regulation of Civil Society Organizations in China," *International Journal of Civil Society Law* 7, no. 4 (2009): 51–6.

76. Ronald S. Burt, *Structural Holes: The Social Structure of Competition* (Cambridge, MA: Harvard University Press, 1992).

77. See also Jürgen Habermas, *Between Facts and Norms: Contributions to a Discourse Theory of Law and Democracy* (trans. William Rehg) (Cambridge, MA: Polity Press, 1996), 367; Jean L. Cohen and Andrew Arato, *Civil Society and Political Theory* (Cambridge, MA: MIT Press, 1992), ix.

78. See also, Burt, *Structural Holes* (note 76).

79. See, for example, Fu, "Access to Justice and Constitutionalism in China" (note 51); Dowdle, "Public Accountability in Alien Terrain" (note 41).

80. Yanqi Tong and Shaohua Lei, "Large-Scale Mass Incidents and Government Responses in China," *International Journal of China Studies* 1, no. 2 (October 2010): 487–508.

81. Martin King Whyte, *Myth of the Social Volcano: Perceptions of Inequality and Distributive Injustice in Contemporary China* (Palo Alto: Stanford University Press, 2010).

82. Tong and Lei, "Large-Scale Mass Incidents and Government Responses in China," 487 (note 80). See also Murray Scot Tanner, "China Rethinks Unrest," *The Washington Quarterly* 27, no. 3 (2004): 137–56.

83. Guobin Yang, "China's Gradual Revolution," *The New York Times*, 13 March 2011.

84. See also Fei Shen et al., "Online Network Size, Efficacy, and Opinion Expression: Assessing the Impacts of Internet Use in China," *International Journal of Public Opinion Research* 21, no. 4 (2009): 451–76.

85. Fu Hualing, "Challenging Authoritarianism through Law," chap. 9 in this volume.

86. See also Baogang He and Mark E. Warren, "Authoritarian Deliberation: The Deliberative Turn in Chinese Political Development," *Perspectives on Politics* 9, no. 2 (2011): 269–89; Min Jiang, "Authoritarian Deliberation: Public Deliberation in China," proceedings of the 2008 Global Communication Forum (Shanghai, China, 21–22 June 2008), available at Social Science Research Network (SSRN), <http://ssrn.com/abstract=1672887>.

87. The International PEN is a global NGO dedicated to promoting freedom of expression and the press. See "A Brief of Independent Chinese PEN Center", 6 February 2008, <http://www.chinesepen.org/English/AboutUs/AboutUs/200802/english_21410.html>.

88. Eva Pils, "Rights Activism in China: The Case of Lawyer Gao Zhisheng," in Balme and Dowdle (eds.), *Building Constitutionalism in China*, 243–20 (note 36); Hualing Fu and Richard Cullen, "*Weiquan* (Rights Protection) Lawyering in an Authoritarian State: Building a Culture of Public-Interest Lawyering," *The China Journal* 59 (2008): 111–28.

89. MacKinnon, "What Does Charter 08 Mean?," (note 1); Roland Soong, "How Charter 08 Is Being Received," EastSouthWestNorth (blog), 11 January 2009, <http://www.zonaeuropa.com/20090111_1.htm>.

90. Soong, "How Charter 08 Is Being Received", ibid.
91. MacKinnon, "What Does Charter 08 Mean?" (note 1).
92. Paine, "The Rights of Man" (note 3). *The Rights of Man* was originally published in 1791–92.
93. Dror Wahrman, "Public Opinion, Violence and the Limits of Constitutional Politics," in James Vernon (ed.), *Re-Reading the Constitution: New Narratives in the Political History of England's Long Nineteenth Century* (Cambridge: Cambridge University Press, 1996), 83–122; Olivia Smith, *The Politics of Language, 1791–1819* (Oxford: Clarendon Press, 1984).
94. Shoemaker, *The London Mob* (note 35); Wahrman, "Public Opinion" (note 93).
95. James A. Epstein, "Narrating Liberty's Defense: T. J. Wooler and the Law," in *Radical Expression: Political Language, Ritual, and Symbol in England, 1790–1850* (New York: Oxford University Press, 1994), 29–69.
96. Blackstone, *Commentaries on the Laws of England* (note 6).
97. Wahrman, "Public Opinion" (note 93).
98. Thompson, *The Making of the English Working Class* (note 35).
99. See, for example, Paine, "The Rights of Man" (note 3). See generally, ibid.
100. Eric Foner, *Tom Paine and Revolutionary America* (New York: Oxford University Press, 1976), 214–20; Thompson, *The Making of the English Working Class*, 117–8 (note 35).
101. Thompson, *The Making of the English Working Class*, 111–206 (note 35).
102. See generally, Epstein, "Narrating Liberty's Defense" (note 95).
103. See also Thompson, *The Making of the English Working Class*, 140–1 (note 35).
104. MacKinnon, "What Does Charter 08 Mean?" (note 1).
105. Xujun Eberlein, "China: Revolution or Reform? — A Summary of the 'Charter 08' Dispute," Inside-out China (blog), 7 January 2009, <http://www.insideoutchina.com/2009/01/china-revolution-or-reform-summary-of.html>.

Chapter 11 Charter 08 and Violent Resistance

1. A *Wall Street Journal* piece argued that the injustice against Liu Xiaobo would strengthen support for Charter 08 and China's democracy movement. But other commentators such as Feng Chongyi suggested that Charter 08 had created far less momentum than hoped for. John Lee, "The Rebirth of Charter 08," *Wall Street Journal*, 28 December 2009, <http://online.wsj.com/article/SB10001424052748704905704574623042952992458.html>; Feng Chongyi, "Charter 08 and China's Troubled Liberalism," *Asia Times*, 26 February 2010, <http://www.atimes.com/atimes/China/LB26Ad01.html>.

2. Even though over ten thousand people are said to have signed the Charter, this figure represents less than 0.001% of the Chinese population.

3. For examples of uses of "grassroots" and "elite" *weiquan*, see minutes of several meetings of a seminar series entitled *"Caogen Weiquan yu Gongmin Shehui"* [Grassroots *Weiquan* and Civil Society] held by the *Jidutu Falüren Tuanqi* [Christian Legal Professionals' Union] on 20 March, 15 April, and 13 May 2010, available at <http://www.zhongmeng.org/bbs/viewthread.php?tid=12118>.

4. Teng Biao, "What is Rights-Defence?" in Stacy Mosher and Patrick Poon (eds.), *A Sword and a Shield: China's Human Rights Lawyers* (Hong Kong: China Human Rights Lawyers Concern Group, 2009).

5. This, however, is what Elizabeth Perry (裴宜理) and Yu Jianrong (于建嵘) have recently argued, characterizing Chinese people's opposition, e.g., to land grabs as rules-based more than rights-based. Elizabeth Perry, "A New Rights Consciousness?," *Journal of Democracy* 20, no. 3 (2009): 17–20; Elizabeth Perry and Yu Jianrong, "China's Political Tradition and Political Development — Yu Jianrong in Dialogue with Elizabeth Perry," *Nanfengchuang*, 26 February 2010, available at *Meiguo Huayi Jiaoshou Zhuanjia Wang* [The Chinese American Professors and Professionals Network], <http://scholarsupdate.zhongwenlink.com/news_read.asp?NewsID=1077>. For a critical view, see Marina Svensson, "Human Rights in China as an Interdisciplinary Field: History, Current Debates and New Approaches," in Thomas Cushman (ed.), *Handbook of Human Rights* (New York: Routledge, 2012), 685–701.

6. Compare with Article 35 (rights to freedom of expression) and Article 41 (right to complain and make suggestions to the Government) of the PRC Constitution.

7. Keith J. Hand, "Using Law For a Righteous Purpose: The Sun Zhigang Incident and Evolving Forms of Citizen Action in the People's Republic of China," *Columbia Journal of Transnational Law* 45, no. 1 (2007): 159; Thomas E. Kellogg, "The Death of Constitutional Litigation in China?," *China Brief* 9, no. 7 (2009), available at <http://www.jamestown.org/programs/chinabrief/single/?tx_ttnews%5Btt_news%5D=34791&tx_ttnews%5BbackPid%5D=414&no_cache=1>.

8. Donald C. Clarke, "Puzzling Observations in Chinese Law: When Is a Riddle Just a Mistake?," Social Science Research Network (SSRN) (10 December 2001), <http://ssrn.com/abstract=293627>.

9. Ling Bing, "The Case of Liu Xiaobo and Freedom of Speech," *Ming Bao* [Mingpao Daily], 30 December 2009, available at *Xin Shiji Xinwen Wang* [New Century News], <http://www.newcenturynews.com/Article/gd/200912/20091230122127.html> (accessed 8 February 2012).

10. Some scholars even believe that China operates under a "monistic" theory, according to which international human rights treaty norms are directly

applicable in China. On the status of public international law, especially human rights treaties and conventions, see Mo Jihong, Wang Zhenjun, Dai Ruijun and Wang Yi, *Renquanfa de Xin Fazhan* [New Developments in Human Rights Law] (Beijing: Press of Chinese Social Science, 2008), 10–114. On the application of international law more generally, see Sanzhuan Guo, "Implementation of Human Rights Treaties by Chinese Courts: Problems and Prospects," *Chinese Journal of International Law* 8, no. 1 (2009): 161–79; Tang Yingxia, "The Relationship between International Law and Domestic Law and the Application of International Treaties in China's Domestic Law", 5 October 2006, <http://www.100paper.com/100paper/falvfa/guojifa/20070618/5870_2.html>.

11. See, for example, Li Heping et al., "The Supremacy of the Constitution and Freedom of Religion — Joint Defense Plea in the Case of Wang Bo, Wang Xinzhong and Liu Shuqin," in Mosher and Poon (eds.), *Sword and a Shield*, 70–88 (note 4).

12. Cp. Dworkin's account of civil disobedience in an American context. Ronald Dworkin, "Taking Rights Seriously" and "Civil Disobedience," chaps. 7 and 8 in *Taking Rights Seriously* (Cambridge: Harvard University Press, 1977).

13. Article 20, Basic Law of the Federal Republic of Germany (*Grundgesetz für die Bundesrepublik Deutschland*).

14. Hand, "Using Law for a Righteous Purpose" (note 7).

15. Hu Xingdou, "Letter of Suggestion to Conduct Unconstitutionality Review of the Household Registration System and the Rural-Urban Dual System," 6 November 2004, <http://boxun.com/news/gb/pubvp/2004/11/200411090133.shtml> (accessed 8 February 2012). See also Chinese Law Prof Blog (Donald C. Clarke), "The Famous Hukou Editorial," 26 March 2010, <http://lawprofessors.typepad.com/china_law_prof_blog/2010/03/the-famous-hukou-editorial.html> (accessed 8 February 2012).

16. "14070 Chinese Citizens Respectfully Request that the ICCPR Be Ratified in China," *Dajiyuan* [The Epoch Times], 2 January 2008, <http://www.epochtimes.com/gb/8/1/2/n1962413.htm> (accessed 8 February 2012). China Human Rights Lawyers Concern Group (CHRLCG), 2 January 2008, <http://www.chrlcg-hk.org/?cat=20>.

17. For an example, see Zhang Jun, "The Superiority of the Socialist Judicial System with Chinese Characteristics," *Zhongguo Renda Wang* [Website of the National People's Congress of the People's Republic of China], 20 May 2009, <http://www.npc.gov.cn/npc/xinwen/rdlt/fzjs/2009–05/20/content_1503052.htm>.

18. See, for example, "Minister of Public Security Meng Jianzhu: Internet Becoming Major Tool of Anti-Chinese Forces," *Ming Bao* [Mingpao Daily], 2 December 2009.

19. Svensson, "Human Rights in China" (note 5).

20. Of the abovementioned petitions, only the one concerning *shourong qiansong* received a sympathetic hearing in the context of the famous "Sun Zhigang (孙志刚) Case." Hand, "Using Law for a Righteous Purpose" (note 7).

21. See He Yang (何杨), *Diao Zhao Men* [Disbarment, 吊照门] (May 2010), <http://vimeo.com/12938865>.

22. Jerome A. Cohen, "First, They Came for the Lawyers," *Foreign Policy*, 12 July 2011, <http://www.foreignpolicy.com/articles/2011/07/12/first_they_came_for_the_lawyers>.

23. Human Rights Watch, *An Alleyway in Hell: China's Abusive "Black Jails"* (12 November 2009), <http://www.hrw.org/en/reports/2009/11/12/alleyway-hell-0>.

24. For example, one such garment complains, "For heaven's sake, tell me! Are we not citizens of the People's Republic of China? Do we not share in the rights safeguarded by the Constitution, in the basic rights and duties of citizens?" Another reads, "Give me my human rights safeguarded in the Constitution, my basic rights and duties of citizens!" Picture from Liu Zhengyou, 2005 (on file with author). Such slogans are common.

25. For example, the slogans shouted by rights defenders, including petitioners and others, outside the gates of the court trying the "Fujian Three Netizens," namely Fan Yanqiong (范燕琼), Wu Huaying (吴华英) and You Jingyou (游精佑)), for defamation of the police due to their calls for the police to investigate the death of a young woman, included "Down with corrupt officials! Down with corruption! Speech is not a crime! Long live freedom!," and an ironic rendering of the People's Liberation Army song: "All nondemocratic systems shall perish toward the sun! Toward freedom! Shining with boundless radiance toward a new China." See documentary film by He Yang, *Hesuoge de Rizi* [Herzog's Days, 赫索格的日子], available at <http://www.youtube.com/watch?v=iEp5mRgPP7A>; and with English subtitle at <http://globalvoicesonline.org/2010/08/25/china-fan-yanqiong-released/>.

26. For example, "14070 Chinese Citizens" (note 16).

27. CHRLCG, "'Lawyers for Us, and We for the Lawyers' — A Thousand Petitioners Protest at Beijing South Railway Station against Suppression of Human Rights Lawyers," 23 June 2009, <http://www.chrlcg-hk.org/?p=437>; see video clip at < http://www.youmaker.com/video/sv?id=9493ebf7121e421ab92b952712c02ab2001>.

28. Zhao Liang's documentary *Shangfang* [Petition, 上访] (Beijing, 2009) portrays petitioners and their plight over a period of twelve years.

29. "Shenzhen Designates 14 Forms of 'Irregular Petitioning' Conduct, Imposes Heavy Punishments on Leaders," *Guangzhou Ribao* [Guangzhou Daily], 12 November 2009, available at <http://news.sohu.com/20091112/n268139942.shtml>.

30. Melissa Chan, "Screams for Help at China's Secret 'Black Jails'," *Al Jazeera*, 27 April 2009, <http://www.youtube.com/watch?v=NsN4-A1G5zc&feature= player_embedded>, cited in "Video: China's 'Black Jails' Uncovered," China Digital Times, 3 June 2009, <http://chinadigitaltimes.net/2009/04/ chinas-black-jails-uncovered/>; Xu Zhiyong, "A Petitioner's Tale," China Digital Times, 30 April 2009, <http://chinadigitaltimes.net/2009/05/xu-zhiyong-a-petitioners-tale/>.

31. Robin Munro, *Dangerous Minds: Political Psychiatry in China Today and Its Origins in the Mao Era* (New York: Human Rights Watch, 2002); Robin Munro, "The Ankang: China's Special Psychiatric Hospitals," *Journal of Comparative Law* 1, no. 1 (2007): 41–87, <http://www.thejcl.com/pdfs/ munro.pdf>.

32. See, for example, Tang Fuzhen's case (唐福珍). Roger Cohen, "A Woman Burns," China Digital Times, <http://chinadigitaltimes.net/2010/01/roger-cohen-a-woman-burns/>.

33. The website of this organization is <http://thelcv.org/en/> (site discontinued).

34. "China League of *Yuanmin* Sues Shanghai Government in France," Radio Free Asia (Cantonese Service), 6 May 2009, <http://www.rfa.org/canton-ese/news/petitioner_rights-05062009111903.html?encoding>.

35. "Cause of Death of LCV Member Remains Unclear, Shen Ting Calls for Thorough Investigation by Authorities," Radio Free Asia (Cantonese Service), 4 September 2009, <http://www.rfa.org/mandarin/yataibaodao/ yuanmeng-09042009085929.html>.

36. Author conversation, Beijing, April 2010.

37. Ibid.

38. Statement by writers of such a coerced "guarantee letter," Spring 2010, copy on file with author.

39. Author conversations, Beijing, May and July 2010.

40. Author conversations, Beijing, April–July 2010.

41. Ibid.

42. Ibid.

43. Fu Hualing analyzes this relationship of enmity by discussing characteri-zation by the state as "individual terrorism." See Fu Hualing, "Responses to Terrorism in China," in Victor V. Ramraj, Michael Hor, Kent Roach and George Williams (eds.), *Global Anti-Terrorism Law and Policy* (2nd Edition) (Cambridge: Cambridge University Press, 2012), 334–56.

44. "Anthology of Songs for Revolutionary Heroes: 'Learning from Model Yang Jia'," 9 July 2008, <http://freshrain.7.forumer.com/a/_post1375.html>.

45. Eva Pils, "Yang Jia and China's Unpopular Criminal Justice System," *China Rights Forum* 1 (2009): 59–66.

46. The song celebrating him as a "model" was circulated on the Internet, and is an obvious satire on a Party eulogy for the "model worker" Lei Feng (雷锋), celebrated for his altruism in the 1960s and 1970s.

47. The original term used is "renlei yizhong" (人类异种), literally, "non-human race."

48. "Ba Shu's Voice: Part of Yang Jia's Statements during Criminal Investigation Stage Leaked," Boxun, 9 May 2010, <http://news.boxun.com/forum/201005/boxun2010/130889.shtml>.

49. Ai Weiwei, Yige Gupi de Ren [A Lonely Person] (Beijing, 2010), <http://www.youtube.com/playlist?list=PLFE3600BEBB04E10A&feature=plcp>.

50. "Yongzhou Attack on Judges Leads to Surge of Petitions, Memorial for Perpetrator, Resistance to Official Corruption," Radio Free Asia (Mandarin Desk), 3 June 2010, <http://www.rfa.org/mandarin/yataibaodao/yz-06032010163340.html>. See also online comments on the incident, <http://www.peacehall.com/forum/201006/boxun2010/134487.shtml>.

51. Joshua Rosenzweig, "The Sky is Falling: Inciting Subversion and the Defense of Liu Xiaobo," chap. 2 in this volume; Mo Shaoping, Gao Xia, Lü Xi, and Chen Zerui, "Criminal Defense in Sensitive Cases: Yao Fuxin, Yang Jianli, Jiang Lijun, Du Daobin, Liu Xiaobo, and Others," chap. 3 in this volume.

52. See Hugo Adam Bedau and Erin Kelly, "Punishment" (in Edward N. Zalta (ed.), Stanford Encyclopedia of Philosophy (Stanford: The Metaphysics Research Lab. Stanford University, 2004-), <http://plato.stanford.edu/entries/punishment/>), for this way of differentiating between retributivist and liberal justifications of punishment.

53. For a recent editorial, see "Warning on Wrong Cases: Police Exhibits 'Presumption of Guilt' Principle," Xinjing Bao [Beijing News], 4 June 2010, <http://comment.bjnews.com.cn/2010/0604/22183.shtml>.

54. Though it may serve to decide how much punishment is deserved.

55. See Munro, Dangerous Minds and "The Ankang" (note 31).

56. Jerome A. Cohen, "Body Blow for the Judiciary," South China Morning Post, 18 October 2008, available at Council on Foreign Relations, <http://www.cfr.org/publication/17565/body_blow_for_the_judiciary.html?breadcrumb=%2Fbios%2F14%2Fjerome_a_cohen>.

57. Author conversation, Beijing, April 2010.

58. "Peking University Professor Sun Dongdong: Professional Petitioners Have Mental Problems," Fenghuang Zixun [Phoenix Information], 3 April 2010 (on file with author) ; Sky Canaves, "Comments on Mental Illness Draw Ire in China," 3 April 2010 (on file with author) ; "Sun Dongdong's Comments on Mental Illness Produce Strong Reaction, Petitioners Confront Him, Plan to Sue Him," Radio Free Asia (Mandarin Desk), 1 April 2009, <http://www.rfa.org/mandarin/yataibaodao/fangmin-04012009084816.html>; "Petitioners Protest at 'Insane' Label," Associated Press/South China Morning Post, 11 April 2009 (on file with author).

59. Author conversation, Beijing, April 2010.

60. Ibid. For a case in which the victim's family ask for the death penalty, see Li Ming, "Hebei: Sentence Reduced to Death Penalty with Reprieve, Young Girl Victim's Father Endures Twelve Years of Hardship while Bringing Complaints," *Zhongguo Weiquan Fuwu Wang* [China Rights-Defense Service Net], 14 May 2009 (on file with author). For a widely discussed case in which the public apparently demanded the death penalty, see "China: The Murder case of Yao Jiaxin," Global Voices, 21 April 2011, <http://globalvoicesonline.org/2011/04/21/china-the-murder-case-of-yao-jiaxin/>.

61. "Incessantly Hitting the Keyboard, Making those Corrupt Elements Tremble with Fear," *Zhongguo Yulun Jiandu Wang* [China Public Opinion Watch], 5 June 2008 (on file with author).

62. Discussed in Benjamin Liebman, "Assessing China's Legal Reforms," *Columbia Journal of Asian Law* 23 (2009): 17.

63. Author conversation, Beijing, May 2010.

64. He Xin, "Lawyer's Retraction Written into Plea Bargain," Caixin Online, 2 October 2010, <http://english.caing.com/2010–02-10/100117225.html>.

65. Jerome A. Cohen and Eva Pils, "Rules and Reality. New Guidelines to Ban Coerced Confessions Will Be Tested in a Case before China's Top Court," *South China Morning Post*, 2 September 2010, <http://www.usasialaw.org/wp-content/uploads/2010/08/20100902-Rule-and-Reality.pdf> (Chinese translation is available at <http://www.usasialaw.org/?p=4102>).

66. See, for example, interview with Chongqing citizens in the film by He Yang, *Zhu Mingyong Lüshi Zhuanfang — Heida* [Conversation with Lawyer Zhu Mingyong on Torture] (August 2010, on file with author).

67. This is a reference to Shi Nai'an's (施耐庵) *Shuihuzhuan* [水浒传, Stories from the Water Margin], a serial novel from the late Northern Song Dynasty, which tells the individual stories of 108 heroes who suffer various wrongs at the hands of local potentates, and leave their homes for the Liang Mountain range (梁山) to become bandits.

68. Liu Xiaobo, "Violent Revenge after Yang Jia Is Merely 'Primeval Justice'" (21 August 2008), *Zhengming* [Chengming Magazine], September 2008, available at <http://blog.boxun.com/hero/200809/liuxb/1_1.shtml>.

69. Perry Link (trans.), "China's Charter 08," *New York Review of Books* 56, no. 1 (15 January 2009), <http://www.nybooks.com/articles/archives/2009/jan/15/chinas-charter-08/>.

70. For a further discussion of the relationship between Kang Youwei (康有为) and Liang Qichao (梁启超) as early constitutional drafters, see Yu Jie, "Civil Rights Are Justice, Constitution Is Good Plan — Viewing the Idea of Reforming Charter 08 in the Context of the Debate between Kang Youwei and Zhang Taiyan," in *Liu Xiaobo yu Hu Jintao de Duizhi* [The Confrontation between Liu Xiaobo and Hu Jintao] (Hong Kong: Chenzhong Bookstore, 2009), 98–111.

71. Human Rights in China (trans.), "Charter 08," <http://www.hrichina.org/public/contents/press?revision_id=89851&item_id=85717>. The author slightly changed the translation of Human Rights in China here.
72. Link (trans.), "China's Charter 08" (note 69).
73. Author conversations, Beijing, April–July 2010.
74. Liu, "Violent Revenge after Yang Jia" (note 68).
75. Cui Weiping, "Conscientious Objection and Civil Disobedience," 2001, available at <http://www.china-review.com/sao.asp?id=1458>.
76. He Weifang, "The Origins of the Tragic Belief in Violence as a Value — Lecture at a Seminar on the Case of Cui Yingjie, Urban Governance and Harmonious Society," 4 December 2007, available at <http://www.chinese-pen.org/Article/hyxz/200712/Article_20071204230911.shtml>.
77. Liu Liu, "Independent Intellectual Teng Biao," *Jingji Guancha Bao* [The Economic Observer], 24 November 2008, available at <http://www.tianya.cn/publicforum/content/no01/1/394515.shtml>. See also, Teng Biao, "Let Us Stop Living in Fear" (1 February 2004), *Duli Zhongwen Bihui* [Independent Chinese PEN Center], <http://blog.boxun.com/hero/tengb/3_1.shtml>.
78. Xiao Han, "Toward Non-Violence," 15 May 2010, available at Xiao Han's blog, <http://xiaohan.blog.caixin.com/archives/7628>.
79. See, for example, "Online Debate Between Xu Zhiyong, Teng Biao, Wang Xiaoyang, Zhao Mu (Part 2)," 5 May 2010, at Xu Zhiyong's blog, <http://blog.sina.com.cn/s/blog_63810a3b0100idkk.html>.
80. He, *Hesuoge de Rizi* (note 25).
81. Xu Youyu, "From 1989 to 2009 — Intellectual Change in China over the Past 20 Years," *Boxun*, 16 May 2009, <http://www.peacehall.com/news/gb/pubvp/2009/05/200905160630.shtml>.
82. Xiao, "Towards Non-Violence" (note 78).
83. Xiao Han, "Anxious Reflections, No. 11: About Charter 08," in Li Xiaorong and Zhang Zuhua (eds.), *Lingba Xianzhang* [Charter 08] (Hong Kong: Kaifang Press, 2009), 109–14.
84. "Online Debate" (note 79).
85. Ibid.
86. Ibid.
87. Ibid.
88. Liu Xiaobo, "I Have No Enemies: My Final Statement," available in English and Chinese in Human Rights in China, *Freedom of Expression on Trial in China* (*China Rights Forum* No. 1 of 2010), 116–21.
89. Xiao, "Anxious Reflections" (note 83).

Chapter 12 The Politics of Liu Xiaobo's Trial

1. Cited in Simon Hooper, "Imprisoned Liu Follows in Footsteps of Suu Kyi, Sakharov," CNN.com, 8 October 2010, <http://edition.cnn.com/

2010/LIVING/10/08/nobel.prize.detainees/?hpt=C1>; Wojciech Moskwa and Ben Blanchard, "China Livid as Dissident Liu Wins Nobel Peace Prize," Reuters, 8 October 2010, <http://www.reuters.com/article/idUSTRE6964LP20101008>.

2. See Charles Hutzler, "China Remains Uncompromising in Response to Nobel," Associated Press, 9 October 2010, available at *Washington Post*, <http://www.washingtontimes.com/news/2010/oct/9/china-remains-uncompromising-response-nobel/>.

3. For a discussion of Liu's political beliefs, see, for example, Megan Stack, "Nobel Peace Prize Winner Liu Xiaobo: Inside the Heart of a Gentle 'Subversive'," *Los Angeles Times*, 9 October 2010, <http://articles.latimes.com/2010/oct/09/world/la-fg-liu-profile-20101009>; *Andrew Leonard*, "The Extraordinary Passion of Liu Xiaobo," *Salon*, 8 October 2010, <http://www.salon.com/technology/how_the_world_works/2010/10/08/the_extraordinary_passion_of_liu_xiaobo/index.html>.

4. For a discussion of Liu's stature in the dissident movement, see, for example, Bao Pu, "The Nobel Peace Prize for Liu Xiaobo," *Asia Sentinel*, 9 October 2010, <http://www.asiasentinel.com/index.php?option=com_content&task=view&id=2746&Itemid=206>.

5. For a discussion of the contributions and fate of Hu Jia, Gao Zhisheng, and their colleagues, see "Profiles in Courage: China's Rights Defenders," Human Rights Watch, 2008, <http://china.hrw.org/chinas_rights_defenders>.

6. For a discussion of the fate of the China Democracy Party, see, for example, Human Rights Watch, *Nipped in the Bud: The Suppression of the China Democracy Party*, vol. 12, no. 5 (New York: Human Rights Watch, September 2000), <http://www.hrw.org/legacy/reports/2000/china/>.

7. For a discussion between the links of Charter 08 to the Czech 77 campaign, see, for example, Václav Havel, Dana Nemcova, and Václav Malý, "A Nobel Prize for a Chinese Dissident," *New York Times*, 20 September 2010, <http://www.nytimes.com/2010/09/21/opinion/21iht-edhavel.html>.

8. Cited in Willy Wo-Lap Lam, "Beijing Cornered by HK People Power," CNN.com, 8 July 2003, <http://edition.cnn.com/2003/WORLD/asiapcf/east/07/07/willy.column/index.html>.

9. For a discussion of Beijing's views on the "color revolutions," see, for example, Thomas Lum and Hannah Fischer, *Human Rights in China: Trends and Policy Implications* (Washington DC: US Congressional Research Service, 31 October 2008), <http://www.isn.ethz.ch/isn/Digital-Library/Publications/Detail/?lng=en&id=100261>. Also see "Political Advisory System Can Help China Avoid 'Color Revolution'," Xinhua News Agency, 10 March 2006.

10. For a discussion of the Great Firewall of China, see, for example, Alexei Oreskovic and Melanie Lee, "Google Says China's 'Great Firewall' Blocked

Search," Reuters, 30 March 2010, <http://www.reuters.com/article/idUS-TRE62T22L20100330>; Abigail Cutler, "Penetrating the Great Firewall," *The Atlantic*, February 2008, <http://www.theatlantic.com/magazine/archive/2008/02/penetrating-the-great-firewall/6690/>.

11. Cited in "Minister of Public Security Meng Jianzhu: The Internet Has Become a Principal Vehicle of Anti-Chinese Forces," *Ming Bao* [Mingpao Daily], 2 December 2009.

12. For a discussion of the "new culture movement" in 2010, see, for example, "Party Poopers: China's Rulers Get Sniffy about Popular Culture," *The Economist*, 12 August 2010, <http://www.economist.com/node/16793041?story_id=16793041>; "Movement against the 'Three Vulgarities' Gather Support in Society," Xinhua News Agency, 13 August 2010, <http://news.xinhuanet.com/politics/2010–08/13/c_12441887.htm>.

13. For a discussion of the impact of Charter 08, see, for example, Perry Link, "Charter 08, One Year On," *Wall Street Journal*, 8 December 2009, <http://online.wsj.com/article/SB10001424052748703558004574582773035958350.html>.

14. For discussion between Internet-enabled Chinese nationalism, see, for example, Paul Mooney, "Internet Fans Flames of Chinese Nationalism," *YaleGlobal Online*, 4 April 2005, <http://yaleglobal.yale.edu/content/internet-fans-flames-chinese-nationalism>.

15. Cited in Jonathan Watts, "Chinese Human Rights Activist Liu Xiaobo Sentenced to 11 Years in Jail," *The Guardian*, 25 December 2009, <http://www.guardian.co.uk/world/2009/dec/25/china-jails-liu-xiaobo>.

16. Cited in David Kenner, "Nobel Peace Prize Also-Rans," *Foreign Policy*, 8 October 2009, <http://www.foreignpolicy.com/articles/2010/10/08/nobel_peace_prize_also_rans>; "Herta Müller Recommends Liu Xiaobo for Nobel Peace Prize," signandsight.com, 8 February 2010, <http://www.signandsight.com/features/1988.html>.

17. Cited in Wojciech Moskwa, "China Warns Norway against Peace Nobel for Dissident," Reuters, 27 September 2010.

18. For the Norwegian government's response to Beijing's anger at the prize, see Walter Gibbs, "Norway Seeks to Pre-Empt Chinese Anger over Nobel," Reuters, 8 October 2010, <http://www.reuters.com/article/idUSTRE6971NT20101008>.

19. Cited in "Premier Wen Vows 'Utmost' Efforts to Redress Injustice, Says Equity Brighter than Sun," Xinhua News Agency, 14 March 2010, <http://news.xinhuanet.com/english2010/china/2010–03/14/c_13210331.htm>; Willy Lam, "Record Revenues Fuel Tensions," *Asia Times Online*, 14 July 2010, <http://www.atimes.com/atimes/China_Business/LG14Cb01.html>.

20. Cited in "18 Provinces Have Raised Their Minimum Wages," *Changjiang Ribao* [Changjiang Daily], 3 July 2010, available at *Zhongguo Xinwen Wang* [China News Service], <http://www.chinanews.com.cn/cj/2010/07–03/2378935.shtml>.

21. For a discussion of collective contracts and collective bargaining, see Willy Lam, "Shaking up China's Labor Movement," *Wall Street Journal*, 14 June 2010, <http://online.wsj.com/article/SB1000142405274870338900457530571 2086031490.html?mod=googlenews_wsj>. Also see "Strike Action Ushers in New Era of Work Relations, Says Expert," *China Daily*, 3 June 2010, <http://english.people.com.cn/90001/90776/90882/7010231.html>.

22. Author's interview conducted in Hong Kong, July 2010.

23. Cited in "Strikes Call for Collective Bargaining," *Global Times*, 2 June 2010, <http://opinion.globaltimes.cn/editorial/2010–06/537625.html>.

24. For a discussion of the treatment of migrant workers, see, for example, "Chinese Premier Calls for Improving Migrant Workers' Living Conditions in Cities," Xinhua News Agency, 25 June 2010, <http://news.xinhuanet.com/english2010/china/2010–06/15/c_13350414.htm>; Wang Ke, "Pay Hikes, Industry Upgrade to Solve Labor Shortage," *Zhongguo Wang* [China.org.cn], 10 March 2010, <http://www.china.org.cn/china/NPC_CPPCC_2010/2010–03/10/content_19575112.htm>.

25. Cited in "Wen Jiabao Writes Article to Remember Hu Yaobang," *Zhongguo Xinwen Wang* [China News Service], 15 April 2010, <http://www.chinanews.com.cn/gn/news/2010/04–15/2226730.shtml>.

26. For a discussion of the repercussions of Wen's essay, see, for example, Jason Dean, "Chinese Eulogy Bares Party Intrigue," *Wall Street Journal*, 15 April 2010, <http://online.wsj.com/article/SB1000142405270230462870457 5185861979803430.html>.

27. Cited in Chris Buckley, "Chinese Magazine Praises Ousted Zhao in Test of Taboo," Reuters, 8 July 2010, <http://in.reuters.com/article/idINIndia-49969920100708>.

28. Cited in Verna Yu, "China's Party Hardliners Want the Last Word," *Asia Times Online*, 22 November 2008, <http://www.atimes.com/atimes/China/JK22Ad01.html>.

29. For a discussion of the political views of Du Daozheng, see, for example, Willy Lam, "Wen, Hu Speeches Hint at Ideological Rift," *Asia Times Online*, 30 September 2010, <http://www.atimes.com/atimes/China/LI30Ad01.html>; "Selections from an Interview with Du Daozheng," *New York Times*, 16 October 2009, <http://www.nytimes.com/2009/10/17/world/asia/17du-transcript.html>.

30. Cited in Sharon LaFraniere, "Chinese Premier Offers a Tribute to a Reformer," *New York Times*, 15 April 2010, <http://www.nytimes.com/2010/04/16/world/asia/16china.html>; HKTVB News, Hong Kong, 15 April 2010.

31. Cited in Allen T. Cheng, "China's Tribute to Ousted Chief Signals Confidence," Bloomberg, 1 December 2005, <http://www.bloomberg.com/apps/news?pid=newsarchive&sid=aTU0Wk93YEcc&refer=germany>.

32. Cited in "Chinese Politburo Meets to Discuss How to Implement Leap-Forward Style Development in Xinjiang and to Maintain Long-Term

Stability," CCTV Net, 23 April 2010, available at *Renmin Wang* [People's Daily website], <http://tv.people.com.cn/GB/166419/11442435.html>.

33. For a discussion of Beijing's latest strategies toward Xinjiang, see, for example, "Stability, Prosperity Linked in Xinjiang: Beijing," Agence France Presse, 20 May 2010, <http://www.google.com/hostednews/afp/article/ALeqM5jg6cKiQ-nVrw6Oq2tZdpBHxlC3vA>; Chris Buckley, "China in Growth Push for Restive Xinjiang Region," Reuters, 20 May 2010, <http://in.reuters.com/articlePrint?articleId=INIndia-48662420100520>.

34. Cited in "Zhang Chunxian: After Running Xinjiang for 70 Days, 'A Departure from the Toughness-Softness Cycle'," *Zhongguo Xinwen Wang* [China News Service], 6 July 2010, <http://www.chinanews.com.cn/gn/2010/07–06/2383986.shtml>.

35. Cited in Cui Jia, "Xinjiang Security Funding Increased by 90 Percent," *China Daily*, 13 January 2010, <http://www.chinadaily.com.cn/china/2010–01/13/content_9311035.htm>.

36. For a discussion of the security situation in Xinjiang, see "Chinese Police Crack a Major Terrorist Case, More than 10 People Arrested," *Zhongguo Xinwen Wang* [China News Service], 24 June 2010, <http://www.chinanews.com.cn/gn/news/2010/06–24/2360302.shtml>; Shi Jiangtao, "Hukou Blitz in Lead-Up to Xinjiang Anniversary Three-Month Clampdown on Mobile Population," *South China Morning Post*, 14 June 2010.

37. For a discussion of programs to aid Xinjiang, see, for example, "Central Authorities Inaugurate Largest-ever Plan to Help Xinjiang," *Zhongguo Xinwen Wang* [China News Service], 4 May 2010, <http://www.chinanews.com.cn/gn/news/2010/05–04/2261068.shtml>; also see Dai Feng, "A New Wave of Programs to Help Xinjiang Has Begun: To Speed up Development in Xinjiang in Five Years," *Renmin Ribao* [People's Daily], 17 May 2010, <http://politics.people.com.cn/GB/14562/11608201.html>.

38. For a discussion of the security apparatus under the CCPLA, see, for example, Willy Lam, "China's New Security State," *Wall Street Journal*, 9 December 2009, <http://online.wsj.com/article/SB10001424052748704240504574585120857399040.html?mod=googlenews_wsj>.

39. Cited in "China Pays High Price for Maintaining Stability: Public Security Expenditure Catching up with Military Budget," *Ming Bao* [Mingpao Daily], 6 March 2010; for a discussion of Beijing's new control mechanisms, see, for example, "Changes in China's Control Mechanisms," *Nanfang Zhoumo* [Southern Weekend], 3 March 2010, <http://news.sina.com.cn/c/2010–03-03/212419788094.shtml>.

40. Cited in "Zhang Gaoli: The Survival of the Party and State Depends on State Security," *Tianjin Ribao* [Tianjin Daily], 3 December 2009, available at *Renmin Wang* [People's Daily website], <http://politics.people.com.cn/GB/14562/10501397.html>.

41. Ibid.

42. Cited in Song Liangliang, "Various Cities and Counties to Set up Offices to Maintain Social Stability and to Rectify Law and Order," *Nanguo Dushi Bao* [Nanguo Metropolitan News], 22 May 2009.

43. For a discussion of the mass mobilization of citizens for maintaining stability, see, for example, Tania Branigan, "Chinese Police Chief Boasts of Recruiting One in 33 residents as Informants," *The Guardian*, 10 February 2010; "Zhou Yongkang: Rely on the Masses to Construct a Steel Wall to Uphold Social Harmony and Stability," *People's Daily*, 5 November 2009.

44. Cited in Lam, "China's New Security State" (note 38).

45. "Minister of Public Security Meng Jianzhu" (note 11).

46. Cited in "Meng Jianzhu Stresses while Touring Anhui that the Fruits of IT Research Should Be Applied to the Construction of a System of Law-Enforcement," *People's Daily*, 1 November 2009.

47. Cited in "Wang Shengjun: Firmly Grasp the Principles of the 'Three Top Priorities' and Open up New Vistas for Judicial Work," *Renmin Fayuan Bao* [People's Court Daily], 23 June 2008. For a discussion of the politicization of the judicial apparatus, see Willy Lam, "The Politicization of China's Law-Enforcement and Judicial Apparatus," *China Perspectives* 2 (2009): 42–51.

48. Cited in "Wang Shengjun: Maximize the Harmonious factors, and Decrease Disharmonious Factors," *Guangming Ribao* [Guangming Daily], 23 June 2008.

49. Cited in "Hu Jintao Sums up Experience as China Celebrates 30 Years of Reform and Open Door Policy," *Zhongguo Xinwen Wang* [China News Service], 18 December 2008, <http://www.chinanews.com.cn/gn/news/2008/12-18/1493307.shtml>.

50. Cited in "Communiqué of the Fourth Plenary Session of the 17th CCP Central Committee," Xinhua News Agency, 18 September 2009.

51. "Hu Jintao Sums up Experience" (note 49).

52. Vice-President Xi Jinping (习近平), who is favored to take over the position of General Secretary in 2012, has also suffused his speeches with references to the imperative of upholding Party power in the past, present, and future. See, for example, "Xi Jinping's Speech at the Autumn Graduation Ceremony of the Central Party School," *Zhongguo Xinwen Wang* [China News Service], 18 November 2009.

53. Cited in Liu Yunshan, "How to Better Use the Newest Fruits in the Sinicization of Marxism to Guide the Masses," *Zhongguo Guangbo Wang* [China National Radio Net], 25 March 2010, <http://www.cnr.cn/allnews/201003/t20100325_506204576.html>.

54. Cited in Li Xiaochun, "Draw a Line of Demarcation between Marxism and Anti-Marxism," *Hongqi Wengao* [Red Flag Manuscripts], 23 March 2010, available at *Zhongguo Gongchandang Xinwen Wang — Renmin Wang* [News of the Chinese Communist Party — People's Daily website], <http://theory.people.com.cn/GB/11201415.html>.

55. Cited in Liu Yunshan, "Deeply Implement Patriotic Education around Celebrations of the 60th Anniversary of the Founding of the People's Republic," Xinhua News Agency, 15 April 2009, <http://politics.people.com.cn/GB/1024/9133769.html>.

56. "Directive of the CCP Central Committee on Propagating 'Principles on the Implementation of Patriotic Education'," Xinhua News Agency, 17 June 2007, available at *Zhongguo Jingji Wang* [www.ce.cn], <http://big5.ce.cn/xwzx/gnsz/szyw/200706/17/t20070617_11789126_1.shtml>.

57. For a discussion of Wen Jiabao's views on "universal values," see Sean Ding and Jingjing Wu, "Universal Values in China: A Domestic Debate," China Elections & Governance, 28 June 2008, <http://chinaelectionsblog.net/?p=13298>.

58. For a discussion of conservatives' views about "universal values," see Chen Kuiyuan, "Take Hold of Opportunities to Push Forward Research and Innovation of Philosophy and Social Science," *Zhongguo Shehui Kexueyuan Bao* [Journal of the Chinese Academy of Social Sciences], 19 March 2009, available at <http://www.wyzxsx.com/Article/Class16/200903/75599.html>.

59. "Veteran Dissident Liu Xianbin Placed in Criminal Detention Again," Human Rights in China, 29 June 2010, <http://www.hrichina.org/public/contents/press?revision_id=174985&item_id=174982>.

60. Cited in "'Using Money to Buy Stability' Is a Dangerous Vicious Cycle," SINA.com, 26 August 2010, <http://news.sina.com.cn/c/2010–08–26/025718021304s.shtml>.

61. Yin Yuzhi, "Using Money to Buy Stability is Tantamount to Drinking Poison to Quench Thirst," *Qianlong Wang* [qianlong.com], 26 August 2010 (on file with author).

62. Cited in "China Implements People's Mediation Law; Disputes Among the People Are Resolved in Good Time," *Zhongguo Xinwen Wang* [China News Service], 28 August 2010, <http://www.chinanews.com.cn/gn/2010/08–28/2497435.shtml>.

63. For a discussion of the plight of petitioners, see Lucy Hornby, "China Says to Handle Petitioners More 'Kindly'," Reuters, 25 January 2010, <http://www.reuters.com/article/idUSTRE60P0M020100126>; "Chinese Officials Required to Meet Local Petitioners," Associated Press, 20 August 2009, available at *Taipei Times*, <http://www.taipeitimes.com/News/world/archives/2009/08/20/2003451539>.

64. For a discussion of "black jails," see, for example, Andrew Jacobs, "China Investigates Company Linked to 'Black Jails'," *New York Times*, 27 September 2010, <http://www.nytimes.com/2010/09/28/world/asia/28china.html>; "'Black Jails' Investigated for Illegally Holding Petitioners," *China Daily*, 27 September 2010, <http://www.chinadaily.com.cn/china/2010–09/27/content_11351127.htm>.

65. Cited in "Xi Jinping: Leading Cadres Must Raise the Comprehensive Quality of their Cultivation on Party Culture," Xinhua News Agency, 1

March 2009, <http://news.xinhuanet.com/newscenter/2009–03/01/content_10923334.htm>; "Looking Back on Xi Jinping's Seven Talks to the Central Party School," *Zhongguo Gongchandang Xinwen Wang — Renmin Wang* [News of the Chinese Communist Party — People's Daily website], 8 September 2009, <http://cpc.people.com.cn/GB/164113/10006898.html>; "Xi Jinping: Use the Spirit of Reform and Innovation in Doing Well the Work of Propagating and Selecting Young Cadres," Xinhua News Agency, 30 March 2009, <http://news.xinhuanet.com/newscenter/2009–03/30/content_11101506_1.htm>.

66. Cited in "Sun Liping: The Re-Establishment of Order in a Changing Society," *Qingnian Shibao* [Youth Times], 17 April 2010, available at *Fenghuang Wang* [ifeng.com], <http://news.ifeng.com/opinion/politics/detail_2010_04/17/1312664_0.shtml>.

Chapter 13 The Political Meaning of the Crime of "Subverting State Power"

1. [Editors' note:] Ai Weiwei, the contemporary Chinese artist and rights activist, was himself detained "on suspicion of tax evasion" in 2011, after this essay was completed. After his release, he detailed aspects of his coercive interrogation at the hands of the authorities. See for example, Sui-wei Lee, "Ai Weiwei Endured 'Immense Pressure' in Detention: Source," Reuters, 10 August 2011, <http://in.reuters.com/article/2011/08/10/us-china-artist-idINTRE7793E620110810> (accessed 3 September 2011).

2. "Crimes of Treason": the crime of conspiracy to subvert the government; the crime of splitting the country; the crime of plotting subversion or sedition; the crime of defection to the enemy, treason, or rebellion; the defection or rebellion with armed forces; the crime of raiding a prison or breaking prison; the crime of espionage; the crime of supplying arms or other military materials to the enemy; the crime of organizing or leading a counter-revolutionary group; the crime of counter-revolutionary killing or personal injury; the crime of counter-revolutionary propaganda and instigation. [Editors' note:] See Articles 90–104, 1979 Criminal Law (no longer in force).

3. [Editors' note:] The original Chinese text is available at the website of Congressional-Executive Commission on China, <http://www.cecc.gov/pages/selectLaws/laws/criminalLaw.php>. This English translation is available at the same website, <http://www.cecc.gov/pages/newLaws/criminalLawENG.php>. An amendment of the Criminal Law of the People's Republic of China, not affecting these provisions, was passed in March 2011.

4. Where it is not stated otherwise, this chapter refers by "subversion crimes" to the crime of "subverting state power" as well as that of "inciting subversion of state power."

5. On totalitarianism, see Hannah Arendt, *Jiquan Zhuyi de Qiyuan* [The Origins of Totalitarianism] (trans. Lin Xianghua) (Taipei: Taiwan Times Press, 1995). On China's Despotism, see Zhang Boshu, *Cong Wusi Dao Liusi: 20 Shiji Zhongguo Zhuanzhi Zhuyi Pipan* [From May Fourth to June Fourth: Criticism of Authoritarianism in 20th Century China], vol. 1 (Hong Kong: Chenzhong Publishing, 2008). [Editors' note:] Hannah Arendts' work was originally published in English language in 1951 in New York with *Schocken* Publishing.

6. [Editors' note:] See, for example, John Locke, *Two Treatises on Government* (1680–1690), bk. 2, chap. 19, para. 232, available at LONANG, <http://www.lonang.com/exlibris/locke/loc-219.htm>:

   Whosoever uses force without right — as every one does in society who does it without law — puts himself into a state of war with those against whom he so uses it, and in that state all former ties are cancelled, all other rights cease, and every one has a right to defend himself, and to resist the aggressor.

7. Declaration of Independence:

   Governments are instituted among Men, deriving their just powers from the consent of the governed. That whenever any Form of Government becomes destructive of these ends, it is the Right of the People to alter or to abolish it, and to institute new Government, laying its foundation on such principles and organizing its powers in such form, as to them shall seem most likely to effect their Safety and Happiness.

   Engels wrote: "The right to revolution is, after all, the only real 'historical right' the only right on which all modern states without exception rest." Frederick Engels, "Introduction to Karl Marx's *The Class Struggles in France, 1848 to 1850*," in Karl Marx and Frederick Engels, *Collected Works, vol. 27, Engels: 1890–1895* (trans. John Peet et al.) (New York: International Publishers, 1990), 521, available at <http://www.marxists.org/archive/marx/works/1850/class-struggles-france/intro.htm>.

8. Hannah Arendt, *Lun Geming* [On Revolution] (trans. Chen Zhouwang) (Nanjing: Yilin Publishing House, 2007), 2.

9. For an analysis of the concepts of "state power," "government," "incitement," "subversion," etc., see Guo Guoting, "Legal Analysis of the Crime of Subverting the State Power," 21 December 2008, available at Guo Guoting's blog, <http://thomasgguo.world.edoors.com/CLoTy6iAPKP0>.

10. [Editors' note:] The author draws on the distinction between "justification" and "legitimacy" as used by John Simmons, in whose work "justification" is understood roughly in the sense of *"ex post* justification" or *"ex post* rationalization." John Simmons, *Justification and Legitimacy: Essays on Rights and Obligations* (Cambridge: Cambridge University Press, 2001), especially chap. 7 ("Justification and Legitimacy").

11. Teng Biao, "Political Legitimacy and 'Charter 08'," *China Rights Forum* 2 (2009).

12. [Editors' note:] Li Shenzhi (李慎之, 1923–2003), a liberal social scientist and public intellectual affiliated with the China Academy of Social Sciences, had become openly critical of authoritarianism from the 1990s.

13. Li Shenzhi, "The Power of the Powerless and Anti-Political Politics — Life Philosophy in a Post-Totalitarian Era," <http://www.aisixiang.com/data/detail.php?id=1724>.

14. [Editors' note:] Xu Ben (徐贲, Ben Xu), professor of literature at the English Department of St Mary's College, California.

15. Xu Ben, "China's New Totalitarianism and Its Apocalypse," *Dangdai Zhongguo Yanjiu* [Contemporary Chinese Studies] 4 (2005). Xu Ben summarizes as follows:

    The "new totalitarianism" era is one of superficial prosperity but actual decline of humanity. In the real world of "new totalitarianism," there is writing, but no speech; there is rule but no shared knowledge/values, there are magazines but no information, there are newspapers but no news, there is scholarship but no thought, there are prospects/there is hope but no goals. The "neo-totalitarian" regime is even more specter-ridden than the post-totalitarian one. The "neo-totalitarian" society is one without shared political concepts, without shared value outlooks.

16. Naazneen H. Barma and others use the concept of "open authoritarianism" to explain countries that develop economically but suppress political freedoms and the continued maintenance of authoritarianism in such countries. These regimes deliver economic success to their populations through versions of state-controlled capitalism, and excel at plugging into the international system in ways that allow them to benefit from global connectivity while retaining their grip on domestic power. It is their very openness to the liberal international order that sustains their authoritarian model. Naazneen H. Barma, Ely Ratner, and Regine A. Spector, "Open Authoritarian Regimes: Surviving and Thriving in the Liberal International Order," *Democracy & Society* 6, no. 2 (Spring 2009): 8–11. Titus C. Chen (陈至洁) discusses how the Communist Party has increased its collective consciousness of external risk as a consequence of its understanding of the Color Revolutions and how it has taken measures to increase its coercive potential. The Party has strengthened its control of the liberal media, of intellectuals, and of civil society. These pre-emptive measures, described as "adaptive authoritarianism," may extend the period of authoritarian rule. Titus C. Chen, "China's Reaction to the Color Revolutions: Adaptive Authoritarianism in Full Swing," *Asian Perspectives* 34, no. 2 (2010): 5–51.

17. [Editors' note:] The idea of "Three Represents" was put forward by then President Jiang Zemin (江泽民) in 2000: "[The Chinese Communist Party] represents the development trends of advanced productive forces. It

represents the orientations of an advanced culture. It represents the fundamental interests of the overwhelming majority of the people of China." For an official explanation, see "What is 'Three Represents' CPC Theory?," China Internet Information Center, <http://www.china.org.cn/english/zhuanti/3represents/68735.htm>.

18. [Editors' note:] The term "Harmonious Society" was first used prominently in a resolution by the Party Central meeting of October 2006 and quickly became a dominant political slogan. See "Party Central Resolution on the Construction of a Socialist Harmonious Society," Xinhua News, 18 October 2006, <http://news.xinhuanet.com/politics/2006–10/18/content_5218639.htm>.

19. [Editors' note:] For various formulations of the Scientific Development Perspective by President Hu Jintao (胡锦涛) and Premier Wen Jiabao (温家宝), see "Scientific Development Perspective," Xinhuanet, <http://news.xinhuanet.com/ziliao/2005–03/16/content_2704537.htm>.

20. Hu Ping, *Quanru Bing — Dangdai Zhongguo de Jingshen Weiji* [The Malady of Cynicism — Contemporary China's Mental Crisis] (CA: Boda Publishing House, 2005), 5 and 24. For a study of the transformation of thought in the post-Mao era, see Chen Yan, *Zhongguo zhi Juexing — Wenge Hou Zhongguo Sixiang Yanbian Licheng (1976–2002)* [China's Awakening — A Chronicle of China's Intellectual Transformation after the Cultural Revolution (1976–2002)] (trans. Xiong Peiyun) (Hong Kong: Tianyuan Publishing, 2006).

21. Teng Biao, "Civic Virtues and Civic Responsibilities in the Age of Post-Totalitarianism," *Gongmin* [Citizen] (February 2008).

22. See Sun Liping's *"Duanlie Sanbuqu"* [The Three Themes of Cleavage]: *Duanlie — 20 Shiji 90 Niandai Yilai de Zhongguo Shehui* [Cleavage — Chinese Society since the 1990s] (Social Sciences Publishing House, 2003); *Shiheng — Duanlie Shehui de Yunzuo Luoji* [Imbalance — The Operational Logic of a Society Experiencing Cleavage] (Social Sciences Publishing House, 2004); and *Boyi — Duanlie Shehui de Liyi Chongtu yu Hexie* [Game — Conflicts of Interest and Harmony in a Cleaved Society] (Social Sciences Publishing House, 2006).

23. The 2008 Yang Jia (杨佳) case and the 2010 cases of amok killings of children in schools have made it very clear that the conflict between officials and the people has already reached an extreme state. If the elites of power and wealth put political transition off indefinitely, then further, unforeseeable, irrational terror incidents will keep occurring. As a result, the entire society will be gripped by fear and trembling. He Qinglian (何清涟) believes, "Since the end of the 1990s, characteristics of a failed state have been emerging in China: public power has been gradually privatized, government behavior has gradually become more mafia-like, and political violence has been legalized, etc." See He Qinglian, "The Blind Spots in China's 'Stability Preservation' Logic," *Zhongguo Renquan Shuangzhoukan*

[Human Rights in China Biweekly] 29 (1 July 2010), <http://biweekly.hrichina.org/article/523>.

24. Chen Ziming (陈子明) treats the Chinese dissident movement, social movement, and political movement as three main branches of the democratic movement in China. Chen Ziming, "Social Movement and Political Formation," *Zhongguo Renquan Shuangzhoukan* [Human Rights in China Biweekly] 35 (20 September 2010), <http://biweekly.hrichina.org/article/661>.

25. This by no means implies that the number of people arrested and convicted of "crimes of endangering state security" is decreasing. According to the *Zhongguo Falü Nianjian* [China Law Yearbook] (1999–2009), the number of people arrested for "crimes of endangering state security" has been, for each year respectively from 1998–2008: 532, 769, 690, 725, 686, 336, 426, 296, 604, 742, and 1,712. The number of people indicted for "crimes of endangering state security" has been, for each year respectively from 1998–2008: 555, 660, 683, 886, 766, 455, 467, 349, 561, 619, and 1,407. These figures are cited in The Duihua Foundation, "'Endangering State Security' Arrests, Prosecutions Jumped in 2008, More High Numbers Expected for 2009," *Dialogue* 38 (Winter 2010): 7.

26. Before 1998, among those sentenced to upward of ten years for crimes of counter-revolution or "subversion of state power" have been Wei Jingsheng (魏京生), Chen Yanbin (陈晏彬), Liu Jingsheng (刘京生), Wang Xizhe (王希哲), Xu Wenli (徐文立), Hu Shigen (胡石根), Chen Ziming (陈子明), Wang Youcai (王有才), Wang Juntao (王军涛), Yang Tianshui (杨天水), Chen Xi (陈西), Qin Yongmin (秦永敏), Xu Wanping (许万平), Zheng Qiuwu (郑酉午), Yu Zhijian (余志坚), Yu Dongyue (喻东岳), Lu Decheng (鲁德成), etc. Many citizens who were regarded as "June Fourth Rascals" were sentenced to death, lifelong imprisonment, or other heavy sentences. In 1997, the death penalty for the crime of "subversion of state power" was abolished.

27. After 2001, cases of "incitement to subvert state power" have included the following, with the respective prison terms. In some of the "incitement to subversion of state power" cases, the sentences were as follows: Guo Qinghai (郭庆海): 4 years; Tao Jun (陶君): 3 years; Yan Peng (燕鹏): 1½ years; Wang Jinbo (王金波): 4 years; Lü Xinhua (吕新华): 4 years; Mou Chuanhang (牟传珩): 3 years; Huang Qi (黄琦): 5 years; Tao Haidong (陶海东): 7 years; Yan Jun (颜钧): 2 years; Zhao Changqing (赵常青): 5 years; Cai Lujun (蔡陆军): 3 years; Sun Gang (孙刚): 5 years; Lan Yupeng (蓝于鹏): 3 years; Wang Xiaoning (王小宁): 10 years; Luo Yongzhong (罗永忠): 3 years; He Depu (何德普): 8 years; Luo Changfu (罗长福): 3 years; Sang Jiancheng (桑坚成): 3 years; Ouyang Yi (欧阳懿): 2 years; Du Daobin (杜导斌): 3 years (suspended for 4 years); Zhang Lin (张林): 5 years; Zheng Yichun (郑贻春): 7 years; Ren Ziyuan (任自元): 10 years; Li Yuanlong (李元龙): 2 years;

Guo Qizhen (郭起真): 4 years; Li Jianping (李建平): 2 years; Gao Zhisheng (高智晟): 3 years (suspended for 5 years); Lai Jindong (赖锦东): 3 years; Li Changqing (李长青): 3 years; Zhang Jianhong (张建红): 6 years; Chen Shuqing (陈树庆): 4 years; Yang Chunlin (杨春林): 5 years; Yuan Xianchen (袁显臣): 4 years; Hu Jia (胡佳): 3½ years; Lü Gengsong (吕耿松): 4 years; Chen Daojun (陈道军): 3 years; Liu Xiaobo (刘晓波): 11 years; Zhang Qi (张起): 4 years; and Tan Zuoren (谭作人): 5 years.

In some of the "subversion of state power" cases the sentences were as follows: Jiang Lijun (姜立军): 4 years; Runggye Adak (荣杰阿扎): 8 years; Xie Changfa (谢长发): 13 years; Guo Quan (郭泉): 10 years; Wang Rongqing (王荣清): 6 years; Yan Zhengxue (严正学): 3 years; Yang Zili (杨子立): 8 years; Zhang Honghai (张宏海): 8 years; Xu Wei (徐伟): 10 years; Jin Haike (靳海科): 10 years; Huang Jinqiu (黄金秋): 12 years; Kong Youping (孔佑平): 10 years; Ning Xianhua (宁先华): 7 years; Wu Yilong (吴义龙): 11 years; Zhang Yuhui (张玉辉): 10 years; Shi Shaoping (时绍平): 10 years; Yao Yue (姚悦): 12 years; Meng Jun (孟军): 10 years; Zhu Yufu (朱虞夫): 7 years; Xu Wanping (许万平): 12 years; Yao Fuxin (姚福信): 7 years; Xiao Yunliang (肖云良): 4 years; Li Zhi (李智): 8 years; Mao Qingxiang (毛庆祥): 8 years; Xu Guang (徐光): 5 years; Yang Tianshui (杨天水): 12 years; Hu Mingjun (胡明军): 11 years; Wang Sen (王森): 10 years; Yue Tianxiang (岳天祥): 10 years; Guo Xinmin (郭新民): 2 years; Wang Fengshan (王凤山): 2 years; Li Dawei (李大伟): 11 years; Wang Rongqing (王荣清): 6 years; and Xue Mingkai (薛明凯): 1½ years.

28. Teng Biao, "What Is Rights Defense?," in Stacy Mosher and Patrick Poon (eds.), *A Sword and a Shield: China's Human Rights Lawyers* (Hong Kong: China Human Rights Lawyers Concern Group, 2009), 122–8.

29. For instance, Gao Zhisheng (高智晟), Yan Zhengxue (严正学), Hu Jia (胡佳), Huang Qi (黄琦), Tan Zuoren (谭作人), etc. are well known and command great authority among petitioners and Falun Gong disciples, peasants deprived of their land, those affected by demolitions, earthquake victims, the HIV-infected, and other such groups.

30. In a 1995 essay, Chen Ziming wrote:

In the current phase "the opposition party" (政治反对派) is primarily a concept of a political affiliation/identification, not one of an organization. The time is not yet ripe for establishing a political opposition party. It is not yet a ripe time for establishing an opposition party. One must not emulate the Communist Party by creating a superstitious organization and shrouding it in a veil of secrecy. The organization must be formed on the basis of a common recognition and trend in society; it requires a [common] faith, principles governing it, leaders, a network of connections as important elements and can only be established if these are in place. Only at a time when a reasonable and responsible political opposition [party] believes that an organization is indispensable and that the external conditions [for establishing an organization] are in place — only then is there a need to establish a democratic political party. When the time is ripe, it will not be a difficult thing to do. (Chen Ziming, "China's Political Opposition in 1995," cited in "Social Movement and Political Formation" (note 24).)

At that time, this kind of view received little acclaim but is rather common nowadays.

31. Guo Guoting, "On Subverting and Inciting to Subvert State Power," 15 December 2008, available at Guo Guoting's blog, <http://thomasgguo. world.edoors.com/CrIR5oBTObm8>.

32. [Editors' note] A special unit of the ordinary police under the Ministry of Public Security.

33. [Editors' note] Officers under the Ministry of State Security.

34. In July 2003, lawyer Li Jianqiang (李建强) and other persons publicly proposed the abolition of the crime of "inciting subversion of state power." In February 2004, 102 persons signed an open letter calling for [restrictive] judicial interpretation of the "crime of inciting to subvert state power." The procurator [public prosecutor] in Du Daobin's (杜导斌) case said to Du: "Even if you just paste a slogan 'Down with the Communist Party' upon a wall, you're already in trouble. Even if no one has seen that slogan, even if you tear it off again the next morning, by that time your conduct already amounts to a crime under Article 105 subsection 2 of the Criminal Law." Du Daobin, "Two Arguments — Defense and Last Statement at My Second Instance Trial" (12 July 2004), <http://www.epochtimes.com/ b5/4/7/13/n594671.htm>. But this clearly is not the standard used by the majority of procurators or police officers. There is another case — the mentally disabled boy Liu Weiqiang (刘伟强) was induced by somebody to post anti-government slogans, and was charged with inciting subversion of state power. "Mentally Disabled Boy, Instigated by Another, Pastes up Opposition Slogan, Stands Trial," *Guangzhou Ribao* [Guangzhou Daily], 25 June 2008.

35. An example of the former is the case of Liu Shaokun (刘绍坤) in Sichuan; an example of the latter is the case of Jing Chu (荆楚) in Guangxi.

36. Political criminal cases in which the crime convicted of was not a political crime include: Chen Guangcheng (陈光诚): organizing a mob to disturb traffic order; Guo Feixiong (郭飞雄): illegal business operation; Phurbu Tsering Rinpoche (普布泽仁仁波切): unlawful exercise of a profession and illegal possession of firearms and ammunition; Zhao Yan (赵岩): fraud; Zhao Lianhai (赵连海): creating a disturbance; Zhu Yufu (朱虞夫): obstructing public duty; Gao Qinrong (高勤荣): taking bribes, pimping, and fraud.

37. For instance, the cases of Nurmemet Yasin (Uighur, sentenced to 10 years); Tohti Tunyaz (Uighur, sentenced to 11 years); Hada (Mongol, sentenced

to 15 years); Gheyret Niyaz (Uighur, sentenced to 15 years); Abdulghani Memetemin (Uighur, sentenced to 9 years); Runggye Adak (Tibetan, sentenced to 8 years); Dolma Kyab (Tibetan, sentenced to 10½ years); Tsultrim Gyatso (Tibetan, sentenced to lifelong imprisonment); Thabkey Gyatso (Tibetan, sentenced to 15 years). To be sure, these cases are not in their entirety cases of subversion of state power; they also include those of sedition, incitement to sedition, divulging state secrets, etc.

38. Gao Zhisheng (高智晟) was given a sentence of 3 years' imprisonment suspended for 5 years, but was subjected to brutal torture. Since his release from detention, he has been forcibly "disappeared" for a long time. Guo Feixiong (郭飞雄), Yan Zhengxue (严正学), Li Hong (力虹), Chen Guangcheng (陈光诚), Huang Qi (黄琦), Yu Dongyue (喻东岳), Liao Yiwu (廖亦武), Lu Decheng (鲁德成), Yu Zhijian (余志坚), He Depu (何德普), Yang Chunlin (杨春林), Yuan Xianchen (袁显臣), Yao Fuxin (姚福信), and many other political prisoners have been exposed to torture and mistreatment while incarcerated. See <http://www.penchinese.com/wipc>. Li Heping (李和平), Liu Shasha (刘沙沙), Liu Dejun (刘德军), Hua Ze (华泽), and other human rights defenders have in the past experienced being hooded and beaten.

39. As Wang Ying (王英) stated:

The Beijing Municipal Police State Security Protection Squad has already marked out the youths Xu Wei (徐伟), Yang Zili (杨子立), Jin Haike (靳海科), Zhang Yanhua (张彦华) and Zhang Honghai (张宏海), etc. They had already spent a great amount of human, financial and other resources on this case. If there had been no outcome whatsoever, they would have been unable to explain the expenditure of several years to their superiors. So therefore on 13 March 2001 they carried out their vicious strike against Yang Zili, Jin Haike, Zhang Yanhua, and Zhang Honghai.

See Wang Ying, "My Friend Xu Wei — A Passionate Young Chinese Man," 20 May 2001, <http://xinsheng.net/xs/gb/da4print.asp?ID=7009>. Further, the people monitoring blind barefoot lawyer Chen Guangcheng (陈光诚) said that "at the local level, 5 million yuan have been allocated to control the family of Chen Guangcheng. They have used up 1.5 million already. What is left of that sum they are certainly not willing to give back, so they have now turned to controlling Chen Guangcheng into a sort of economic development program." See Liu Shasha's Tweet, <https://twitter.com/lss007/status/25027914756>. Chen Guangcheng is a blind rights activist who, since his release from prison in September 2010, has been kept under strictest house arrest in the village of Dongshigu (东师古村) in Linyi (临沂), Shandong Province (山东省). Many friends and supporters have tried to visit him there, thus far without success, as the government employs hired thugs to prevent outsiders from accessing the village. See, e.g.,

"Chen Guangcheng," Wikipedia, <http://en.wikipedia.org/wiki/Chen_ Guangcheng> (accessed 2 April 2012).

40. As Kong Youping (孔佑平) stated in his statement before his first instance trial:

> We all honestly ask ourselves, this kind of state power that is opposed to the people, to history, surely it must undergo change? "Change" is not equal to "subversion," it is merely getting it genuinely to stand on the people's side, genuinely to represent the people's will, to reflect the people's will! We who have a conscience, who cherish open, reasonable, peaceful, and non-violent strategies, when we use the form of dialogue to express our different political views within the boundaries set by the Constitution and the law, that is our only goal! That is to say, we want the state power to be healthier, in better order; and we want to change its current status of abnormality and deformity. Establishing a political party is entirely to make the state's political power a better one! If a state power has no effective constraints, no supervision mechanisms, then it is of necessity imperfect.

Kong Youping, "Whose Crime — Kong Youping's Statement at First Instance Trial at Anshan City Intermediate Court, Liaoning Province," 8 March 2001, <http://boxun.com/news/gb/pubvp/2010/04/201004191724. shtml>.

41. [Editors note:] Liu Xianbin, rights activist, China Democracy Party organizer, and Charter 08 signatory, detained on suspicion of inciting subversion in June 2010.

42. [Editors' note:] Chen Guangcheng, a well-known rights advocate, released from prison in September 2010 and subsequently detained in his home in Dongshigu Village, Linyi City, Shandong Province.

43. Kang Xiaoguang, *90 Niandai Zhongguo Dalu Zhengzhi Wendingxing Yanjiu* [A Study of the Political Stability of Mainland China in the 1990s] (Hong Kong: 21st Century Press, CUHK Chinese Cultural Studies Institute, August 2002).

Appendix: Charter 08

1. [Translator's note:] Announced on 27 August 1908, in the late Qing dynasty, the first Chinese "constitution" was in fact an outline of principles for a constitution that was meant to go into effect nine years later. As part of an ambitious government program to modernize China, the constitution was aimed at strengthening the state while preserving the power of the emperor. See Andrew J. Nathan, "Political Rights in Chinese Constitutions," in Randle Edwards, Louis Henkin, and Andrew J. Nathan, *Human Rights in Contemporary China* (New York: Columbia University Press, 1996), 77–124.

2. [Translator's note:] China signed the International Covenant on Economic, Social and Cultural Rights (ICESCR) in 1997, which it ratified in 2001; it signed the International Covenant on Civil and Political Rights (ICCPR) in 1998, but has not yet ratified this covenant.

Index